THE OXFORD BOOK OF
NARRATIVE VERSE

The Oxford Book of
Narrative Verse

Chosen and edited by
Iona and Peter Opie

Oxford New York

OXFORD UNIVERSITY PRESS

Oxford University Press, Walton Street, Oxford OX2 6DP
Oxford New York Toronto
Delhi Bombay Calcutta Madras Karachi
Petaling Jaya Singapore Hong Kong Tokyo
Nairobi Dar es Salaam Cape Town
Melbourne Auckland
and associated companies in
Berlin Ibadan

Oxford is a trade mark of Oxford University Press

First published 1983
First issued as an Oxford University Press paperback 1989
Reprinted 1989, 1990

British Library Cataloguing in Publication Data
The Oxford book of narrative verse.
1. Narrative poetry in English, 1300–
1980–Anthologies
I. Opie, Iona, 1923– II. Opie, Peter 1918–1982 821′.03′08
ISBN 0–19–282243–8

Library of Congress Cataloging in Publication Data
The Oxford book of narrative verse/chosen and edited by Iona and Peter Opie.
p. cm.
bibliography: p.
Includes indexes.
1. Narrative poetry, English. 2. Narrative poetry, American.
I. Opie, Iona Archibald. II. Opie, Peter.
PR1195.N209 1988
821′.03′08—dc19 88–23262
ISBN 0–19–282243–8

Printed in Great Britain by
The Guernsey Press Co. Ltd.
Guernsey, Channel Islands

PREFACE

Geographically this anthology has come back nearly to its starting place. In *A Book of Narrative Verse*, published by the Oxford University Press in 1930, Vere Collins thanked Helen Thomas for unreservedly placing at his service 'a scheme for an anthology of narrative verse drawn up provisionally in 1914 by her husband, Edward Thomas, who was killed before he could complete it'. And now we, in this house at the foot of Edward Thomas's hill, have been compiling a successor to the book he did not live to finish.

In the same tradition, we have chosen poems that tell a straightforward and complete story; or are, like Chaucer's 'Death and the Three Revellers', stories within a story; or, as with the extracts from the *Faerie Queene* and *Paradise Lost*, are episodes from longer poems complete in themselves. In a few cases, for instance 'Beppo', we have abridged poems to strengthen the narrative element (Byron himself admitted he was too discursive). Narrative verse can range from the succinctness of 'Little Miss Muffet' and 'Georgie Porgie' to the amplitude of Browning's 'The Ring and the Book', Tennyson's 'Locksley Hall', and Stephen Vincent Benét's 'John Brown's Body'. Extracts from long, sometimes book-length, poems such as these would have meant that readers were sampling a style rather than enjoying a story; and for the same reason we decided against including excerpts from poetic drama.

Much verse that has at one time or another been described as 'narrative' did not fit our criterion. We have excluded character studies (such as Charlotte Mew's 'Ken'), biographies (such as Francis Warner's 'Ballad of Brendan Behan'), stories in dialogue with the action off-stage (such as Robert Graves's 'A Frosty Night'), meditations (such as T. S. Eliot's 'Journey of the Magi'), introspections (such as Louis MacNeice's 'Burnt Bridge'), and celebrations (such as Thomas Love Peacock's 'War Song of Dinas Vawr'). Some pieces, such as Blake's 'William Bond' and Swinburne's 'Ballad of Dead Men's Bay' were simply pronounced to be 'not enough of a story'. Then, having gathered together what we considered to be the best of the story poems, we applied Horace's test from the *Art of Poetry*, 'One poem pleases but once, another, called for many a time, yet still will please', but, kinder than Horace, gave each poem six chances of survival. In this manner Pratt's 'Ice-Floes', Yeats's 'Cuchulain's Fight with the Sea', Whittier's 'Pipes of Lucknow', Wilfred Gibson's 'The Hare' and 'Flannan Isle', and many others, disappeared from the anthology. We thought Edward Thomas would agree with us that Binyon's narrative poems, such as 'The Battle of Stamford Bridge', were only for their own time; and we hoped he would forgive us for not including anything by his friend

PREFACE

Henry Newbolt. On the other hand, ballads like 'The Wreck of the Hesperus' and 'The Inchcape Rock' which, in 1914, seemed hackneyed through too much recitation, are not only part of the language's terms of reference, but can now be seen to be imbued with a saltiness quite extra to their maritime subject-matter.

In fact, this book pretends to be nothing more than a story-book. It is a book of tales of various kinds, romantic, humorous, ghostly, and gory, written at any time over the past six hundred years, but with this in common, that each of them has been made, through the peculiar alchemy of verse, more memorable and significant, so that their music and meaning become stronger at the second and third reading than at the first. Here is a classic tale of cunning, Chaucer's 'Cock and Hen'; and a classic tale of greed, Chaucer's 'Three Revellers', said to be the best story in the world. Here are tales of King Arthur, never far from a story-teller's mind—Tennyson's 'Lady of Shalott' and 'Morte d'Arthur'. Here are songs in praise of bravery on land and on the sea, Drayton's 'Ballad of Agincourt', Macaulay's 'Horatius', and Day-Lewis's 'Nabara'. There can be few more hilarious witch stories than 'Tam o' Shanter', and few more riveting Gothic tales than Poe's 'Raven' (the essence of a Gothic tale is its artificiality). 'Tam Lin' is a fairy-tale in the traditional manner; 'Goblin Market' in the literary. Southey's two tales of 'divine justice', and Browning's 'Pied Piper', hand out retribution as satisfyingly as the grimmest of the old folk-tales—which is not surprising since all three are based on such tales. Henryson's 'Upland Mouse and Burgess Mouse' is a fable which for two thousand years has reassured the frugal that their way of life is right. Robert Service's 'Sam McGee' must be amongst the tallest of tall tales; and 'The Eve of St. Agnes' and 'King Estmere' amongst the most romantic of love stories. 'Sohrab and Rustum' and Hardy's 'Trampwoman' are tragedies in the Greek sense, in which the characters carry the seeds of doom in their own natures, and the tragedy is inevitable.

Tragedy, passion, and heroism, the frequent themes of narrative verse, are large themes requiring a large canvas. Humanity seems to want excitement more than it wants security, but often compromises by experiencing it vicariously in comfort. The Hardy family, gathered round the cottage fireside in Bockhampton when Hardy was a boy, telling tales of hangings and suicides which he was never to forget; the matrons in Bournemouth hotel lounges, retailing narratives of cancer and marital cruelty; the Western–film addict, casually watching six cowboys being shot dead on the television screen—are all cosily aware that these events have happened to other people, or are not real, and can say to themselves with Cowper:

How calm is my recess! and how the frost
Raging abroad, and the rough wind, endear
The silence and the warmth enjoyed within.

PREFACE

Sometimes, however, the bitter pain in a poem cuts sharply through any distance that seems to exist between oneself and it. When we first read Charles Causley's 'Samuel Sweet' we felt we could not bring ourselves to go through the agony of reading it again. Yet, curiously, though poetry heightens the emotion in a story, at the same time it shapes and controls suffering, and makes a harmony between cause and effect. It is also one of the purposes of poetry to teach wisdom to the human heart. Chaucer pleads with us:

> Taketh the morality, good men,
> For Saint Paul saith that all that written is,
> To our doctrine it is y-writ.

One finds oneself learning from Causley and Coleridge that evil, once let loose, will hurt the innocent as well as the guilty; and from Spenser that a man may not leave this life 'until his Captain bid'. But often 'black tragedy lets slip her grim disguise' and turns to black comedy instead. The more we tried to balance the anthology between tragedy and comedy the faster it spun like a thaumatrope and the two masks merged into one. Milton's *Paradise Lost* is by no means unrelieved tragedy: some incidents might come straight from horror comics. William Plomer, writing satires in which 'the terrifying coincides with the absurd', and Marriott Edgar, were only the latest in a succession of poets who have treated death with levity. Thomas Hood and Richard Barham out-clowned them long before, and the author of the exuberant 'Babes in the Wood' long before that.

This anthology, like *The Oxford Book of Children's Verse*, is arranged chronologically not by the date of a poet's birth but by the date of publication of the earliest of his pieces here included. Only two poems presented any difficulty: the anonymous, unprovenanced ballad of 'Tam Lin', which has been placed beside its likely coeval 'Robin Hood and the Monk' of *c.* 1450; and the magnificent ballad of 'King Estmere'. The only source of 'King Estmere' is the mid-seventeenth-century manuscript now called the Percy Folio, upon which Thomas Percy based his *Reliques of Ancient English Poetry*, 1765. The extent of Percy's emendations to the ballad is not known, since he sent the manuscript pages on which the ballad appeared direct to the printer when the fourth edition was in preparation and they were inadvertently destroyed (he probably did no more than tidy up the wording and supply, most skilfully, stanzas 63–6). For this reason we decided to place the ballad in the mid-eighteenth century, and its inclusion here serves to highlight the influence his collection had on poets such as Coleridge and Scott. In the same way, the publication of Professor Child's eight volumes of traditional ballads in 1857–9 started a spate of imitation-antique ballads (Robert Buchanan's 'Ballad of Judas Iscariot' was one we reluctantly rejected), and Charles Dodgson, gleefully making fun of balladry in

PREFACE

'The Hunting of the Snark' produced one of the best ballads ever
written, in which the reader feels impelled to move eagerly from one
stanza to the next, for 141 stanzas, although perfectly aware—if he has
any sense—that what he is reading is nonsense. The classic ballad form
of short rhymed stanzas is, however, so excellently suited to the telling
of stories that poets have turned to it naturally without any sense of
archaism: for instance, and to name only those in this book, Goldsmith,
Cowper, Spencer, Macaulay, Longfellow, Hood, Oscar Wilde, and
Robert Service—and Kipling, the greatest ballad-writer of all, who
made the metre his own by doubling up the lines.

In keeping with other Oxford books in the series care has been taken
with the texts, the different readings have been collated, and spelling
and punctuation have been modernized. We have followed *The New
Oxford Book of English Verse* in bringing Chaucer's lines as near to
present-day orthography as is possible without, we hope, spoiling the
wonder that must be felt at this deliciously human verse having been
written six hundred years ago. We have also brought Henryson's fable
of the 'Upland Mouse and the Burgess Mouse' as near to modern
Scots as seemed allowable, thinking it would be a pity if it was not read
because of what W. E. Henley called its 'distressingly quaint and
crabbed' dialect. We even felt that in an anthology for the general reader
it was permissible to modernize slightly Spenser's deliberately archaic
spelling in the *Faerie Queene*; for someone reading 'The Cave of Despair'
as a story, it seems unnecessarily irritating to find 'persuade' spelt
'perswade' and 'melt'th' spelt 'mealt'th'. Glosses have been given for
any words that, left unexplained, might have impeded the
understanding of a poem. We have, in fact, tried to present the poems
in a form that would be comfortable for a modern reader.

One of the interests to us, in assembling the anthology, has been in
discovering where the narrative poets found their stories, and how
astonishingly often the stories they used were traditional. Emerson was
right when he said 'The poet needs a ground in popular tradition on
which he may work, and which, again, may restrain his art within the
due temperance. It holds him to the people, supplies a foundation for
his edifice; and, in furnishing so much work done to his hand, leaves
him at leisure, and in full strength for the audacities of his imagination.
In short, the poet owes to his legend what sculpture owed to the
temple.' Of the fifty-nine stories in this book, nearly half are from
tradition, and less than that number from real life; seven are borrowed
from other authors, and only ten could conceivably be considered the
products of the poet's imagination. We hope the notes at the back of
the book will be found interesting not only because they trace,
whenever possible, the story or incident which inspired a poem, but
because they sometimes also show the creative process by which a poet
fashioned his poem from a prose source; and we hope they will not be

painfully disillusioning to those who believe that a dog hero is buried beneath the cairn of stones at Beddgelert; or that the Lady of Shalott drifted along the river Wey to many-towered Guildford.

It may also be helpful to point out that narrative verse needs a different reading technique from lyric and reflective poetry. The second reading of these poems is the time to pause at lines like 'Nervous the sea crawled and twitched like the skin of a beast', and to be dazzled by the brilliance of Arnold's metaphors. A narrative poem is in the nature of a sea voyage, and it is no good poking about in the rock pools waiting for the sea anemones to unfold their fronds. The reader of 'The Nabara' must launch himself boldly on to the Mar Cantabrico; the adventurer must hasten with Sohrab and Rustum to the glittering sands by the far-distant Oxus (and if he feels no sense of excitement he would do better to have a day at Bognor Regis instead). He will find the rewards are great: he will bring home not only the memory of the voyage but a rich cargo of experience and laughter.

I. O. & P. O.

West Liss in Hampshire

CONTENTS

CONTENTS

CONTENTS

CONTENTS

GEOFFREY CHAUCER

c.1343–1400

The Cock and the Hen

A POORÈ widow, somedeal stape in age,
Was whilom dwelling in a narrow cottáge,
Beside a grovè, standing in a dale.
This widow, of which I tell you my tale,
Since thilkè day that she was last a wife,   5
In patiénce led a full simple life,
For little was her cattle and her rent.
By husbandry of such as God her sent
She found herself and eek her daughtrèn two.
Three largè sowès had she, and na mo,   10
Three kine, and eek a sheep that hightè Mall.
Full sooty was her bower and eek her hall,
In which she eat full many a slender meal.
Of poignant sauce her needed never a deal.
No dainty morsel passèd through her throat;   15
Her diet was accordant to her coat.
Repletión ne made her never sick;
A temperate diet was all her physíc,
And exercise, and heartès suffisánce.
The goutè let her nothing for to dance,   20
Ne apoplexy shentè not her head.
No wine ne drank she, neither white ne red;
Her board was servèd most with white and black—
Milk and brown bread, in which she found no lack—
Seynd bacon, and sometime an egg or tway;   25
For she was, as it were, a manner dey.
A yard she had, enclosèd all about
With stickès, and a dryè ditch without,
In which she had a cock, hight Chanticleer.
In all the land, of crowing n'as his peer;   30
His voice was merrier than the merry orgán
On massè-days that in the churchè gone.
Well sikerer was his crowing in his lodge
Than is a clock or an abbey horologe.

somedeal stape in age] somewhat advanced in age   whilom] once   thilkè] that, that same
cattle] goods   rent] income   found] provided for   eek] also   hightè] was named
deal] bit   let] hindered   shentè] injured   Seynd] broiled
a manner dey] a kind of dairy-woman   n'as] none was   Well sikerer] more reliable

By nature knew he each ascensión 35
Of the equinoxial in thilkè town;
For when degrees fifteen weren ascended,
Then crew he, that it might not ben amended.
His comb was redder than the fine corál,
And batailled, as it were a castle wall; 40
His bill was black, and as the jet it shone;
Like azure were his leggès, and his toon;
His nailès whiter than the lily flower,
And like the burnèd gold was his colóur.
This gentle cock had in his governánce 45
Seven hennès for to doon all his pleasánce,
Which were his sisters and his paramours,
And wonder like to him, as of colóurs;
Of which the fairest huèd on her throat
Was cleped fair damoisellè Pertelote. 50
Courteous she was, discreet, and debonair,
And compaignable, and bore herself so fair,
Since thilkè day that she was seven night old,
That truèly she hath the heart in hold
Of Chanticleer, locken in every lith; 55
He loved her so, that well was him therewith.
But such a joy was it to hear them sing,
When that the brightè sunnè gan to spring,
In sweet accord, 'My lief is faren in land.'
For thilkè time, as I have understood, 60
Beastès and birdès couldè speak and sing.
    And so befell that in a dawèning,
As Chanticleer among his wivès all
Sat on his perchè, that was in the hall,
And next him sat this fairè Pertelote, 65
This Chanticleer gan groanen in his throat
As man that in his dream is dretchèd sore.
And when that Pertelote thus heard him roar,
She was aghast, and said, 'O heartè dear,
What aileth you, to groan in this mannér? 70
Ye been a very sleeper; fie, for shame!'
    And he answered, and saidè thus: 'Madame,
I pray you that ye take it not agrief.
By God, me met I was in such mischíef

batailled] battlemented   toon] toes   cleped] called   discreet] wise   debonair] meek
locken in every lith] locked in every limb
'My lief is faren in land'] 'My love has gone to foreign lands'   dretchèd] troubled
Ye been a very sleeper] what a sleeper you are   met] dreamed

2

Right now, that yet mine heart is sore afright. 75
Now God,' quod he, 'my sweven reck aright,
And keep my body out of foul prisón!
Me met how that I roamèd up and down
Within our yard, where as I saw a beast
Was like an hound, and would han made arrest 80
Upon my body, and would han had me dead.
His colour was betwix yellòw and red,
And tippèd was his tail and both his ears
With black, unlike the remnant of his hairs;
His snoutè small, with glowing eyen tway. 85
Yet of his look for fear almost I die;
This causèd me my groaning, doubtèless.'
 'Avoy!' quod she, 'fie on you, heartèless!
Alas,' quod she, 'for, by that God above,
Now han ye lost mine heart and all my love. 90
I can not love a coward, by my faith!
For certès, what so any woman saith,
We all desiren, if it mightè be,
To han husbandès hardy, wise, and free,
And secret, and no niggard, ne no fool, 95
Ne him that is aghast of every tool,
Ne none avaunter, by that God above!
How durst ye say, for shame, unto your love
That any thing might makè you afeared?
Have ye no mannès heart, and han a beard? 100
Alas! and can ye been aghast of swevenis?
Nothing, God wot, but vanity in sweven is.
Swevens engendren of repletións,
And oft of fume and of complexións,
When humours been too abundant in a wight. 105
Certès this dream, which ye han met tonight,
Cometh of the great superfluity
Of your reddè colera, pardie,
Which causeth folk to dreaden in their dreams
Of arrows, and of fire with reddè leams, 110
Of reddè beastès, that they will them bite,
Of conteck, and of whelpès, great and lite;
Right as the humour of meláncholỵ
Causeth full many a man in sleep to cry

my sweven reck aright] interpret my dream favourably eyen] eyes heartèless] spiritless
secret] discreet aghast of every tool] frightened of every weapon avaunter] boaster
fume] vapour from the stomach complexións] natural bodily constitutions
humours] vapours tonight] last night colera] bile leams] flames conteck] strife
lite] little Right as] just as

For fear of blackè bears, or bullès black,   115
Or ellès blackè devils will them take.
Of other humours could I tell alsó
That wirken many a man in sleep full woe;
But I will pass as lightly as I can.
 'Lo Cato, which that was so wise a man, 120
Said he not thus, "Ne do no force of dreams"?
 'Now sire,' quod she, 'when we fly from the beams,
For Goddès love, as take some laxative.
Up peril of my soul and of my life,
I counsel you the best, I will not lie,   125
That both of colere and of melancholy
Ye purge you; and for ye shall not tarry,
Though in this town is none apothecary,
I shall myself to herbès teachen you
That shall be for your heal and for your prow; 130
And in our yard those herbès shall I find
The which han of their property, by kind,
To purgè you beneath and eek above.
Forget not this, for Goddès owen love!
Ye been full coleric of complexión.   135
Ware the sun in his ascensión
Ne find you not replete of humours hot;
And if it do, I dare well lay a groat,
That ye shall have a fever terciáne,
Or an ague, that may be your bane.   140
A day or two ye shall have digestíves
Of wormès, ere ye take your laxatives
Of laureole, centaury, and fumitory,
Or else of hellebore, that groweth there,
Of catapucè, or of goat-tree's berries,   145
Of herb ivy, growing in our yard, there merry is;
Peck them up right as they grow, and eat them in.
Be merry, husband, for your father kin!
Dreadeth no dream; I can say you no more.'
 'Madame,' quod he, 'gramercy of your lore. 150
But nathèless, as touching Don Cato,
That hath of wisdom such a great renown,
Though that he bad no dreamès for to dread,
By God, men may in oldè bookès read

wirken] make Lo Cato] look at Cato Ne do no force] take no notice Up peril of] at
the peril of heal] health prow] benefit terciáne] tertian, recurring every third day
laureole] spurge laurel catapucè] caper-spurge goat-tree] dogwood, or possibly buckthorn
herb ivy] ground ivy for your father kin] for the sake of your fathers
gramercy] many thanks

Of many a man more of authority 155
Than ever Cato was, so moot I thee,
That all the reverse sayen of this sentence,
And han well founden by experience
That dreamès been significatións
As well of joyè as of tribulatións 160
That folk enduren in this life present.
There needeth make of this none argument;
The very proofè showeth it indeed.
   'One of the greatest authors that men read
Saith thus: that whilom two fellowès went 165
On pilgrimage, in a full good intent;
And happened so, they comen in a town
Where as there was such congregatión
Of people, and eek so strait of harbourage,
That they ne found as much as one cottáge 170
In which they bothè might y-lodgèd be.
Wherefore they mosten of necessitý,
As for that night, departen companý;
And each of them goeth to his hostelrý,
And took his lodging as it wouldè fall. 175
That one of them was lodgèd in a stall,
Far in a yard, with oxen of the plough;
That other man was lodgèd well enough,
As was his aventúre or his fortúne,
That us governeth all as in commúne. 180
   'And so befell that, long ere it were day,
This man met in his bed, there as he lay,
How that his fellow gan upon him call,
And said, "Alas, for in an oxès stall
This night I shall be murdered there I lie. 185
Now help me, dearè brother, or I die.
In allè hastè come to me!" he said.
This man out of his sleep for fear abraid;
But when that he was wakened of his sleep,
He turnèd him, and took of this no keep. 190
Him thought his dream n'as but a vanity.
Thus twiès in his sleeping dreamèd he;
And at the third time yet his fellow
Came, as him thought, and said, "I am now slawe.
Behold my bloody woundès deep and wide! 195
Arise up early in the morning-tide,

so moot I thee] so may I thrive   sentence] opinion   so strait of harbourage] so short of
lodgings   met] dreamed   abraid] awoke

And at the west gate of the town," quod he,
"A cartė full of dung there shalt thou see,
In which my body is hid full privily;
Do thilkė cart arresten boldėly.   200
My gold caused my murder, sooth to sayn."
And told him every point how he was slain,
With a full piteous facė, pale of hue.
And trustė well, his dream he found full true;
For on the morrow, as soon as it was day,   205
To his fellowės inn he took the way;
And when that he came to this oxės stall,
After his fellow he began to call.

    'The hosteler answered him anon,
And saidė, "Sire, your fellow is a-gone;   210
As soon as day he went out of the town."

    'This man gan fallen in suspición,
Remembering on his dreamės that he met,
And forth he goeth—no longer would he let—
Unto the west gate of the town, and found   215
A dung-cart, as it were to dungė land,
That was arrayėd in the samė wise
As ye han heard the deadė man devise.
And with an hardy heart he gan to cry
Vengeance and justice of this felony.   220
"My fellow murdered is this samė night,
And in this cart he lieth gaping upright.
I cry out on the ministers," quod he,
"That shoulden keep and rulen this citý.
Harrow! alas! here lieth my fellow slain!"   225
What should I more unto this talė sayn?
The people out start and cast the cart to ground,
And in the middle of the dung they found
The deadė man, that murdered was all new.

    'O blissful God, that art so just and true,   230
Lo, how that thou bewrayest murder alway!
Murder will out, that see we day by day.
Murder is so wlatsom and abominable
To God, that is so just and reasonable,
That he ne will not suffer it helėd be,   235
Though it abide a year, or two, or three.
Murder will out, this my conclusión.
And right anon, ministers of that town

sooth to sayn] truth to tell   anon] at once   gaping upright] i.e. on his back
    bewrayest] makest known   wlatsom] odious   helėd] concealed

6

Han hent the carter and so sore him pyned,
And eek the hosteler so sore engynèd, 240
That they biknewe their wickedness anon,
And were anhangèd by the neckè-bone.
  'Here may men seen that dreamès been to dread.
And certès in the samè book I read,
Right in the nextè chapter after this— 245
I gabbè not, so have I joy or bliss—
Two men that would han passèd over sea,
For certain cause, into a far countrý,
If that the wind ne had been contrarý,
That made them in a city for to tarry 250
That stood full merry upon an haven-side.
But on a day, again the eventide,
The wind gan change, and blew right as them lest.
Jolif and glad they went unto their rest,
And casten them full early for to sail. 255
But to that one man fell a great marvél:
That one of them, in sleeping as he lay,
Him met a wonder dream again the day.
Him thought a man stood by his beddès side,
And him commanded that he should abide, 260
And said him thus: "If thou tomorrow wend,
Thou shall be drowned; my tale is at an end."
He woke, and told his fellow what he met,
And prayèd him his voyage for to let;
As for that day, he prayèd him to bide. 265
His fellow, that lay by his beddès side,
Gan for to laugh, and scornèd him full fast.
"No dream," quod he, "may so mine heart aghast
That I will lettè for to do my things.
I settè not a straw by thy dreamíngs, 270
For swevens been but vanitics and japes.
Men dream all day of owlès and of apes,
And eek of many a mazè therewithal;
Men dream of thing that never was ne shall.
But sith I see that thou wilt here abide, 275
And thus forslewthen wilfully thy tide,
God wot, it rueth me; and have good day!"
And thus he took his leave, and went his way.

hent] seized pyned] tortured engyned] racked biknewe] confessed
  I gabbè not, so have I. . .] If I lie, may I never have joy or bliss
right as them lest] just as they wished jolif] jolly casten] planned
    mazè] delusion forslewthen] lose through sloth

7

But ere that he had half his course y-sailed,
Noot I not why, ne what mischance it ailed,   280
But casually the shippės bottom rent,
And ship and man under the water went
In sight of other shippės it beside,
And with them sailèd at the same tide.
And therefore, fairė Pertelote so dear,   285
By such examples oldė mayst thou lear
That no man shouldė been too reckėless
Of dreamės; for I say thee, doubtėless,
That many a dream full sore is for to dread.
   'Lo, in the life of Saint Kenelm I read,   290
That was Kenulphus' son, the noble king
Of Mercia, how Kenelm met a thing.
A little ere he was murdered, on a day,
His murderer in his avisión he say.
His norice him expounded every deal   295
His sweven, and bad him for to keep him well
For treason; but he n'as but seven year old,
And therefore little talė hath he told
Of any dream, so holy was his heart.
By God! I haddė liefer than my shirt   300
That you had read his legend, as have I.
   'Dame Pertelote, I say you truėly,
Macrobius, that writ the avisión
In Afrique of the worthy Scipio,
Affirmeth dreams, and sayeth that they been   305
Warning of thingės that men after seen.
And furthermore, I pray you, looketh well
In the old testament, of Daniel,
If he held dreamės any vanity.
Read eek of Joseph, and there shall ye see   310
Where dreamės ben sometime—I say not all—
Warning of thingės that shall after fall.
Look of Egýpt the king, Don Pharaoh,
His baker and his butiller also,
Where they ne feltė no effect in dreams?   315
Whoso will seeken acts of sundry realms
May read of dreamės many a wonder thing.
Lo Croesus, which that was of Lydia king,
Met he not that he sat upon a tree,
Which signified he should anhangèd be?   320

Noot I] I know not   casually] accidentally   lear] learn   reckėless] heedless
say (l.294)] saw   norice] nurse   deal] part   little tale hath he told] little heed has he paid

Lo here Andrómache, Hectórès wife,
That day that Hector shouldè lose his life,
She dreamèd on the samè night beforn
How that the life of Hector should be lorn,
If thilkè day he went into bataille. 325
She warnèd him, but it might not avail;
He wentè for to fightè nathèless,
But he was slain anon of Achilles.
But thilkè tale is all too long to tell,
And eek it is nigh day, I may not dwell. 330
Shortly I say, as for conclusión,
That I shall han of this avisión
Adversity; and I say furthermore,
That I ne tell of laxatives no store,
For they been venomous, I wot it well; 335
I them defy, I love them never a deal.
    'Now let us speak of mirth and stint all this.
Madamè Pertelote, so have I bliss,
Of one thing God hath sent me largè grace;
For when I see the beauty of your face, 340
Ye been so scarlet red about your eyen,
It maketh all my dreadè for to dyen;
For all so siker as *In principio*,
Mulier est hominis confusio—
Madame, the sentence of this Latin is, 345
"Woman is mannès joy and all his bliss."*
For when I feel a-night your softè side,
Albeit that I may not on you ride,
For that our perch is made so narrowè, alas!
I am so full of joy and of soláce 350
That I defyè bothè sweven and dream.'
And with that word he flew down from the beam,
For it was day, and eek his hennès all;
And with a chuck he gan them for to call,
For he had found a corn, lay in the yard. 355
Royal he was, he was no more afeard.
He feathered Pertelotè twenty time,
And trod her eek as oft, ere it was prime.
He looketh as it were a grim lión,
And on his toes he roameth up and down; 360

lorn] lost   tell . . . no store] set no store   so siker as *In principio*] as true as the Gospel

* The uneducated Pertelote is not to know *Mulier est hominis confusio* really means 'Woman is man's undoing'.

Him deignèd not to set his foot to ground.
He chucketh when he hath a corn y-found,
And to him runnen then his wivès all.
Thus royal, as a prince is in his hall,
Leave I this Chanticleer in his pastúre; 365
And after will I tell his aventúre.
    When that the month in which the world began,
That hightè March, when God first makèd man,
Was cómplete, and passèd were also,
Since March begannè, thirty days and two, 370
Befell that Chanticleer in all his pride,
His seven wivès walking by his side,
Cast up his eyen to the brightè sun,
That in the sign of Taurus had y-run
Twenty degrees and one, and somewhat more, 375
And knew by kind, and by none other lore,
That it was prime, and crew with blissful steven.
'The sun,' he said, 'is clomben up on heaven
Forty degrees and one, and more ywis.
Madamè Pertelote, my worldès bliss, 380
Harkneth these blissful birdès how they sing,
And see the freshè flowers how they spring;
Full is mine heart of revel and soláce!'
But suddenly him fell a sorrowful case,
For ever the latter end of joy is woe. 385
God wot that worldly joy is soon ago;
And if a rhetor couldè fair indite,
He in a chronique safely might it write
As for a sovereign notability.
Now every wise man, let him harken me; 390
This story is all so true, I undertake,
As is the book of Launcelot de Lake,
That women hold in full great reverence.
Now will I turn again to my sentence.
    A coal-fox, full of sly iniquity, 395
That in the grove had wonèd yearès three,
By high imaginatión forncast,
The samè night throughout the hedges brast
Into the yard there Chanticleer the fair
Was wont, and eek his wivès, to repair; 400
And in a bed of wortès still he lay,
Till it was passèd undren of the day,

by kind] by instinct steven] voice ywis] surely rhetor] writer coal-fox] fox with black-tipped ears wonèd] dwelt By high imaginatión forncast] By divine imagination ordained throughout] out through wortès] herbs undren of the day] the middle of the day

10

Waiting his time on Chanticleer to fall,
As gladly doon these homicidès all
That in await liggen to murder men.   405
O false murderer, lurking in thy den!
O new Iscariot, newè Ganelon!
False dissimuler, O Greek Sinon,
That broughtest Troy all utterly to sorrow!
O Chanticleer, accursèd be that morrow   410
That thou into that yard flew from the beams!
Thou were full well y-warnèd by thy dreams
That thilkè day was perilous to thee;
But what that God forwoot must needès be,
After the opiniòn of certain clerkès.   415
Witness on him that any perfect clerk is,
That in school is great altercation
In this mattèr, and great disputation,
And hath been of an hundred thousand men.
But I ne can not bult it to the bren   420
As can the holy doctor Augustine,
Or Boethius, or the Bishop Bradwardine,
Whether that Goddès worthy forwitting
Straineth me needly for to doon a thing—
'Needly' clepe I simple necessity;   425
Or ellès, if free choice be granted me
To do that samè thing, or do it nought,
Though God forwoot it ere that it was wrought;
Or if his witting straineth never a deal
But by necessity conditionàl.   430
I will not han to do of such mattèr;
My tale is of a cock, as ye may hear,
That took his counsel of his wife, with sorrow,
To walken in the yard upon that morrow
That he had met the dream that I you told.   435
Womenès counsels been full oftè cold;
Womenès counsel brought us first to woe,
And made Adam from Paradise to go,
There as he was full merry and well at ease.
But for I noot to whom it might displease,   440
If I counsel of women wouldè blame,
Pass over, for I said it in my game.
Read authors, where they treat of such mattèr,
And what they sayn of women ye may hear.

forwoot] foreknew   clerk] scholar   bult it to the bren] sift it to the bran, i.e. to the bottom
   Goddès worthy forwitting] God's excellent foreknowing   Straineth me needly] forces
   me necessarily   clepe] call   cold] fatal   for I noot] for I know not

These been the cockès wordès, and not mine;   445
I can none harm of no woman divine.
   Fair in the sand, to bathe her merrily,
Lay Pertelote, and all her sisters by,
Again the sun, and Chanticleer so free
Sang merrier than the mermaid in the sea;   450
For Physiologus saith sikerly
How that they singen well and merrily.
And so befell that, as he cast his eye
Among the wortès on a butterfly,
He was ware of this fox that lay full low.   455
Nothing ne list him thennè for to crow,
But cried anon, 'Cok! cok!' and up he start
As man that was affrayèd in his heart.
For naturally a beast desireth flee
From his contráry, if he may it see,   460
Though he never erst had seen it with his eye.
   This Chanticleer, when he gan him espy,
He would han fled, but that the fox anon
Said, 'Gentle sire, alas! where will ye gon?
Be ye afraid of me that am your friend?   465
Now certès, I were worsè than a fiend,
If I to you would harm or villainy!
I am not come your council for t'espy,
But truèly, the cause of my comíng
Was only for to harken how that ye sing.   470
For truèly, ye have as merry a steven
As any angel hath that is in heaven;
Therewith ye han in music more feelíng
Than had Boethius, or any that can sing.
My lord your father—God his soulè bless!—   475
And eek your mother, of her gentleness,
Han in mine house y-been, to my great ease;
And certès, sire, full fain would I you please.
But, for men speak of singing, I will say—
So moot I brookè well mine eyen tway—   480
Save you, I heardè never man so sing
As did your father in the morwening.
Certès, it was of heart, all that he sung.
And for to make his voice the morè strong,
He would so peyn him that with both his eyen   485
He mostè wink, so loudè he would cryen,

divine] perceive   erst] before
So moot I brookè well mine eyen tway] so may I enjoy my two eyes   morwening] morning
so peyn him] make such an effort   mostè wink] must close his eyes

12

And standen on his tiptoon therewithal,
And stretchè forth his neckè long and small.
And eek he was of such discretión
That there n'as no man in no región   490
That him in song or wisdom mightè pass.
I have well read in "Don Burnel the Ass",
Among his verse, how that there was a cock,
For that a priestès son gave him a knock
Upon his leg while he was young and nice,   495
He made him for to lose his benefice.
But certain, there n'is no comparisón
Betwixt the wisdom and discretión
Of your father, and of his subtlety.
Now singeth, sire, for Saintè Charity;   500
Let see, can ye your father counterfeit?'
      This Chanticleer his wingès gan to beat,
As man that could his treason not espy,
So was he ravished with his flattery.
      Alas! ye lordès, many a false flatterer   505
Is in your courts, and many a losenger,
That pleasen you well moré, by my faith,
Than he that soothfastness unto you saith.
Readeth Ecclesiasticus of flattery;
Beeth ware, ye lordès, of her treachery.   510
      This Chanticleer stood high upon his toes,
Stretching his neck, and held his eyen close,
And gan to crowè loudè for the nonce;
And Don Russell the fox start up at once,
And by the garget hentè Chanticleer   515
And on his back toward the wood him bare,
For yet ne was there no man that him 'sued.
      O destiny, that mayst not been eschewed!
Alas, that Chanticleer flew from the beams!
Alas, his wife ne reckèd not of dreams!   520
And on a Friday fell all this mischance.
      O Venus, that art goddess of pleasánce,
Since that thy servant was this Chanticleer,
And in thy service didè all his power,
More for delight than world to multiply,   525
Why wouldst thou suffer him on thy day to die?
      O Geoffrey, dear master sovereign,
That, when thy worthy king Richard was slain

nice] foolish   losenger] deceiver
soothfastness] truth   Beeth ware] be wary   garget] throat   'sued] pursued

With shot, complainèdest his death so sore,
Why ne had I now thy sentence and thy lore,   530
The Friday for to chide, as diden ye?
For on a Friday, soothly, slain was he.
Then would I show you how that I could 'plain
For Chanticleerès dread and for his pain.

    Certès, such cry ne lamentatión   535
Was never of ladies made when Ilium
Was won, and Pyrrhus with his straightè sword,
When he had hent king Priam by the beard,
And slain him, as saith us *Aeneid*,
As maden all the hennès in the close,   540
When they had seen of Chanticleer the sight.
But sovereignly Dame Pertelotè shright
Full louder than did Hasdrubalès wife,
When that her husband haddè lost his life,
And that the Romans haddè burnt Carthage.   545
She was so full of torment and of rage
That wilfully into the fire she start,
And burned herselfen with a steadfast heart.

    O woeful hennès, right so cryden ye,
As, when that Nero burnèd the cití   550
Of Rome, cryden senatorès wives
For that their husbands losten all their lives—
Withouten guilt this Nero hath them slain.
Now will I turnè to my tale again.

    This silly widowè and eek her daughters two   555
Hearden these hennès cry and maken woe,
And out at doorès starten they anon,
And seen the fox toward the grovè gone,
And bore upon his back the cock away,
And cryden, 'Out! harrow! and well-away!   560
Ha! ha! the fox!' and after him they ran,
And eek with stavès many another man.
Ran Coll our dog, and Talbot and Garlánd,
And Malkin, with a distaff in her hand;
Ran cow and calf, and eek the very hogs,   565
So fearèd for the barking of the dogs
And shouting of the men and women eek,
They rannè so them thought their heartè break.
They yélleden as fiendès doon in hell;
The duckès cryden as men would them quell;   570

sentence] judgement   'plain] complain   shright] shrieked   silly] simple   quell] kill

The geese for fearė flewen over the trees;
Out of the hivė came the swarm of bees.
So hideous was the noise, ah! *benedicite*!
Certės, he Jackė Straw and his meinie
Ne madė never shoutės half so shrill   575
When that they woulden any Fleming kill,
As thilkė day was made upon the fox.
Of brass they broughten bemės, and of box,
Of horn, of bone, in which they blew and pooped,
And therewithal they skrikèd and they whooped;   580
It seemėd as that heaven shouldė fall.

   Now, goodė men, I pray you harkneth all:
Lo, how Fortunė turneth suddenly
The hope and pride eek of her enemy!
This cock, that lay upon the foxės back,   585
In all his dread unto the fox he spake,
And saidė, 'Sire, if that I were as ye,
Yet should I sayen, as wise God helpė me,
"Turneth again, ye proudė churlės all!
A very pestilence upon you fall!   590
Now am I come unto this woodės side;
Maugrė your heed, the cock shall here abide.
I will him eat, in faith, and that anon!" '

   The fox answéred, 'In faith, it shall be done.'
And as he spoke that word, all suddenly   595
This cock brake from his mouth deliverly,
And high upon a tree he flew anon.
And when the fox saw that the cock was gone,
  'Alas,' quod he, 'O Chanticleer, alas!
I have to you,' quod he, 'y-done trespáss,   600
In as much as I makèd you afeard
When I you hent and brought out of the yard.
But, sire, I did it in no wikke intent;
Come down, and I shall tell you what I meant.
I shall say sooth to you, God help me so!'   605
  'Nay then,' quod he, 'I shrew us bothė two.
And first I shrew myself, both blood and bones,
If thou beguilė me ofter than once.
Thou shalt no morė, through thy flattery,
Do me to sing and winkė with mine eye;   610
For he that winketh, when he shouldė see,
All wilfully, God let him never thee!'

     meinie] mob bemės] trumpets skrikèd] screeched
Maugrė your heed] in spite of all you can do deliverly] quickly wikke] wicked
     shrew] beshrew, blame thee] thrive

15

'Nay,' quod the fox, 'but God give him mischance,
That is so indiscreet of governance
That jangleth when he shoulde hold his peace.'   615
   Lo, such it is for to be reckeless,
And negligent, and trust on flattery.
   But ye that holden this tale a folly,
As of a fox, or of a cock and hen,
Taketh the morality, good men.   620
For Saint Paul saith that all that written is,
To our doctrine it is y-writ, ywis;
Taketh the fruit, and let the chaff be still.
Now, goode God, if that it be thy will,
As saith my Lord, so make us all good men,   625
And bring us to his highe blisss! Amen.

Death and the Three Revellers

THESE rioteres three of which I tell,
Long erst ere prime rang of any bell
Were set them in a tavern for to drink;
And as they sat, they heard a belle clink
Beforn a corpse, was carried to his grave.   5
That one of them gan callen to his knave:
'Go bet,' quod he, 'and aske readily
What corpse is this that passeth here forby;
And look that thou report his name well.'
   'Sire,' quod this boy, 'it needeth never-a-deal.   10
It was me told, ere ye came here, two hours.
He was, pardie, an old fellow of yours;
And suddenly he was y-slain tonight,
Fordrunk, as he sat on his bench upright.
There came a privy thief men clepeth Death,   15
That in this country all the people slayeth,
And with his spear he smote his heart a-two
And went his way withouten wordes mo.
He hath a thousand slain, this pestilence.
And, master, ere ye come in his presence,   20
Me thinketh that it were necessary
For to be ware of such an adversary.

To our doctrine it is y-writ] it is written to teach us
Long erst ere. . .] Long before the first ringing of any church bell 'Go bet'] go quickly
it needeth never-a-deal] it is not a bit necessary pardie] by God Fordrunk] very drunk

Beeth ready for to meet him evermore;
Thus taughtè me my dame; I say no more.'
'By Saintè Mary!' said this taverner,   25
'The child saith sooth, for he has slain this year,
Hence over a mile, within a great village,
Both man and woman, child, and hind, and page.
I trow his habitatión be there.
To been avisèd great wisdóm it were,   30
Ere that he did a man a dishonour.'
      'Yea, Goddès armès!' quod this rioter,
'Is it such peril with him for to meet?
I shall him seek by way and eek by street,
I make avow to Goddès dignè bones!   35
Harkeneth, fellows, we three been all ones;
Let each of us hold up his hand till other,
And each of us becomen others brother,
And we will slayen this false traitor Death.
He shall be slain, which that so many slayeth,   40
By Goddès dignity, ere it be night!'
      Together han these three their trothès plight
To live and dyen each of them for other,
As though he were his own y-boren brother;
And up they start, all drunken in this rage,   45
And forth they goon towardès that village
Of which the taverner had spoke beforn.
And many a grisly oath then han they sworn,
And Christès blessèd body they to-rent:
Death shall be dead, if that they may him hent!   50
      When they han goon not fully half a mile,
Right as they would han trodden over a stile,
An old man and a poorè with them met.
This oldè man full meekèly them gret,
And saidè thus, 'Now, lordès, God you see!'   55
      The proudest of these rioterès three
Answered again, 'What, carl, with sorry grace!
Why art thou all forwrappèd save thy face?
Why livest thou so long in so great age?'
      This oldè man gan look in his viságe,   60
And saidè thus: 'For I ne can not find
A man, though that I walkèd into Ind,
Neither in city nor in no villáge,
That wouldè change his youthè for mine age;

sooth] truth   avisèd] forewarned   Yea] Indeed   dignè] honoured
                        hent] catch

And therefore moot I han mine agè still,   65
As longè time as it is Goddès will.
Ne Death, alas! ne will not han my life.
Thus walk I, like a restèless caitiff,
And on the ground, which is my mother's gate,
I knockè with my staff, both early and late,   70
And sayè "Liefè mother, let me in!
Lo how I vanish, flesh, and blood, and skin!
Alas! when shall my bonès been at rest?
Mother, with you would I change my chest
That in my chamber longè time hath be,   75
Yea, for an hairè clout to wrappè me!"
But yet to me she will not do that grace,
For which full pale and welkèd is my face.
   'But, sires, to you it is no courtesy
To speaken to an old man villainy,   80
But he trespass in word, or else in deed.
In Holy Writ ye may yourself well read:
"Against an old man, hoar upon his head,
Ye should arise;" wherefore I give you rede,
Ne doeth unto an old man none harm now,   85
No more than that ye would men did to you
In agè, if that ye so long abide—
And God be with you, where ye go or ride!
I moot go thither as I have to go.'
   'Nay, oldè churl, by God, thou shalt not so,'   90
Said this other hazarder anon,
'Thou partest not so lightly, by Saint John!
Thou spake right now of thilkè traitor Death,
That in this country all our friendès slayeth.
Have here my troth, as thou art his espy,   95
Tell where he is, or thou shalt it abye,
By God, and by the holy sacrament!
For soothly thou art one of his a-sent
To slain us youngè folk, thou falsè thief!'
   'Now, sires,' quod he, 'if that you be so lief   100
To findè Death, turn up this crooked way,
For in that grove I left him, by my fay,
Under a tree, and there he will abide;
Not for your boast he will him nothing hide.

caitiff] captive liefè] dear chest] chest of clothes hairè clout] hair cloth (for a shroud)
welkèd] withered speaken...villainy, But] speak...uncivilly, Unless Ye should
arise] a reference to Leviticus (19:32) 'Thou shalt rise up before the hoary head, and
honour the face of the old man' rede] counsel thilkè] that abye] pay the penalty
fay] faith Not for your boast...hide] He will not hide in spite of your noise

See ye that oak? Right there ye shall him find.   105
God savė you, that bought again mankind,
And you amend!' Thus said this oldė man;
And everich of these rioterės ran
Till he came to that tree, and there they found
Of florins fine of gold y-coinèd round   110
Well nigh an eightė bushels, as them thought.
No longer thennė after Death they sought,
But each of them so glad was of that sight,
For that the florins been so fair and bright,
That down they set them by this precious hoard.   115
The worst of them, he spake the firstė word.
'Brethren,' quod he, 'take keepė what I say;
My wit is great, though that I bourd and play.
This treasure hath Fortune unto us given,
In mirth and jollity our life to liven,   120
And lightly as it cometh, so will we spend.
Ey! Goddės precious dignity! who wend
Today that we should han so fair a grace?
But might this gold be carried from this place
Home to mine house, or ellės unto yours—   125
For well ye woot that all this gold is ours—
Then werė we in high felicity.
But truėly, by day it may not be.
Men wouldė sayen that we were thievės strong,
And for our owėn treasure doon us hung.   130
This treasure must y-carried be by night
As wisely and as slyly as it might.
Wherefore I rede that cut among us all
Be draw, and let see where the cut will fall;
And he that hath the cut with heartė blithe   135
Shall runnė to the town, and that full swithe,
And bring us bread and wine full privily.
And two of us shall keepen subtėly
This treasure well; and if he will not tarry,
When it is night we will this treasure carry,   140
By one assent, where as us thinketh best.'
That one of them the cut brought in his fist,
And bad them draw, and look where it will fall;
And it fell on the youngest of them all,
And forth toward the town he went anon.   145
And all so soonė as that he was gone,

everich] each   bourd] jest   who wend] who would have imagined
rede] advise   cut among us all be draw] we draw lots   swithe] quickly

That one of them spake thus unto that other:
'Thou knowest well thou art my swornè brother;
Thy profit will I tellè thee anon.
Thou woost well that our fellow is agone;   150
And here is gold, and that full great plentý,
That shall departed been among us three.
But nathèless, if I can shape it so
That it departed were among us two,
Had I not done a friendès turn to thee?'   155
    That other answered, 'I noot how that may be;
He woot how that the gold is with us tway.
What shall we doon? What shall we to him say?'
    'Shall it be counsel?' said the firstè shrew,
'And shall I tellen thee in wordès few   160
What we shall doon, and bring it well about?'
    'I grantè,' quod that other, 'out of doubt,
That, by my troth, I will thee not betray.'
    'Now,' quod the first, 'thou woost well we be tway,
And two of us shall stronger be than one.   165
Look when that he is set, and right anon
Arise as though thou wouldest with him play,
And I shall rive him through the sidès tway
While that thou strugglest with him as in game,
And with thy dagger look thou do the same;   170
And then shall all this gold departed be,
My dearè friend, betwixen me and thee.
Then may we both our lustès all fulfil,
And play at dice right at our owèn will.'
And thus accorded been these shrewès tway   175
To slain the third, as ye han heard me say.
    This youngest, which that went unto the town,
Full oft in heart he rolleth up and down
The beauty of these florins new and bright.
'O Lord,' quod he, 'if so were that I might   180
Have all this treasure to myself alone,
There is no man that liveth under the throne
Of God that shouldè live so merry as I!'
And attè last the fiend, our enemy,
Put in his thought that he should poison buy,   185
With which he mightè slain his fellows tway;
For-why the fiend found him in such living
That he had leavè him to sorrow bring;

departed] divided   counsel] secret   shrew] villain   rive] pierce

20

For this was utterly his full intent,
To slay them both and never to repent.   190
And forth he goeth, no longer would he tarry,
Into the town, unto a pothecary.
And prayèd him that he him wouldè sell
Some poison, that he might his rattès quell;
And eek there was a polecat in his hawe,   195
That, as he said, his capons had y-slawe,
And fain he wouldè wreak him, if he might,
On vermin that destroyèd him by night.

    The pothecary answered, 'And thou shalt have
A thing that, all so God my soulè save,   200
In all this world there is no créatúre,
That eat or drunk hath of this confiture
Nought but the mountance of a corn of wheat,
That he ne shall his life anon forlete;
Yea, sterve he shall, and that in lessè while   205
Than thou wilt goon apace not but a mile,
This poison is so strong and violent.'

    This cursèd man hath in his hand y-hent
This poison in a box, and sith he ran
Into the nextè street unto a man,   210
And borrowed of him largè bottles three;
And in the two his poison pourèd he;
The third he keptè cleanè for his drink.
For all the night he shoop him for to swink
In carrying of the gold out of that place.   215
And when this rioter, with sorry grace,
Had filled with wine his greatè bottles three,
To his fellows again repaireth he.

    What needeth it to sermon of it more?
For right as they had cast his death before,   220
Right so they han him slain, and that anon.
And when that this was done, thus spake that one:
'Now let us sit and drink, and make us merry,
And afterward we will his body bury.'
And with that word it happèd him, par cas,   225
To take the bottle there the poison was,
And drank, and gave his fellow drink also,
For which anon they storven bothè two.

    But certès, I suppose that Avycen
Wrote never in no canon, ne in no fen,   230

hawe] yard   confiture] confection   mountance] amount   forlete] give up   sterve] die
sith] thereupon   he shoop him for to swink] he intended to labour   par cas] by chance
    storven] died   fen] section in Avicenna's *Canon of Medicine*

More wonder signés of empoisoning
Than had these wretches two, ere their ending.
Thus ended been these homicidés two,
And eek the false empoisoner also.

ANONYMOUS

*c.*1475

Robin Hood and the Monk

IN summer, when the shaws be sheen
   And leaves be large and long,
Hit is full merry in fair forest
   To hear the fowlis song;

To see the deer draw to the dale   5
   And leave the hillés hee,
And shadow them in the leavés green
   Under the greenwood tree.

Hit befell on Whitsontide,
   Early in a May morning,   10
The sun up fair can shine
   And the birdés merry can sing.

'This is a merry morning,' said Little John,
   'Be Him that died on tree;
A more merry man than I am one   15
   Lives not in Christiantie.'

'Pluck up thy heart, my dear master,'
   Little John can say,
'And think hit is a full fair time
   In a morning of May.'   20

'Yea, on thing grieves me,' said Robin,
   'And does my heart much woe—
That I may not no solemn day
   To mass nor matins go.'

sheen] bright

'Hit is a fortnight and more,' said he,   25
  'Sin I my saviour see;
Today will I to Nottingham,' said Robin,
  'With the might of mild Mary.'

Then spake Much, the milner son,
  Ever more well him betide: 30
'Take twelve of thy wight yeomen,
  Well weaponed, be thy side.
Such on would thy selfe slon,
  That twelve dare not abide.'

'Of all my merry men,' said Robin,   35
  'Be my faith I will non have,
But Little John shall bear my bow
  Till that me list to draw.'

'Thou shall bear thine own,' said Little John,
  'Master, and I will bear mine,   40
And we will shoot a penny,' said Little John,
  'Under the greenwood lyne.'

'I will not shoot a penny,' said Robin Hood,
  'I' faith, Little John, with thee,
But ever for one as thou shootis,' said Robin,   45
  'In faith I hold thee three.'

Thus shoot they forth, these yeomen two,
  Both at busk and broom,
Till Little John won of his master
  Five shillings to hose and shoon.   50

A ferly strife fell them between,
  As they went be the way;
Little John said he had won five shillings,
  And Robin Hood said shortly 'Nay'.

       55

With that Robin Hood lyed Little John,
  And smote him with his hand;
Little John waxed wroth therewith,
  And pulled out his bright brand.

slon] slay abide] withstand
lyne] linden busk] bush shoon] shoes ferly] wonderful lyed] called a liar

'Were thou not my master,' said Little John,
   'Thou shouldis be hit full sore;   60
Get thee a man where thou wilt,
   For thou getis me no more.'

Then Robin goes to Nottingham,
   Him self mourning alone,
And Little John to merry Sherwood,   65
   The paths he knew ilkone.

When Robin came to Nottingham,
   Certainly withouten layn,
He prayed to God and mild Mary
   To bring him home safe again.   70

He goes into Saint Mary church
   And kneeled down before the rood;
All that ever were the church within
   Beheld well Robin Hood.

Beside him stood a great-headed monk,   75
   I pray to God woe he be!
Full soon he knew good Robin,
   As soon as he him see.

Out at the door he ran,
   Full soon and anon;   80
All the gates of Nottingham
   He made to be sparred every one.

'Rise up,' he said, 'thou proud sheriff,
   Busk thee and make thee bowne;
I have spied the kingis felon   85
   For sooth he is in this town.

'I have spied the false felon,
   As he stands at his mass;
Hit is long of thee,' said the monk,
   'And ever he fro us pass.   90

'This traitor name is Robin Hood,
   Under the greenwood lynde;
He robbit me once of a hundred pound,
   Hit shall never out of my mind.'

ilkone] each one   layn] disguise   busk thee] dress yourself   bowne] ready

Up then rose this proud sheriff,　　　　　　95
　　And radly made him yare;
Many was the mother son
　　To the kirk with him can fare.

In at the doors they throly thrust,
　　With staves full good wone;　　　　　100
'Alas, alas,' said Robin Hood,
　　'Now miss I Little John.'

But Robin took out a two-hand sword,
　　That hangit down by his knee;
There as the sheriff and his men stood thickest,　　105
　　Thitherward would he.

Thrice through at them he ran,
　　For sooth as I yow say,
And woundit many a mother son,
　　And twelve he slew that day.　　　　110

His sword upon the sheriff head
　　Certainly he brake in two;
'The smith that thee made,' said Robin,
　　'I pray to God work him woe!

'For now am I weaponless,' said Robin,　　115
　　'Alas! again' my will;
But if I may flee these traitors fro,
　　I wot they will me kill.'

[Here Robin's men come to his rescue]

Some fell in swooning as they were dead,
　　And lay still as any stone;　　　　120
Non of them were in their mind
　　But only Little John.

'Let be your rule,' said Little John,
　　'For his life that died on tree,
Ye that should be doughty men—　　　125
　　It is great shame to see.

radly] quickly　yare] ready　good wone] plenty　But if] Unless　rule] confusion

25

'Our master has been hard bystood
  And yet 'scaped away;
Pluck up your heartis, and leave this moan,
  And hearken what I shall say.   130

'He has served Our Lady many a day
  And yet will, securly;
Therefore I trust in her specially
  No wicked death shall he die.

'Therefore be glad,' said Little John,   135
  'And let this mourning be;
And I shall be the monkis guide
  With the might of mild Mary.'

[Then spake Much, the milner son,]
  'We will go but we two;'   140
['And I meet him,' said Little John,
  'I trust to work him woe.']

[*They go to Much's uncle's house, which overlooks the highway*]

'Be my faith,' said Little John to Much,
  'I can thee tell tidings good;
I see where the monk comes riding,   145
  I know him be his wide hood.'

They went into the way, these yeomen both,
  As courteous men and hend,
They speired tidings at the monk,
  As they had been his friend.   150

'Fro whence come ye?' said Little John,
  'Tell us tidings, I yow pray,
Of a false outlaw, called Robin Hood,
  Was taken yesterday.

'He robbit me and my fellows both   155
  Of twenty mark in certain;
If that false outlaw be taken,
  For sooth we would be fain.'

hend] kind

26

'So did he me,' said the monk,
  'Of a hundred pound and more;   160
I laid first hand him upon,
  Ye may thank me therefore.'

'I pray God thank you,' said Little John,
  'And we will when we may;
We will go with you, with your leave,   165
  And bring yow on your way.

'For Robin Hood has many a wild fellow,
  I tell you in certain;
If they wist ye rode this way,
  In faith ye should be slain.'   170

As they went talking be the way,
  The monk and Little John,
John took the monkis horse be the head,
  Full soon and anon.

John took the monkis horse be the head,   175
  For sooth as I yow say;
So did Much the little page,
  For he should not 'scape away.

By the golett of the hood
  John pulled the monkè down;   180
John was nothing of him aghast,
  He let him fall on his crown.

Little John was so sore aggrieved,
  And drew out his sword in high;
This monk saw he should be dead,   185
  Loud mercy can he cry.

'He was my master,' said Little John,
  'That thou hast brought in bale;
Shall thou never come at our king,
  For to tell him tale.'   190

John smote off the monkis head,
  No longer would he dwell;
So did Much the little page,
  For fear lest he would tell.

golett] neck

27

There they buried them both,
  In neither moss nor ling,
And Little John and Much in fere
  Bare the letters to the king.

195

[When John came unto the king]
  He kneeled down upon his knee:
'God yow save, my liege lord,
  Jesus yow save and see!

200

'God yow save, my liege king!'
  To speak John was full bold;
He gave him the letters in his hand,
  And the king did hit unfold.

205

The king read the letters anon,
  And said 'So might I thee,
There was never yeoman in merry England
  I longed so sore to see.

210

'Where is the monk that these should have brought?'
  Our king can say:
'Be my troth,' said Little John,
  'He died after the way.'

The king gave Much and Little John
  Twenty pound in certain,
And made them yeomen of the crown,
  And bade them go again.

215

He gave John the seal in hand,
  The sheriff for to bear,
To bring Robin him to,
  And no man do him dere.

220

John took his leave at our king,
  The sooth as I yow say;
The next way to Nottingham
  To take, he yede the way.

225

When John came to Nottingham
  The gates were sparred each one;
John callèd up the porter,
  He answered soon anon.

230

    in fere] together thee] thrive dere] harm yede] went

'What is the cause,' said Little John,
  'Thou sparris the gates so fast?'
'Because of Robin Hood,' said the porter,
  'In deep prison is cast.

'John and Much and Will Scathlok,   235
  For sooth as I yow say,
They slew our men upon our walls,
  And sawten us every day.'

Little John spurred after the sheriff,
  And soon he him found;   240
He opened the kingis privy seal,
  And gave him in his hand.

When the sheriff saw the kingis seal,
  He did off his hood anon;
'Where is the monk that bare the letters?'   245
  He said to Little John.

'He is so fain of him,' said Little John,
  'For sooth as I yow say,
He has made him Abbot of Westminster,
  A lord of that Abbey.'   250

The sheriff made John good cheer,
  And gave him wine of the best;
At night they went to their bed,
  And every man to his rest.

When the sheriff was on sleep,   255
  Drunken of wine and ale,
Little John and Much for sooth
  Took the way unto the jail.

Little John called up the jailer,
  And bade him rise anon;   260
He said Robin Hood had broken prison,
  And out of it was gone.

The porter rose anon certain,
  As soon as he heard John call;
Little John was ready with a sword,   265
  And bare him to the wall.

sawten] assault

29

'Now will I be porter,' said Little John,
  'And take the keys in hand.'
He took the way to Robin Hood,
  And soon he him unbound. 270

He gave him a good sword in his hand,
  His head therewith to keep,
And there as the wall was lowest
  Anon down can they leap.

Be that the cock began to crow, 275
  The day began to spring;
The sheriff found the jailer dead,
  The common-bell made he ring.

He made a cry throughout all the town,
  Whether he be yeoman or knave, 280
That could bring him Robin Hood,
  His warison he should have.

'For I dare never,' said the sheriff,
  'Come before our king;
For if I do, I wot certain 285
  For sooth he will me hang.'

The sheriff made to seek Nottingham,
  Both be street and sty,
And Robin was in merry Sherwood,
  As light as leaf on lynde. 290

Then bespake good Little John,
  To Robin can he say,
'I have done thee a good turn for an evil,
  Quite thee when thou may.

'I have done thee a good turn,' said Little John, 295
  'For sooth as I yow say;
I have brought thee under greenwood lyne;
  Fare well, and have good-day.'

'Nay, be my troth,' said Robin Hood,
  'So shall it never be; 300
I make thee master,' said Robin Hood,
  'Of all my men and me.'

common-bell] town bell warison] reward Quite] requite

'Nay, be my troth,' said Little John,
  'So shall it never be;
But let me be a fellow,' said Little John,   305
  'No n'other keep I be.'

Thus John gate Robin Hood out of prison,
  Certain withouten layn,
When his men saw him whole and sound,
  For sooth they were full fain.   310

They filled in wine, and made them glad,
  Under the leavès small,
And ate pastes of venison,
  That good was with ale.

Then word came to our king   315
  How Robin Hood was gone,
And how the sheriff of Nottingham
  Durst never look him upon.

Then spake our comely king,
  In an anger high: 320
'Little John has beguiled the sheriff,
  In faith, so has he me.

'Little John has beguiled us both,
  And that full well I see;
Or else the sheriff of Nottingham   325
  High hangèd should he be.

'I made them yeomen of the crown,
  And gave them fee with my hand;
I gave them grith,' said our king,
  'Throughout all merry Englànd.   330

'I gave them grith,' then said our king;
  'I say, so might I thee,
For sooth such a yeoman as he is on
  In all England are not three.

'He is true to his master,' said our king;   335
  'I say, be sweet Saint John,
He loves better Robin Hood
  Than he does us each one.

No n'other keep I be] Nothing else do I care to be layn] disguise grith] safe conduct

31

'Robin Hood is ever bond to him,
    Both a street and stall;   340
Speak no more of this matter,' said our king,
    'But John has beguiled us all.'

Thus ends the talking of the monk
    And Robin Hood i-wis;
God, that is ever a crownèd king,   345
    Bring us all to his bliss!

ANONYMOUS

Tam Lin

'O I FORBID you, maidens a',
    That wear gowd on your hair,
To come or gae by Carterhaugh,
    For young Tam Lin is there.

'There's nane that gaes by Carterhaugh   5
    But they leave him a wad,
Either their rings, or green mantles,
    Or else their maidenhead.'

Janet has kilted her green kirtle
    A little aboon her knee,   10
And she has broded her yellow hair
    A little aboon her bree,
And she's awa to Carterhaugh,
    As fast as she can hie.

When she came to Carterhaugh   15
    Tam Lin was at the well,
And there she fand his steed standing,
    But awa was himsel.

She had na pu'd a double rose,
    A rose but only twae,   20
Till up then started young Tam Lin,
    Says, 'Lady, thou's pu' nae mae.

gowd] gold   wad] forfeit   bree] eyebrow

'Why pu's thou the rose, Janet,
  And why breaks thou the wand?
Or why comes thou to Carterhaugh   25
  Withouten my command?'

'Carterhaugh, it is my ain,
  My daddie gave it me;
I'll come and gang by Carterhaugh,
  And ask nae leave at thee.'   30

Janet has kilted her green kirtle
  A little aboon her knee,
And she has snooded her yellow hair
  A little aboon her bree,
And she is to her father's ha',   35
  As fast as she can hie.

Four and twenty ladies fair
  Were playing at the ba',
And out then cam the fair Janet,
  Ance the flower amang them a'.   40

Four and twenty ladies fair
  Were playing at the chess,
And out then cam the fair Janet,
  As green as onie glass.

Out then spak an auld grey knight,   45
  Lay o'er the castle wa',
And says, 'Alas, fair Janet, for thee,
  But we'll be blamed a'.'

'Haud your tongue, ye auld faced knight,
  Some ill death may ye die!   50
Father my bairn on whom I will,
  I'll father nane on thee.'

Out then spak her father dear,
  And he spak meek and mild;
'And ever alas, sweet Janet,' he says,   55
  'I think thou gaes wi' child.'

snooded] tied back with a band

33

'If that I gae wi' child, father,
  Mysel maun bear the blame;
There's ne'er a laird about your ha'
  Shall get the bairn's name.   60

'If my love were an earthly knight,
  As he's an elfin grey,
I wad na gie my ain true-love
  For nae lord that ye hae.

'The steed that my true-love rides on   65
  Is lighter than the wind;
Wi' siller he is shod before,
  Wi' burning gowd behind.'

Janet has kilted her green kirtle
  A little aboon her knee,   70
And she has snooded her yellow hair
  A little aboon her bree,
And she's awa to Carterhaugh,
  As fast as she can hie.

When she cam to Carterhaugh,   75
  Tam Lin was at the well,
And there she fand his steed standing,
  But away was himsel.

She had na pu'd a double rose,
  A rose but only twae,   80
Till up then started young Tam Lin,
  Says, 'Lady, thou pu's nae mae.

'Why pu's thou the rose, Janet,
  Amang the groves sae green,
And a' to kill the bonnie babe   85
  That we gat us between?'

'O tell me, tell me, Tam Lin,' she says,
  'For's sake that died on tree,
If e'er ye was in holy chapel,
  Or Christendom did see?'   90

'Roxbrugh he was my grandfather,
  Took me with him to bide,
And ance it fell upon a day
  That wae did me betide.

'And ance it fell upon a day,   95
  A cauld day and a snell,
When we were frae the hunting come,
  That frae my horse I fell;
The Queen o' Fairies she caught me,
  In yon green hill to dwell.   100

'And pleasant is the fairy land,
  But, an eerie tale to tell,
Ay at the end of seven years
  We pay a tiend to hell;
I am sae fair and fu' o' flesh,   105
  I'm feard it be mysel.

'But the night is Halloween, lady,
  The morn is Hallowday;
Then win, win me, an' ye will,
  For weel I wat ye may.   110

'Just at the mirk and midnight hour
  The fairy folk will ride,
And they that wad their true-love win,
  At Miles Cross they maun bide.'

'But how shall I thee ken, Tam Lin,   115
  Or how my true-love know,
Amang sae mony unco knights
  The like I never saw?'

'O first let pass the black, lady,
  And syne let pass the brown,   120
But quickly run to the milk-white steed,
  Pu' ye his rider down.

'For I'll ride on the milk-white steed,
  And ay nearest the town;
Because I was an earthly knight   125
  They gie me that renown.

'My right hand will be gloved, lady,
  My left hand will be bare,
Cockt up shall my bonnet be,
  And kaimed down shall my hair;   130
And thae's the takens I gie thee,
  Nae doubt I will be there.

    snell] bitter   tiend] tithe   unco] strange

35

ANONYMOUS

'They'll turn me in your arms, lady,
   Into an esk and adder;
But hold me fast, and fear me not,   135
   I am your bairn's father.

'They'll turn me to a bear sae grim,
   And then a lion bold;
But hold me fast, and fear me not,
   As ye shall love your child.   140

'Again they'll turn me in your arms
   To a red het gaud of airn;
But hold me fast, and fear me not,
   I'll do to you nae harm.

'And last they'll turn me in your arms   145
   Into the burning gleed;
Then throw me into well water,
   O throw me in wi' speed.

'And then I'll be your ain true-love,
   I'll turn a naked knight;   150
Then cover me wi' your green mantle,
   And cover me out o' sight.'

Gloomy, gloomy was the night,
   And eerie was the way,
As fair Jenny in her green mantle
   To Miles Cross she did gae.   155

About the middle o' the night
   She heard the bridles ring;
This lady was as glad at that
   As any earthly thing.   160

First she let the black pass by,
   And syne she let the brown;
But quickly she ran to the milk-white steed,
   And pu'd the rider down.

Sae weel she minded what he did say,   165
   And young Tam Lin did win;
Syne covered him wi' her green mantle,
   As blythe's a bird in spring.

esk] newt   gaud of airn] bar of iron   gleed] red-hot coal

36

Out then spak the Queen o' Fairies,
  Out of a bush o' broom: 170
'Them that has gotten young Tam Lin
  Has gotten a stately groom.'

Out then spak the Queen o' Fairies,
  And an angry woman was she:
'Shame betide her ill-fared face,   175
  And an ill death may she die,
For she's taen awa the bonniest knight
  In a' my companie.

'But had I kend, Tam Lin,' she says,
  'What now this night I see,   180
I wad hae taen out thy twa grey een,
  And put in twa een o' tree.'

ROBERT HENRYSON
?1430–1506

From *The Tale of the Upland Mouse and the Burgess Mouse*

AESOP, mine author, makis mention
  Of twa mice, and they were sisteris dear,
Of whom the eldest dwelt in ane borough's-town;
  The other winnit upon land, well near,
  Solitary, whiles under bush, whiles under brier,   5
Whiles in the corn and other mennis scathe,
As outlawis does, and livis on their waith.

This rural mouse into the winter-tide
  Had hunger, cauld, and tholit great distress;
The other mouse that in the burgh can bide   10
  Was guild-brother and made ane free burgèss;
  Toll-free also, but custom mair or less,
And freedom had to ga wherever she list
Amang the cheese in ark and meal in chest.

tree] wood
winnit] dwelt   whiles] at times   scathe] harm   waith] hunting   tholit] suffered
custom mair or less] free of dues great or small

Ane time when she was full and unfoot-sair,   15
  She took in mind her sister upon land,
And langit for to hear of her welfare,
  To see what life she had under the wand;
  Barefoot, alone, with pikestaff in her hand,
As puir pilgrim she passit out of town   20
To seek her sister baith ower dale and down.

Forth mony wilsum wayis can she walk;
  Through moss and muir, through bankis, bush and brier,
She ran crying till she come to a baulk,
  'Come forth to me, my owin sister dear—   25
  Cry "peep" aince!' With that the mouse could hear
And knew her voice, as kinnisman will do
By very kind; and forth she come her to.

The heartly joy, God! if ye had seen,
  Beis kith when that these sisteris met!   30
And great kindness was showin them between,
  For whiles they leuch, and whiles for joy they gret,
  Whiles kissit sweet, whiles in armis plet;
And thus they fure till soberit was their mind,
Syne foot for foot unto the chamber wend.   35

When they were lodgit thus, these silly mice,
  The youngest sister into her buttery gaed,
And brought forth nuttis and candle instead of spice:
  If this was guid fare, I do it on them beside.
  The burgess-mouse prompit forth in pride,   40
And said, 'Sister, is this your daily food?'
'Why not?' quod she, 'Is not this meat right guid?'

'Na, by my soul! I think it but ane scorn.'
  'Madame,' quod she, 'ye be the mair to blame.
My mother said, sister, when we were born,   45
  That I and ye lay baith within ane wame.
  I keep the rate and custom of my dame,
And of my living into poverty;
For landis have we nane in property.'

'My fair sister,' quod she, 'have me excusit;   50
  This rude diet and I can not accord.

under the wand] in the open wilsum] bewildering baulk] ridge
leuch] laughed gret] cried plet] folded fure] carried on silly] simple I do
it on them beside] I leave it to them to answer wame] womb

To tender meat my stomach is aye usit,
  For whiles I fare als well as ony lord.
These withered peas and nuttis, ere they be bored,
Will break my teeth, and make my wame full slender,   55
Whilk was before usit to meatis tender.'

'Well, well, sister,' quod the rural mouse,
  'If it please you, such things as ye see here,
Both meat and drink, harbery and house,
  Shall be your owin, will ye remain all year;   60
  Ye shall it have with blithe and merry cheer,
And that should make the messes that are rude,
Among friendis, right tender and wonder guid.'

For all her merry exhortation,
  This burgess-mouse had little will to sing;   65
But heavily she cast her browis down,
  For all the dainteis that she could her bring.
  Yet at the last she said, half in hething,
'Sister, this victual and your royal feast
May well suffice unto ane rural beast.   70

'Let be this holc, and come into my place.
  I shall to you show by experience
My Good Friday is better nor your Pace:
  My dish-lickings is worth your whole expence.
  I have housis eneuch of great defence;   75
Of cat nor fall-trap I have na dread.'
'I grant,' quod she; and on together they gaed.

In stubble array through gorse and corn
  And under bushis privily could they creep;
The eldest was the guide and went beforn,   80
  The younger to her wayis took guid keep.
  On night they ran, and on the day can sleep;
Till in the morning, ere the laverock sang,
They found the town and in blithely could gang.

After, when they disposit were to dine,   85
  Withoutin grace they wash and went to meat,
With all coursis that cookis could divine:
  Mutton and beef, strickin in tailyeis great;
  And lordis fare thus could they counterfeit,

harbery] lodging   messes that are rude] dishes that are coarse
hething] derision   Pace] Easter   divine] contrive   strickin in tailyeis] cut in slices

Except ane thing, they drank the water clear   90
Instead of wine; but yet they made guid cheer.

Thus made they merry till they might na mair,
    And 'Hail, yule, hail!' cryit upon high.
Yet after joy ofttimes comis care,
    And trouble after great prosperity;   95
    Thus as they sat in all their jollity,
The spenser come with keyis in his hand,
Openit the door, and them at dinner fand.

They tarryit not to wash, as I suppose,
    But on to ga who that might foremost win.   100
The burgess had ane hole, and in she goes;
    Her sister had na hole to hide her in:
    To see that silly mouse it was great sin,
So desolate and will of ane guid rede!
For very dread she fell in swoon near deid.   105

But as God would, it fell ane happy case:
    The spenser had na leisure for to bide,
Neither to seek nor search, to scare nor chase,
    But on he went and left the door up wide.
    The bold burgess his passing weel has spied;   110
Out of her hole she come and cryit on high,
'How fare ye, sister? Cry "Peep", wherever ye be!

'Why lie ye thus? Rise up, my sister dear!
    Come to your meat, this peril is overpast.'
The other answerit her with heavy cheer,   115
    'I may not eat, sa sair I am aghast;
    I had liefer these forty dayis fast
With water-kail, and to gnaw beans or peas,
Than all your feast in this dread and dis-ease.'

With fair treaty yet she gart her uprise,   120
    And to the board they went and together sat.
And scantly had they drunkin aince or twice
    When in come Gib Hunter, our jolly cat,
    And bad 'God speed!' The burgess up with that,
And till the hole she went as fire on flint;   125
Baudrons the other by the back has hint.

spenser] dispenser, i.e. steward
will of ane guid rede] at a loss for one good plan   water-kail] cabbage-water
treaty] entreaty   gart] made   Baudrons] Puss   hint] caught

40

THE UPLAND MOUSE AND THE BURGESS MOUSE

Fra foot to foot he cast her to and fra,
   Whiles up, whiles down, als cant as ony kid;
Whiles would he let her run under the straw,
   Whiles would he wink, and play with her buck-hid.   130
   Thus to the silly mouse great pain he did,
Till at the last, through fortune and guid hap,
Betwix ane board and the wall she crap.

And up in haste behind ane parralling
   She clam so high that Gilbert might not get her;   135
Syne by the cluke there craftily can hing
   Till he was gone: her cheer was all the better.
   Syne down she lap when there was nane to let her,
And to the burgess-mouse loud can she cry,
'Farewell, sister, thy feast here I defy!   140

'Were I into the kith that I come fra,
   For weal nor woe should I never come again.'
With that she took her leave and forth can ga,
   Whiles through the corn and whiles through the plain.
   When she was forth and free she was full fain,   145
And merrily markit unto the muir:
I can not tell how well thereafter she fure.

But I heard say she passit to her den,
   Als warm as wool, suppose it was not great,
Full beinly stuffit, baith but and ben,   150
   Of beanis, and nuttis, peas, rye, and wheat.
   Whenever she list she had enough to eat
In quiet and ease withoutin ony dread;
But to her sisteris feast na mair she gaed.

    cant] brisk wink] shut his eyes buck-hid] hide-and-seek
  parralling] partition wall cluke] claw let] hinder kith] country
markit] marched fure] journeyed beinly] snugly but and ben] outer
       and inner rooms

ANONYMOUS

1595

The Babes in the Wood

Now ponder well, you parents dear,
   These words which I shall write;
A doleful story you shall hear,
   In time brought forth to light.
A gentleman of good account   5
   In Norfolk dwelt of late,
Who did in honour far surmount
   Most men of his estate.

Sore sick he was, and like to die,
   No help his life could save;   10
His wife by him as sick did lie,
   And both possessed one grave.
No love between these two was lost,
   Each was to other kind,
In love they lived, in love they died,   15
   And left two babes behind:

The one a fine and pretty boy,
   Not passing three years old;
The other a girl more young than he,
   And framed in beauty's mould.   20
The father left his little son,
   As plainly doth appear,
When he to perfect age should come,
   Three hundred pounds a year.

And to his little daughter Jane   25
   Five hundred pounds in gold,
To be paid down on marriage-day,
   Which might not be controlled.
But if the children chance to die,
   Ere they to age should come,   30
Their uncle should possess their wealth,
   For so the will did run.

'Now, brother,' said the dying man,
  'Look to my children dear;
Be good unto my boy and girl,   35
  No friends else have they here.
To God and you I recommend
  My children dear this day;
But little while be sure we have
  Within this world to stay.   40

'You must be father and mother both,
  And uncle all in one;
God knows what will become of them,
  When I am dead and gone.'
With that bespake their mother dear,   45
  'O brother kind,' quoth she,
'You are the man must bring our babes
  To wealth or misery:

'And if you keep them carefully,
  Then God will you reward;   50
But if you otherwise should deal,
  God will your deeds regard.'
With lips as cold as any stone
  They kissed their children small:
'God bless you both, my children dear';   55
  With that the tears did fall.

These speeches then their brother spake
  To this sick couple there,
'The keeping of your little ones,
  Sweet sister, do not fear;   60
God never prosper me nor mine,
  Nor aught else that I have,
If I do wrong your children dear,
  When you are laid in grave.'

The parents being dead and gone,   65
  The children home he takes,
And brings them straight unto his house,
  Where much of them he makes.
He had not kept these pretty babes
  A twelvemonth and a day,   70
But, for their wealth, he did devise
  To make them both away.

He bargained with two ruffians strong,
　　Which were of furious mood,
That they should take these children young,　　75
　　And slay them in a wood.
He told his wife an artful tale,
　　He would the children send
To be brought up in fair Londòn,
　　With one that was his friend.　　80

Away then went those pretty babes,
　　Rejoicing at that tide,
Rejoicing with a merry mind
　　They should on cock-horse ride.
They prate and prattle pleasantly,　　85
　　As they rode on the way,
To those that should their butchers be,
　　And work their lives' decay:

So that the pretty speech they had,
　　Made Murder's heart relent;　　90
And they that undertook the deed,
　　Full sore did now repent.
Yet one of them more hard of heart,
　　Did vow to do his charge,
Because the wretch that hired him　　95
　　Had paid him very large.

The other won't agree thereto,
　　So here they fall to strife;
With one another they did fight
　　About the children's life.　　100
And he that was of mildest mood
　　Did slay the other there,
Within an unfrequented wood—
　　The babes did quake for fear.

He took the children by the hand,　　105
　　Tears standing in their eye,
And bad them straightway follow him,
　　And look they did not cry.
And two long miles he led them on,
　　While they for food complain:　　110
'Stay here,' quoth he, 'I'll bring you bread,
　　When I come back again.'

44

These pretty babes, with hand in hand,
  Went wandering up and down;
But never more could see the man   115
  Approaching from the town.
Their pretty lips with blackberries
  Were all besmeared and dyed,
And when they saw the darksome night
  They sat them down and cried.   120

Thus wandered these poor innocents,
  Till death did end their grief;
In one another's arms they died,
  As wanting due relief.
No burial this pretty pair   125
  Of any man receives,
Till Robin Redbreast piously
  Did cover them with leaves.

And now the heavy wrath of God
  Upon their uncle fell;   130
Yea, fearful fiends did haunt his house,
  His conscience felt an hell;
His barns were fired, his goods consumed,
  His lands were barren made,
His cattle died within the field,   135
  And nothing with him stayed.

And in a voyage to Portugal
  Two of his sons did die;
And to conclude, himself was brought
  To want and misery.   140
He pawned and mortgaged all his land
  Ere seven years came about;
And now at length this wicked act
  Did by this means come out:

The fellow that did take in hand   145
  These children for to kill,
Was for a robbery judged to die—
  Such was God's blessed will:
Who did confess the very truth,
  As here hath been displayed;   150
Their uncle having died in gaol,
  Where he for debt was laid.

You that executors be made,
  And overseers eke
Of children that be fatherless,   155
  And infants mild and meek;
Take you example by this thing,
  And yield to each his right,
Lest God with such like misery
  Your wicked minds requite.   160

EDMUND SPENSER
?1552–1599

The Cave of Despair

THUS been they parted, Arthur on his way
  To seek his love, and th'other for to fight
With Una's foe, that all her realm did prey.
But she now weighing the decayed plight,
And shrunken sinews of her chosen knight,   5
  Would not awhile her forward course pursue,
Ne bring him forth in face of dreadful fight,
  Till he recovered had his former hue:
For him to be yet weak and weary well she knew.

So as they travelled, lo they gan espy   10
  An armed knight towards them gallop fast,
That seemed from some feared foe to fly,
Or other grisly thing, that him aghast.
Still as he fled, his eye was backward cast,
As if his fear still followed him behind;   15
  Als flew his steed, as he his bands had brast,
  And with his winged heels did tread the wind,
As he had been a foal of Pegasus his kind.

Nigh as he drew, they might perceive his head
  To be unarmed, and curled uncombed hairs   20
Upstaring stiff, dismayed with uncouth dread;
Nor drop of blood in all his face appears
Nor life in limb: and to increase his fears,
In foul reproach of knighthood's fair degree,
About his neck an hempen rope he wears,   25
  That with his glist'ring arms does ill agree;
But he of rope or arms has now no memory.

The Red Cross Knight toward him crossed fast,
  To weet, what mister wight was so dismayed:
  There him he finds all senseless and aghast,   30
  That of himself he seemed to be afraid;
  Whom hardly he from flying forward stayed,
  Till he these words to him deliver might:
  'Sir Knight, aread who hath ye thus arrayed,
  And eke from whom make ye this hasty flight: 35
For never knight I saw in such mis-seeming plight.'

He answered nought at all, but adding new
  Fear to his first amazement, staring wide
  With stony eyes, and heartless hollow hue,
  Astonished stood, as one that had espied   40
  Infernal furies, with their chains untied.
  Him yet again, and yet again bespake
  The gentle knight; who nought to him replied,
  But trembling every joint did inly quake,
And faltering tongue at last these words seemed forth to shake. 45

'For God's dear love, Sir Knight, do me not stay;
  For lo he comes, he comes fast after me.'
  Eft looking back would fain have run away;
  But he him forced to stay, and tellen free
  The secret cause of his perplexity: 50
  Yet nathemore by his bold hearty speech,
  Could his blood-frozen heart emboldened be,
  But through his boldness rather fear did reach,
Yet forced, at last he made through silence sudden breach.

'And am I now in safety sure,' quoth he,   55
  'From him, that would have forced me to die?
  And is the point of death now turned fro me,
  That I may tell this hapless history?'
  'Fear nought,' quoth he, 'no danger now is nigh.'
  'Then shall I you recount a rueful case,'   60
  Said he, 'the which with this unlucky eye
  I late beheld, and had not greater grace
Me reft from it, had been partaker of the place.

'I lately chanced (Would I had never chanced)
  With a fair knight to keepen company,   65
  Sir Terwin hight, that well himself advanced

        weet] know   mister] kind of   aread] tell   hight] called

In all affairs, and was both bold and free,
But not so happy as mote happy be:
He loved, as was his lot, a lady gent,
That him again loved in the least degree;   70
For she was proud, and of too high intent,
And joyed to see her lover languish and lament.

'From whom returning sad and comfortless,
  As on the way together we did fare,
  We met that villain (God from him me bless)   75
  That cursed wight, from whom I 'scaped whilere,
  A man of hell, that calls himself Despair:
  Who first us greets, and after fair areads
  Of tidings strange, and of adventures rare:
  So creeping close, as snake in hidden weeds,   80
Inquireth of our states, and of our knightly deeds.

'Which when he knew, and felt our feeble hearts
  Embossed with bale, and bitter biting grief,
  Which love had launched with his deadly darts,
  With wounding words and terms of foul reproof   85
  He plucked from us all hope of due relief,
  That erst us held in love of ling'ring life;
  Then hopeless heartless, gan the cunning thief
  Persuade us die, to stint all further strife:
To me he lent this rope, to him a rustie knife.   90

'With which sad instrument of hasty death,
  That woeful lover, loathing longer light,
  A wide way made to let forth living breath.
  But I more fearful, or more lucky wight,
  Dismayed with that deformed dismal sight,   95
  Fled fast away, half dead with dying fear:
  Ne yet assured of life by you, Sir Knight,
  Whose like infirmity like chance may bear:
But God you never let his charmed speeches hear.'

'How may a man,' said he, 'with idle speech   100
  Be won, to spoil the castle of his health?'
  'I wote,' quoth he, 'whom trial late did teach,
  That like would not for all this worldes wealth:
  His subtle tongue, like dropping honey, melt'th
  Into the heart, and searcheth every vein,   105

bale] woe

48

That ere one be aware, by secret stealth
His power is reft, and weakness doth remain.
O never, Sir, desire to try his guileful train.'

'Certes,' said he, 'hence shall I never rest,
  Till I that treacherous art have heard and tried;   110
  And you, Sir Knight, whose name mote I request,
  Of grace do me unto his cabin guide.'
  'I that hight Trevisan,' quoth he, 'will ride
  Against my liking back, to do you grace:
  But nor for gold nor glee will I abide   115
  By you, when ye arrive in that same place;
For liefer had I die, than see his deadly face.'

Ere long they come, where that same wicked wight
  His dwelling has, low in an hollow cave,
  Far underneath a craggy cliff ypight,   120
  Dark, doleful, dreary, like a greedy grave,
  That still for carrion carcases doth crave:
  On top whereof aye dwelt the ghastly owl,
  Shrieking his baleful note, which ever drave
  Far from that haunt all other cheerful fowl;   125
And all about it wand'ring ghosts did wail and howl.

And all about old stocks and stubs of trees,
  Whereon nor fruit, nor leaf was ever seen,
  Did hang upon the ragged rocky knees;
  On which had many wretches hanged been,   130
  Whose carcases were scattered on the green,
  And thrown about the cliffs. Arrived there,
  That bare-head knight for dread and doleful teen
  Would fain have fled, ne durst approchen near,
But th'other forced him stay, and comforted in fear.   135

That darksome cave they enter, where they find
  That cursed man, low sitting on the ground,
  Musing full sadly in his sullen mind;
  His greasy locks, long growen, and unbound,
  Disordered hung about his shoulders round,   140
  And hid his face; through which his hollow eyne
  Looked deadly dull, and stared as astound;
  His raw-bone cheeks through penury and pine,
Were shrunk into his jaws, as he did never dine.

teen] distress

49

His garment nought but many ragged clouts,   145
  With thorns together pinned and patched was,
  The which his naked sides he wrapped abouts;
  And him beside there lay upon the grass
  A dreary corse, whose life away did pass,
  All wallowed in his own yet lukewarm blood,   150
  That from his wound yet welled fresh alas;
  In which a rusty knife fast fixed stood,
And made an open passage for the gushing flood.

Which piteous spectacle, approving true
  The woeful tale that Trevisan had told,   155
  When as the gentle Red Cross Knight did view,
  With fiery zeal he burnt in courage bold,
  Him to avenge, before his blood were cold,
  And to the villain said, 'Thou damned wight,
  The author of this fact we here behold,   160
  What justice can but judge against thee right,
With thine own blood to price his blood, here shed in sight?'

'What frantic fit,' quoth he, 'hath thus distraught
  Thee, foolish man, so rash a doom to give?
  What justice ever other judgement taught,   165
  But he should die, who merits not to live?
  None else to death this man despairing drive,
  But his own guilty mind deserving death.
  Is then unjust to each his due to give?
  Or let him die, that loatheth living breath?   170
Or let him die at ease, that liveth here uneath?

'Who travels by the weary wand'ring way,
  To come unto his wished home in haste,
  And meets a flood, that doth his passage stay,
  Is not great grace to help him overpast,   175
  Or free his feet, that in the mire stick fast?
  Most envious man, that grieves at neighbour's good,
  And fond, that joyest in the woe thou hast,
  Why wilt not let him pass, that long hath stood
Upon the bank, yet wilt thyself not pass the flood?   180

'He there does now enjoy eternal rest
  And happy ease, which thou dost want and crave,
  And further from it daily wanderest:

uneath] only with difficulty

What if some little pain the passage have,
That makes frail flesh to fear the bitter wave?   185
Is not short pain well borne, that brings long ease,
And lays the soul to sleep in quiet grave?
Sleep after toil, port after stormy seas,
Ease after war, death after life does greatly please.'

The knight much wondered at his sudden wit,   190
And said, 'The term of life is limited,
Ne may a man prolong, nor shorten it;
The soldier may not move from watchful stead,
Nor leave his stand, until his Captain bid.'
'Who life did limit by almighty doom,'   195
Quoth he, 'knows best the terms established;
And he, that 'points the sentinel his room,
Doth license him depart at sound of morning drum.

'Is not his deed, whatever thing is done,
In heaven and earth? did not he all create   200
To die again? All ends that was begun.
Their times in his eternal book of fate
Are written sure, and have their certain date.
Who then can strive with strong necessity,
That holds the world in his still changing state,   205
Or shun the death ordained by destiny?
When hour of death is come, let none ask whence, nor why.

'The longer life, I wote the greater sin,
The greater sin, the greater punishment:
All those great battles, which thou boasts to win,   210
Through strife, and bloodshed, and avengement,
Now praised, hereafter dear thou shalt repent:
For life must life, and blood must blood repay.
Is not enough thy evil life forespent?
For he, that once hath missed the right way,   215
The further he doth go, the further he doth stray.

'Then do no further go, no further stray,
But here lie down, and to thy rest betake,
Th'ill to prevent, that life ensuen may.
For what hath life, that may it loved make,   220
And gives not rather cause it to forsake?
Fear, sickness, age, loss, labour, sorrow, strife,
Pain, hunger, cold, that makes the heart to quake;
And ever fickle fortune rageth rife,
All which, and thousands mo do make a loathsome life.   225

51

'Thou wretched man, of death hast greatest need,
    If in true balance thou wilt weigh thy state:
    For never knight, that dared warlike deed,
    More luckless disadventures did amate:
    Witness the dungeon deep, wherein of late   230
    Thy life shut up, for death so oft did call;
    And though good luck prolonged hath thy date,
    Yet death then, would the like mishaps forestall,
Into the which hereafter thou mayest happen fall.

'Why then dost thou, O man of sin, desire   235
    To draw thy days forth to their last degree?
    Is not the measure of thy sinful hire
    High heaped up with huge iniquity,
    Against the day of wrath, to burden thee?
    Is not enough, that to this lady mild   240
    Thou falsed hast thy faith with perjury,
    And sold thyself to serve Duessa vild,
With whom in all abuse thou hast thyself defiled?

'Is he not just, that all this doth behold
    From highest heaven, and bears an equal eye?   245
    Shall he thy sins up in his knowledge fold,
    And guilty be of thy impiety?
    Is not his law, Let every sinner die:
    Die shall all flesh? What then must needs be done,
    Is it not better to do willingly,   250
    Than linger, till the glass be all out run?
Death is the end of woes: die soon, O fairies' son.'

The knight was much enmoved with his speech,
    That as a sword's point through his heart did pierce,
    And in his conscience made a secret breach,   255
    Well knowing true all that he did rehearse;
    And to his fresh remembrance did reverse
    The ugly view of his deformed crimes,
    That all his manly powers it did disperse,
    As he were charmed with enchanted rhymes,   260
That oftentimes he quaked, and fainted oftentimes.

In which amazement, when the miscreant
    Perceived him to waver weak and frail,
    Whiles trembling horror did his conscience daunt,

vild] vile

52

And hellish anguish did his soul assail,   265
  To drive him to despair, and quite to quail,
  He showed him painted in a table plain
  The damned ghosts, that do in torments wail,
  And thousand fiends that do them endless pain
With fire and brimstone, which for ever shall remain.   270

The sight whereof so throughly him dismayed,
  That nought but death before his eyes he saw,
  And ever burning wrath before him laid,
  By righteous sentence of th'Almighty's law:
  Then gan the villain him to overcraw,   275
  And brought unto him swords, ropes, poison, fire,
  And all that might him to perdition draw;
  And bad him choose, what death he would desire:
For death was due to him, that had provoked God's ire.

But when as none of them he saw him take,   280
  He to him raught a dagger sharp and keen,
  And gave it him in hand: his hand did quake,
  And tremble like a leaf of aspen green,
  And troubled blood through his pale face was seen
  To come, and go with tidings from the heart,   285
  As it a running messenger had been.
  At last resolved to work his final smart,
He lifted up his hand, that back again did start.

Which when as Una saw, through every vein
  The cruddled cold ran to her well of life,   290
  As in a swoon; but soon relived again,
  Out of his hand she snatched the cursed knife,
  And threw it to the ground, enraged rife,
  And to him said, 'Fie, fie, faint-hearted knight,
  What meanest thou by this reproachful strife?   295
  Is this the battle which thou vauntst to fight
With that fire-mouthed dragon, horrible and bright?

'Come, come away, frail, feeble, fleshly wight,
  Ne let vain words bewitch thy manly heart,
  Ne devilish thoughts dismay thy constant spright.   300
  In heavenly mercies hast thou not a part?
  Why shouldst thou then despair, that chosen art?
  Where justice grows, there grows eke greater grace,
  The which doth quench the brand of hellish smart,
  And that accurst hand-writing doth deface.   305
Arise, Sir Knight arise, and leave this cursed place.'

So up he rose, and thence amounted straight.
  Which when the carl beheld, and saw his guest
  Would safe depart, for all his subtle sleight,
  He chose an halter from among the rest,   310
  And with it hung himself, unbid unblest.
  But death he could not work himself thereby;
  For thousand times he so himself had dressed,
  Yet natheless it could not do him die,
Till he should die his last, that is eternally.   315

MICHAEL DRAYTON
1563–1631

The Ballad of Agincourt

FAIR stood the wind for France,
When we our sails advance,
Nor now to prove our chance
    Longer will tarry;
But putting to the main,   5
At Caux, the mouth of Seine,
With all his martial train,
    Landed King Harry.

And taking many a fort,
Furnished in warlike sort,   10
Marcheth towards Agincourt
    In happy hour;
Skirmishing day by day
With those that stopped his way,
Where the French general lay   15
    With all his power:

Which, in his height of pride,
King Henry to deride,
His ransom to provide
    To the king sending;   20
Which he neglects the while
As from a nation vile,
Yet with an angry smile
    Their fall portending.

And turning to his men,   25
Quoth our brave Henry then,
'Though they to one be ten,
    Be not amazèd.
Yet have we well begun,
Battles so bravely won   30
Have ever to the sun
    By fame been raisèd.

'And for myself,' quoth he,
'This my full rest shall be;
England ne'er mourn for me,   35
    Nor more esteem me.
Victor I will remain
Or on this earth lie slain;
Never shall she sustain
    Loss to redeem me.   40

'Poitiers and Cressy tell,
When most their pride did swell,
Under our swords they fell;
    No less our skill is
Than when our grandsire great,   45
Claiming the regal seat,
By many a warlike feat
    Lopped the French lilies.'

The Duke of York so dread
The eager vaward led;   50
With the main Henry sped,
    Amongst his henchmen;
Excester had the rear,
A braver man not there:
O Lord, how hot they were   55
    On the false Frenchmen!

They now to fight are gone,
Armour on armour shone,
Drum now to drum did groan,
    To hear was wonder;   60
That with the cries they make
The very earth did shake,
Trumpet to trumpet spake,
    Thunder to thunder.

vaward] vanguard

MICHAEL DRAYTON

Well it thine age became,
O noble Erpingham,
Which did the signal aim
   To our hid forces!
When from a meadow by,
Like a storm suddenly,
The English archery
   Struck the French horses:

With Spanish yew so strong,
Arrows a cloth-yard long,
That like to serpents stung,
   Piercing the weather;
None from his fellow starts,
But playing manly parts,
And like true English hearts
   Stuck close together.

When down their bows they threw,
And forth their bilbos drew,
And on the French they flew,
   Not one was tardy;
Arms were from shoulders sent,
Scalps to the teeth were rent,
Down the French peasants went;
   Our men were hardy.

This while our noble king,
His broadsword brandishing,
Down the French host did ding
   As to o'erwhelm it;
And many a deep wound lent,
His arms with blood besprent,
And many a cruel dent
   Bruisèd his helmet.

Glo'ster, that duke so good,
Next of the royal blood,
For famous England stood,
   With his brave brother;
Clarence, in steel so bright,
Though but a maiden knight,
Yet in that furious fight
   Scarce such another!

56

Warwick in blood did wade,   105
Oxford the foe invade,
And cruel slaughter made,
    Still as they ran up;
Suffolk his axe did ply,
Beaumont and Willoughby   110
Bare them right doughtily,
    Ferrers and Fanhope.

Upon Saint Crispin's Day
Fought was this noble fray,
Which fame did not delay,   115
    To England to carry.
O when shall Englishmen
With such acts fill a pen,
Or England breed again
    Such a King Harry?   120

JOHN MILTON
1608–1674

Sin and Death

MEANWHILE the adversary of God and man,
Satan with thoughts inflamed of highest design,
Puts on swift wings, and toward the gates of Hell
Explores his solitary flight; sometimes
He scours the right hand coast, sometimes the left,   5
Now shaves with level wing the deep, then soars
Up to the fiery concave towering high.
As when far off at sea a fleet descried
Hangs in the clouds, by equinoctial winds
Close sailing from Bengala, or the isles   10
Of Ternate and Tidore, whence merchants bring
Their spicy drugs: they on the trading flood
Through the wide Ethiopian to the Cape
Ply stemming nightly toward the pole. So seemed
Far off the flying fiend: at last appear   15
Hell bounds high reaching to the horrid roof,
And thrice threefold the gates; three folds were brass,
Three iron, three of adamantine rock,
Impenetrable, impaled with circling fire,

Yet unconsumed. Before the gates there sat   20
On either side a formidable shape;
The one seemed woman to the waist, and fair,
But ended foul in many a scaly fold
Voluminous and vast, a serpent armed
With mortal sting: about her middle round   25
A cry of hell hounds never ceasing barked
With wide Cerberean mouths full loud, and rung
A hideous peal: yet, when they list, would creep,
If aught disturbed their noise, into her womb,
And kennel there, yet there still barked and howled   30
Within unseen. Far less abhorred than these
Vexed Scylla bathing in the sea that parts
Calabria from the hoarse Trinacrian shore:
Nor uglier follow the night-hag, when called
In secret, riding through the air she comes   35
Lured with the smell of infant blood, to dance
With Lapland witches, while the labouring moon
Eclipses at their charms. The other shape,
If shape it might be called that shape had none
Distinguishable in member, joint, or limb,   40
Or substance might be called that shadow seemed,
For each seemed either; black it stood as night,
Fierce as ten Furies, terrible as Hell,
And shook a dreadful dart; what seemed his head
The likeness of a kingly crown had on.   45
Satan was now at hand, and from his seat
The monster moving onwards came as fast
With horrid strides; Hell trembled as he strode.
The undaunted fiend what this might be admired,
Admired, not feared; God and his son except,   50
Created thing nought valued he nor shunned;
And with disdainful look thus first began.

'Whence and what art thou, execrable shape,
That dar'st, though grim and terrible, advance
Thy miscreated front athwart my way   55
To yonder gates? through them I mean to pass,
That be assured, without leave asked of thee:
Retire, or taste thy folly, and learn by proof,
Hell-born, not to contend with spirits of Heaven.'

  To whom the goblin full of wrath replied,   60
'Art thou that traitor angel, art thou he,

Who first broke peace in Heaven and faith, till then
Unbroken, and in proud rebellious arms
Drew after him the third part of Heaven's sons
Conjured against the Highest, for which both thou   65
And they outcast from God, are here condemned
To waste eternal days in woe and pain?
And reckon'st thou thyself with spirits of Heaven,
Hell-doomed, and breath'st defiance here and scorn,
Where I reign King, and to enrage thee more,   70
Thy King and Lord? Back to thy punishment,
False fugitive, and to thy speed add wings,
Lest with a whip of scorpions I pursue
Thy lingering, or with one stroke of this dart
Strange horror seize thee, and pangs unfelt before.'   75

So spake the grisly terror, and in shape,
So speaking and so threatening, grew tenfold
More dreadful and deform: on the other side
Incensed with indignation Satan stood
Unterrified, and like a comet burned,   80
That fires the length of Ophiúcus huge
In the arctic sky, and from his horrid hair
Shakes pestilence and war. Each at the head
Levelled his deadly aim; their fatal hands
No second stroke intend, and such a frown   85
Each cast at the other, as when two black clouds
With Heaven's artillery fraught, come rattling on
Over the Caspian, then stand front to front
Hovering a space, till winds the signal blow
To join their dark encounter in mid air: 90
So frowned the mighty combatants, that Hell
Grew darker at their frown, so matched they stood;
For never but once more was either like
To meet so great a foe: and now great deeds
Had been achieved, whereof all Hell had rung,   95
Had not the snaky sorceress that sat
Fast by Hell gate, and kept the fatal key,
Risen, and with hideous outcry rushed between.

'O father, what intends thy hand,' she cried,
'Against thy only son? What fury, O son,   100
Possesses thee to bend that mortal dart
Against thy father's head? and know'st for whom?
For him who sits above and laughs the while

At thee ordained his drudge, to execute
Whate'er his wrath, which he calls justice, bids,   105
His wrath which one day will destroy ye both.'

She spake, and at her words the hellish pest
Forbore, then these to her Satan returned:

'So strange thy outcry, and thy words so strange
Thou interposest, that my sudden hand   110
Prevented spares to tell thee yet by deeds
What it intends; till first I know of thee,
What thing thou art, thus double-formed, and why
In this infernal vale first met thou call'st
Me father, and that phantasm call'st my son.   115
I know thee not, nor ever saw till now
Sight more detestable than him and thee.'

To whom thus the portress of Hell gate replied,
'Hast thou forgot me then, and do I seem
Now in thine eye so foul, once deemed so fair   120
In Heaven, when at the assembly, and in sight
Of all the seraphim with thee combined
In bold conspiracy against Heaven's King,
All on a sudden miserable pain
Surprised thee, dim thine eyes, and dizzy swum   125
In darkness, while thy head flames thick and fast
Threw forth, till on the left side opening wide,
Likest to thee in shape and countenance bright,
Then shining heavenly fair, a goddess armed
Out of thy head I sprung: amazement seized   130
All the Host of Heaven; back they recoiled afraid
At first, and called me Sin, and for a sign
Portentous held me; but familiar grown,
I pleased, and with attractive graces won
The most averse, thee chiefly, who full oft   135
Thyself in me thy perfect image viewing
Becam'st enamoured, and such joy thou took'st
With me in secret, that my womb conceived
A growing burden. Meanwhile war arose,
And fields were fought in Heaven; wherein remained   140
(For what could else) to our Almighty Foe
Clear victory, to our part loss and rout
Through all the empyrean: down they fell
Driven headlong from the pitch of Heaven, down
Into this deep, and in the general fall   145

I also; at which time this powerful key
Into my hand was given, with charge to keep
These gates for ever shut, which none can pass
Without my opening. Pensive here I sat
Alone, but long I sat not, till my womb   150
Pregnant by thee, and now excessive grown
Prodigious motion felt and rueful throes.
At last this odious offspring whom thou seest
Thine own begotten, breaking violent way
Tore through my entrails, that with fear and pain   155
Distorted, all my nether shape thus grew
Transformed: but he my inbred enemy
Forth issued, brandishing his fatal dart
Made to destroy: I fled, and cried out "Death!";
Hell trembled at the hideous name, and sighed   160
From all her caves, and back resounded "Death!"
I fled, but he pursued (though more, it seems,
Inflamed with lust than rage) and swifter far,
Me overtook, his mother, all dismayed,
And in embraces forcible and foul   165
Engendering with me, of that rape begot
These yelling monsters that with ceaseless cry
Surround me, as thou saw'st, hourly conceived
And hourly born, with sorrow infinite
To me, for when they list, into the womb   170
That bred them they return, and howl and gnaw
My bowels, their repast; then bursting forth
Afresh with conscious terrors vex me round,
That rest or intermission none I find.
Before mine eyes in opposition sits   175
Grim Death my son and foe, who sets them on,
And me his parent would full soon devour
For want of other prey, but that he knows
His end with mine involved; and knows that I
Should prove a bitter morsel, and his bane,   180
Whenever that shall be; so Fate pronounced.
But thou, O father, I forewarn thee, shun
His deadly arrow; neither vainly hope
To be invulnerable in those bright arms,
Though tempered heavenly, for that mortal dint,   185
Save he who reigns above, none can resist.'

    She finished, and the subtle fiend his lore
Soon learned, now milder, and thus answered smooth.
'Dear daughter, since thou claim'st me for thy sire,

And my fair son here show'st me, the dear pledge 190
Of dalliance had with thee in Heaven, and joys
Then sweet, now sad to mention, through dire change
Befallen us unforeseen, unthought of, know
I come no enemy, but to set free
From out this dark and dismal house of pain, 195
Both him and thee, and all the heavenly host
Of spirits that in our just pretences armed
Fell with us from on high: from them I go
This uncouth errand sole, and one for all
Myself expose, with lonely steps to tread 200
The unfounded deep, and through the void immense
To search with wandering quest a place foretold
Should be, and, by concurring signs, ere now
Created vast and round, a place of bliss
In the purlieus of Heaven, and therein placed 205
A race of upstart creatures, to supply
Perhaps our vacant room, though more removed,
Lest Heaven surcharged with potent multitude
Might hap to move new broils. Be this or aught
Than this more secret now designed, I haste 210
To know, and this once known, shall soon return,
And bring ye to the place where thou and Death
Shall dwell at ease, and up and down unseen
Wing silently the buxom air, embalmed
With odours; there ye shall be fed and filled 215
Immeasurably; all things shall be your prey.'

He ceased, for both seemed highly pleased, and Death
Grinned horrible a ghastly smile, to hear
His famine should be filled, and blessed his maw
Destined to that good hour: no less rejoiced 220
His mother bad, and thus bespake her sire.

'The key of this infernal pit by due,
And by command of Heaven's all-powerful King
I keep, by him forbidden to unlock
These adamantine gates; against all force 225
Death ready stands to interpose his dart,
Fearless to be o'ermatched by living might.
But what owe I to his commands above
Who hates me, and hath hither thrust me down
Into this gloom of Tartarus profound, 230
To sit in hateful office here confined,
Inhabitant of Heaven, and heavenly-born,
Here in perpetual agony and pain,

With terrors and with clamours compassed round
Of mine own brood, that on my bowels feed?   235
Thou art my father, thou my author, thou
My being gav'st me; whom should I obey
But thee, whom follow? thou wilt bring me soon
To that new world of light and bliss, among
The gods who live at ease, where I shall reign   240
At thy right hand voluptuous, as beseems
Thy daughter and thy darling, without end.'

   Thus saying, from her side the fatal key,
Sad instrument of all our woe, she took;
And towards the gate rolling her bestial train,   245
Forthwith the huge portcullis high updrew,
Which but herself not all the Stygian powers
Could once have moved; then in the keyhole turns
The intricate wards, and every bolt and bar
Of massy iron or solid rock with ease   250
Unfastens: on a sudden open fly
With impetuous recoil and jarring sound
The infernal doors, and on their hinges grate
Harsh thunder, that the lowest bottom shook
Of Erebus. She opened, but to shut   255
Excelled her power; the gates wide open stood,
That with extended wings a bannered host
Under spread ensigns marching might pass through
With horse and chariots ranked in loose array;
So wide they stood, and like a furnace mouth   260
Cast forth redounding smoke and ruddy flame.

JOHN DRYDEN

1631-1700

Cymon and Iphigenia

OLD as I am, for ladies' love unfit,
The power of beauty I remember yet,
Which once inflamed my soul, and still inspires my wit.
If Love be folly, the severe Divine
Has felt that folly, tho' he censures mine;   5
Pollutes the pleasures of a chaste embrace,
Acts what I write, and propagates in grace
With riotous excess, a priestly race:

Suppose him free, and that I forge the offence,
He showed the way, perverting first my sense: 10
In malice witty, and with venom fraught,
He makes me speak the things I never thought.
Compute the gains of his ungoverned zeal;
Ill suits his cloth the praise of railing well!
The world will think that what we loosely write,   15
Tho' now arraigned, he read with some delight;
Because he seems to chew the cud again,
When his broad comment makes the text too plain,
And teaches more in one explaining page,
Than all the double meanings of the stage.   20
    What needs he paraphrase on what we mean?
We were at worst but wanton; he's obscene.
I, nor my fellows, nor myself excuse;
But Love's the subject of the comic muse:
Nor can we write without it, nor would you   25
A tale of only dry instruction view;
Nor Love is always of a vicious kind,
But oft to virtuous acts inflames the mind,
Awakes the sleepy vigour of the soul,
And, brushing o'er, adds motion to the pool.   30
Love, studious how to please, improves our parts
With polished manners, and adorns with arts.
Love first invented verse, and formed the rhyme,
The motion measured, harmonized the chime;
To liberal acts enlarged the narrow-souled,   35
Softened the fierce, and made the coward bold:
The world when wast, he peopled with increase,
And warring nations reconciled in peace.
Ormond, the first and all the fair may find
In this one legend to their fame designed,   40
When beauty fires the blood, how Love exalts the mind.

In that sweet isle where Venus keeps her court,
And every grace, and all the loves resort;
Where either sex is formed of softer earth,
And takes the bent of pleasure from their birth;   45
There lived a Cyprian lord, above the rest,
Wise, wealthy, with a numerous issue blest.
    But as no gift of fortune is sincere,
Was only wanting in a worthy heir:

Ormond] the Duchess of Ormond, Dryden's patron

His eldest born, a goodly youth to view,   50
Excelled the rest in shape, and outward show;
Fair, tall, his limbs with due proportion joined,
But of a heavy, dull, degenerate mind.
His soul belied the features of his face;
Beauty was there, but beauty in disgrace.   55
A clownish mien, a voice with rustic sound,
And stupid eyes, that ever loved the ground.
He looked like Nature's error; as the mind
And body were not of a piece designed,
And made for two, and by mistake in one were joined.   60
    The ruling rod, the father's forming care,
Were exercised in vain on wit's despair;
The more informed the less he understood,
And deeper sunk by floundering in the mud.
Now scorned of all, and grown the public shame,   65
The people from Galesus changed his name,
And Cymon called, which signifies a brute;
So well his name did with his nature suit.
    His father when he found his labour lost,
And care employed that answered not the cost,   70
Chose an ungrateful object to remove,
And loathed to see what Nature made him love;
So to his country farm the fool confined:
Rude work well suited with a rustic mind.
Thus to the wilds the sturdy Cymon went,   75
A squire among the swains, and pleased with banishment.
His corn and cattle were his only care,
And his supreme delight a country fair.
    It happened on a summer's holiday,
That to the greenwood shade he took his way;   80
For Cymon shunned the church, and used not much to pray.
His quarter-staff, which he could ne'er forsake,
Hung half before, and half behind his back.
He trudged along, unknowing what he sought,
And whistled as he went, for want of thought.   85
    By chance conducted, or by thirst constrained,
The deep recesses of the grove he gained;
Where in a plain, defended by the wood,
Crept through the matted grass a crystal flood,
By which an alabaster fountain stood: 90
And on the margin of the fount was laid
(Attended by her slaves) a sleeping maid;
Like Dian and her nymphs, when, tired with sport,
To rest by cool Eurotas they resort:

The dame herself the goddess well expressed,   95
Not more distinguished by her purple vest,
Than by the charming features of her face,
And even in slumber a superior grace:
Her comely limbs composed with decent care,
Her body shaded with a slight cymar;   100
Her bosom to the view was only bare:
Where two beginning paps were scarcely spied,
For yet their places were but signified:
The fanning wind upon her bosom blows,
To meet the fanning wind the bosom rose;   105
The fanning wind and purling streams continue her repose.
   The fool of Nature stood with stupid eyes
And gaping mouth, that testified surprise,
Fixed on her face, nor could remove his sight,
New as he was to love, and novice in delight: 110
Long mute he stood, and leaning on his staff,
His wonder witnessed with an idiot laugh;
Then would have spoke, but by his glimmering sense
First found his want of words, and feared offence:
Doubted for what he was he should be known,   115
By his clown accent, and his country tone.
   Through the rude chaos thus the running light
Shot the first ray that pierced the native night:
Then day and darkness in the mass were mixed,
Till gathered in a globe, the beams were fixed: 120
Last shone the sun, who radiant in his sphere
Illumined heaven and earth, and rolled around the year.
So reason in this brutal soul began:
Love made him first suspect he was a man;
Love made him doubt his broad barbarian sound;   125
By Love his want of words and wit he found:
That sense of want prepared the future way
To knowledge, and disclosed the promise of a day.
   What not his father's care, nor tutor's art
Could plant with pains in his unpolished heart,   130
The best instructor Love at once inspired,
As barren grounds to fruitfulness are fired;
Love taught him shame, and shame with Love at strife
Soon taught the sweet civilities of life;
His gross material soul at once could find   135
Somewhat in her excelling all her kind:
Exciting a desire till then unknown,
Somewhat unfound, or found in her alone.

           cymar] chemise

This made the first impression in his mind,
Above, but just above, the brutal kind.   140
For beasts can like, but not distinguish too,
Nor their own liking by reflection know;
Nor why they like or this or t'other face
Or judge of this or that peculiar grace,
But love in gross, and stupidly admire;   145
As flies allured by light approach the fire.
Thus our man-beast advancing by degrees
First likes the whole, then separates what he sees;
On several parts a several praise bestows,
The ruby lips, the well-proportioned nose,   150
The snowy skin, the raven-glossy hair,
The dimpled cheek, the forehead rising fair,
And even in sleep itself a smiling air.
From thence his eyes descending viewed the rest,
Her plump round arms, white hands, and heaving breast.   155
Long on the last he dwelt, though every part
A pointed arrow sped to pierce his heart.
    Thus in a trice a judge of beauty grown,
(A judge erected from a country clown)
He longed to see her eyes, in slumber hid,   160
And wished his own could pierce within the lid:
He would have waked her, but restrained his thought,
And love new-born the first good manners taught.
An awful fear his ardent wish withstood,
Nor durst disturb the goddess of the wood;   165
For such she seemed by her celestial face,
Excelling all the rest of human race:
And things divine, by common sense he knew,
Must be devoutly seen at distant view:
So checking his desire, with trembling heart   170
Gazing he stood, nor would, nor could depart;
Fixed as a pilgrim wildered in his way,
Who dares not stir by night for fear to stray;
But stands with awful eyes to watch the dawn of day.
    At length awaking, Iphigene the fair   175
(So was the beauty called who caused his care)
Unclosed her eyes, and double day revealed,
While those of all her slaves in sleep were sealed.
    The slavering cudden, propped upon his staff,
Stood ready gaping with a grinning laugh   180
To welcome her awake, nor durst begin
To speak, but wisely kept the fool within.

cudden] fool

67

Then she: 'What make you Cymon here alone?'
(For Cymon's name was round the country known
Because descended of a noble race,   185
And for a soul ill sorted with his face.)
    But still the sot stood silent with surprise,
With fixed regard on her new-opened eyes,
And in his breast received the envenomed dart,
A tickling pain that pleased amid the smart.   190
But conscious of her form, with quick distrust
She saw his sparkling eyes, and feared his brutal lust:
This to prevent she waked her sleepy crew,
And rising hasty took a short adieu.
    Then Cymon first his rustic voice essayed,   195
With proffered service to the parting maid
To see her safe; his hand she long denied,
But took at length, ashamed of such a guide.
So Cymon led her home, and leaving there
No more would to his country clowns repair,   200
But sought his father's house with better mind,
Refusing in the farm to be confined.
    The father wondered at the son's return,
And knew not whether to rejoice or mourn;
But doubtfully received, expecting still   205
To learn the secret causes of his altered will.
Nor was he long delayed; the first request
He made, was, like his brothers to be dressed,
And, as his birth required, above the rest.
    With ease his suit was granted by his sire,   210
Distinguishing his heir by rich attire:
His body thus adorned, he next designed
With liberal arts to cultivate his mind:
He sought a tutor of his own accord,
And studied lessons he before abhorred.   215
    Thus the man-child advanced, and learned so fast
That in short time his equals he surpassed:
His brutal manners from his breast exiled,
His mien he fashioned, and his tongue he filed;
In every exercise of all admired,   220
He seemed, nor only seemed, but was inspired:
Inspired by Love, whose business is to please;
He rode, he fenced, he moved with graceful ease,
More famed for sense, for courtly carriage more,
Than for his brutal folly known before.   225
    What then of altered Cymon shall we say,
But that the fire which choked in ashes lay,

A load too heavy for his soul to move,
Was upward blown below, and brushed away by Love?
Love made an active progress through his mind,   230
The dusky parts he cleared, the gross refined;
The drowsy waked; and as he went impressed
The Maker's image on the human beast.
Thus was the man amended by desire,
And, though he loved perhaps with too much fire,   235
His father all his faults with reason scanned,
And liked an error of the better hand;
Excused the excess of passion in his mind,
By flames too fierce, perhaps too much refined:
So Cymon, since his sire indulged his will,   240
Impetuous loved, and would be Cymon still;
Galesus he disowned, and chose to bear
The name of Fool confirmed and bishoped by the fair.

    To Cipseus by his friends his suit he moved,
Cipseus the father of the fair he loved: 245
But he was pre-engaged by former ties,
While Cymon was endeavouring to be wise:
And Iphigene, obliged by former vows,
Had given her faith to wed a foreign spouse:
Her sire and she to Rhodian Pasimond,   250
Though both repenting, were by promise bound,
Nor could retract; and thus, as Fate decreed,
Though better loved, he spoke too late to speed.

    The doom was past, the ship already sent
Did all his tardy diligence prevent: 255
Sighed to herself the fair unhappy maid,
While stormy Cymon thus in secret said:
'The time is come for Iphigene to find
The miracle she wrought upon my mind;
Her charms have made me man, her ravished love   260
In rank shall place me with the blessed above.
For mine by love, by force she shall be mine,
Or death, if force should fail, shall finish my design.'

    Resolved he said: and rigged with speedy care
A vessel strong, and well equipped for war.   265
The secret ship with chosen friends he stored,
And bent to die, or conquer, went aboard.
Ambushed he lay behind the Cyprian shore,
Waiting the sail that all his wishes bore;
Nor long expected, for the following tide   270
Sent out the hostile ship and beauteous bride.

To Rhodes the rival bark directly steered,
When Cymon sudden at her back appeared
And stopped her flight: then standing on his prow
In haughty terms he thus defied the foe: 275
'Or strike your sails at summons, or prepare
To prove the last extremities of war.'
Thus warned, the Rhodians for the fight provide;
Already were the vessels side by side,
These obstinate to save, and those to seize the bride. 280
But Cymon soon his crooked grapples cast,
Which with tenacious hold his foes embraced,
And armed with sword and shield, amid the press he passed.
Fierce was the fight, but hastening to his prey,
By force the furious lover freed his way: 285
Himself alone dispersed the Rhodian crew,
The weak disdained, the valiant overthrew;
Cheap conquest for his following friends remained,
He reaped the field, and they but only gleaned.

His victory confessed, the foes retreat, 290
And cast their weapons at the victor's feet.
Whom thus he cheered: 'O Rhodian youth, I fought
For love alone, nor other booty sought;
Your lives are safe; your vessel I resign,
Yours be your own, restoring what is mine: 295
In Iphigene I claim my rightful due,
Robbed by my rival, and detained by you:
Your Pasimond a lawless bargain drove,
The parent could not sell the daughter's love;
Or if he could, my love disdains the laws, 300
And like a king by conquest gains his cause:
Where arms take place, all other pleas are vain;
Love taught me force, and force shall Love maintain.
You, what by strength you could not keep, release
And at an easy ransom buy your peace.' 305
Fear on the conquered side soon signed the accord,
And Iphigene to Cymon was restored:
While to his arms the blushing bride he took,
To seeming sadness she composed her look;
As if by force subjected to his will, 310
Though pleased, dissembling, and a woman still.
And, for she wept, he wiped her falling tears,
And prayed her to dismiss her empty fears;
'For yours I am,' he said, 'and have deserved
Your love much better, whom so long I served, 315

Than he to whom your formal father tied
Your vows; and sold a slave, not sent a bride.'
Thus while he spoke he seized the willing prey,
As Paris bore the Spartan spouse away:
Faintly she screamed, and even her eyes confessed   320
She rather would be thought, than was distressed.
   Who now exults but Cymon in his mind?
Vain hopes and empty joys of human kind,
Proud of the present, to the future blind!
Secure of fate while Cymon ploughs the sea   325
And steers to Candy with his conquered prey,
Scarce the third glass of measured hours was run,
When like a fiery meteor sunk the sun;
The promise of a storm; the shifting gales
Forsake by fits and fill the flagging sails: 330
Hoarse murmurs of the main from far were heard,
And night came on, not by degrees prepared,
But all at once; at once the winds arise,
The thunders roll, the forky lightning flies:
In vain the master issues out commands,   335
In vain the trembling sailors ply their hands:
The tempest unforeseen prevents their care,
And from the first they labour in despair.
The giddy ship, betwixt the winds and tides
Forced back and forwards, in a circle rides,   340
Stunned with the different blows; then shoots amain
Till counterbuffed she stops, and sleeps again.
Not more aghast the proud archangel fell,
Plunged from the height of Heaven to deepest Hell,
Than stood the lover of his love possessed,   345
Now cursed the more, the more he had been blessed;
More anxious for her danger than his own,
Death he defies; but would be lost alone.
   Sad Iphigene to womanish complaints
Adds pious prayers, and wearies all the saints;   350
Even if she could, her love she would repent,
But since she cannot, dreads the punishment:
Her forfeit faith, and Pasimond betrayed,
Are ever present, and her crime upbraid.
She blames herself, nor blames her lover less,   355
Augments her anger as her fears increase;
From her own back the burden would remove,
And lays the load on his ungoverned love,
Which interposing durst in Heaven's despite
Invade, and violate another's right: 360

The powers incensed awhile deferred his pain,
And made him master of his vows in vain:
But soon they punished his presumptuous pride,
That for his daring enterprise she died,
Who rather not resisted, than complied.   365
    Then impotent of mind, with altered sense,
She hugged the offender, and forgave the offence,
Sex to the last: meantime with sails declined
The wandering vessel drove before the wind:
Tossed, and retossed, aloft, and then alow;   370
Nor port they seek, nor certain course they know,
But every moment wait the coming blow.
Thus blindly driven, by breaking day they viewed
The land before them, and their fears renewed;
The land was welcome, but the tempest bore   375
The threatened ship against a rocky shore.
    A winding bay was near; to this they bent,
And just escaped; their force already spent;
Secure from storms and panting from the sea,
The land unknown at leisure they survey;   380
And saw (but soon their sickly sight withdrew)
The rising towers of Rhodes at distant view;
And cursed the hostile shore of Pasimond,
Saved from the seas, and shipwrecked on the ground.
    The frightened sailors tried their strength in vain   385
To turn the stern, and tempt the stormy main;
But the stiff wind withstood the labouring oar,
And forced them forward on the fatal shore!
The crooked keel now bites the Rhodian strand,
And the ship moored constrains the crew to land: 390
Yet still they might be safe because unknown;
But as ill fortune seldom comes alone,
The vessel they dismissed was driven before,
Already sheltered on their native shore;
Known each, they know: but each with change of cheer;   395
The vanquished side exults; the victors fear;
Not them but theirs, made prisoners ere they fight,
Despairing conquest, and deprived of flight.
    The country rings around with loud alarms,
And raw in fields the rude militia swarms;   400
Mouths without hands; maintained at vast expense,
In peace a charge, in war a weak defence:
Stout once a month they march, a blustering band,
And ever, but in times of need, at hand:

This was the morn when, issuing on the guard, 405
Drawn up in rank and file they stood prepared
Of seeming arms to make a short essay,
Then hasten to be drunk, the business of the day.
    The cowards would have fled, but that they knew
Themselves so many, and their foes so few; 410
But crowding on, the last the first impel;
Till overborne with weight the Cyprians fell.
Cymon enslaved, who first the war begun,
And Iphigene once more is lost and won.
    Deep in a dungeon was the captive cast, 415
Deprived of day, and held in fetters fast;
His life was only spared at their request,
Whom taken he so nobly had released:
But Iphigenia was the ladies' care,
Each in their turn addressed to treat the fair; 420
While Pasimond and his, the nuptial feast prepare.
    Her secret soul to Cymon was inclined,
But she must suffer what her fates assigned;
So passive is the church of womankind.
What worse to Cymon could his fortune deal, 425
Rolled to the lowest spoke of all her wheel?
It rested to dismiss the downward weight,
Or raise him upward to his former height;
The latter pleased; and Love (concerned the most)
Prepared the amends, for what by Love he lost. 430
    The sire of Pasimond had left a son,
Though younger, yet for courage early known,
Ormisda called; to whom, by promise tied,
A Rhodian beauty was the destined bride:
Cassandra was her name, above the rest 435
Renowned for birth, with fortune amply blessed.
Lysymachus, who ruled the Rhodian state,
Was then by choice their annual magistrate:
He loved Cassandra too with equal fire,
But fortune had not favoured his desire; 440
Crossed by her friends, by her not disapproved,
Nor yet preferred, or like Ormisda loved:
So stood the affair: some little hope remained,
That should his rival chance to lose, he gained.
    Meantime young Pasimond his marriage pressed, 445
Ordained the nuptial day, prepared the feast;
And frugally resolved (the charge to shun,
Which would be double should he wed alone)
To join his brother's bridal with his own.

Lysymachus oppressed with mortal grief   450
Received the news, and studied quick relief:
The fatal day approached: if force were used,
The magistrate his public trust abused;
To justice, liable as law required;
For when his office ceased, his power expired: 455
While power remained, the means were in his hand
By force to seize, and then forsake the land:
Betwixt extremes he knew not how to move,
A slave to fame, but more a slave to love:
Restraining others, yet himself not free,   460
Made impotent by power, debased by dignity!
Both sides he weighed: but after much debate,
The man prevailed above the magistrate.
    Love never fails to master what he finds,
But works a different way in different minds,   465
The fool enlightens, and the wise he blinds.
This youth proposing to possess, and scape,
Began in murder, to conclude in rape:
Unpraised by me, though Heaven sometime may bless
An impious act with undeserved success: 470
The great, it seems, are privileged alone
To punish all injustice but their own.
But here I stop, not daring to proceed,
Yet blush to flatter an unrighteous deed:
For crimes are but permitted, not decreed.   475
    Resolved on force, his wit the praetor bent
To find the means that might secure the event;
Nor long he laboured, for his lucky thought
In captive Cymon found the friend he sought;
The example pleased: the cause and crime the same;   480
An injured lover and a ravished dame.
How much he durst he knew by what he dared;
The less he had to lose, the less he cared
To menage loathsome life when love was the reward.
    This pondered well, and fixed on his intent   485
In depth of night he for the prisoner sent;
In secret sent, the public view to shun,
Then with a sober smile he thus begun:
'The powers above, who bounteously bestow
Their gifts and graces on mankind below,
Yet prove our merit first, nor blindly give   490
To such as are not worthy to receive:

To menage] to be careful of

74

For valour and for virtue they provide
Their due reward, but first they must be tried:
These fruitful seeds within your mind they sowed;   495
'Twas yours to improve the talent they bestowed:
They gave you to be born of noble kind,
They gave you Love to lighten up your mind
And purge the grosser parts; they gave you care
To please, and courage to deserve the fair.   500
    'Thus far they tried you, and by proof they found
The grain entrusted in a grateful ground:
But still the great experiment remained,
They suffered you to lose the prize you gained;
That you might learn the gift was theirs alone,   505
And, when restored, to them the blessing own.
Restored it soon will be; the means prepared,
The difficulty smoothed, the danger shared:
Be but yourself, the care to me resign,
Then Iphigene is yours, Cassandra mine.   510
Your rival Pasimond pursues your life,
Impatient to revenge his ravished wife,
But yet not his; tomorrow is behind,
And Love our fortunes in one band has joined:
Two brothers are our foes; Ormisda mine,   515
As much declared, as Pasimond is thine:
Tomorrow must their common vows be tied;
With Love to friend, and Fortune for our guide,
Let both resolve to die, or each redeem a bride.
    'Right I have none, nor hast thou much to plead;   520
'Tis force when done must justify the deed:
Our task performed, we next prepare for flight;
And let the losers talk in vain of right:
We with the fair will sail before the wind;
If they are grieved, I leave the laws behind.   525
Speak thy resolves; if now thy courage droop,
Despair in prison and abandon hope;
But if thou dar'st in arms thy love regain
(For liberty without thy love were vain)
Then second my design to seize the prey,   530
Or lead to second rape, for well thou know'st the way.'
    Said Cymon, overjoyed, 'Do thou propose
The means to fight, and only show the foes;
For from the first, when Love had fired my mind,
Resolved I left the care of life behind.'   535
    To this the bold Lysymachus replied,
'Let Heaven be neuter, and the sword decide:

75

The spousals are prepared, already play
The minstrels, and provoke the tardy day:
By this the brides are waked, their grooms are dressed;   540
All Rhodes is summoned to the nuptial feast,
All but myself, the sole unbidden guest.
Unbidden though I am, I will be there,
And joined by thee, intend to joy the fair.
  'Now hear the rest; when day resigns the light,   545
And cheerful torches gild the jolly night,
Be ready at my call; my chosen few
With arms administered shall aid thy crew.
Then entering unexpected will we seize
Our destined prey, from men dissolved in ease,   550
By wine disabled, unprepared for fight;
And hastening to the seas suborn our flight:
The seas are ours, for I command the fort,
A ship well manned expects us in the port:
If they, or if their friends the prize contest,   555
Death shall attend the man who dares resist.'
  It pleased! the prisoner to his hold retired,
His troop with equal emulation fired,
All fixed to fight, and all their wonted work required.
  The sun arose; the streets were thronged around,   560
The palace opened, and the posts were crowned:
The double bridegroom at the door attends
The expected spouse, and entertains the friends:
They meet, they lead to church; the priests invoke
The powers, and feed the flames with fragrant smoke: 565
This done they feast, and at the close of night
By kindled torches vary their delight,
These lead the lively dance, and those the brimming bowls
      invite.
  Now at the appointed place and hour assigned,
With souls resolved the ravishers were joined: 570
Three bands are formed: the first is sent before
To favour the retreat and guard the shore:
The second at the palace gate is placed,
And up the lofty stairs ascend the last:
A peaceful troop they seem with shining vests,   575
But coats of mail beneath secure their breasts.
  Dauntless they enter, Cymon at their head,
And find the feast renewed, the table spread:
Sweet voices mixed with instrumental sounds
Ascend the vaulted roof, the vaulted roof rebounds.   580

When like the harpies rushing through the hall
The sudden troop appears, the tables fall,
Their smoking load is on the pavement thrown;
Each ravisher prepares to seize his own:
The brides invaded with a rude embrace   585
Shriek out for aid, confusion fills the place:
Quick to redeem the prey their plighted lords
Advance, the palace gleams with shining swords.
    But late is all defence, and succour vain;
The rape is made, the ravishers remain: 590
Two sturdy slaves were only sent before
To bear the purchased prize in safety to the shore.
The troop retires, the lovers close the rear,
With forward faces not confessing fear:
Backward they move, but scorn their pace to mend,   595
Then seek the stairs, and with slow haste descend.
    Fierce Pasimond their passage to prevent
Thrust full on Cymon's back in his descent,
The blade returned unbathed, and to the handle bent:
Stout Cymon soon remounts, and cleft in two   600
His rival's head with one descending blow:
And as the next in rank Ormisda stood,
He turned the point; the sword inured to blood
Bored his unguarded breast, which poured a purple flood.
    With vowed revenge the gathering crowd pursues,   605
The ravishers turn head, the fight renews;
The hall is heaped with corps; the sprinkled gore
Besmears the walls, and floats the marble floor.
Dispersed at length the drunken squadron flies,
The victors to their vessel bear the prize,   610
And hear behind loud groans, and lamentable cries.
    The crew with merry shouts their anchors weigh,
Then ply their oars, and brush the buxom sea,
While troops of gathered Rhodians crowd the quay.
What should the people do, when left alone?   615
The governor and government are gone;
The public wealth to foreign parts conveyed;
Some troops disbanded, and the rest unpaid.
Rhodes is the sovereign of the sea no more;
Their ships unrigged, and spent their naval store;   620
They neither could defend, nor can pursue,
But grind their teeth, and cast a helpless view:
In vain with darts a distant war they try,
Short, and more short the missive weapons fly.

Meanwhile the ravishers their crimes enjoy,   625
And flying sails, and sweeping oars employ:
The cliffs of Rhodes in little space are lost;
Jove's Isle they seek; nor Jove denies his coast.
   In safety landed on the Candian shore,
With generous wines their spirits they restore;   630
There Cymon with his Rhodian friend resides,
Both court and wed at once the willing brides.
A war ensues, the Cretans own their cause,
Stiff to defend their hospitable laws:
Both parties lose by turns; and neither wins,   635
Till peace propounded by a truce begins.
The kindred of the slain forgive the deed,
But a short exile must for show precede;
The term expired, from Candia they remove;
And happy each at home enjoys his love.   640

ALEXANDER POPE
1688–1744

The Rape of the Lock

CANTO I

WHAT dire offence from amorous causes springs,
What mighty contests rise from trivial things,
I sing—This verse to CARYL, Muse! is due:
This, even Belinda may vouchsafe to view:
Slight is the subject, but not so the praise,   5
If she inspire, and he approve my lays.
   Say what strange motive, Goddess! could compel
A well-bred lord to assault a gentle belle?
O say what stranger cause, yet unexplored,
Could make a gentle belle reject a lord?   10
In tasks so bold, can little men engage,
And in soft bosoms dwells such mighty rage?
   Sol through white curtains shot a timorous ray,
And oped those eyes that must eclipse the day:
Now lapdogs give themselves the rousing shake,   15
And sleepless lovers, just at twelve, awake:
Thrice rung the bell, the slipper knocked the ground,
And the pressed watch returned a silver sound.

Belinda still her downy pillow pressed,
Her guardian sylph prolonged the balmy rest: 20
'Twas he had summoned to her silent bed
The morning dream that hovered o'er her head;
A youth more glittering than a birth-night beau
(That even in slumber caused her cheek to glow)
Seemed to her ear his winning lips to lay,   25
And thus in whispers said, or seemed to say:
   'Fairest of mortals, thou distinguished care
Of thousand bright inhabitants of air!
If e'er one vision touched thy infant thought,
Of all the nurse and all the priest have taught;   30
Of airy elves by moonlight shadows seen,
The silver token, and the circled green,
Or virgins visited by angel powers,
With golden crowns and wreaths of heavenly flowers;
Hear and believe! thy own importance know,   35
Nor bound thy narrow views to things below.
Some secret truths, from learned pride concealed,
To maids alone and children are revealed:
What though no credit doubting wits may give?
The fair and innocent shall still believe.   40
Know, then, unnumbered spirits round thee fly,
The light militia of the lower sky;
These, though unseen, are ever on the wing,
Hang o'er the box, and hover round the ring:
Think what an equipage thou hast in air,   45
And view with scorn two pages and a chair.
As now your own, our beings were of old,
And once inclosed in woman's beauteous mould;
Thence, by a soft transition, we repair
From earthly vehicles to these of air.   50
Think not, when woman's transient breath is fled,
That all her vanities at once are dead;
Succeeding vanities she still regards,
And though she plays no more, o'erlooks the cards.
Her joy in gilded chariots, when alive,   55
And love of ombre, after death survive.
For when the fair in all their pride expire,
To their first elements their souls retire:
The sprites of fiery termagants in flame
Mount up, and take a salamander's name.   60
Soft yielding minds to water glide away,
And sip, with nymphs, their elemental tea.

ombre] a card game

79

The graver prude sinks downward to a gnome,
In search of mischief still on earth to roam.
The light coquettes in sylphs aloft repair,   65
And sport and flutter in the fields of air.
    'Know farther yet; whoever fair and chaste
Rejects mankind, is by some sylph embraced:
For spirits, freed from mortal laws, with ease
Assume what sexes and what shapes they please.   70
What guards the purity of melting maids,
In courtly balls, and midnight masquerades,
Safe from the treacherous friend, the daring spark,
The glance by day, the whisper in the dark,
When kind occasion prompts their warm desires,   75
When music softens, and when dancing fires?
'Tis but their sylph, the wise celestials know,
Though honour is the word with men below.
    'Some nymphs there are, too conscious of their face,
For life predestined to the gnomes' embrace.   80
These swell their prospects and exalt their pride,
When offers are disdained, and love denied.
Then gay ideas crowd the vacant brain,
While peers, and dukes, and all their sweeping train,
And garters, stars, and coronets appear,   85
And in soft sounds, "Your Grace" salutes their ear.
'Tis these that early taint the female soul,
Instruct the eyes of young coquettes to roll,
Teach infant cheeks a bidden blush to know,
And little hearts to flutter at a beau.   90
    'Oft, when the world imagine women stray,
The sylphs through mystic mazes guide their way,
Through all the giddy circle they pursue,
And old impertinence expel by new.
What tender maid but must a victim fall   95
To one man's treat, but for another's ball?
When Florio speaks, what virgin could withstand,
If gentle Damon did not squeeze her hand?
With varying vanities, from every part,
They shift the moving toyshop of their heart;   100
Where wigs with wigs, with sword-knots sword-knots strive,
Beaux banish beaux, and coaches coaches drive.
This erring mortals levity may call;
Oh blind to truth! the sylphs contrive it all.
    'Of these am I, who thy protection claim,   105
A watchful sprite, and Ariel is my name.

Late, as I ranged the crystal wilds of air,
In the clear mirror of thy ruling star
I saw, alas! some dread event impend,
Ere to the main this morning sun descend,   110
But heaven reveals not what, or how, or where:
Warned by the sylph, oh pious maid, beware!
This to disclose is all thy guardian can:
Beware of all, but most beware of man!'
    He said; when Shock, who thought she slept too long,   115
Leaped up, and waked his mistress with his tongue.
'Twas then, Belinda, if report say true,
Thy eyes first opened on a billet-doux;
Wounds, charms, and ardours were no sooner read,
But all the vision vanished from thy head.   120
  And now, unveiled, the toilet stands displayed,
Each silver vase in mystic order laid.
First, robed in white, the nymph intent adores,
With head uncovered, the cosmetic powers.
A heavenly image in the glass appears,   125
To that she bends, to that her eyes she rears;
The inferior priestess, at her altar's side,
Trembling, begins the sacred rites of pride.
Unnumbered treasures ope at once, and here
The various offerings of the world appear;   130
From each she nicely culls with curious toil,
And decks the Goddess with the glittering spoil.
This casket India's glowing gems unlocks,
And all Arabia breathes from yonder box.
The tortoise here and elephant unite,   135
Transformed to combs, the speckled, and the white.
Here files of pins extend their shining rows,
Puffs, powders, patches, bibles, billet-doux.
Now awful beauty puts on all its arms;
The fair each moment rises in her charms,   140
Repairs her smiles, awakens every grace,
And calls forth all the wonders of her face;
Sees by degrees a purer blush arise,
And keener lightnings quicken in her eyes.
The busy sylphs surround their darling care,   145
These set the head and those divide the hair,
Some fold the sleeve, whilst others plait the gown;
And Betty's praised for labours not her own.

Canto ii

Not with more glories, in the ethereal plain,
The sun first rises o'er the purpled main,
Than, issuing forth, the rival of his beams
Launched on the bosom of the silver Thames.
Fair nymphs, and well-dressed youths around her shone,   5
But every eye was fixed on her alone.
On her white breast a sparkling cross she wore,
Which Jews might kiss, and infidels adore.
Her lively looks a sprightly mind disclose,
Quick as her eyes, and as unfixed as those: 10
Favours to none, to all she smiles extends;
Oft she rejects, but never once offends.
Bright as the sun, her eyes the gazers strike,
And, like the sun, they shine on all alike.
Yet graceful ease, and sweetness void of pride,   15
Might hide her faults, if belles had faults to hide:
If to her share some female errors fall,
Look on her face, and you'll forget 'em all.
    This nymph, to the destruction of mankind,
Nourished two locks, which graceful hung behind   20
In equal curls, and well conspired to deck
With shining ringlets her smooth ivory neck.
Love in these labyrinths his slaves detains,
And mighty hearts are held in slender chains.
With hairy springes we the birds betray,   25
Slight lines of hair surprise the finny prey,
Fair tresses man's imperial race ensnare,
And beauty draws us with a single hair.
    The adventurous Baron the bright locks admired;
He saw, he wished, and to the prize aspired.   30
Resolved to win, he meditates the way,
By force to ravish, or by fraud betray;
For when success a lover's toil attends,
Few ask, if fraud or force attained his ends.
    For this, ere Phoebus rose, he had implored   35
Propitious heaven, and every power adored,
But chiefly Love—to Love an altar built,
Of twelve vast French romances, neatly gilt.
There lay three garters, half a pair of gloves;
And all the trophies of his former loves;   40
With tender billet-doux he lights the pyre,
And breathes three amorous sighs to raise the fire.

Then prostrate falls, and begs with ardent eyes
Soon to obtain, and long possess the prize:
The powers gave ear, and granted half his prayer,   45
The rest the winds dispersed in empty air.
  But now secure the painted vessel glides,
The sunbeams trembling on the floating tides:
While melting music steals upon the sky,
And softened sounds along the waters die;   50
Smooth flow the waves, the zephyrs gently play,
Belinda smiled, and all the world was gay.
All but the sylph—with careful thoughts oppressed,
The impending woe sat heavy on his breast.
He summons straight his denizens of air;   55
The lucid squadrons round the sails repair:
Soft o'er the shrouds aerial whispers breathe,
That seemed but zephyrs to the train beneath.
Some to the sun their insect-wings unfold,
Waft on the breeze, or sink in clouds of gold;   60
Transparent forms, too fine for mortal sight,
Their fluid bodies half dissolved in light;
Loose to the wind their airy garments flew,
Thin glittering textures of the filmy dew,
Dipped in the richest tincture of the skies,   65
Where light disports in ever-mingling dyes,
While every beam new transient colours flings,
Colours that change whene'er they wave their wings.
Amid the circle, on the gilded mast,
Superior by the head, was Ariel placed;   70
His purple pinions opening to the sun,
He raised his azure wand, and thus begun:
  'Ye sylphs and sylphids, to your chief give ear!
Fays, fairies, genii, elves, and demons, hear!
Ye know the spheres and various tasks assigned   75
By laws eternal to the aerial kind.
Some in the fields of purest ether play,
And bask and whiten in the blaze of day.
Some guide the course of wandering orbs on high,
Or roll the planets through the boundless sky.   80
Some less refined, beneath the moon's pale light
Pursue the stars that shoot athwart the night,
Or suck the mists in grosser air below,
Or dip their pinions in the painted bow,
Or brew fierce tempests on the wintry main,   85
Or o'er the glebe distil the kindly rain.

Others on earth o'er human race preside,
Watch all their ways, and all their actions guide:
Of these the chief the care of nations own,
And guard with arms divine the British throne.   90
  'Our humbler province is to tend the fair,
Not a less pleasing, though less glorious care;
To save the powder from too rude a gale,
Nor let the imprisoned essences exhale;
To draw fresh colours from the vernal flowers;   95
To steal from rainbows ere they drop in showers
A brighter wash; to curl their waving hairs,
Assist their blushes, and inspire their airs;
Nay oft, in dreams, invention we bestow,
To change a flounce, or add a furbelow.   100
  'This day, black omens threat the brightest fair
That e'er deserved a watchful spirit's care;
Some dire disaster, or by force, or slight;
But what, or where, the fates have wrapped in night.
Whether the nymph shall break Diana's law,   105
Or some frail china jar receive a flaw;
Or stain her honour or her new brocade;
Forget her prayers, or miss a masquerade;
Or lose her heart, or necklace, at a ball;
Or whether Heaven has doomed that Shock must fall.   110
Haste, then, ye spirits! to your charge repair:
The fluttering fan be Zephyretta's care;
The drops to thee, Brillante, we consign;
And, Momentilla, let the watch be thine;
Do thou, Crispissa, tend her favourite lock;   115
Ariel himself shall be the guard of Shock.
  'To fifty chosen sylphs, of special note,
We trust the important charge, the petticoat;
Oft have we known that sevenfold fence to fail,
Though stiff with hoops, and armed with ribs of whale: 120
Form a strong line about the silver bound,
And guard the wide circumference around.
  'Whatever spirit, careless of his charge,
His post neglects, or leaves the fair at large,
Shall feel sharp vengeance soon o'ertake his sins,   125
Be stopped in vials, or transfixed with pins;
Or plunged in lakes of bitter washes lie,
Or wedged whole ages in a bodkin's eye:
Gums and pomatums shall his flight restrain,
While clogged he beats his silken wings in vain;   130

Or alum styptics with contracting power
Shrink his thin essence like a rivelled flower:
Or, as Ixion fixed, the wretch shall feel
The giddy motion of the whirling mill,
In fumes of burning chocolate shall glow,   135
And tremble at the sea that froths below!'
  He spoke; the spirits from the sails descend;
Some, orb in orb, around the nymph extend;
Some thread the mazy ringlets of her hair;
Some hang upon the pendants of her ear: 140
With beating hearts the dire event they wait,
Anxious, and trembling for the birth of Fate.

CANTO III

Close by those meads, for ever crowned with flowers,
Where Thames with pride surveys his rising towers,
There stands a structure of majestic frame,
Which from the neighbouring Hampton takes its name.
Here Britain's statesmen oft the fall foredoom   5
Of foreign tyrants and of nymphs at home;
Here thou, great ANNA! whom three realms obey,
Dost sometimes counsel take—and sometimes tea.
  Hither the heroes and the nymphs resort,
To taste awhile the pleasures of a court;   10
In various talk the instructive hours they passed,
Who gave the ball, or paid the visit last;
One speaks the glory of the British queen,
And one describes a charming Indian screen;
A third interprets motions, looks, and eyes;   15
At every word a reputation dies.
Snuff, or the fan, supply each pause of chat,
With singing, laughing, ogling, and all that.
  Meanwhile, declining from the noon of day,
The sun obliquely shoots his burning ray;   20
The hungry judges soon the sentence sign,
And wretches hang that jurymen may dine;
The merchant from the Exchange returns in peace,
And the long labours of the toilet cease.
Belinda now, whom thirst of fame invites,   25
Burns to encounter two adventurous knights,
At ombre singly to decide their doom;
And swells her breast with conquests yet to come.
Straight the three bands prepare in arms to join,
Each band the number of the sacred nine.   30

Soon as she spreads her hand, the aerial guard
Descend, and sit on each important card:
First Ariel perched upon a Matadore,
Then each, according to the rank they bore;
For sylphs, yet mindful of their ancient race,   35
Are, as when women, wondrous fond of place.
  Behold, four kings in majesty revered,
With hoary whiskers and a forky beard;
And four fair queens whose hands sustain a flower,
The expressive emblem of their softer power;   40
Four knaves in garbs succinct, a trusty band,
Caps on their heads, and halberts in their hand;
And particoloured troops, a shining train,
Draw forth to combat on the velvet plain.
  The skilful nymph reviews her force with care: 45
'Let spades be trumps!' she said, and trumps they were.
  Now move to war her sable Matadores,
In show like leaders of the swarthy Moors.
Spadillio first, unconquerable lord!
Led off two captive trumps, and swept the board.   50
As many more Manillio forced to yield,
And marched a victor from the verdant field.
Him Basto followed, but his fate more hard
Gained but one trump and one plebeian card.
With his broad sabre next, a chief in years,   55
The hoary majesty of spades appears,
Puts forth one manly leg, to sight revealed,
The rest, in many-coloured robe concealed.
The rebel knave, who dares his prince engage,
Proves the just victim of his royal rage.   60
Even mighty Pam, that kings and queens o'erthrew,
And mowed down armies in the fights of Lu,
Sad chance of war! now destitute of aid
Falls undistinguished by the victor spade!
  Thus far both armies to Belinda yield;   65
Now to the Baron fate inclines the field.
His warlike Amazon her host invades,
The imperial consort of the crown of spades.
The club's black tyrant first her victim died,
Spite of his haughty mien, and barbarous pride: 70
What boots the regal circle on his head,
His giant limbs, in state unwieldy spread;

Pam] the Jack of Clubs, highest trump in the five-card version of Lu, or Loo

That long behind he trails his pompous robe,
And, of all monarchs, only grasps the globe?
The Baron now his diamonds pours apace;   75
The embroidered king who shows but half his face,
And his refulgent queen, with powers combined,
Of broken troops an easy conquest find.
Clubs, diamonds, hearts, in wild disorder seen,
With throngs promiscuous strew the level green.   80
Thus when dispersed a routed army runs,
Of Asia's troops, and Afric's sable sons;
With like confusion different nations fly,
Of various habit, and of various dye;
The pierced battalions disunited fall,   85
In heaps on heaps: one fate o'erwhelms them all.
The knave of diamonds tries his wily arts,
And wins (oh shameful chance!) the queen of hearts.
At this, the blood the virgin's cheek forsook,
A livid paleness spreads o'er all her look;   90
She sees, and trembles at the approaching ill,
Just in the jaws of ruin, and codille.
And now (as oft in some distempered state)
On one nice trick depends the general fate:
An ace of hearts steps forth: the king unseen   95
Lurked in her hand, and mourned his captive queen:
He springs to vengeance with an eager pace,
And falls like thunder on the prostrate ace.
The nymph exulting fills with shouts the sky;
The walls, the woods, and long canals reply.   100
O thoughtless mortals! ever blind to fate,
Too soon dejected, and too soon elate.
Sudden, these honours shall be snatched away,
And cursed for ever this victorious day.
For lo! the board with cups and spoons is crowned,   105
The berries crackle, and the mill turns round;
On shining altars of Japan they raise
The silver lamp; the fiery spirits blaze:
From silver spouts the grateful liquors glide,
While China's earth receives the smoking tide: 110
At once they gratify their scent and taste,
And frequent cups prolong the rich repast.
Straight hover round the fair her airy band;
Some, as she sipped, the fuming liquor fanned,

codille] term used when the game is lost by the challenger

Some o'er her lap their careful plumes displayed,   115
Trembling, and conscious of the rich brocade.
Coffee (which makes the politician wise,
And see through all things with his half-shut eyes)
Sent up in vapours to the Baron's brain
New stratagems, the radiant lock to gain.   120
Ah cease, rash youth! desist ere 'tis too late,
Fear the just Gods, and think of Scylla's fate!
Changed to a bird, and sent to flit in air,
She dearly pays for Nisus' injured hair!
    But when to mischief mortals bend their will,   125
How soon they find fit instruments of ill!
Just then, Clarissa drew with tempting grace
A two-edged weapon from her shining case:
So ladies in romance assist their knight,
Present the spear, and arm him for the fight.   130
He takes the gift with reverence, and extends
The little engine on his fingers' ends;
This just behind Belinda's neck he spread,
As o'er the fragrant steams she bends her head.
Swift to the lock a thousand sprites repair,   135
A thousand wings, by turns, blow back the hair;
And thrice they twitched the diamond in her ear;
Thrice she looked back, and thrice the foe drew near.
Just in that instant, anxious Ariel sought
The close recesses of the virgin's thought;   140
As on the nosegay in her breast reclined,
He watched the ideas rising in her mind,
Sudden he viewed, in spite of all her art,
An earthly lover lurking at her heart.
Amazed, confused, he found his power expired,   145
Resigned to fate, and with a sigh retired.
    The peer now spreads the glittering forfex wide,
To inclose the lock; now joins it, to divide.
Even then, before the fatal engine closed,
A wretched sylph too fondly interposed;   150
Fate urged the shears, and cut the sylph in twain
(But airy substance soon unites again):
The meeting points the sacred hair dissever
From the fair head, for ever, and for ever!
    Then flashed the living lightning from her eyes,   155
And screams of horror rend the affrighted skies.
Not louder shrieks to pitying heaven are cast,
When husbands, or when lapdogs breathe their last;

Or when rich china vessels, fallen from high,
In glittering dust and painted fragments lie!   160
  'Let wreaths of triumph now my temples twine'
(The victor cried) 'the glorious prize is mine!
While fish in streams, or birds delight in air,
Or in a coach and six the British fair,
As long as Atalantis shall be read,   165
Or the small pillow grace a lady's bed,
While visits shall be paid on solemn days,
When numerous wax-lights in bright order blaze,
While nymphs take treats, or assignations give,
So long my honour, name, and praise shall live!   170
What time would spare, from steel receives its date,
And monuments, like men, submit to fate!
Steel could the labour of the Gods destroy,
And strike to dust the imperial towers of Troy;
Steel could the works of mortal pride confound,   175
And hew triumphal arches to the ground.
What wonder then, fair nymph! thy hairs should feel
The conquering force of unresisted steel?'

Canto IV

But anxious cares the pensive nymph oppressed,
And secret passions laboured in her breast.
Not youthful kings in battle seized alive,
Not scornful virgins who their charms survive,
Not ardent lovers robbed of all their bliss,   5
Not ancient ladies when refused a kiss,
Not tyrants fierce that unrepenting die,
Not Cynthia when her manteau's pinned awry,
E'er felt such rage, resentment, and despair,
As thou, sad virgin! for thy ravished hair.   10
  For, that sad moment, when the sylphs withdrew
And Ariel weeping from Belinda flew,
Umbriel, a dusky, melancholy sprite,
As ever sullied the fair face of light,
Down to the central earth, his proper scene,   15
Repaired to search the gloomy Cave of Spleen.
  Swift on his sooty pinions flits the gnome,
And in a vapour reached the dismal dome.
No cheerful breeze this sullen region knows,
The dreaded east is all the wind that blows.   20
Here in a grotto, sheltered close from air,
And screened in shades from day's detested glare,

She sighs for ever on her pensive bed,
Pain at her side, and Megrim at her head.
    Two handmaids wait the throne: alike in place,   25
But differing far in figure and in face.
Here stood Ill-nature like an ancient maid,
Her wrinkled form in black and white arrayed;
With store of prayers, for mornings, nights, and noons,
Her hand is filled; her bosom with lampoons.   30
    There Affectation, with a sickly mien,
Shows in her cheek the roses of eighteen,
Practised to lisp, and hang the head aside,
Faints into airs, and languishes with pride;
On the rich quilt sinks with becoming woe,   35
Wrapped in a gown, for sickness, and for show.
The fair ones feel such maladies as these,
When each new nightdress gives a new disease.
    A constant vapour o'er the palace flies;
Strange phantoms rising as the mists arise;   40
Dreadful, as hermit's dreams in haunted shades,
Or bright, as visions of expiring maids.
Now glaring fiends, and snakes on rolling spires,
Pale spectres, gaping tombs, and purple fires:
Now lakes of liquid gold, Elysian scenes,   45
And crystal domes, and angels in machines.
    Unnumbered throngs on every side are seen,
Of bodies changed to various forms by Spleen.
Here living teapots stand, one arm held out,
One bent; the handle this, and that the spout: 50
A pipkin there, like Homer's tripod, walks;
Here sighs a jar, and there a goose pie talks;
Men prove with child, as powerful fancy works,
And maids turned bottles, call aloud for corks.
    Safe passed the gnome through this fantastic band,   55
A branch of healing spleenwort in his hand.
Then thus addressed the power: 'Hail, wayward Queen!
Who rule the sex to fifty from fifteen:
Parent of vapours and of female wit,
Who give the hysteric, or poetic fit,   60
On various tempers act by various ways,
Make some take physic, others scribble plays;
Who cause the proud their visits to delay,
And send the godly in a pet to pray.
A nymph there is, that all thy power disdains,   65
And thousands more in equal mirth maintains.

But oh! if e'er thy gnome could spoil a grace,
Or raise a pimple on a beauteous face,
Like citron-waters matrons' cheeks inflame,
Or change complexions at a losing game;   70
If e'er with airy horns I planted heads,
Or rumpled petticoats, or tumbled beds,
Or caused suspicion when no soul was rude,
Or discomposed the head-dress of a prude,
Or e'er to costive lapdog gave disease,   75
Which not the tears of brightest eyes could ease:
Hear me, and touch Belinda with chagrin,
That single act gives half the world the spleen.'
   The Goddess with a discontented air
Seems to reject him, though she grants his prayer.   80
A wondrous bag with both her hands she binds,
Like that where once Ulysses held the winds;
There she collects the force of female lungs,
Sighs, sobs, and passions, and the war of tongues.
A vial next she fills with fainting fears,   85
Soft sorrows, melting griefs, and flowing tears.
The gnome rejoicing bears her gifts away,
Spreads his black wings, and slowly mounts to day.
   Sunk in Thalestris' arms the nymph he found,
Her eyes dejected and her hair unbound.   90
Full o'er their heads the swelling bag he rent,
And all the Furies issued at the vent.
Belinda burns with more than mortal ire,
And fierce Thalestris fans the rising fire.
'O wretched maid!' she spread her hands and cried   95
(While Hampton's echoes 'Wretched maid!' replied),
'Was it for this you took such constant care
The bodkin, comb, and essence to prepare?
For this your locks in paper durance bound,
For this with torturing irons wreathed around?   100
For this with fillets strained your tender head,
And bravely bore the double loads of lead?
Gods! shall the ravisher display your hair,
While the fops envy, and the ladies stare?
Honour forbid! at whose unrivalled shrine   105
Ease, pleasure, virtue, all our sex resign.
Methinks already I your tears survey,
Already hear the horrid things they say,
Already see you a degraded toast,
And all your honour in a whisper lost!   110

How shall I, then, your helpless fame defend?
'Twill then be infamy to seem your friend!
And shall this prize, the inestimable prize,
Exposed through crystal to the gazing eyes,
And heightened by the diamond's circling rays,   115
On that rapacious hand for ever blaze?
Sooner shall grass in Hyde Park Circus grow,
And wits take lodgings in the sound of Bow;
Sooner let earth, air, sea, to chaos fall,
Men, monkeys, lapdogs, parrots, perish all!'   120
   She said; then raging to Sir Plume repairs,
And bids her beau demand the precious hairs
(Sir Plume of amber snuff-box justly vain,
And the nice conduct of a clouded cane):
With earnest eyes, and round unthinking face,   125
He first the snuff-box opened, then the case,
And thus broke out—'My Lord, why, what the devil?
Zounds! damn the lock! 'fore Gad, you must be civil!
Plague on't! 'tis past a jest—nay prithee, pox!
Give her the hair'—he spoke, and rapped his box.   130
   'It grieves me much' (replied the Peer again)
'Who speaks so well should ever speak in vain.
But by this lock, this sacred lock I swear
(Which never more shall join its parted hair;
Which never more its honours shall renew,   135
Clipped from the lovely head where late it grew),
That while my nostrils draw the vital air,
This hand, which won it, shall for ever wear.'
He spoke; and speaking, in proud triumph spread
The long-contended honours of her head.   140
   But Umbriel, hateful gnome! forbears not so;
He breaks the vial whence the sorrows flow.
Then see! the nymph in beauteous grief appears,
Her eyes half-languishing, half-drowned in tears;
On her heaved bosom hung her drooping head,   145
Which, with a sigh, she raised; and thus she said:
   'For ever cursed be this detested day,
Which snatched my best, my favourite curl away!
Happy! ah ten times happy had I been,
If Hampton Court these eyes had never seen!   150
Yet am not I the first mistaken maid,
By love of courts to numerous ills betrayed.
Oh had I rather unadmired remained
In some lone isle, or distant northern land;

Where the gilt chariot never marks the way,   155
Where none learn ombre, none e'er taste bohea!
There kept my charms concealed from mortal eye,
Like roses that in deserts bloom and die.
What moved my mind with youthful lords to roam?
Oh had I stayed, and said my prayers at home!   160
'Twas this, the morning omens seemed to tell;
Thrice from my trembling hand the patch-box fell;
The tottering china shook without a wind,
Nay, Poll sat mute, and Shock was most unkind!
A sylph too warned me of the threats of fate,   165
In mystic visions, now believed too late!
See the poor remnants of these slighted hairs!
My hands shall rend what even thy rapine spares:
These in two sable ringlets taught to break,
Once gave new beauties to the snowy neck;   170
The sister-lock now sits uncouth, alone,
And in its fellow's fate foresees its own;
Uncurled it hangs, the fatal shears demands,
And tempts once more thy sacrilegious hands.
Oh hadst thou, cruel! been content to seize   175
Hairs less in sight, or any hairs but these!'

Canto v

She said: the pitying audience melt in tears,
But fate and Jove had stopped the Baron's ears.
In vain Thalestris with reproach assails,
For who can move when fair Belinda fails?
Not half so fixed the Trojan could remain,   5
While Anna begged and Dido raged in vain.
Then grave Clarissa graceful waved her fan;
Silence ensued, and thus the nymph began:
  'Say, why are beauties praised and honoured most,
The wise man's passion, and the vain man's toast?   10
Why decked with all that land and sea afford,
Why Angels called, and Angel-like adored?
Why round our coaches crowd the white-gloved beaux,
Why bows the side-box from its inmost rows?
How vain are all these glories, all our pains,   15
Unless good sense preserve what beauty gains:
That men may say, when we the front-box grace:
"Behold the first in virtue as in face!"
Oh! if to dance all night, and dress all day,
Charmed the smallpox, or chased old age away,   20

93

Who would not scorn what housewife's cares produce,
Or who would learn one earthly thing of use?
To patch, nay ogle, might become a saint,
Nor could it sure be such a sin to paint.
But since, alas! frail beauty must decay,   25
Curled or uncurled, since locks will turn to grey;
Since painted, or not painted, all shall fade,
And she who scorns a man must die a maid;
What then remains but well our power to use,
And keep good humour still whate'er we lose?   30
And trust me, dear! good humour can prevail,
When airs, and flights, and screams, and scolding fail.
Beauties in vain their pretty eyes may roll;
Charms strike the sight, but merit wins the soul.'

So spoke the dame, but no applause ensued;   35
Belinda frowned, Thalestris called her prude.
'To arms, to arms!' the fierce virago cries,
And swift as lightning to the combat flies.
All side in parties, and begin the attack;
Fans clap, silks rustle, and tough whalebones crack;   40
Heroes' and heroines' shouts confusedly rise,
And base and treble voices strike the skies.
No common weapons in their hands are found,
Like gods they fight, nor dread a mortal wound.

So when bold Homer makes the gods engage,   45
And heavenly breasts with human passions rage;
'Gainst Pallas, Mars; Latona, Hermes arms,
And all Olympus rings with loud alarms:
Jove's thunder roars, heaven trembles all around,
Blue Neptune storms, the bellowing deeps resound: 50
Earth shakes her nodding towers, the ground gives way,
And the pale ghosts start at the flash of day!

Triumphant Umbriel on a sconce's height
Clapped his glad wings, and sat to view the fight:
Propped on their bodkin spears, the sprites survey   55
The growing combat, or assist the fray.

While through the press enraged Thalestris flies,
And scatters death around from both her eyes,
A beau and witling perished in the throng,
One died in metaphor, and one in song.   60
'O cruel nymph! a living death I bear,'
Cried Dapperwit, and sunk beside his chair.
A mournful glance Sir Fopling upwards cast,
'Those eyes are made so killing'—was his last.

Thus on Mæander's flowery margin lies   65
The expiring swan, and as he sings he dies.
  When bold Sir Plume had drawn Clarissa down,
Chloe stepped in, and killed him with a frown;
She smiled to see the doughty hero slain,
But, at her smile, the beau revived again.   70
  Now Jove suspends his golden scales in air,
Weighs the men's wits against the lady's hair;
The doubtful beam long nods from side to side;
At length the wits mount up, the hairs subside.
  See, fierce Belinda on the Baron flies,   75
With more than usual lightning in her eyes:
Nor feared the chief the unequal fight to try,
Who sought no more than on his foe to die.
But this bold lord with manly strength endued,
She with one finger and a thumb subdued: 80
Just where the breath of life his nostrils drew,
A charge of snuff the wily virgin threw;
The gnomes direct, to every atom just,
The pungent grains of titillating dust.
Sudden, with starting tears each eye o'erflows,   85
And the high dome re-echoes to his nose.
  'Now meet thy fate,' incensed Belinda cried,
And drew a deadly bodkin from her side.
(The same, his ancient personage to deck,
Her great-great-grandsire wore about his neck,   90
In three seal-rings; which after, melted down,
Formed a vast buckle for his widow's gown:
Her infant grandame's whistle next it grew,
The bells she jingled, and the whistle blew;
Then in a bodkin graced her mother's hairs,   95
Which long she wore, and now Belinda wears.)
  'Boast not my fall' (he cried) 'insulting foe!
Thou by some other shalt be laid as low;
Nor think, to die dejects my lofty mind:
All that I dread is leaving you behind!   100
Rather than so, ah let me still survive,
And burn in Cupid's flames—but burn alive.'
  'Restore the lock!' she cries; and all around
'Restore the lock!' the vaulted roofs rebound.
Nor fierce Othello in so loud a strain   105
Roared for the handkerchief that caused his pain;
But see how oft ambitious aims are crossed,
And chiefs contend till all the prize is lost!

The lock, obtained with guilt, and kept with pain,
In every place is sought, but sought in vain: 110
With such a prize no mortal must be blest,
So heaven decrees! with heaven who can contest?
   Some thought it mounted to the lunar sphere,
Since all things lost on earth are treasured there.
There heroes' wits are kept in ponderous vases,   115
And beaux' in snuff-boxes and tweezer-cases.
There broken vows and deathbed alms are found,
And lovers' hearts with ends of ribband bound,
The courtier's promises, and sick man's prayers,
The smiles of harlots, and the tears of heirs,   120
Cages for gnats, and chains to yoke a flea,
Dried butterflies, and tomes of casuistry.
   But trust the Muse—she saw it upward rise,
Though marked by none but quick, poetic eyes
(So Rome's great founder to the heavens withdrew,   125
To Proculus alone confessed in view):
A sudden star, it shot through liquid air,
And drew behind a radiant trail of hair.
Not Berenice's locks first rose so bright,
The heavens bespangling with dishevelled light.   130
The sylphs behold it kindling as it flies,
And pleased pursue its progress through the skies.
   This the beau monde shall from the Mall survey,
And hail with music its propitious ray.
This the blest lover shall for Venus take,   135
And send up vows from Rosamonda's lake.
This Partridge soon shall view in cloudless skies,
When next he looks through Galileo's eyes;
And hence the egregious wizard shall foredoom
The fate of Louis, and the fall of Rome.   140
   Then cease, bright nymph! to mourn thy ravished hair,
Which adds new glory to the shining sphere!
Not all the tresses that fair head can boast,
Shall draw such envy as the lock you lost.
For, after all the murders of your eye,   145
When, after millions slain, yourself shall die;
When those fair suns shall set, as set they must,
And all those tresses shall be laid in dust,
This lock, the Muse shall consecrate to fame,
And 'midst the stars inscribe Belinda's name.   150

OLIVER GOLDSMITH

1730–1774

Elegy on the Death of a Mad Dog

GOOD people all, of every sort,
   Give ear unto my song;
And if you find it wondrous short,
   It cannot hold you long.

In Islington there was a man,   5
   Of whom the world might say,
That still a godly race he ran,
   Whene'er he went to pray.

A kind and gentle heart he had,
   To comfort friends and foes;   10
The naked every day he clad,
   When he put on his clothes.

And in that town a dog was found,
   As many dogs there be,
Both mongrel, puppy, whelp, and hound,   15
   And curs of low degree.

This dog and man at first were friends;
   But when a pique began,
The dog, to gain some private ends,
   Went mad and bit the man.   20

Around from all the neighbouring streets
   The wondering neighbours ran,
And swore the dog had lost his wits,
   To bite so good a man.

The wound it seemed both sore and sad   25
   To every Christian eye;
And while they swore the dog was mad,
   They swore the man would die.

But soon a wonder came to light,
   That showed the rogues they lied: 30
The man recovered of the bite—
   The dog it was that died.

The Double Transformation

SECLUDED from domestic strife,
Jack Bookworm led a college life;
A fellowship at twenty-five
Made him the happiest man alive;
He drank his glass and cracked his joke,   5
And freshmen wondered as he spoke.

  Such pleasures, unalloyed with care,
Could any accident impair?
Could Cupid's shaft at length transfix
Our swain, arrived at thirty-six?   10
O had the archer ne'er come down
To ravage in a country town!
Or Flavia been content to stop
At triumphs in a Fleet Street shop.
O had her eyes forgot to blaze!   15
Or Jack had wanted eyes to gaze.
O !—But let exclamation cease,
Her presence banished all his peace.
So with decorum all things carried;
Miss frowned, and blushed, and then was—married. 20

  Need we expose to vulgar sight
The raptures of the bridal night?
Need we intrude on hallowed ground,
Or draw the curtains closed around?
Let it suffice, that each had charms;   25
He clasped a goddess in his arms;
And, though she felt his usage rough,
Yet in a man 'twas well enough.

  The honeymoon like lightning flew,
The second brought its transports too.   30
A third, a fourth, were not amiss,
The fifth was friendship mixed with bliss:
But, when a twelvemonth passed away,
Jack found his goddess made of clay;
Found half the charms that decked her face   35
Arose from powder, shreds, or lace;
But still the worst remained behind,
That very face had robbed her mind.

Skilled in no other arts was she
But dressing, patching, repartee,   40
And, just as humour rose or fell,
By turns a slattern or a belle:
'Tis true she dressed with modern grace,
Half naked at a ball or race;
But when at home, at board or bed,   45
Five greasy nightcaps wrapped her head.
Could so much beauty condescend
To be a dull domestic friend?
Could any curtain-lectures bring
To decency so fine a thing?   50
In short, by night, 'twas fits or fretting;
By day, 'twas gadding or coquetting.
Fond to be seen, she kept a bevy
Of powdered coxcombs at her levy;
The squire and captain took their stations,   55
And twenty other near relations:
Jack sucked his pipe, and often broke
A sigh in suffocating smoke;
While all their hours were passed between
Insulting repartee or spleen.   60

Thus as her faults each day were known,
He thinks her features coarser grown;
He fancies every vice she shows,
Or thins her lip, or points her nose:
Whenever rage or envy rise,   65
How wide her mouth, how wild her eyes!
He knows not how, but so it is,
Her face is grown a knowing phiz;
And, though her fops are wondrous civil,
He thinks her ugly as the devil.   70

Now, to perplex the ravelled noose,
As each a different way pursues,
While sullen or loquacious strife,
Promised to hold them on for life,
That dire disease, whose ruthless power   75
Withers the beauty's transient flower:
Lo! the smallpox, whose horrid glare
Levelled its terrors at the fair;
And, rifling every youthful grace,
Left but the remnant of a face.   80

The glass, grown hateful to her sight,
Reflected now a perfect fright:
Each former art she vainly tries
To bring back lustre to her eyes.
In vain she tries her paste and creams,   85
To smooth her skin, or hide its seams;
Her country beaux and city cousins,
Lovers no more, flew off by dozens:
The squire himself was seen to yield,
And e'en the captain quit the field.   90

  Poor Madam, now condemned to hack
The rest of life with anxious Jack,
Perceiving others fairly flown,
Attempted pleasing him alone.
Jack soon was dazzled to behold   95
Her present face surpass the old;
With modesty her cheeks are dyed,
Humility displaces pride;
For tawdry finery is seen
A person ever neatly clean: 100
No more presuming on her sway,
She learns good nature every day;
Serenely gay, and strict in duty,
Jack finds his wife a perfect beauty.

ANONYMOUS
1765

King Estmere

HEARKEN to me, gentlemen,
  Come and you shall hear;
I'll tell you of two of the boldest brethren
  That ever born y-were.

The t'one of them was Adler young,   5
  The t'other was King Estmere;
They were as bold men in their deeds
  As any were far and near.

As they were drinking ale and wine
   Within King Estmere's hall: 10
'When will ye marry a wife, brother,
   A wife to glad us all?'

Then bespake him King Estmere,
   And answered him hastily:
'I know not that lady in any land   15
   That's able to marry with me.'

'King Adland hath a daughter, brother,
   Men call her bright and sheen;
If I were king here in your stead,
   That lady should be my queen.'   20

Says, 'Rede me, rede me, dear brother,
   Throughout merry England,
Where we might find a messenger
   Betwixt us two to send.'

Says, 'You shall ride yourself, brother,   25
   I'll bear you company;
Many through false messengers are deceived,
   And I fear lest so should we.'

Thus they renisht them to ride
   Of two good renisht steeds,   30
And when they came to King Adland's hall,
   Of red gold shone their weeds.

And when they came to King Adland's hall
   Before the goodly gate,
There they found good King Adland   35
   Rearing himself thereat.

'Now Christ thee save, good King Adland;
   Now Christ you save and see.'
Said, 'You be welcome, King Estmere,
   Right heartily to me.'   40

'You have a daughter,' said Adler young,
   'Men call her bright and sheen,
My brother would marry her to his wife,
   Of England to be queen.'

sheen] beautiful   Rede] advise   renisht] ?accoutred   weeds] garments   Rearing] Leaning

ANONYMOUS

'Yesterday was at my dear daughter
   Sir Bremor the king of Spain;
And then she nickèd him of nay,
   And I doubt she'll do you the same.'

'The king of Spain is a foul paynim,
   And 'lieveth on Mahound;
And pity it were that fair lady
   Should marry a heathen hound.

'But grant to me,' says King Estmere,
   For my love I you pray;
That I may see your daughter dear
   Before I go hence away.'

'Although it is seven years and more
   Since my daughter was in hall,
She shall come once down for your sake
   To glad my guestès all.'

Down then came that maiden fair,
   With ladies laced in pall,
And half a hundred of bold knights,
   To bring her from bower to hall;
And as many gentle squires,
   To tend upon them all.

The talents of gold were on her head set,
   Hanged low down to her knee;
And every ring on her small finger,
   Shone of the crystal free.

Says, 'God you save, my dear madam;'
   Says, 'God you save and see.'
Said, 'You be welcome, King Estmere,
   Right welcome unto me.

'And if you love me, as you say,
   So well and heartily,
All that ever you are comen about
   Soon sped now it shall be.'

45

50

55

60

65

70

75

nickèd him of nay] refused him with 'Nay'   pall] fine cloth   talents] gold ornaments

Then bespake her father dear:
  'My daughter, I say nay;   80
Remember well the king of Spain,
  What he said yesterday.

'He would pull down my halls and castles,
  And reave me of my life.
I cannot blame him if he do,   85
  If I reave him of his wife.'

'Your castles and your towers, father,
  Are strongly built about;
And therefore of the king of Spain
  We need not stand in doubt.   90

'Plight me your troth, now, King Estmere,
  By heaven and your right hand,
That you will marry me to your wife,
  And make me queen of your land.'

Then King Estmere he plight his troth   95
  By heaven and his right hand,
That he would marry her to his wife,
  And make her queen of his land.

And he took leave of that lady fair,
  To go to his own country,   100
To fetch him dukes and lords and knights,
  That married they might be.

They had not ridden scant a mile,
  A mile forth of the town,
But in did come the king of Spain,   105
  With kempès many one.

But in did come the king of Spain,
  With many a bold baròn,
T'one day to marry King Adland's daughter,
  T'other day to carry her home.   110

She sent one after King Estmere
  In all the speed might be,
That he must either turn again and fight,
  Or go home and lose his ladý.

reave] rob   kempès] warriors

One while then the page he went,
 Another while he ran;
Till he had o'ertaken King Estmere,
 I wis, he never blan.   115

'Tidings, tidings, King Estmere!'
 'What tidings now, my boy?'   120
'O, tidings I can tell to you,
 That will you sore annoy.

'You had not ridden scant a mile,
 A mile out of the town,
But in did come the king of Spain   125
 With kempès many a one:

'But in did come the king of Spain
 With many a bold barón,
T'one day to marry King Adland's daughter,
 T'other day to carry her home.   130

'My lady fair she greets you well,
 And evermore well by me:
You must either turn again and fight,
 Or go home and lose your lady.'

Says, 'Rede me, rede me, dear brother,   135
 My rede shall rise at thee,
Whether it is better to turn and fight,
 Or go home and lose my lady.'

'Now hearken to me,' says Adler young,
 'And your rede must rise at me,   140
I quickly will devise a way
 To set thy lady free.

'My mother was a western woman,
 And learned in gramarye,
And when I learned at the school,   145
 Something she taught it me.

'There grows an herb within this field,
 And if it were but known,
His colour, which is white and red,
 It will make black and brown: 150

blan] stopped   My rede shall rise at thee] My counsel shall come from thee   gramarye] magic

'His colour, which is brown and black,
  It will make red and white;
That sword is not in all England,
  Upon his coat will bite.

'And you shall be a harper, brother,   155
  Out of the north countrý;
And I'll be your boy, so fain of fight,
  And bear your harp by your knee.

'And you shall be the best harper,
  That ever took harp in hand;   160
And I will be the best singer,
  That ever sung in this land.

'It shall be written in our foreheads
  All and in gramarye,
That we two are the boldest men   165
  That are in all Christentye.'

And thus they renisht them to ride,
  On two good renisht steeds:
And when they came to King Adland's hall,
  Of red gold shone their weeds.   170

And when they came to King Adland's hall,
  Until the fair hall yate,
There they found a proud porter
  Rearing himself thereat.

Says, 'Christ thee save, thou proud porter;'   175
  Says, 'Christ thee save and see.'
'Now you be welcome,' said the porter,
  'Of what land soever ye be.'

'We been harpers,' said Adler young,
  'Come out of the north country;   180
We been come hither until this place,
  This proud wedding for to see.'

Said, 'And your colour were white and red,
  As it is black and brown,
I would say King Estmere and his brother   185
  Were comen until this town.'

yate] gate

105

Then they pulled out a ring of gold,
   Laid it on the porter's arm:
'And ever we will thee, proud porter,
   Thou wilt say us no harm.'   190

Sore he looked on King Estmere,
   And sore he handled the ring,
Then opened to them the fair hall yates,
   He let for no kind of thing.

King Estmere he stabled his steed   195
   So fair at the hall board;
The froth, that came from his bridle bit,
   Light in King Bremor's beard.

Says, 'Stable thy steed, thou proud harper,'
   Says, 'Stable him in the stall;   200
It doth not beseem a proud harper
   To stable him in a king's hall.'

'My lad he is so lither,' he said,
   'He will do nought that's meet;
And is there any man in this hall   205
   Were able him to beat?'

'Thou speakst proud words,' says the king of Spain,
   'Thou harper here to me;
There is a man within this hall,
   Will beat thy lad and thee.'   210

'O let that man come down,' he said,
   'A sight of him would I see;
And when he hath beaten well my lad,
   Then he shall beat of me.'

Down then came the kempery-man,   215
   And looked him in the ear;
For all the gold that was under heaven,
   He durst not nigh him near.

'And how now, kemp,' said the king of Spain,
   'And how, what aileth thee?'   220

lither] rascally   kempery-man] champion

He says, 'It is writ in his forehead,
    All and in gramarye,
That for all the gold that is under heaven,
    I dare not nigh him nigh.'

Then King Estmere pulled forth his harp,   225
    And played a pretty thing:
The lady upstart from the board,
    And would have gone from the king.

'Stay thy harp, thou proud harper,
    For God's love I pray thee;   230
For and thou plays as thou begins,
    Thou'lt till my bride from me.'

He stroke upon his harp again,
    And played a pretty thing:
The lady lough a loud laughter,   235
    As she sate by the king.

Says, 'Sell me thy harp, thou proud harper,
    And thy stringès all;
For as many gold nobles thou shalt have
    As here be rings in the hall.'   240

'What would ye do with my harp,' he said,
    'If I did sell it ye?'
'To play my wife and me a fit,
    When abed together we be.'

'Now sell me,' quoth he, 'thy bride so gay,   245
    As she sits by thy knee;
And as many gold nobles I will give
    As leaves been on a tree.'

'And what would ye do with my bride so gay,
    If I did sell her thee?   250
More seemly it is for her fair body
    To lie by me than thee.'

He played again both loud and shrill,
    And Adler he did sing,
'O lady, this is thy own true love;   255
    No harper, but a king.

till] entice   fit] strain of music

'O lady, this is thy own true love,
  As plainly thou mayst see,
And I'll rid thee of that foul paynim
  Who parts thy love and thee.'   260

The lady looked, the lady blushed,
  And blushed and looked again,
While Adler he hath drawn his brand,
  And hath the sowdan slain.

Up then rose the kempery-men,   265
  And loud they gan to cry:
'Ah! traitors, ye have slain our king,
  And therefore ye shall die.'

King Estmere threw the harp aside,
  And swith he drew his brand,   270
And Estmere he, and Adler Young
  Right stiff in stour can stand.

And aye their swords so sore can bite,
  Through help of gramarye,
That soon they have slain the kempery-men,   275
  Or forced them forth to flee.

King Estmere took that fair lady,
  And married her to his wife,
And brought her home to merry England,
  With her to lead his life.   280

WILLIAM COWPER
1731–1800

*The Diverting History of John Gilpin: showing how he went
farther than he intended and came safe home again*

JOHN GILPIN was a citizen
  Of credit and renown,
A train-band captain eke was he
  Of famous London town.

sowdan] sultan   stiff in stour] unyielding in fight

John Gilpin's spouse said to her dear,　　　　5
　'Though wedded we have been
These twice ten tedious years, yet we
　No holiday have seen.

'Tomorrow is our wedding day,
　And we will then repair　　　　　　　10
Unto the Bell at Edmonton,
　All in a chaise and pair.

'My sister and my sister's child,
　Myself and children three,
Will fill the chaise; so you must ride　　15
　On horseback after we.'

He soon replied, 'I do admire
　Of womankind but one,
And you are she, my dearest dear,
　Therefore it shall be done.　　　　　20

'I am a linen-draper bold,
　As all the world doth know,
And my good friend the calender
　Will lend his horse to go.'

Quoth Mrs Gilpin, 'That's well said;　　25
　And, for that wine is dear,
We will be furnished with our own,
　Which is both bright and clear.'

John Gilpin kissed his loving wife;
　O'erjoyed was he to find　　　　　　30
That, though on pleasure she was bent,
　She had a frugal mind.

The morning came, the chaise was brought,
　But yet was not allowed
To drive up to the door, lest all　　　　35
　Should say that she was proud.

So three doors off the chaise was stayed,
　Where they did all get in;
Six precious souls, and all agog
　To dash through thick and thin.　　　40

calender] a cloth processor

Smack went the whip, round went the wheels,
  Were never folk so glad;
The stones did rattle underneath
  As if Cheapside were mad.

John Gilpin at his horse's side   45
  Seized fast the flowing mane,
And up he got in haste to ride,
  But soon came down again.

For saddle-tree scarce reached had he,
  His journey to begin,   50
When, turning round his head, he saw
  Three customers come in.

So down he came; for loss of time,
  Although it grieved him sore,
Yet loss of pence, full well he knew,   55
  Would trouble him much more.

'Twas long before the customers
  Were suited to their mind,
When Betty screaming came downstairs,
  'The wine is left behind!'   60

'Good lack!' quoth he, 'yet bring it me,
  My leathern belt likewise,
In which I bear my trusty sword
  When I do exercise.'

Now Mistress Gilpin, careful soul,   65
  Had two stone bottles found,
To hold the liquor that she loved,
  And keep it safe and sound.

Each bottle had a curling ear,
  Through which the belt he drew,   70
And hung a bottle on each side,
  To make his balance true.

Then over all, that he might be
  Equipped from top to toe,
His long red cloak, well brushed and neat,   75
  He manfully did throw.

Now see him mounted once again
　　Upon his nimble steed,
Full slowly pacing o'er the stones,
　　With caution and good heed.　　　　　　　80

But finding soon a smoother road
　　Beneath his well-shod feet,
The snorting beast began to trot,
　　Which galled him in his seat.

So, 'Fair and softly!' John he cried,　　　85
　　But John he cried in vain;
That trot became a gallop soon,
　　In spite of curb and rein.

So stooping down, as needs he must
　　Who cannot sit upright,　　　　　　　90
He grasped the mane with both his hands,
　　And eke with all his might.

His horse, who never in that sort
　　Had handled been before,
What thing upon his back had got　　　　95
　　Did wonder more and more.

Away went Gilpin, neck or nought,
　　Away went hat and wig!
He little dreamt when he set out
　　Of running such a rig.　　　　　　　100

The wind did blow, the cloak did fly,
　　Like streamer long and gay,
Till, loop and button failing both,
　　At last it flew away.

Then might all people well discern　　　105
　　The bottles he had slung;
A bottle swinging at each side,
　　As hath been said or sung.

The dogs did bark, the children screamed,
　　Up flew the windows all,　　　　　　110
And every soul cried out, 'Well done!'
　　As loud as he could bawl.

Away went Gilpin—who but he?
  His fame soon spread around—
'He carries weight!' 'He rides a race!'   115
  ''Tis for a thousand pound!'

And still, as fast as he drew near,
  'Twas wonderful to view
How in a trice the turnpike-men
  Their gates wide open threw.   120

And now, as he went bowing down
  His reeking head full low,
The bottles twain behind his back
  Were shattered at a blow.

Down ran the wine into the road,   125
  Most piteous to be seen,
Which made his horse's flanks to smoke
  As they had basted been.

But still he seemed to carry weight,
  With leathern girdle braced,   130
For all might see the bottle-necks
  Still dangling at his waist.

Thus all through merry Islington
  These gambols he did play,
And till he came unto the Wash   135
  Of Edmonton so gay.

And there he threw the wash about
  On both sides of the way,
Just like unto a trundling mop,
  Or a wild goose at play.   140

At Edmonton his loving wife
  From the balcony spied
Her tender husband, wondering much
  To see how he did ride.

'Stop, stop, John Gilpin! Here's the house!'   145
  They all at once did cry;
'The dinner waits, and we are tired!'
  Said Gilpin, 'So am I!'

But yet his horse was not a whit
   Inclined to tarry there;   150
For why?—his owner had a house
   Full ten miles off, at Ware.

So, like an arrow swift he flew,
   Shot by an archer strong;
So did he fly—which brings me to   155
   The middle of my song.

Away went Gilpin, out of breath,
   And sore against his will,
Till at his friend the calender's
   His horse at last stood still.   160

The calender, amazed to see
   His neighbour in such trim,
Laid down his pipe, flew to the gate,
   And thus accosted him:

'What news? What news? Your tidings tell,   165
   Tell me you must and shall—
Say why bare-headed you are come,
   Or why you come at all?'

Now Gilpin had a pleasant wit,
   And loved a timely joke,   170
And thus unto the calender
   In merry guise he spoke:

'I came because your horse would come,
   And, if I well forebode,
My hat and wig will soon be here,   175
   They are upon the road.'

The calender, right glad to find
   His friend in merry pin,
Returned him not a single word,
   But to the house went in.   180

Whence straight he came with hat and wig;
   A wig that flowed behind,
A hat not much the worse for wear,
   Each comely in its kind.

He held them up, and in his turn   185
  Thus showed his ready wit,
'My head is twice as big as yours,
  They therefore needs must fit.

'But let me scrape the dirt away
  That hangs upon your face;   190
And stop and eat, for well you may
  Be in a hungry case.'

Said John, 'It is my wedding day,
  And all the world would stare
If wife should dine at Edmonton   195
  And I should dine at Ware.'

So, turning to his horse, he said,
  'I am in haste to dine;
'Twas for your pleasure you came here,
  You shall go back for mine.'   200

Ah luckless speech, and bootless boast!
  For which he paid full dear;
For, while he spake, a braying ass
  Did sing most loud and clear;

Whereat his horse did snort, as he   205
  Had heard a lion roar,
And galloped off with all his might,
  As he had done before.

Away went Gilpin, and away
  Went Gilpin's hat and wig!   210
He lost them sooner than at first;
  For why?—they were too big.

Now Mistress Gilpin, when she saw
  Her husband posting down
Into the country far away,   215
  She pulled out half-a-crown;

And thus unto the youth she said
  That drove them to the Bell,
'This shall be yours when you bring back
  My husband safe and well.'   220

The youth did ride, and soon did meet
    John coming back amain;
Whom in a trice he tried to stop,
    By catching at his rein.

But not performing what he meant,   225
    And gladly would have done,
The frightened steed he frightened more,
    And made him faster run.

Away went Gilpin, and away
    Went postboy at his heels,   230
The postboy's horse right glad to miss
    The lumbering of the wheels.

Six gentlemen upon the road
    Thus seeing Gilpin fly,
With postboy scampering in the rear,   235
    They raised the hue and cry:

'Stop thief! Stop thief! A highwayman!'
    Not one of them was mute;
And all and each that passed that way
    Did join in the pursuit.   240

And now the turnpike gates again
    Flew open in short space;
The toll-men thinking, as before,
    That Gilpin rode a race.

And so he did, and won it too,   245
    For he got first to town;
Nor stopped till where he had got up
    He did again get down.

Now let us sing, Long live the king,
    And Gilpin long live he;   250
And when he next doth ride abroad,
    May I be there to see!

ROBERT BURNS
1759–1796

Tam o'Shanter

WHEN chapman billies leave the street,
And drouthy neebors neebors meet;
As market days are wearing late,
An' folk begin to tak the gate;
While we sit bousing at the nappy,   5
An' getting fou and unco happy,
We think na on the lang Scots miles,
The mosses, waters, slaps, and stiles,
That lie between us and our hame,
Whare sits our sulky, sullen dame,   10
Gathering her brows like gathering storm,
Nursing her wrath to keep it warm.

 This truth fand honest Tam o' Shanter,
As he frae Ayr ae night did canter:
(Auld Ayr, wham ne'er a town surpasses,   15
For honest men and bonnie lasses).

 O Tam, had'st thou but been sae wise
As taen thy ain wife Kate's advice!
She tauld thee weel thou was a skellum,
A blethering, blustering, drunken blellum;   20
That frae November till October,
Ae market day thou was nae sober;
That ilka melder wi' the miller,
Thou sat as lang as thou had siller;
That every naig was ca'd a shoe on,   25
The smith and thee gat roaring fou on;
That at the Lord's house, even on Sunday,
Thou drank wi' Kirkton Jean till Monday.
She prophesied, that, late or soon,
Thou would be found deep drowned in Doon, 30
Or catched wi' warlocks in the mirk
By Alloway's auld, haunted kirk.

chapman billies] pedlar fellows drouthy] thirsty gate] road nappy] ale
fou] full unco] uncommon slaps] gaps skellum] good-for-nothing
blellum] babbler melder] grinding ca'd] driven mirk] dark

Ah! gentle dames, it gars me greet
To think how monie counsels sweet,
How monie lengthened, sage advices   35
The husband frae the wife despises!

But to our tale: Ae market-night,
Tam had got planted unco right,
Fast by an ingle, bleezing finely,
Wi' reaming swats, that drank divinely;   40
And at his elbow, Souter Johnnie,
His ancient, trusty, drouthy cronie:
Tam lo'ed him like a very brither;
They had been fou for weeks thegither.
The night drave on wi' sangs and clatter;   45
And ay the ale was growing better:
The landlady and Tam grew gracious
Wi' secret favours, sweet and precious:
The Souter tauld his queerest stories;
The landlord's laugh was ready chorus: 50
The storm without might rair and rustle,
Tam did na mind the storm a whistle.

Care, mad to see a man sae happy,
E'en drowned himsel amang the nappy.
As bees flee hame wi' lades o' treasure,   55
The minutes winged their way wi' pleasure:
Kings may be blest, but Tam was glorious,
O'er a' the ills o' life victorious!

But pleasures are like poppies spread:
You seize the flower, its bloom is shed;   60
Or like the snow falls in the river,
A moment white—then melts for ever;
Or like the borealis race,
That flit ere you can point their place;
Or like the rainbow's lovely form   65
Evanishing amid the storm.
Nae man can tether time or tide;
The hour approaches Tam maun ride:
That hour, o' night's black arch the key-stane,
That dreary hour he mounts his beast in;   70
And sic a night he taks the road in,
As ne'er poor sinner was abroad in.

gars me greet] makes me weep   ingle] fire   bleezing] blazing   reaming swats] foaming
new ale   Souter] Cobbler

The wind blew as 'twad blawn its last;
The rattling showers rose on the blast;
The speedy gleams the darkness swallowed;   75
Loud, deep, and lang the thunder bellowed:
That night, a child might understand,
The Deil had business on his hand.

Weel mounted on his gray mare Meg,
A better never lifted leg,   80
Tam skelpit on thro' dub and mire,
Despising wind, and rain, and fire;
Whiles holding fast his guid blue bonnet,
Whiles crooning o'er some auld Scots sonnet,
Whiles glow'ring round wi' prudent cares,   85
Lest bogles catch him unawares:
Kirk-Alloway was drawing nigh,
Whare ghaists and houlets nightly cry.

By this time he was 'cross the ford,
Whare in the snaw the chapman smoored;   90
And past the birks and meikle stane,
Whare drunken Charlie brak's neck-bane;
And thro' the whins, and by the cairn,
Whare hunters fand the murdered bairn;
And near the thorn, aboon the well,   95
Whare Mungo's mither hanged hersel.
Before him Doon pours all his floods;
The doubling storm roars thro' the woods;
The lightnings flash frae pole to pole;
Near and more near the thunders roll: 100
When, glimmering thro' the groaning trees,
Kirk-Alloway seemed in a bleeze,
Thro' ilka bore the beams were glancing,
And loud resounded mirth and dancing.

Inspiring bold John Barleycorn,   105
What dangers thou canst make us scorn!
Wi' tippenny, we fear nae evil;
Wi' usquabae, we'll face the Devil!
The swats sae reamed in Tammie's noddle,
Fair play, he cared na deils a boddle.   110
But Maggie stood, right sair astonished,
Till, by the heel and hand admonished,

skelpit] hurried   dub] puddle   smoored] smothered   birks and meikle stane] birches and
big stone   ilka bore] every chink   tippenny] twopenny ale   usquabae] whisky
cared na deils a boddle] cared not a farthing for devils

She ventured forward on the light;
And, vow! Tam saw an unco sight!

Warlocks and witches in a dance: 115
Nae cotillion, brent new frae France,
But hornpipes, jigs, strathspeys, and reels,
Put life and mettle in their heels.
A winnock-bunker in the east,
There sat Auld Nick, in shape o' beast;   120
A tousie tyke, black, grim, and large,
To gie them music was his charge:
He screwed the pipes and gart them skirl,
Till roof and rafters a' did dirl.
Coffins stood round, like open presses,   125
That shawed the dead in their last dresses;
And, by some devilish cantraip sleight,
Each in its cauld hand held a light:
By which heroic Tam was able
To note upon the haly table,   130
A murderer's banes, in gibbet-airns;
Twa span-lang, wee, unchristened bairns;
A thief new-cutted frae a rape—
Wi' his last gasp his gab did gape;
Five tomahawks wi' bluid red-rusted;   135
Five scymitars wi' murder crusted;
A garter which a babe had strangled;
A knife a father's throat had mangled—
Whom his ain son o' life bereft—
The grey hairs yet stack to the heft;   140
Wi' mair of horrible and awfu',
Which even to name wad be unlawfu'.

As Tammie glowered, amazed and curious,
The mirth and fun grew fast and furious;
The piper loud and louder blew,   145
The dancers quick and quicker flew,
They reeled, they set, they crossed, they cleekit,
Till ilka carlin swat and reekit,
And coost her duddies to the wark,
And linket at it in her sark!   150

brent] brand   winnock-bunker] window seat   tousie tyke] unkempt fellow
dirl] ring   presses] cupboards   cantraip sleight] magic trick   glowered] stared
cleekit] hooked arms   carlin] old hag   coost her duddies] cast off her clothes
linket] tripped   sark] shift

Now Tam, O Tam! had thae been queans,
A' plump and strapping in their teens!
Their sarks, instead o' creeshie flannen,
Been snaw-white seventeen hunder linen!
Thir breeks o' mine, my only pair,   155
That ance were plush, o' guid blue hair,
I wad hae gi'en them off my hurdies
For ae blink o' the bonnie burdies!

But withered beldams, auld and droll,
Rigwoodie hags wad spean a foal,   160
Louping and flinging on a crummock,
I wonder did na turn thy stomach!

But Tam kend what was what fu' brawlie:
There was ae winsome wench and wawlie,
That night enlisted in the core,   165
Lang after kend on Carrick shore
(For monie a beast to dead she shot,
An' perished monie a bonnie boat,
And shook baith meikle corn and bear,
And kept the countryside in fear).   170
Her cutty sark, o' Paisley harn,
That while a lassie she had worn,
In longitude tho' sorely scanty,
It was her best, and she was vauntie.
Ah! little kend thy reverend grannie,   175
That sark she coft for her wee Nannie,
Wi' twa pund Scots ('twas a' her riches),
Wad ever graced a dance of witches!

But here my Muse her wing maun cour,
Sic flights are far beyond her power: 180
To sing how Nannie lap and flang
(A souple jade she was and strang),
And how Tam stood like ane bewitched,
And thought his very een enriched;
Even Satan glowered, and fidged fu' fain,   185
And hotched and blew wi' might and main;

queans] lasses   creeshie flannen] greasy flannel   Thir breeks] These breeches
hurdies] buttocks Rigwoodie] ill-shapen spean] wean (in disgust) crummock] staff with
crooked head brawlie] well wawlie] nimble core] company kend] known meikle corn
and bear] much corn and barley cutty] short harn] coarse cloth vauntie] proud
coft] bought   cour] stoop fidged fu' fain] fidgeted with eagerness hotched] jerked

Till first ae caper, syne anither,
Tam tint his reason a' thegither,
And roars out 'Weel done, Cutty-sark!'
And in an instant all was dark;   190
And scarcely had he Maggie rallied,
When out the hellish legion sallied.

   As bees bizz out wi' angry fyke,
When plundering herds assail their byke;
As open pussie's mortal foes,   195
When, pop! she starts before their nose;
As eager runs the market-crowd,
When 'Catch the thief!' resounds aloud:
So Maggie runs, the witches follow,
Wi' monie an eldritch skreech and hollo.   200

   Ah, Tam! Ah, Tam! thou'll get thy fairin'!
In hell they'll roast thee like a herrin'!
In vain thy Kate awaits thy comin'!
Kate soon will be a woefu' woman!
Now, do thy speedy utmost, Meg,   205
And win the key-stane of the brig;
There, at them thou thy tail may toss,
A running stream they dare na cross!
But ere the key-stane she could make,
The fient a tail she had to shake!   210
For Nannie, far before the rest,
Hard upon noble Maggie prest,
And flew at Tam wi' furious ettle;
But little wist she Maggie's mettle—
Ae spring brought off her master hale,   215
But left behind her ain grey tail:
The carlin claught her by the rump,
And left poor Maggie scarce a stump.

   Now, wha this tale o' truth shall read,
Ilk man, and mother's son, take heed: 220
Whene'er to drink you are inclined,
Or cutty sarks run in your mind,
Think! ye may buy the joys o'er dear:
Remember Tam o' Shanter's mare.

     tint] lost fyke] fuss herds] herd boys byke] nest
           pussie's] the hare's eldritch] unearthly
brig] bridge fient] devil ettle] intent claught] clutched

SAMUEL TAYLOR COLERIDGE
1772–1834

The Rime of the Ancient Mariner

PART I

An ancient Mariner
meeteth three
Gallants bidden to a
wedding-feast, and
detaineth one.

IT is an ancient Mariner
And he stoppeth one of three.
'By thy long grey beard and glittering eye,
Now wherefore stopp'st thou me?

The Bridegroom's doors are opened wide,   5
And I am next of kin;
The guests are met, the feast is set:
Mayst hear the merry din.'

He holds him with his skinny hand,
'There was a ship,' quoth he.   10
'Hold off! unhand me, grey-beard loon!'
Eftsoons his hand dropt he.

The Wedding-Guest
is spellbound by the
eye of the old
seafaring man, and
constrained to hear
his tale.

He holds him with his glittering eye—
The Wedding-Guest stood still,
And listens like a three years' child: 15
The Mariner hath his will.

The Wedding-Guest sat on a stone:
He cannot choose but hear;
And thus spake on that ancient man,
The bright-eyed Mariner.   20

'The ship was cheered, the harbour cleared,
Merrily did we drop
Below the kirk, below the hill,
Below the lighthouse top.

The Mariner tells
how the ship sailed
southward with a
good wind and fair
weather, till it
reached the Line.

The Sun came up upon the left,   25
Out of the sea came he!
And he shone bright, and on the right
Went down into the sea.

Higher and higher every day,
Till over the mast at noon—'
The Wedding-Guest here beat his breast,   30
For he heard the loud bassoon.

The Wedding-Guest heareth the bridal music; but the Mariner continueth his tale.

The bride hath paced into the hall,
Red as a rose is she;
Nodding their heads before her goes   35
The merry minstrelsy.

The Wedding-Guest he beat his breast,
Yet he cannot choose but hear;
And thus spake on that ancient man,
The bright-eyed Mariner.   40

The ship driven by a storm toward the South Pole.

'And now the STORM-BLAST came, and he
Was tyrannous and strong:
He struck with his o'ertaking wings,
And chased us south along.

With sloping masts and dipping prow,   45
As who pursued with yell and blow
Still treads the shadow of his foe,
And forward bends his head,
The ship drove fast, loud roared the blast,
And southward aye we fled.   50

And now there came both mist and snow,
And it grew wondrous cold:
And ice, mast-high, came floating by,
As green as emerald.

The land of ice, and of fearful sounds, where no living thing was to be seen.

And through the drifts the snowy clifts   55
Did send a dismal sheen:
Nor shapes of men nor beasts we ken—
The ice was all between.

The ice was here, the ice was there,
The ice was all around: 60
It cracked and growled, and roared and howled,
Like noises in a swound!

Till a great sea-bird, called the Albatross, came through the snow-fog, and was received with great joy and hospitality.

At length did cross an Albatross,
Thorough the fog it came;
As if it had been a Christian soul,   65
We hailed it in God's name.

It ate the food it ne'er had eat,
And round and round it flew.
The ice did split with a thunder-fit;
The helmsman steered us through!   70

And a good south wind sprung up behind;
The Albatross did follow,
And every day, for food or play,
Came to the mariners' hollo!

                                                     75
In mist or cloud, on mast or shroud,
It perched for vespers nine;
Whiles all the night, through fog-smoke white,
Glimmered the white Moon-shine.'

'God save thee, ancient Mariner!
From the fiends, that plague thee thus!—   80
Why look'st thou so?'—'With my cross-bow
I shot the ALBATROSS.'

PART II

'The Sun now rose upon the right:
Out of the sea came he,
Still hid in mist, and on the left   85
Went down into the sea.

And the good south wind still blew behind,
But no sweet bird did follow,
Nor any day for food or play
Came to the mariners' hollo!   90

And I had done a hellish thing,
And it would work 'em woe:
For all averred, I had killed the bird
That made the breeze to blow.
Ah wretch! said they, the bird to slay,   95
That made the breeze to blow!

Nor dim nor red, like God's own head,
The glorious Sun uprist:
Then all averred, I had killed the bird
That brought the fog and mist.   100
'Twas right, said they, such birds to slay,
That bring the fog and mist.

The margin glosses (left column):

And lo! the Albatross proveth a bird of good omen, and followeth the ship as it returned northward through fog and floating ice.

The ancient Mariner inhospitably killeth the pious bird of good omen.

His shipmates cry out against the ancient Mariner, for killing the bird of good luck.

But when the fog cleared off, they justify the same, and thus make themselves accomplices in the crime.

The fair breeze continues; the ship enters the Pacific Ocean, and sails northward, even till it reaches the Line.

The fair breeze blew, the white foam flew,
The furrow followed free;
We were the first that ever burst
Into that silent sea.

105

Down dropt the breeze, the sails dropt down,
'Twas sad as sad could be;
And we did speak only to break
The silence of the sea!

110

The ship hath been suddenly becalmed.

All in a hot and copper sky,
The bloody Sun, at noon,
Right up above the mast did stand,
No bigger than the Moon.

Day after day, day after day,
We stuck, nor breath nor motion;
As idle as a painted ship
Upon a painted ocean.

115

And the Albatross begins to be avenged.

Water, water, everywhere,
And all the boards did shrink;
Water, water, everywhere,
Nor any drop to drink.

120

The very deep did rot: O Christ!
That ever this should be!
Yea, slimy things did crawl with legs
Upon the slimy sea.

125

About, about, in reel and rout
The death-fires danced at night;
The water, like a witch's oils,
Burnt green, and blue and white.

130

A Spirit had followed them; one of the invisible inhabitants of this planet, neither

And some in dreams assurèd were
Of the Spirit that plagued us so;
Nine fathom deep he had followed us
From the land of mist and snow.

departed souls nor angels; concerning whom the learned Jew Josephus, and the Platonic Constantinopolitan, Michael Psellus, may be consulted. They are very numerous, and there is no climate or element without one or more.

And every tongue, through utter drought,   135
Was withered at the root;
We could not speak, no more than if
We had been choked with soot.

The shipmates in
their sore distress,
would fain throw the
whole guilt on the
ancient Mariner: in
sign whereof they hang

Ah! well a-day! What evil looks
Had I from old and young!   140
Instead of the cross, the Albatross
About my neck was hung.'

the dead seabird round his neck.

PART III

'There passed a weary time. Each throat
Was parched, and glazed each eye.
A weary time! a weary time!   145
How glazed each weary eye,
When looking westward, I beheld
A something in the sky.

The ancient Mariner
beholdeth a sign in
the element afar off.

At first it seemed a little speck,
And then it seemed a mist;   150
It moved and moved, and took at last
A certain shape, I wist.

A speck, a mist, a shape, I wist!
And still it neared and neared:
As if it dodged a water-sprite,   155
It plunged and tacked and veered.

At its nearer
approach, it seemeth
him to be a ship; and
at a dear ransom he
freeth his speech
from the bonds of
thirst.

With throats unslaked, with black lips baked,
We could nor laugh nor wail;
Through utter drought all dumb we stood!
I bit my arm, I sucked the blood,   160
And cried, A sail! a sail!

A flash of joy;

With throats unslaked, with black lips baked,
Agape they heard me call:
Gramercy! they for joy did grin,
And all at once their breath drew in,   165
As they were drinking all.

And horror follows.
For can it be a ship
that comes onward
without wind or tide?

"See! see!" (I cried) "she tacks no more!
Hither to work us weal;
Without a breeze, without a tide,
She steadies with upright keel!"   170

The western wave was all a-flame.
The day was well nigh done!
Almost upon the western wave
Rested the broad bright Sun;
When that strange shape drove suddenly 175
Betwixt us and the Sun.

It seemeth him but the skeleton of a ship.

And straight the Sun was flecked with bars,
(Heaven's Mother send us grace!)
As if through a dungeon-grate he peered
With broad and burning face. 180

And its ribs are seen as bars on the face of the setting Sun. The Spectre-Woman and her Death-mate, and no other on board the skeleton ship.

Alas! (thought I, and my heart beat loud)
How fast she nears and nears!
Are those *her* sails that glance in the Sun,
Like restless gossameres?

Are those *her* ribs through which the Sun 185
Did peer, as through a grate?
And is that Woman all her crew?
Is that a DEATH? and are there two?
Is DEATH that woman's mate?

Like vessel, like crew! Death and Life-in-Death have diced for the ship's crew, and she (the latter) winneth the ancient Mariner.

Her lips were red, *her* looks were free, 190
Her locks were yellow as gold:
Her skin was as white as leprosy,
The Night-mare LIFE-IN-DEATH was she,
Who thicks man's blood with cold.

The naked hulk alongside came, 195
And the twain were casting dice;
"The game is done! I've won! I've won!"
Quoth she, and whistles thrice.

No twilight within the courts of the Sun.

The Sun's rim dips; the stars rush out:
At one stride comes the dark; 200
With far-heard whisper, o'er the sea,
Off shot the spectre-bark.

At the rising of the Moon,

We listened and looked sideways up!
Fear at my heart, as at a cup,
My life-blood seemed to sip! 205
The stars were dim, and thick the night,
The steersman's face by his lamp gleamed white;

From the sails the dew did drip—
Till clomb above the eastern bar
The hornèd Moon, with one bright star   210
Within the nether tip.

One after another,

One after one, by the star-dogged Moon,
Too quick for groan or sigh,
Each turned his face with a ghastly pang,
And cursed me with his eye.   215

His shipmates drop
down dead.

Four times fifty living men,
(And I heard nor sign nor groan)
With heavy thump, a lifeless lump,
They dropped down one by one.

But Life-in-Death
begins her work on
the ancient Mariner.

The souls did from their bodies fly—   220
They fled to bliss or woe!
And every soul, it passed me by,
Like the whizz of my cross-bow!'

PART IV

The Wedding-Guest
feareth that a Spirit
is talking to him;

'I fear thee, ancient Mariner!
I fear thy skinny hand!   225
And thou art long, and lank, and brown,
As is the ribbed sea-sand.

I fear thee and thy glittering eye,
And thy skinny hand, so brown.'—

But the ancient
Mariner assureth
him of his bodily life,
and proceedeth to
relate his horrible
penance.

'Fear not, fear not, thou Wedding-Guest!   230
This body dropt not down.

Alone, alone, all, all alone,
Alone on a wide wide sea!
And never a saint took pity on
My soul in agony.   235

He despiseth the
creatures of the
calm,

The many men, so beautiful!
And they all dead did lie:
And a thousand thousand slimy things
Lived on; and so did I.

And envieth that *they*
should live, and so
many lie dead.

I looked upon the rotting sea,   240
And drew my eyes away;
I looked upon the rotting deck,
And there the dead men lay.

I looked to Heaven, and tried to pray;
But or ever a prayer had gusht,   245
A wicked whisper came, and made
My heart as dry as dust.

I closed my lids, and kept them close,
And the balls like pulses beat;
For the sky and the sea, and the sea and the sky
Lay like a load on my weary eye,   251
And the dead were at my feet.

But the curse liveth
for him in the eye of
the dead men.

The cold sweat melted from their limbs,
Nor rot nor reek did they:
The look with which they looked on me   255
Had never passed away.

An orphan's curse would drag to hell
A spirit from on high;
But oh! more horrible than that
Is the curse in a dead man's eye!   260
Seven days, seven nights, I saw that curse,
And yet I could not die.

In his loneliness and
fixedness he yearneth
towards the
journeying Moon,
and the stars that
still sojourn, yet still
move onward; and
everywhere the blue
sky belongs to them,
and is their
appointed rest, and
their native country

The moving Moon went up the sky,
And nowhere did abide:
Softly she was going up,   265
And a star or two beside—

Her beams bemocked the sultry main,
Like April hoar-frost spread;
But where the ship's huge shadow lay,
The charmèd water burnt alway   270
A still and awful red.

and their own natural homes, which they enter unannounced, as lords that are
certainly expected and yet there is a silent joy at their arrival.

By the light of the
Moon he beholdeth
God's creatures of
the great calm.

Beyond the shadow of the ship,
I watched the water-snakes:
They moved in tracks of shining white,
And when they reared, the elfish light   275
Fell off in hoary flakes.

Within the shadow of the ship
I watched their rich attire:
Blue, glossy green, and velvet black,
They coiled and swam; and every track   280
Was a flash of golden fire.

*Their beauty and
their happiness.*

O happy living things! no tongue
Their beauty might declare:
A spring of love gushed from my heart,

*He blesseth them in
his heart.*

And I blessed them unaware: 285
Sure my kind Saint took pity on me,
And I blessed them unaware.

The self-same moment I could pray;

*The spell begins to
break.*

And from my neck so free
The Albatross fell off, and sank   290
Like lead into the sea.'

PART V

'Oh sleep! it is a gentle thing,
Beloved from pole to pole!
To Mary Queen the praise be given!
She sent the gentle sleep from Heaven,   295
That slid into my soul.

*By grace of the holy
Mother, the ancient
Mariner is refreshed
with rain.*

The silly buckets on the deck,
That had so long remained,
I dreamt that they were filled with dew;
And when I awoke, it rained.   300

My lips were wet, my throat was cold,
My garments all were dank;
Sure I had drunken in my dreams,
And still my body drank.

I moved, and could not feel my limbs: 305
I was so light—almost
I thought that I had died in sleep,
And was a blessèd ghost.

*He heareth sounds
and seeth strange
sights and
commotions in the
sky and the element.*

And soon I heard a roaring wind:
It did not come anear;   310
But with its sound it shook the sails,
That were so thin and sere.

The upper air burst into life!
And a hundred fire-flags sheen,
To and fro they were hurried about!   315
And to and fro, and in and out,
The wan stars danced between.

And the coming wind did roar more loud,
And the sails did sigh like sedge;
And the rain poured down from one black cloud;
The Moon was at its edge.   321

The thick black cloud was cleft, and still
The Moon was at its side:
Like waters shot from some high crag,
The lightning fell with never a jag,   325
A river steep and wide.

The bodies of the
ship's crew are
inspired and the ship
moves on;

The loud wind never reached the ship,
Yet now the ship moved on!
Beneath the lightning and the Moon
The dead men gave a groan.   330

They groaned, they stirred, they all uprose,
Nor spake, nor moved their eyes;
It had been strange, even in a dream,
To have seen those dead men rise.

The helmsman steered, the ship moved on;   335
Yet never a breeze up-blew;
The mariners all 'gan work the ropes,
Where they were wont to do;
They raised their limbs like lifeless tools—
We were a ghastly crew.   340

The body of my brother's son
Stood by me, knee to knee:
The body and I pulled at one rope,
But he said nought to me.'

'I fear thee, ancient Mariner!'   345

But not by the souls
of the men, nor by
daemons of earth or
middle air, but by a
blessed troop of
angelic spirits, sent down by the invocation of the guardian saint.

'Be calm, thou Wedding-Guest!
'Twas not those souls that fled in pain,
Which to their corses came again,
But a troop of spirits blest:

For when it dawned—they dropped their arms,   350
And clustered round the mast;
Sweet sounds rose slowly through their mouths,
And from their bodies passed.

Around, around, flew each sweet sound,
Then darted to the Sun;   355
Slowly the sounds came back again,
Now mixed, now one by one.

Sometimes a-dropping from the sky
I heard the sky-lark sing;
Sometimes all little birds that are,   360
How they seemed to fill the sea and air
With their sweet jargoning!

And now 'twas like all instruments,
Now like a lonely flute;
And now it is an angel's song,   365
That makes the heavens be mute.

It ceased; yet still the sails made on
A pleasant noise till noon,
A noise like of a hidden brook
In the leafy month of June,   370
That to the sleeping woods all night
Singeth a quiet tune.

Till noon we quietly sailed on,
Yet never a breeze did breathe:
Slowly and smoothly went the ship,   375
Moved onward from beneath.

The lonesome Spirit from the South Pole carries on the ship as far as the Line, in obedience to the angelic troop, but still requireth vengeance.

Under the keel nine fathom deep,
From the land of mist and snow,
The spirit slid: and it was he
That made the ship to go.   380
The sails at noon left off their tune,
And the ship stood still also.

The Sun, right up above the mast,
Had fixed her to the ocean:
But in a minute she 'gan stir,   385
With a short uneasy motion—
Backwards and forwards half her length
With a short uneasy motion.

Then like a pawing horse let go,
She made a sudden bound:
It flung the blood into my head, 390
And I fell down in a swound.

How long in that same fit I lay,
I have not to declare;
But ere my living life returned, 395
I heard and in my soul discerned
Two voices in the air.

"Is it he?" quoth one, "Is this the man?
By him who died on cross,
With his cruel bow he laid full low 400
The harmless Albatross.

The spirit who bideth by himself
In the land of mist and snow,
He loved the bird that loved the man
Who shot him with his bow." 405

The other was a softer voice,
As soft as honey-dew:
Quoth he, "The man hath penance done,
And penance more will do." '

PART VI

FIRST VOICE

' "But tell me, tell me! speak again, 410
Thy soft response renewing—
What makes that ship drive on so fast?
What is the ocean doing?"

SECOND VOICE

"Still as a slave before his lord,
The ocean hath no blast;
His great bright eye most silently 415
Up to the Moon is cast—

If he may know which way to go;
For she guides him smooth or grim.
See, brother, see! how graciously 420
She looketh down on him."

FIRST VOICE

"But why drives on that ship so fast,
Without or wave or wind?"

SECOND VOICE

"The air is cut away before,
And closes from behind.   425

Fly, brother, fly! more high, more high!
Or we shall be belated:
For slow and slow that ship will go,
When the Mariner's trance is abated."

I woke, and we were sailing on   430
As in a gentle weather:
'Twas night, calm night, the moon was high;
The dead men stood together.

All stood together on the deck,
For a charnel-dungeon fitter: 435
All fixed on me their stony eyes,
That in the Moon did glitter.

The pang, the curse, with which they died,
Had never passed away:
I could not draw my eyes from theirs,   440
Nor turn them up to pray.

And now this spell was snapt: once more
I viewed the ocean green,
And looked far forth, yet little saw
Of what had else been seen—   445

Like one, that on a lonesome road
Doth walk in fear and dread,
And having once turned round walks on,
And turns no more his head;
Because he knows, a frightful fiend   450
Doth close behind him tread.

But soon there breathed a wind on me,
Nor sound nor motion made:
Its path was not upon the sea,
In ripple or in shade.   455

The Mariner hath been cast into a trance; for the angelic power causeth the vessel to drive northward faster than human life could endure.

The supernatural motion is retarded; the Mariner awakes, and his penance begins anew.

The curse is finally expiated.

It raised my hair, it fanned my cheek
Like a meadow-gale of spring—
It mingled strangely with my fears,
Yet it felt like a welcoming.

Swiftly, swiftly flew the ship,   460
Yet she sailed softly too:
Sweetly, sweetly blew the breeze—
On me alone it blew.

And the ancient Mariner beholdeth his native country.

Oh! dream of joy! is this indeed
The light-house top I see?   465
Is this the hill? is this the kirk?
Is this mine own countree?

We drifted o'er the harbour-bar,
And I with sobs did pray—
O let me be awake, my God!   470
Or let me sleep alway.

The harbour-bay was clear as glass,
So smoothly it was strewn!
And on the bay the moonlight lay,
And the shadow of the Moon.   475

The rock shone bright, the kirk no less,
That stands above the rock:
The moonlight steeped in silentness
The steady weathercock.

And the bay was white with silent light,   480
Till rising from the same,

The angelic spirits leave the dead bodies,

Full many shapes, that shadows were,
In crimson colours came.

And appear in their own forms of light.

A little distance from the prow
Those crimson shadows were: 485
I turned my eyes upon the deck—
Oh, Christ! what saw I there!

Each corse lay flat, lifeless and flat,
And, by the holy rood!
A man all light, a seraph-man,   490
On every corse there stood.

This seraph-band, each waved his hand:
It was a heavenly sight!
They stood as signals to the land,
Each one a lovely light;   495

This seraph-band, each waved his hand,
No voice did they impart—
No voice; but oh! the silence sank
Like music on my heart.

But soon I heard the dash of oars,   500
I heard the Pilot's cheer;
My head was turned perforce away
And I saw a boat appear.

The Pilot and the Pilot's boy,
I heard them coming fast: 505
Dear Lord in Heaven! it was a joy
The dead men could not blast.

I saw a third—I heard his voice:
It is the Hermit good!
He singeth loud his godly hymns   510
That he makes in the wood.
He'll shrieve my soul, he'll wash away
The Albatross's blood.'

PART VII

The Hermit of the Wood,

'This Hermit good lives in that wood
Which slopes down to the sea.   515
How loudly his sweet voice he rears!
He loves to talk with marineres
That come from a far countree.

He kneels at morn, and noon, and eve—
He hath a cushion plump: 520
It is the moss that wholly hides
The rotted old oak-stump.

The skiff-boat neared: I heard them talk,
"Why, this is strange, I trow!
Where are those lights so many and fair,   525
That signal made but now?"

Approacheth the ship with wonder.	"Strange, by my faith!" the Hermit said— "And they answered not our cheer! The planks looked warped! and see those sails, How thin they are and sere! 530 I never saw aught like to them, Unless perchance it were

Brown skeletons of leaves that lag
My forest-brook along;
When the ivy-tod is heavy with snow,   535
And the owlet whoops to the wolf below,
That eats the she-wolf's young."

"Dear Lord! it hath a fiendish look—"
(The Pilot made reply)
"I am a-feared"—"Push on, push on!"   540
Said the Hermit cheerily.

The boat came closer to the ship,
But I nor spake nor stirred;
The boat came close beneath the ship,
And straight a sound was heard.   545

The ship suddenly sinketh.	Under the water it rumbled on, Still louder and more dread: It reached the ship, it split the bay; The ship went down like lead.

The ancient Mariner is saved in the Pilot's boat.	Stunned by that loud and dreadful sound, 550 Which sky and ocean smote, Like one that hath been seven days drowned My body lay afloat; But swift as dreams, myself I found Within the Pilot's boat. 555

Upon the whirl, where sank the ship,
The boat spun round and round;
And all was still, save that the hill
Was telling of the sound.

I moved my lips—the Pilot shrieked   560
And fell down in a fit;
The holy Hermit raised his eyes,
And prayed where he did sit.

I took the oars: the Pilot's boy,
Who now doth crazy go,   565
Laughed loud and long, and all the while
His eyes went to and fro.
"Ha! Ha!" quoth he, "full plain I see,
The Devil knows how to row."

And now, all in my own countree,   570
I stood on the firm land!
The Hermit stepped forth from the boat,
And scarcely he could stand.

The ancient Mariner   "O shrieve me, shrieve me, holy man!"
earnestly entreateth   The Hermit crossed his brow.   575
the Hermit to   "Say quick," quoth he, "I bid thee say—
shrieve him; and the   What manner of man art thou?"
penance of life falls
on him.

Forthwith this frame of mine was wrenched
With a woeful agony,
Which forced me to begin my tale;   580
And then it left me free.

And ever and anon   Since then, at an uncertain hour,
throughout his future   That agony returns:
life an agony   And till my ghastly tale is told,
constraineth him to   This heart within me burns.   585
travel from land to
land;

I pass, like night, from land to land;
I have strange power of speech;
That moment that his face I see,
I know the man that must hear me:
To him my tale I teach.   590

What loud uproar bursts from that door!
The wedding-guests are there:
But in the garden-bower the bride
And bride-maids singing are:
And hark the little vesper bell,   595
Which biddeth me to prayer!

O Wedding-Guest! this soul hath been
Alone on a wide wide sea:
So lonely 'twas, that God himself
Scarce seemèd there to be.   600

O sweeter than the marriage-feast,
'Tis sweeter far to me,
To walk together to the kirk
With a goodly company!—

To walk together to the kirk   605
And all together pray,
While each to his great Father bends,
Old men, and babes, and loving friends
And youths and maidens gay!

And to teach, by his own example, love and reverence to all things that God made and loveth.

Farewell, farewell! but this I tell   610
To thee, thou Wedding-Guest!
He prayeth well, who loveth well
Both man and bird and beast.

He prayeth best, who loveth best
All things both great and small;   615
For the dear God who loveth us,
He made and loveth all.'

The Mariner, whose eye is bright,
Whose beard with age is hoar,
Is gone: and now the Wedding-Guest   620
Turned from the bridegroom's door.

He went like one that hath been stunned,
And is of sense forlorn:
A sadder and a wiser man,
He rose the morrow morn.   625

WILLIAM WORDSWORTH

1770–1850

The Idiot Boy

'TIS eight o'clock—a clear March night,
The moon is up—the sky is blue,
The owlet, in the moonlight air,
Shouts from nobody knows where;
He lengthens out his lonely shout,   5
Halloo! halloo! a long halloo!

—Why bustle thus about your door,
What means this bustle, Betty Foy?
Why are you in this mighty fret?
And why on horseback have you set   10
Him whom you love, your idiot boy?

Scarcely a soul is out of bed;
Good Betty, put him down again;
His lips with joy they burr at you;
But, Betty, what has he to do   15
With stirrup, saddle, or with rein?

But Betty's bent on her intent;
For her good neighbour Susan Gale,
Old Susan, she who dwells alone,
Is sick, and makes a piteous moan,   20
As if her very life would fail.

There's not a house within a mile,
No hand to help them in distress;
Old Susan lies a-bed in pain,
And sorely puzzled are the twain,   25
For what she ails they cannot guess.

And Betty's husband's at the wood,
Where by the week he doth abide,
A woodman in the distant vale;
There's none to help poor Susan Gale;   30
What must be done? what will betide?

And Betty from the lane has fetched
Her pony, that is mild and good;
Whether he be in joy or pain,
Feeding at will along the lane,   35
Or bringing faggots from the wood.

And he is all in travelling trim,
And, by the moonlight, Betty Foy
Has on the well-girt saddle set
(The like was never heard of yet)   40
Him whom she loves, her idiot boy.

And he must post without delay
Across the bridge and through the dale,
And by the church, and o'er the down,
To bring a doctor from the town,   45
Or she will die, old Susan Gale.

There is no need of boot or spur,
There is no need of whip or wand;
For Johnny has his holly-bough,
And with a *hurly-burly* now   50
He shakes the green bough in his hand.

And Betty o'er and o'er has told
The boy, who is her best delight,
Both what to follow, what to shun,
What do, and what to leave undone,   55
How turn to left, and how to right.

And Betty's most especial charge,
Was, 'Johnny! Johnny! mind that you
Come home again, nor stop at all—
Come home again, whate'er befall,   60
My Johnny, do, I pray you, do.'

To this did Johnny answer make,
Both with his head and with his hand,
And proudly shook the bridle too;
And then! his words were not a few,   65
Which Betty well could understand.

And now that Johnny is just going,
Though Betty's in a mighty flurry,
She gently pats the pony's side,
On which her idiot boy must ride,   70
And seems no longer in a hurry.

But when the pony moved his legs,
Oh! then for the poor idiot boy!
For joy he cannot hold the bridle,
For joy his head and heels are idle,   75
He's idle all for very joy.

And, while the pony moves his legs,
In Johnny's left hand you may see
The green bough motionless and dead:
The moon that shines above his head   80
Is not more still and mute than he.

His heart it was so full of glee
That, till full fifty yards were gone,
He quite forgot his holly whip,
And all his skill in horsemanship: 85
Oh! happy, happy, happy John.

And while the mother, at the door,
Stands fixed, her face with joy o'erflows,
Proud of herself, and proud of him,
She sees him in his travelling trim,   90
How quietly her Johnny goes.

The silence of her idiot boy,
What hopes it sends to Betty's heart!
He's at the guide-post—he turns right;
She watches till he's out of sight,   95
And Betty will not then depart.

Burr, burr—now Johnny's lips they burr,
As loud as any mill, or near it;
Meek as a lamb the pony moves,
And Johnny makes the noise he loves,   100
And Betty listens, glad to hear it.

Away she hies to Susan Gale:
Her messenger's in merry tune;
The owlets hoot, the owlets curr,
And Johnny's lips they burr, burr, burr,   105
As on he goes beneath the moon.

His steed and he right well agree;
For of this pony there's a rumour
That, should he lose his eyes and ears,
And should he live a thousand years,   110
He never will be out of humour.

But then he is a horse that thinks!
And, when he thinks, his pace is slack;
Now, though he knows poor Johnny well,
Yet, for his life, he cannot tell   115
What he has got upon his back.

So through the moonlight lanes they go,
And far into the moonlight dale,
And by the church, and o'er the down,
To bring a doctor from the town,   120
To comfort poor old Susan Gale.

And Betty, now at Susan's side,
Is in the middle of her story,
What speedy help her boy will bring,
With many a most diverting thing,   125
Of Johnny's wit, and Johnny's glory.

And Betty, still at Susan's side,
By this time is not quite so flurried:
Demure with porringer and plate
She sits, as if in Susan's fate   130
Her life and soul were buried.

But Betty, poor good woman! she,
You plainly in her face may read it,
Could lend out of that moment's store
Five years of happiness or more   135
To any that might need it.

But yet I guess that now and then
With Betty all was not so well;
And to the road she turns her ears,
And thence full many a sound she hears,   140
Which she to Susan will not tell.

Poor Susan moans, poor Susan groans;
'As sure as there's a moon in heaven,'
Cries Betty, 'he'll be back again;
They'll both be here—'tis almost ten—   145
Both will be here before eleven.'

Poor Susan moans, poor Susan groans;
The clock gives warning for eleven;
'Tis on the stroke—'He must be near,'
Quoth Betty, 'and will soon be here,   150
As sure as there's a moon in heaven.'

The clock is on the stroke of twelve,
And Johnny is not yet in sight:
—The moon's in heaven, as Betty sees,
But Betty is not quite at ease;   155
And Susan has a dreadful night.

And Betty, half an hour ago,
On Johnny vile reflections cast:
'A little idle sauntering thing!'
With other names, an endless string;   160
But now that time is gone and past.

And Betty's drooping at the heart,
That happy time all past and gone,
'How can it be he is so late?
The doctor, he has made him wait;   165
Susan! they'll both be here anon.'

And Susan's growing worse and worse,
And Betty's in a sad *quandary*;
And then there's nobody to say
If she must go, or she must stay!   170
—She's in a sad *quandary*.

The clock is on the stroke of one;
But neither doctor nor his guide
Appears along the moonlight road;
There's neither horse nor man abroad,   175
And Betty's still at Susan's side.

And Susan now begins to fear
Of sad mischances not a few,
That Johnny may perhaps be drowned;
Or lost, perhaps, and never found;   180
Which they must both for ever rue.

She prefaced half a hint of this
With, 'God forbid it should be true!'
At the first word that Susan said
Cried Betty, rising from the bed,   185
'Susan, I'd gladly stay with you.

'I must be gone, I must away:
Consider, Johnny's but half-wise;
Susan, we must take care of him,
If he is hurt in life or limb'—   190
'Oh God forbid!' poor Susan cries.

'What can I do?' says Betty, going,
'What can I do to ease your pain?
Good Susan tell me, and I'll stay;
I fear you're in a dreadful way,   195
But I shall soon be back again.'

'Nay, Betty, go! good Betty, go!
There's nothing that can ease my pain.'
Then off she hies; but with a prayer,
That God poor Susan's life would spare,   200
Till she comes back again.

So, through the moonlight lane she goes,
And far into the moonlight dale;
And how she ran, and how she walked,
And all that to herself she talked,   205
Would surely be a tedious tale.

144

In high and low, above, below,
In great and small, in round and square,
In tree and tower was Johnny seen,
In bush and brake, in black and green;   210
'Twas Johnny, Johnny, everywhere.

And while she crossed the bridge, there came
A thought with which her heart is sore—
Johnny perhaps his horse forsook,
To hunt the moon within the brook,   215
And never will be heard of more.

Now is she high upon the down,
Alone amid a prospect wide;
There's neither Johnny nor his horse
Among the fern or in the gorse;   220
There's neither doctor nor his guide.

'Oh saints! what is become of him?
Perhaps he's climbed into an oak,
Where he will stay till he is dead;
Or sadly he has been misled,   225
And joined the wandering gipsy folk.

'Or him that wicked pony's carried
To the dark cave, the goblin's hall;
Or in the castle he's pursuing
Among the ghosts his own undoing;   230
Or playing with the waterfall.'

At poor old Susan then she railed,
While to the town she posts away;
'If Susan had not been so ill,
Alas! I should have had him still,   235
My Johnny, till my dying day.'

Poor Betty, in this sad distemper,
The doctor's self could hardly spare:
Unworthy things she talked, and wild;
Even he, of cattle the most mild,   240
The pony had his share.

But now she's fairly in the town,
And to the doctor's door she hies;
'Tis silence all on every side;
The town so long, the town so wide,   245
Is silent as the skies.

And now she's at the doctor's door,
She lifts the knocker, rap, rap, rap;
The doctor at the casement shows
His glimmering eyes that peep and doze,   250
And one hand rubs his old night-cap.

'Oh doctor! doctor! where's my Johnny?'
'I'm here, what is't you want with me?'
'Oh sir! you know I'm Betty Foy,
And I have lost my poor dear boy,   255
You know him—him you often see;

He's not so wise as some folks be.'
'The devil take his wisdom!' said
The doctor, looking somewhat grim,
'What, woman, should I know of him?'   260
And, grumbling, he went back to bed.

'O woe is me! O woe is me!
Here will I die; here will I die;
I thought to find my lost one here,
But he is neither far nor near,   265
Oh! what a wretched mother I!'

She stops, she stands, she looks about;
Which way to turn she cannot tell.
Poor Betty! it would ease her pain
If she had heart to knock again;   270
—The clock strikes three—a dismal knell!

Then up along the town she hies,
No wonder if her senses fail;
This piteous news so much it shocked her,
She quite forgot to send the doctor   275
To comfort poor old Susan Gale.

And now she's high upon the down,
And she can see a mile of road:
'O cruel! I'm almost threescore;
Such night as this was ne'er before,   280
There's not a single soul abroad.'

She listens, but she cannot hear
The foot of horse, the voice of man;
The streams with softest sound are flowing,
The grass you almost hear it growing,   285
You hear it now, if e'er you can.

The owlets through the long blue night
Are shouting to each other still:
Fond lovers! yet not quite hob nob,
They lengthen out the tremulous sob,   290
That echoes far from hill to hill.

Poor Betty now has lost all hope,
Her thoughts are bent on deadly sin,
A green-grown pond she just has past,
And from the brink she hurries fast,   295
Lest she should drown herself therein.

And now she sits her down and weeps;
Such tears she never shed before;
'Oh dear, dear pony! my sweet joy!
Oh carry back my idiot boy!   300
And we will ne'er o'erload thee more.'

A thought is come into her head:
The pony he is mild and good,
And we have always used him well;
Perhaps he's gone along the dell,   305
And carried Johnny to the wood.

Then up she springs as if on wings;
She thinks no more of deadly sin;
If Betty fifty ponds should see,
The last of all her thoughts would be   310
To drown herself therein.

Oh reader, now that I might tell
What Johnny and his horse are doing!
What they've been doing all this time,
Oh could I put it into rhyme,   315
A most delightful tale pursuing!

Perhaps, and no unlikely thought!
He with his pony now doth roam
The cliffs and peaks so high that are,
To lay his hands upon a star,   320
And in his pocket bring it home.

Perhaps he's turned himself about,
His face unto his horse's tail,
And, still and mute, in wonder lost,
All silent as a horseman-ghost,   325
He travels slowly down the vale.

147

And now, perhaps, is hunting sheep,
A fierce and dreadful hunter he;
Yon valley, now so trim and green,
In five months' time, should he be seen,   330
A desert wilderness will be.

Perhaps, with head and heels on fire,
And like the very soul of evil,
He's galloping away, away,
And so will gallop on for aye,   335
The bane of all that dread the devil.

I to the Muses have been bound
These fourteen years, by strong indentures:
O gentle Muses! let me tell
But half of what to him befell;   340
He surely met with strange adventures.

O gentle Muses! is this kind?
Why will ye thus my suit repel?
Why of your further aid bereave me?
And can ye thus unfriended leave me;   345
Ye Muses! whom I love so well?

Who's yon, that, near the waterfall,
Which thunders down with headlong force,
Beneath the moon, yet shining fair,
As careless as if nothing were,   350
Sits upright on a feeding horse?

Unto his horse—there feeding free,
He seems, I think, the rein to give;
Of moon or stars he takes no heed;
Of such we in romances read: 355
—'Tis Johnny! Johnny! as I live.

And that's the very pony, too!
Where is she, where is Betty Foy?
She hardly can sustain her fears;
The roaring waterfall she hears,   360
And cannot find her idiot boy.

Your pony's worth his weight in gold:
Then calm your terrors, Betty Foy!
She's coming from among the trees,
And now all full in view she sees   365
Him whom she loves, her idiot boy.

And Betty sees the pony too:
Why stand you thus, good Betty Foy?
It is no goblin, 'tis no ghost,
'Tis he whom you so long have lost,
He whom you love, your idiot boy.   370

She looks again—her arms are up—
She screams—she cannot move for joy;
She darts, as with a torrent's force,
She almost has o'erturned the horse,   375
And fast she holds her idiot boy.

And Johnny burrs, and laughs aloud;
Whether in cunning or in joy
I cannot tell; but, while he laughs,
Betty a drunken pleasure quaffs   380
To hear again her idiot boy.

And now she's at the pony's tail,
And now is at the pony's head—
On that side now, and now on this;
And, almost stifled with her bliss,   385
A few sad tears does Betty shed.

She kisses o'er and o'er again
Him whom she loves, her idiot boy;
She's happy here, is happy there,
She is uneasy everywhere;   390
Her limbs are all alive with joy.

She pats the pony, where or when
She knows not, happy Betty Foy!
The little pony glad may be,
But he is milder far than she,   395
You hardly can perceive his joy.

'Oh! Johnny, never mind the doctor;
You've done your best, and that is all.'
She took the reins, when this was said,
And gently turned the pony's head   400
From the loud waterfall.

By this the stars were almost gone,
The moon was setting on the hill,
So pale you scarcely looked at her:
The little birds began to stir,   405
Though yet their tongues were still.

The pony, Betty, and her boy,
Wind slowly through the woody dale;
And who is she, betimes abroad,
That hobbles up the steep rough road?   410
Who is it, but old Susan Gale?

Long time lay Susan lost in thought;
And many dreadful fears beset her,
Both for her messenger and nurse;
And, as her mind grew worse and worse,   415
Her body—it grew better.

She turned, she tossed herself in bed,
On all sides doubts and terrors met her;
Point after point did she discuss;
And, while her mind was fighting thus,   420
Her body still grew better.

'Alas! what is become of them?
These fears can never be endured;
I'll to the wood.' The word scarce said,
Did Susan rise up from her bed,   425
As if by magic cured.

Away she goes up hill and down,
And to the wood at length is come;
She spies her friends, she shouts a greeting;
Oh me! it is a merry meeting   430
As ever was in Christendom.

The owls have hardly sung their last,
While our four travellers homeward wend;
The owls have hooted all night long,
And with the owls began my song,   435
And with the owls must end.

For, while they all were travelling home,
Cried Betty, 'Tell us, Johnny, do,
Where all this long night you have been,
What you have heard, what you have seen: 440
And, Johnny, mind you tell us true.'

Now Johnny all night long had heard
The owls in tuneful concert strive;
No doubt too he the moon had seen;
For in the moonlight he had been   445
From eight o'clock till five.

And thus, to Betty's question, he
Made answer, like a traveller bold,
(His very words I give to you)
'The cocks did crow to-whoo, to-whoo,   450
And the sun did shine so cold!'
—Thus answered Johnny in his glory,
And that was all his travel's story.

Alice Fell; or, Poverty

THE post-boy drove with fierce career,
For threatening clouds the moon had drowned;
When, as we hurried on, my ear
Was smitten with a startling sound

As if the wind blew many ways,   5
I heard the sound—and more and more;
It seemed to follow with the chaise,
And still I heard it as before.

At length I to the boy called out;
He stopped his horses at the word,   10
But neither cry, nor voice, nor shout,
Nor aught else like it, could be heard.

The boy then smacked his whip, and fast
The horses scampered through the rain;
But, hearing soon upon the blast   15
The cry, I bade him halt again.

Forthwith alighting on the ground,
'Whence comes,' said I, 'this piteous moan?'
And there a little girl I found,
Sitting behind the chaise, alone.   20

'My cloak!' no other word she spake,
But loud and bitterly she wept,
As if her innocent heart would break;
And down from off her seat she leapt.

'What ails you, child?'—she sobbed, 'Look here!'   25
I saw it in the wheel entangled,
A weather-beaten rag as e'er
From any garden scarecrow dangled.

WILLIAM WORDSWORTH

There, twisted between nave and spoke,
It hung, nor could at once be freed;
But our joint pains unloosed the cloak,
A miserable rag indeed!

'And whither are you going, child,
Tonight along these lonesome ways?'
'To Durham,' answered she, half wild—
'Then come with me into the chaise.'

Insensible to all relief
Sat the poor girl, and forth did send
Sob after sob, as if her grief
Could never, never have an end.

'My child, in Durham do you dwell?'
She checked herself in her distress,
And said, 'My name is Alice Fell;
I'm fatherless and motherless.

'And I to Durham, sir, belong.'
Again, as if the thought would choke
Her very heart, her grief grew strong;
And all was for her tattered cloak!

The chaise drove on; our journey's end
Was nigh; and, sitting by my side,
As if she had lost her only friend
She wept, nor would be pacified.

Up to the tavern door we post;
Of Alice and her grief I told;
And I gave money to the host,
To buy a new cloak for the old.

'And let it be of duffel grey,
As warm a cloak as man can sell!'
Proud creature was she the next day,
The little orphan, Alice Fell!

ROBERT SOUTHEY
1774–1843

Bishop Hatto

THE summer and autumn had been so wet,
That in winter the corn was growing yet,
'Twas a piteous sight to see all around
The grain lie rotting on the ground.

Every day the starving poor   5
Crowded round Bishop Hatto's door,
For he had a plentiful last-year's store,
And all the neighbourhood could tell
His granaries were furnished well.

At last Bishop Hatto appointed a day   10
To quiet the poor without delay;
He bade them to his great barn repair,
And they should have food for the winter there.

Rejoiced such tidings good to hear,
The poor folk flocked from far and near;   15
The great barn was full as it could hold
Of women and children, and young and old.

Then when he saw it could hold no more,
Bishop Hatto he made fast the door;
And while for mercy on Christ they call,   20
He set fire to the barn and burnt them all.

'I'faith 'tis an excellent bonfire!' quoth he,
'And the country is greatly obliged to me,
For ridding it in these times forlorn
Of rats that only consume the corn.'   25

So then to his palace returnèd he,
And he sat down to supper merrily,
And he slept that night like an innocent man;
But Bishop Hatto never slept again.

In the morning as he entered the hall   30
Where his picture hung against the wall,
A sweat like death all over him came,
For the rats had eaten it out of the frame.

As he looked there came a man from his farm—
He had a countenance white with alarm;   35
'My Lord, I opened your granaries this morn,
And the rats had eaten all your corn.'

Another came running presently,
And he was pale as pale could be,
'Fly! my Lord Bishop, fly!' quoth he,   40
'Ten thousand rats are coming this way—
The Lord forgive you for yesterday!'

'I'll go to my tower on the Rhine,' replied he,
''Tis the safest place in Germany;
The walls are high and the shores are steep,   45
And the stream is strong and the water deep.'

Bishop Hatto fearfully hastened away,
And he crossed the Rhine without delay,
And reached his tower, and barred with care
All the windows, doors, and loopholes there.   50

He laid him down and closed his eyes;
But soon a scream made him arise,
He started, and saw two eyes of flame
On his pillow from whence the screaming came.

He listened and looked—it was only the cat;   55
But the Bishop he grew more fearful for that,
For she sat screaming, mad with fear
At the army of rats that were drawing near.

For they have swum over the river so deep,
And they have climbed the shores so steep,   60
And up the tower their way is bent,
To do the work for which they were sent.

They are not to be told by the dozen or score,
By thousands they come, and by myriads and more,
Such numbers had never been heard of before,   65
Such a judgement had never been witnessed of yore.

Down on his knees the Bishop fell,
And faster and faster his beads did he tell,
As louder and louder drawing near
The gnawing of their teeth he could hear.   70

And in at the windows and in at the door,
And through the walls helter-skelter they pour,
And down from the ceiling, and up through the floor,
From the right and the left, from behind and before,
From within and without, from above and below,   75
And all at once to the Bishop they go.

They have whetted their teeth against the stones,
And now they pick the Bishop's bones;
They gnawed the flesh from every limb,
For they were sent to do judgement on him!   80

The Inchcape Rock

No stir in the air, no stir in the sea,
The ship was still as she could be,
Her sails from heaven received no motion,
Her keel was steady in the ocean.

Without either sign or sound of their shock   5
The waves flowed over the Inchcape Rock;
So little they rose, so little they fell,
They did not move the Inchcape Bell.

The Abbot of Aberbrothok
Had placed that bell on the Inchcape Rock;   10
On a buoy in the storm it floated and swung,
And over the waves its warning rung.

When the rock was hid by the surge's swell,
The mariners heard the warning bell;
And then they knew the perilous rock,   15
And blessed the Abbot of Aberbrothok.

The sun in heaven was shining gay,
All things were joyful on that day;
The sea-birds screamed as they wheeled round,
And there was joyance in their sound.   20

The buoy of the Inchcape Bell was seen
A darker speck on the ocean green;
Sir Ralph the Rover walked his deck,
And he fixed his eyes on the darker speck.

He felt the cheering power of spring,   25
It made him whistle, it made him sing;
His heart was mirthful to excess,
But the Rover's mirth was wickedness.

His eye was on the Inchcape float;
Quoth he, 'My men, put out the boat,   30
And row me to the Inchcape Rock,
And I'll plague the Abbot of Aberbrothok.'

The boat is lowered, the boatmen row,
And to the Inchcape Rock they go;
Sir Ralph bent over from the boat,   35
And he cut the bell from the Inchcape float.

Down sunk the bell with a gurgling sound,
The bubbles rose and burst around;
Quoth Sir Ralph, 'The next who comes to the rock
Won't bless the Abbot of Aberbrothok.'   40

Sir Ralph the Rover sailed away,
He scoured the seas for many a day;
And now grown rich with plundered store,
He steers his course for Scotland's shore.

So thick a haze o'erspreads the sky   45
They cannot see the sun on high;
The wind hath blown a gale all day,
At evening it hath died away.

On the deck the Rover takes his stand,
So dark it is they see no land.   50
Quoth Sir Ralph, 'It will be lighter soon,
For there is the dawn of the rising moon.'

'Canst hear,' said one, 'the breakers roar?
For methinks we should be near the shore.'
'Now where we are I cannot tell,   55
But I wish I could hear the Inchcape Bell.'

They hear no sound, the swell is strong;
Though the wind hath fallen they drift along,
Till the vessel strikes with a shivering shock—
'Oh Christ! it is the Inchcape Rock!'   60

Sir Ralph the Rover tore his hair;
He cursed himself in his despair;
The waves rush in on every side,
The ship is sinking beneath the tide.

But even in his dying fear   65
One dreadful sound could the Rover hear,
A sound as if with the Inchcape Bell,
The Devil below was ringing his knell.

WILLIAM ROBERT SPENCER
1769–1834

Beth Gêlert; or, The Grave of the Greyhound

THE spearmen heard the bugle sound,
And cheerly smiled the morn;
And many a brach, and many a hound,
Obeyed Llewelyn's horn.

And still he blew a louder blast,   5
And gave a lustier cheer:
'Come, Gêlert, come, wer't never last
Llewelyn's horn to hear.

'Oh where does faithful Gêlert roam,
The flower of all his race;   10
So true, so brave, a lamb at home,
A lion in the chase?'

'Twas only at Llewelyn's board
The faithful Gêlert fed;
He watched, he served, he cheered his lord,   15
And sentinelled his bed.

In sooth he was a peerless hound,
The gift of royal John;
But now no Gêlert could be found,
And all the chase rode on.   20

And now, as o'er the rocks and dells
The gallant chidings rise,
All Snowdon's craggy chaos yells
The many-mingled cries.

That day Llewelyn little loved   25
The chase of hart and hare;
And scant and small the booty proved,
For Gêlert was not there.

Unpleased Llewelyn homeward hied,
When near the portal seat   30
His truant Gêlert he espied,
Bounding his lord to greet.

But when he gained his castle door
Aghast the chieftain stood;
The hound all o'er was smeared with gore,   35
His lips, his fangs, ran blood.

Llewelyn gazed with fierce surprise;
Unused such looks to meet,
His favourite checked his joyful guise,
And crouched, and licked his feet.   40

Onward in haste Llewelyn passed,
And on went Gêlert too;
And still, where'er his eyes he cast,
Fresh blood-gouts shocked his view.

O'erturned his infant's bed he found,   45
With blood-stained covert rent;
And all around the walls and ground
With recent blood besprent.

He called his child—no voice replied—
He searched with terror wild;   50
Blood, blood he found on every side,
But nowhere found his child.

'Hell hound! my child's by thee devoured,'
The frantic father cried;
And to the hilt his vengeful sword   55
He plunged in Gêlert's side.

His suppliant looks, as prone he fell,
No pity could impart;
But still his Gêlert's dying yell
Passed heavy o'er his heart.   60

Aroused by Gêlert's dying yell,
Some slumberer wakened nigh:
What words the parent's joy could tell
To hear his infant's cry!

Concealed beneath a tumbled heap   65
His hurried search had missed,
All glowing from his rosy sleep,
The cherub boy he kissed.

Nor scathe had he, nor harm, nor dread,
But, the same couch beneath,   70
Lay a gaunt wolf, all torn and dead,
Tremendous still in death.

Ah, what was then Llewelyn's pain!
For now the truth was clear;
His gallant hound the wolf had slain,   75
To save Llewelyn's heir.

Vain, vain was all Llewelyn's woe:
'Best of thy kind, adieu!
The frantic blow, which laid thee low,
This heart shall ever rue.'   80

And now a gallant tomb they raise,
With costly sculpture decked;
And marbles storied with his praise
Poor Gêlert's bones protect.

There never could the spearman pass,   85
Or forester, unmoved;
There, oft the tear-besprinkled grass
Llewelyn's sorrow proved.

And there he hung his horn and spear,
And there, as evening fell,   90
In fancy's ear he oft would hear
Poor Gêlert's dying yell.

And till great Snowdon's rocks grow old,
And cease the storm to brave,
The consecrated spot shall hold   95
The name of 'Gêlert's grave'.

SIR WALTER SCOTT
1771–1832

Young Lochinvar

O, YOUNG Lochinvar is come out of the west,
Through all the wide Border his steed was the best;
And save his good broadsword he weapons had none,
He rode all unarmed, and he rode all alone.
So faithful in love, and so dauntless in war,   5
There never was knight like the young Lochinvar.

He stayed not for brake, and he stopped not for stone,
He swam the Esk river where ford there was none;
But ere he alighted at Netherby gate,
The bride had consented, the gallant came late:
For a laggard in love, and a dastard in war,   10
Was to wed the fair Ellen of brave Lochinvar.

So boldly he entered the Netherby Hall,
Among bridesmen, and kinsmen, and brothers, and all:
Then spoke the bride's father, his hand on his sword
(For the poor craven bridegroom said never a word), 15
'O come ye in peace here, or come ye in war,
Or to dance at our bridal, young Lord·Lochinvar?'

'I long wooed your daughter, my suit you denied—
Love swells like the Solway, but ebbs like its tide— 20
And now am I come, with this lost love of mine,
To lead but one measure, drink one cup of wine.
There are maidens in Scotland more lovely by far,
That would gladly be bride to the young Lochinvar.'

The bride kissed the goblet: the knight took it up, 25
He quaffed off the wine, and he threw down the cup.
She looked down to blush, and she looked up to sigh,
With a smile on her lips, and a tear in her eye.

He took her soft hand, ere her mother could bar—
'Now tread we a measure!' said young Lochinvar.   30

So stately his form, and so lovely her face,
That never a hall such a galliard did grace;
While her mother did fret, and her father did fume,
And the bridegroom stood dangling his bonnet and plume;
And the bride-maidens whispered, ''Twere better by far,   35
To have matched our fair cousin with young Lochinvar.'

One touch to her hand, and one word in her ear,
When they reached the hall door, and the charger stood near;
So light to the croupe the fair lady he swung,
So light to the saddle before her he sprung!   40
'She is won! we are gone, over bank, bush, and scaur;
They'll have fleet steeds that follow,' quoth young Lochinvar.

There was mounting 'mong Graemes of the Netherby clan;
Forsters, Fenwicks, and Musgraves, they rode and they ran:
There was racing and chasing on Cannobie Lee,   45
But the lost bride of Netherby ne'er did they see.
So daring in love, and so dauntless in war,
Have ye e'er heard of gallant like young Lochinvar?

GEORGE CRABBE

1754–1832

Peter Grimes

OLD Peter Grimes made fishing his employ,
His wife he cabined with him and his boy,
And seemed that life laborious to enjoy:
To town came quiet Peter with his fish,
And had of all a civil word and wish.   5
He left his trade upon the Sabbath-day,
And took young Peter in his hand to pray:
But soon the stubborn boy from care broke loose,
At first refused, then added his abuse:
His father's love he scorned, his power defied,   10
But being drunk, wept sorely when he died.
   Yes! then he wept, and to his mind there came
Much of his conduct, and he felt the shame—

How he had oft the good old man reviled,
And never paid the duty of a child;   15
How, when the father in his Bible read,
He in contempt and anger left the shed:
'It is the word of life,' the parent cried;
—'This is the life itself,' the boy replied;
And while old Peter in amazement stood,   20
Gave the hot spirit to his boiling blood:
How he, with oath and furious speech, began
To prove his freedom and assert the man;
And when the parent checked his impious rage,
How he had cursed the tyranny of age—   25
Nay, once had dealt the sacrilegious blow
On his bare head, and laid his parent low;
The father groaned—'If thou art old,' said he,
'And hast a son—thou wilt remember me:
Thy mother left me in a happy time,   30
Thou kill'dst not her—Heaven spares the double crime.'

On an inn-settle, in his maudlin grief,
This he revolved, and drank for his relief.

Now lived the youth in freedom, but debarred
From constant pleasure, and he thought it hard;   35
Hard that he could not every wish obey,
But must awhile relinquish ale and play;
Hard! that he could not to his cards attend,
But must acquire the money he would spend.

With greedy eye he looked on all he saw,   40
He knew not justice, and he laughed at law.
On all he marked, he stretched his ready hand;
He fished by water and he filched by land:
Oft in the night has Peter dropped his oar,
Fled from his boat, and sought for prey on shore;   45
Oft up the hedgerow glided, on his back
Bearing the orchard's produce in a sack,
Or farmyard load, tugged fiercely from the stack;
And as these wrongs to greater numbers rose,
The more he looked on all men as his foes.   50

He built a mud-walled hovel, where he kept
His various wealth, and there he oft-times slept;
But no success could please his cruel soul,
He wished for one to trouble and control;
He wanted some obedient boy to stand   55
And bear the blow of his outrageous hand;
And hoped to find in some propitious hour
A feeling creature subject to his power.

Peter had heard there were in London then—
Still have they being!—workhouse-clearing men,   60
Who, undisturbed by feelings just or kind,
Would parish-boys to needy tradesmen bind:
They in their want a trifling sum would take,
And toiling slaves of piteous orphans make.

Such Peter sought, and when a lad was found,   65
The sum was dealt him, and the slave was bound.
Some few in town observed in Peter's trap
A boy, with jacket blue and woollen cap;
But none inquired how Peter used the rope,
Or what the bruise that made the stripling stoop;   70
None could the ridges on his back behold,
None sought him shivering in the winter's cold;
None put the question—'Peter, dost thou give
The boy his food?—What, man! the lad must live.
Consider, Peter, let the child have bread,   75
He'll serve thee better if he's stroked and fed.'
None reasoned thus—and some, on hearing cries,
Said calmly, 'Grimes is at his exercise.'

Pinned, beaten, cold, pinched, threatened, and abused—
His efforts punished and his food refused—   80
Awake tormented—soon aroused from sleep—
Struck if he wept, and yet compelled to weep,
The trembling boy dropped down and strove to pray,
Received a blow, and trembling turned away,
Or sobbed and hid his piteous face;—while he,   85
The savage master, grinned in horrid glee:
He'd now the power he ever loved to show,
A feeling being subject to his blow.

Thus lived the lad, in hunger, peril, pain,
His tears despised, his supplications vain: 90
Compelled by fear to lie, by need to steal,
His bed uneasy and unblessed his meal,
For three sad years the boy his tortures bore,
And then his pains and trials were no more.

'How died he, Peter?' when the people said,   95
He growled—'I found him lifeless in his bed;'
Then tried for softer tone, and sighed, 'Poor Sam is dead.'
Yet murmurs were there, and some questions asked—
How he was fed, how punished, and how tasked?
Much they suspected, but they little proved,   100
And Peter passed untroubled and unmoved.

Another boy with equal ease was found,
The money granted, and the victim bound;

And what his fate?—One night it chanced he fell
From the boat's mast and perished in her well,   105
Where fish were living kept, and where the boy
(So reasoned men) could not himself destroy:
  'Yes! so it was,' said Peter, 'in his play
(For he was idle both by night and day)
He climbed the main-mast and then fell below'—   110
Then showed his corpse, and pointed to the blow:
'What said the jury?'—they were long in doubt,
But sturdy Peter faced the matter out:
So they dismissed him, saying at the time,
'Keep fast your hatchway when you've boys who climb.'   115
This hit the conscience, and he coloured more
Than for the closest questions put before.
  Thus all his fears the verdict set aside,
And at the slave-shop Peter still applied.
  Then came a boy, of manners soft and mild—   120
Our seamen's wives with grief beheld the child;
All thought (the poor themselves) that he was one
Of gentle blood, some noble sinner's son,
Who had, belike, deceived some humble maid,
Whom he had first seduced and then betrayed:—   125
However this, he seemed a gracious lad,
In grief submissive, and with patience sad.
  Passive he laboured, till his slender frame
Bent with his loads, and he at length was lame:
Strange that a frame so weak could bear so long   130
The grossest insult and the foulest wrong;
But there were causes—in the town they gave
Fire, food, and comfort, to the gentle slave;
And though stern Peter, with a cruel hand,
And knotted rope, enforced the rude command,   135
Yet he considered what he'd lately felt,
And his vile blows with selfish pity dealt.
  One day such draughts the cruel fisher made,
He could not vend them in his borough-trade,
But sailed for London-mart: the boy was ill,   140
But ever humbled to his master's will;
And on the river, where they smoothly sailed,
He strove with terror and awhile prevailed;
But new to danger on the angry sea,
He clung affrighted to his master's knee: 145
The boat grew leaky and the wind was strong,
Rough was the passage and the time was long;

His liquor failed, and Peter's wrath arose—
No more is known—the rest we must suppose,
Or learn of Peter: Peter says, he 'spied   150
The stripling's danger and for harbour tried;
Meantime the fish, and then the apprentice died.'
   The pitying women raised a clamour round,
And weeping said, 'Thou hast thy 'prentice drowned.'
   Now the stern man was summoned to the hall,   155
To tell his tale before the burghers all:
He gave the account; professed the lad he loved,
And kept his brazen features all unmoved.
   The mayor himself with tone severe replied—
'Henceforth with thee shall never boy abide;   160
Hire thee a freeman, whom thou durst not beat,
But who, in thy despite, will sleep and eat:
Free thou art now!—again shouldst thou appear,
Thou'lt find thy sentence, like thy soul, severe.'
   Alas! for Peter not a helping hand,   165
So was he hated, could he now command;
Alone he rowed his boat, alone he cast
His nets beside, or made his anchor fast;
To hold a rope or hear a curse was none—
He toiled and railed; he groaned and swore alone.   170
   Thus by himself compelled to live each day,
To wait for certain hours the tide's delay;
At the same times the same dull views to see,
The bounding marsh-bank and the blighted tree;
The water only, when the tides were high,   175
When low, the mud half-covered and half-dry;
The sun-burnt tar that blisters on the planks,
And bankside stakes in their uneven ranks;
Heaps of entangled weeds that slowly float,
As the tide rolls by the impeded boat.   180
   When tides were neap, and, in the sultry day,
Through the tall bounding mud-banks made their way,
Which on each side rose swelling, and below
The dark warm flood ran silently and slow;
There anchoring, Peter chose from man to hide,   185
There hang his head, and view the lazy tide
In its hot slimy channel slowly glide;
Where the small eels that left the deeper way
For the warm shore, within the shallows play;
Where gaping mussels, left upon the mud,   190
Slope their slow passage to the fallen flood;

Here dull and hopeless he'd lie down and trace
How sidelong crabs had scrawled their crooked race,
Or sadly listen to the tuneless cry
Of fishing gull or clanging golden-eye;   195
What time the sea-birds to the marsh would come,
And the loud bittern, from the bulrush home,
Gave from the salt ditch side the bellowing boom:
He nursed the feelings these dull scenes produce,
And loved to stop beside the opening sluice;   200
Where the small stream, confined in narrow bound,
Ran with a dull, unvaried, saddening sound;
Where all, presented to the eye or ear,
Oppressed the soul with misery, grief, and fear.

    Besides these objects, there were places three,   205
Which Peter seemed with certain dread to see;
When he drew near them he would turn from each,
And loudly whistle till he passed the reach.

    A change of scene to him brought no relief;
In town, 'twas plain, men took him for a thief: 210
The sailors' wives would stop him in the street,
And say, 'Now, Peter, thou'st no boy to beat.'
Infants at play when they perceived him, ran,
Warning each other—'That's the wicked man.'
He growled an oath, and in an angry tone   215
Cursed the whole place and wished to be alone.

    Alone he was, the same dull scenes in view,
And still more gloomy in his sight they grew:
Though man he hated, yet employed alone
At bootless labour, he would swear and groan,   220
Cursing the shoals that glided by the spot,
And gulls that caught them when his arts could not.

    Cold nervous tremblings shook his sturdy frame,
And strange disease—he couldn't say the name;
Wild were his dreams, and oft he rose in fright,   225
Waked by his view of horrors in the night—
Horrors that would the sternest minds amaze,
Horrors that demons might be proud to raise:
And though he felt forsaken, grieved at heart,
To think he lived from all mankind apart;   230
Yet, if a man approached, in terrors he would start.

    A winter passed since Peter saw the town,
And summer-lodgers were again come down;
These, idly curious, with their glasses spied
The ships in bay as anchored for the tide—   235

The river's craft—the bustle of the quay—
And seaport views, which landmen love to see.
  One, up the river, had a man and boat
Seen day by day, now anchored, now afloat;
Fisher he seemed, yet used no net nor hook;   240
Of sea-fowl swimming by no heed he took,
But on the gliding waves still fixed his lazy look:
At certain stations he would view the stream,
As if he stood bewildered in a dream,
Or that some power had chained him for a time,   245
To feel a curse or meditate on crime.
  This known, some curious, some in pity went,
And others questioned—'Wretch, dost thou repent?'
He heard, he trembled, and in fear resigned
His boat: new terror filled his restless mind;   250
Furious he grew, and up the country ran,
And there they seized him—a distempered man:
Him we received, and to a parish-bed,
Followed and cursed, the groaning man was led.
  Here when they saw him, whom they used to shun,   255
A lost, lone man, so harassed and undone;
Our gentle females, ever prompt to feel,
Perceived compassion on their anger steal;
His crimes they could not from their memories blot,
But they were grieved, and trembled at his lot.   260
  A priest too came, to whom his words are told;
And all the signs they shuddered to behold.
  'Look! look!' they cried, 'his limbs with horror shake,
And as he grinds his teeth, what noise they make!
How glare his angry eyes, and yet he's not awake: 265
See! what cold drops upon his forehead stand,
And how he clenches that broad bony hand.'
  The priest attending, found he spoke at times
As one alluding to his fears and crimes;
'It was the fall,' he muttered, 'I can show   270
The manner how—I never struck a blow'—
And then aloud—'Unhand me, free my chain;
On oath, he fell—it struck him to the brain—
Why ask my father?—that old man will swear
Against my life; besides, he wasn't there—   275
What, all agreed?—Am I to die today?—
My Lord, in mercy give me time to pray.'
  Then, as they watched him, calmer he became,
And grew so weak he couldn't move his frame,

But murmuring spake—while they could see and hear   280
The start of terror and the groan of fear;
See the large dew-beads on his forehead rise,
And the cold death-drop glaze his sunken eyes;
Nor yet he died, but with unwonted force
Seemed with some fancied being to discourse: 285
He knew us not, or with accustomed art
He hid the knowledge, yet exposed his heart;
'Twas part confession and the rest defence,
A madman's tale, with gleams of waking sense.

   'I'll tell you all,' he said, 'the very day   290
When the old man first placed them in my way:
My father's spirit—he who always tried
To give me trouble, when he lived and died—
When he was gone he could not be content
To see my days in painful labour spent,   295
But would appoint his meetings, and he made
Me watch at these, and so neglect my trade.

   ''Twas one hot noon, all silent, still, serene,
No living being had I lately seen;
I paddled up and down and dipped my net,   300
But (such his pleasure) I could nothing get—
A father's pleasure, when his toil was done,
To plague and torture thus an only son!
And so I sat and looked upon the stream,
How it ran on, and felt as in a dream: 305
But dream it was not: no!—I fixed my eyes
On the mid stream and saw the spirits rise:
I saw my father on the water stand,
And hold a thin pale boy in either hand;
And there they glided ghastly on the top   310
Of the salt flood, and never touched a drop:
I would have struck them, but they knew th'intent,
And smiled upon the oar, and down they went.

   'Now, from that day, whenever I began
To dip my net, there stood the hard old man—   315
He and those boys: I humbled me and prayed
They would be gone; they heeded not, but stayed:
Nor could I turn, nor would the boat go by,
But, gazing on the spirits, there was I:
They bade me leap to death, but I was loth to die: 320
And every day, as sure as day arose,
Would these three spirits meet me ere the close;
To hear and mark them daily was my doom,
And "Come," they said, with weak, sad voices, "come."

To row away, with all my strength I tried,   325
But there were they, hard by me in the tide,
The three unbodied forms—and "Come," still "come," they cried.
   'Fathers should pity— but this old man shook
His hoary locks, and froze me by a look:
Thrice, when I struck them, through the water came   330
A hollow groan, that weakened all my frame:
"Father!" said I, "have mercy": he replied,
I know not what—the angry spirit lied—
"Didst thou not draw thy knife?" said he. 'Twas true,
But I had pity and my arm withdrew: 335
He cried for mercy, which I kindly gave,
But he has no compassion in his grave.
   'There were three places, where they ever rose—
The whole long river has not such as those—
Places accursed, where, if a man remain,   340
He'll see the things which strike him to the brain;
And there they made me on my paddle lean,
And look at them for hours—accursed scene!
When they would glide to that smooth eddy-space,
Then bid me leap and join them in the place;   345
And at my groans each little villain sprite
Enjoyed my pains and vanished in delight.
   'In one fierce summer day, when my poor brain
Was burning hot, and cruel was my pain,
Then came this father-foe, and there he stood   350
With his two boys again upon the flood:
There was more mischief in their eyes, more glee
In their pale faces when they glared at me:
Still they did force me on the oar to rest,
And when they saw me fainting and oppressed,   355
He, with his hand, the old man, scooped the flood,
And there came flame about him mixed with blood;
He bade me stoop and look upon the place,
Then flung the hot-red liquor in my face;
Burning it blazed, and then I roared for pain,   360
I thought the demons would have turned my brain.
   'Still there they stood, and forced me to behold
A place of horrors—they can not be told—
Where the flood opened, there I heard the shriek
Of tortured guilt—no earthly tongue can speak: 365
"All days alike! for ever!" did they say,
"And unremitted torments every day"—
Yes, so they said'—But here he ceased and gazed
On all around, affrightened and amazed;

And still he tried to speak, and looked in dread   370
  Of frightened females gathering round his bed;
Then dropped exhausted and appeared at rest,
  Till the strong foe the vital powers possessed:
Then with an inward, broken voice he cried,
  'Again they come!' and muttered as he died.   375

GEORGE GORDON NOEL, LORD BYRON

1788–1824

From *Beppo; a Venetian Story*

'TIS known, at least it should be, that throughout
  All countries of the Catholic persuasion,
Some weeks before Shrove Tuesday comes about,
  The people take their fill of recreation,
And buy repentance, ere they grow devout,   5
  However high their rank, or low their station,
With fiddling, feasting, dancing, drinking, masking,
And other things which may be had for asking.

The moment night with dusky mantle covers
  The skies (and the more duskily the better),   10
The time less liked by husbands than by lovers
  Begins, and prudery flings aside her fetter;
And gaiety on restless tiptoe hovers,
  Giggling with all the gallants who beset her;
And there are songs and quavers, roaring, humming,   15
Guitars, and every other sort of strumming.

And there are dresses splendid, but fantastical,
  Masks of all times and nations, Turks and Jews,
And harlequins and clowns, with feats gymnastical,
  Greeks, Romans, Yankee-doodles, and Hindoos;   20
All kinds of dress, except the ecclesiastical,
  All people, as their fancies hit, may choose,
But no one in these parts may quiz the clergy—
Therefore take heed, ye Freethinkers! I charge ye.

This feast is named the Carnival, which being   25
  Interpreted, implies 'farewell to flesh':
So called because the name and thing agreeing,
  Through Lent they live on fish both salt and fresh.

But why they usher Lent with so much glee in,
  Is more than I can tell, although I guess 30
'Tis as we take a glass with friends at parting,
In the stage-coach or packet, just at starting.

Of all the places where the Carnival
  Was most facetious in the days of yore,
For dance, and song, and serenade, and ball, 35
  And masque, and mime, and mystery, and more
Than I have time to tell now, or at all,
  Venice the bell from every city bore—
And at the moment when I fix my story,
That sea-born city was in all her glory. 40

They've pretty faces yet, those same Venetians,
  Black eyes, arched brows, and sweet expressions still;
Such as of old were copied from the Grecians,
  In ancient arts by moderns mimicked ill;
And like so many Venuses of Titian's 45
  (The best's at Florence—see it, if ye will),
They look when leaning over the balcony,
Or stepped from out a picture by Giorgione,

Whose tints are truth and beauty at their best;
  And when you to Manfrini's palace go, 50
That picture (howsoever fine the rest)
  Is loveliest to my mind of all the show;
It may perhaps be also to your zest,
  And that's the cause I rhyme upon it so:
'Tis but a portrait of his son, and wife, 55
And self; but *such* a woman! love in life!

Love in full life and length, not love ideal,
  No, nor ideal beauty, that fine name,
But something better still, so very real,
  That the sweet model must have been the same; 60
A thing that you would purchase, beg, or steal,
  Were't not impossible, besides a shame:
The face recalls some face, as 'twere with pain,
You once have seen, but ne'er will see again.

But to my story. 'Twas some years ago, 65
  It may be thirty, forty, more or less,
The Carnival was at its height, and so
  Were all kinds of buffoonery and dress;

A certain lady went to see the show,
  Her real name I know not, nor can guess,   70
And so we'll call her Laura, if you please,
Because it slips into my verse with ease.

She was not old, nor young, nor at the years
  Which certain people call a '*certain age*,'
Which yet the most uncertain age appears,   75
  Because I never heard, nor could engage
A person yet by prayers, or bribes, or tears,
  To name, define by speech, or write on page,
The period meant precisely by that word—
Which surely is exceedingly absurd.   80

She was a married woman; 'tis convenient,
  Because in Christian countries 'tis a rule
To view their little slips with eyes more lenient;
  Whereas if single ladies play the fool
(Unless within the period intervenient   85
  A well-timed wedding makes the scandal cool),
I don't know how they ever can get over it,
Except they manage never to discover it.

Her husband sailed upon the Adriatic,
  And made some voyages, too, in other seas,   90
And when he lay in quarantine for pratique
  (A forty days' precaution 'gainst disease),
His wife would mount, at times, her highest attic,
  For thence she could discern the ship with ease:
He was a merchant trading to Aleppo,   95
His name Giuseppe, called more briefly, Beppo.

He was a man as dusky as a Spaniard,
  Sunburnt with travel, yet a portly figure;
Though coloured, as it were, within a tanyard,
  He was a person both of sense and vigour—   100
A better seaman never yet did man yard;
  And she, although her manners showed no rigour,
Was deemed a woman of the strictest principle,
So much as to be thought almost invincible.

But several years elapsed since they had met;   105
  Some people thought the ship was lost, and some
That he had somehow blundered into debt,
  And did not like the thought of steering home;

And there were several offered any bet,
   Or that he would, or that he would not come;   110
For most men (till by losing rendered sager)
Will back their own opinions with a wager.

'Tis said that their last parting was pathetic,
   As partings often are, or ought to be,
And their presentiment was quite prophetic,   115
   That they should never more each other see
(A sort of morbid feeling, half poetic,
   Which I have known occur in two or three),
When kneeling on the shore upon her sad knee
He left this Adriatic Ariadne.   120

And Laura waited long, and wept a little,
   And thought of wearing weeds, as well she might;
She almost lost all appetite for victual,
   And could not sleep with ease alone at night;
She deemed the window-frames and shutters brittle   125
   Against a daring housebreaker or sprite,
And so she thought it prudent to connect her
With a vice-husband, *chiefly* to *protect her*.

She chose (and what is there they will not choose,
   If only you will but oppose their choice?),   130
Till Beppo should return from his long cruise,
   And bid once more her faithful heart rejoice,
A man some women like, and yet abuse—
   A coxcomb was he by the public voice;
A Count of wealth, they said, as well as quality,   135
And in his pleasures of great liberality.

Then he was faithful, too, as well as amorous;
   So that no sort of female could complain,
Although they're now and then a little clamorous,
   He never put the pretty souls in pain;   140
His heart was one of those which most enamour us,
   Wax to receive, and marble to retain:
He was a lover of the good old school,
Who still become more constant as they cool.

The Count and Laura made their new arrangement,   145
   Which lasted, as arrangements sometimes do,
For half a dozen years without estrangement;
   They had their little differences, too;

Those jealous whiffs, which never any change meant;
  In such affairs there probably are few   150
Who have not had this pouting sort of squabble,
From sinners of high station to the rabble.

But, on the whole, they were a happy pair,
  As happy as unlawful love could make them;
The gentleman was fond, the lady fair,   155
  Their chains so slight, 'twas not worth while to break them;
The world beheld them with indulgent air;
  The pious only wished 'the devil take them!'
He took them not; he very often waits,
And leaves old sinners to be young ones' baits.   160

They went to the Ridotto—'tis a hall
  Where people dance, and sup, and dance again—
Its proper name, perhaps, were a masked ball,
  But that's of no importance to my strain;
'Tis (on a smaller scale) like our Vauxhall,   165
  Excepting that it can't be spoilt by rain;
The company is 'mixed' (the phrase I quote is
As much as saying they're below your notice);

For a 'mixed company' implies that, save
  Yourself and friends, and half a hundred more,   170
Whom you may bow to without looking grave,
  The rest are but a vulgar set, the bore
Of public places, where they basely brave
  The fashionable stare of twenty score
Of well-bred persons, called 'The World;' but I,   175
Although I know them, really don't know why.

Now Laura moves along the joyous crowd,
  Smiles in her eyes, and simpers on her lips;
To some she whispers, others speaks aloud;
  To some she curtsies, and to some she dips,   180
Complains of warmth, and this complaint avowed,
  Her lover brings the lemonade, she sips;
She then surveys, condemns, but pities still
Her dearest friends for being dressed so ill.

While Laura thus was seen, and seeing, smiling,   185
  Talking, she knew not why, and cared not what,
So that her female friends, with envy broiling,
  Beheld her airs and triumph, and all that;

And well-dressed males still kept before her filing,
   And passing bowed and mingled with her chat;   190
More than the rest one person seemed to stare
With pertinacity that's rather rare.

He was a Turk, the colour of mahogany;
   And Laura saw him, and at first was glad,
Because the Turks so much admire philogyny,   195
   Although their usage of their wives is sad;
'Tis said they use no better than a dog any
   Poor woman, whom they purchase like a pad;
They have a number, though they ne'er exhibit 'em,
Four wives by law, and concubines 'ad libitum.'   200

Our Laura's Turk still kept his eyes upon her,
   Less in the Mussulman than Christian way,
Which seems to say, 'Madam, I do you honour,
   And while I please to stare, you'll please to stay.'
Could staring win a woman, this had won her,   205
   But Laura could not thus be led astray;
She had stood fire too long and well, to boggle
Even at this stranger's most outlandish ogle.

The morning now was on the point of breaking,
   A turn of time at which I would advise   210
Ladies who have been dancing, or partaking
   In any other kind of exercise,
To make their preparations for forsaking
   The ballroom ere the sun begins to rise,
Because when once the lamps and candles fail,   215
His blushes make them look a little pale.

Laura, who knew it would not do at all
   To meet the daylight after seven hours' sitting
Among three thousand people at a ball,
   To make her curtsy thought it right and fitting;   220
The Count was at her elbow with her shawl,
   And they the room were on the point of quitting,
When lo! those cursed gondoliers had got
Just in the very place where they *should not*.

In this they're like our coachmen, and the cause   225
   Is much the same—the crowd, and pulling, hauling,
With blasphemies enough to break their jaws,
   They make a never intermitted bawling.

At home, our Bow-Street gemmen keep the laws,
  And here a sentry stands within your calling; 230
But for all that, there is a deal of swearing,
And nauseous words past mentioning or bearing.

The Count and Laura found their boat at last,
  And homeward floated o'er the silent tide,
Discussing all the dances gone and past; 235
  The dancers and their dresses, too, beside;
Some little scandals eke; but all aghast
  (As to their palace-stairs the rowers glide)
Sate Laura by the side of her Adorer,
When lo! the Mussulman was there before her. 240

'Sir,' said the Count, with brow exceeding grave,
  'Your unexpected presence here will make
It necessary for myself to crave
  Its import? But perhaps 'tis a mistake;
I hope it is so; and, at once to waive 245
  All compliment, I hope so for *your* sake;
You understand my meaning, or you *shall*.'
'Sir' (quoth the Turk), ''tis no mistake at all:

'That lady is *my wife!*' Much wonder paints
  The lady's changing cheek, as well it might; 250
But where an Englishwoman sometimes faints,
  Italian females don't do so outright;
They only call a little on their saints,
  And then come to themselves, almost or quite;
Which saves much hartshorn, salts, and sprinkling faces, 255
And cutting stays, as usual in such cases.

She said—what could she say? Why, not a word:
  But the Count courteously invited in
The stranger, much appeased by what he heard:
  'Such things, perhaps, we'd best discuss within,' 260
Said he; 'don't let us make ourselves absurd
  In public, by a scene, nor raise a din,
For then the chief and only satisfaction
Will be much quizzing on the whole transaction.'

They entered, and for coffee called—it came, 265
  A beverage for Turks and Christians both,
Although the way they make it's not the same.
  Now Laura, much recovered, or less loth

To speak, cries 'Beppo! what's your pagan name?
  Bless me! your beard is of amazing growth!   270
And how came you to keep away so long?
  Are you not sensible 'twas very wrong?

'And are you *really*, *truly*, now a Turk?
  With any other women did you wive?
Is't true they use their fingers for a fork?   275
  Well, that's the prettiest shawl—as I'm alive!
You'll give it me? They say you eat no pork.
  And how so many years did you contrive
To—Bless me! did I ever? No, I never
Saw a man grown so yellow! How's your liver?   280

'Beppo! that beard of yours becomes you not:
  It shall be shaved before you're a day older:
Why do you wear it? Oh! I had forgot—
  Pray don't you think the weather here is colder?
How do I look? You shan't stir from this spot   285
  In that queer dress, for fear that some beholder
Should find you out, and make the story known.
How short your hair is! Lord! how grey it's grown!'

What answer Beppo made to these demands
  Is more than I know. He was cast away   290
About where Troy stood once, and nothing stands;
  Became a slave of course, and for his pay
Had bread and bastinadoes, till some bands
  Of pirates landing in a neighbouring bay,
He joined the rogues and prospered, and became   295
A renegado of indifferent fame.

But he grew rich, and with his riches grew so
  Keen the desire to see his home again
He thought himself in duty bound to do so,
  And not be always thieving on the main;   300
Lonely he felt, at times, as Robin Crusoe,
  And so he hired a vessel come from Spain,
Bound for Corfu: she was a fine polacca,
Manned with twelve hands, and laden with tobacco.

They reached the island, he transferred his lading   305
  And self and live stock to another bottom,
And passed for a true Turkey-merchant, trading
  With goods of various names, but I've forgot 'em.

However, he got off by this evading,
   Or else the people would perhaps have shot him;   310
And thus at Venice landed to reclaim
His wife, religion, house, and Christian name.

His wife received, the patriarch re-baptized him
   (He made the church a present, by the way);
He then threw off the garments which disguised him,   315
   And borrowed the Count's smallclothes for a day:
His friends the more for his long absence prized him,
   Finding he'd wherewithal to make them gay,
With dinners, where he oft became the laugh of them,
For stories—but *I* don't believe the half of them.   320

Whate'er his youth had suffered, his old age
   With wealth and talking made him some amends;
Though Laura sometimes put him in a rage,
   I've heard the Count and he were always friends.
My pen is at the bottom of a page,   325
   Which being finished, here the story ends;
'Tis to be wished it had been sooner done,
But stories somehow lengthen when begun.

JOHN KEATS
1795–1821

The Eve of St. Agnes

St. Agnes' Eve—Ah, bitter chill it was!
The owl, for all his feathers, was a-cold;
The hare limped trembling through the frozen grass,
And silent was the flock in woolly fold:
Numb were the Beadsman's fingers, while he told   5
His rosary, and while his frosted breath,
Like pious incense from a censer old,
Seemed taking flight for heaven, without a death,
Past the sweet Virgin's picture, while his prayer he saith.

His prayer he saith, this patient, holy man;   10
Then takes his lamp, and riseth from his knees,
And back returneth, meagre, barefoot, wan,
Along the chapel aisle by slow degrees:
The sculptured dead, on each side, seem to freeze,

Emprisoned in black, purgatorial rails: 15
Knights, ladies, praying in dumb oratories,
He passeth by; and his weak spirit fails
To think how they may ache in icy hoods and mails.

Northward he turneth through a little door,
And scarce three steps, ere Music's golden tongue   20
Flattered to tears this aged man and poor;
But no—already had his deathbell rung;
The joys of all his life were said and sung:
His was harsh penance on St. Agnes' Eve:
Another way he went, and soon among   25
Rough ashes sat he for his soul's reprieve,
And all night kept awake, for sinners' sake to grieve.

That ancient Beadsman heard the prelude soft;
And so it chanced, for many a door was wide,
From hurry to and fro. Soon, up aloft,   30
The silver, snarling trumpets 'gan to chide:
The level chambers, ready with their pride,
Were glowing to receive a thousand guests:
The carved angels, ever eager-eyed,
Stared, where upon their heads the cornice rests,   35
With hair blown back, and wings put crosswise on their breasts.

At length burst in the argent revelry,
With plume, tiara, and all rich array,
Numerous as shadows haunting fairily
The brain, new stuffed, in youth, with triumphs gay   40
Of old romance. These let us wish away,
And turn, sole-thoughted, to one Lady there,
Whose heart had brooded, all that wintry day,
On love, and winged St. Agnes' saintly care,
As she had heard old dames full many times declare.   45

They told her how, upon St. Agnes' Eve,
Young virgins might have visions of delight,
And soft adorings from their loves receive
Upon the honeyed middle of the night,
If ceremonies due they did aright;   50
As, supperless to bed they must retire,
And couch supine their beauties, lily white;
Nor look behind, nor sideways, but require
Of Heaven with upward eyes for all that they desire.

Full of this whim was thoughtful Madeline: 55
The music, yearning like a God in pain,
She scarcely heard: her maiden eyes divine,
Fixed on the floor, saw many a sweeping train
Pass by—she heeded not at all: in vain
Came many a tiptoe, amorous cavalier,   60
And back retired; not cooled by high disdain,
But she saw not: her heart was otherwhere:
She sighed for Agnes' dreams, the sweetest of the year.

She danced along with vague, regardless eyes,
Anxious her lips, her breathing quick and short: 65
The hallowed hour was near at hand: she sighs
Amid the timbrels, and the thronged resort
Of whisperers in anger, or in sport;
'Mid looks of love, defiance, hate, and scorn,
Hoodwinked with faery fancy; all amort,   70
Save to St. Agnes and her lambs unshorn,
And all the bliss to be before tomorrow morn.

So, purposing each moment to retire,
She lingered still. Meantime, across the moors,
Had come young Porphyro, with heart on fire   75
For Madeline. Beside the portal doors,
Buttressed from moonlight, stands he, and implores
All saints to give him sight of Madeline,
But for one moment in the tedious hours,
That he might gaze and worship all unseen;   80
Perchance speak, kneel, touch, kiss—in sooth such things have been.

He ventures in: let no buzzed whisper tell:
All eyes be muffled, or a hundred swords
Will storm his heart, Love's fev'rous citadel:
For him, those chambers held barbarian hordes,   85
Hyena foemen, and hot-blooded lords,
Whose very dogs would execrations howl
Against his lineage: not one breast affords
Him any mercy, in that mansion foul,
Save one old beldame, weak in body and in soul.   90

Ah, happy chance! the aged creature came,
Shuffling along with ivory-headed wand,
To where he stood, hid from the torch's flame,
Behind a broad hall-pillar, far beyond
The sound of merriment and chorus bland: 95

He startled her; but soon she knew his face,
And grasped his fingers in her palsied hand,
Saying, 'Mercy, Porphyro! hie thee from this place:
They are all here tonight, the whole bloodthirsty race!

'Get hence! get hence! there's dwarfish Hildebrand;   100
He had a fever late, and in the fit
He cursed thee and thine, both house and land:
Then there's that old Lord Maurice, not a whit
More tame for his gray hairs—Alas me! flit!
Flit like a ghost away.' 'Ah, Gossip dear,   105
We're safe enough; here in this armchair sit,
And tell me how–' 'Good Saints! not here, not here;
Follow me, child, or else these stones will be thy bier.'

He followed through a lowly arched way,
Brushing the cobwebs with his lofty plume,   110
And as she muttered 'Well-a—well-a-day!'
He found him in a little moonlight room,
Pale, latticed, chill, and silent as a tomb.
'Now tell me where is Madeline,' said he,
'O tell me, Angela, by the holy loom   115
Which none but secret sisterhood may see,
When they St. Agnes' wool are weaving piously.'

'St. Agnes! Ah! it is St. Agnes' Eve—
Yet men will murder upon holy days:
Thou must hold water in a witch's sieve,   120
And be liege-lord of all the elves and fays,
To venture so: it fills me with amaze
To see thee, Porphyro!—St. Agnes' Eve!
God's help! my lady fair the conjuror plays
This very night: good angels her deceive!   125
But let me laugh awhile, I've mickle time to grieve.'

Feebly she laugheth in the languid moon,
While Porphyro upon her face doth look,
Like puzzled urchin on an aged crone
Who keepeth closed a wondrous riddle book,   130
As spectacled she sits in chimney nook.
But soon his eyes grew brilliant, when she told
His lady's purpose; and he scarce could brook
Tears, at the thought of those enchantments cold,
And Madeline asleep in lap of legends old.   135

Sudden a thought came like a full-blown rose,
Flushing his brow, and in his pained heart
Made purple riot: then doth he propose
A stratagem, that makes the beldame start:
'A cruel man and impious thou art: 140
Sweet lady, let her pray, and sleep, and dream
Alone with her good angels, far apart
From wicked men like thee. Go, go!—I deem
Thou canst not surely be the same that thou didst seem.'

'I will not harm her, by all saints I swear,'   145
Quoth Porphyro: 'O may I ne'er find grace
When my weak voice shall whisper its last prayer,
If one of her soft ringlets I displace,
Or look with ruffian passion in her face:
Good Angela, believe me by these tears;   150
Or I will, even in a moment's space,
Awake, with horrid shout, my foemen's ears,
And beard them, though they be more fanged than wolves
      and bears.'

'Ah! why wilt thou affright a feeble soul?
A poor, weak, palsy-stricken, churchyard thing,   155
Whose passing-bell may ere the midnight toll;
Whose prayers for thee, each morn and evening,
Were never missed.' Thus plaining, doth she bring
A gentler speech from burning Porphyro;
So woeful, and of such deep sorrowing,   160
That Angela gives promise she will do
Whatever he shall wish, betide her weal or woe.

Which was, to lead him, in close secrecy,
Even to Madeline's chamber, and there hide
Him in a closet, of such privacy   165
That he might see her beauty unespied,
And win perhaps that night a peerless bride,
While legioned fairies paced the coverlet,
And pale enchantment held her sleepy-eyed.
Never on such a night have lovers met,   170
Since Merlin paid his Demon all the monstrous debt.

'It shall be as thou wishest,' said the Dame:
'All cates and dainties shall be stored there
Quickly on this feast-night: by the tambour frame
Her own lute thou wilt see: no time to spare,   175
For I am slow and feeble, and scarce dare

On such a catering trust my dizzy head.
Wait here, my child, with patience; kneel in prayer
The while. Ah! thou must needs the lady wed,
Or may I never leave my grave among the dead.'   180

So saying, she hobbled off with busy fear.
The lover's endless minutes slowly passed;
The dame returned, and whispered in his ear
To follow her; with aged eyes aghast
From fright of dim espial. Safe at last,   185
Through many a dusky gallery, they gain
The maiden's chamber, silken, hushed, and chaste;
Where Porphyro took covert, pleased amain.
His poor guide hurried back with agues in her brain.

Her faltering hand upon the balustrade,   190
Old Angela was feeling for the stair,
When Madeline, St. Agnes' charmed maid,
Rose, like a missioned spirit, unaware:
With silver taper's light, and pious care,
She turned, and down the aged gossip led   195
To a safe level matting. Now prepare,
Young Porphyro, for gazing on that bed;
She comes, she comes again, like ring-dove frayed and fled.

Out went the taper as she hurried in;
Its little smoke, in pallid moonshine, died: 200
She closed the door, she panted, all akin
To spirits of the air, and visions wide:
No uttered syllable, or, woe betide!
But to her heart, her heart was voluble,
Paining with eloquence her balmy side;   205
As though a tongueless nightingale should swell
Her throat in vain, and die, heart-stifled, in her dell.

A casement high and triple-arched there was,
All garlanded with carven imageries
Of fruits, and flowers, and bunches of knot-grass,   210
And diamonded with panes of quaint device,
Innumerable of stains and splendid dyes,
As are the tiger-moth's deep-damasked wings;
And in the midst, 'mong thousand heraldries,
And twilight saints, and dim emblazonings,   215
A shielded scutcheon blushed with blood of queens and kings.

Full on this casement shone the wintry moon,
And threw warm gules on Madeline's fair breast,
As down she knelt for heaven's grace and boon;
Rose-bloom fell on her hands, together pressed,   220
And on her silver cross soft amethyst,
And on her hair a glory, like a saint:
She seemed a splendid angel, newly dressed,
Save wings, for heaven. Porphyro grew faint:
She knelt, so pure a thing, so free from mortal taint.   225

Anon his heart revives: her vespers done,
Of all its wreathed pearls her hair she frees;
Unclasps her warmed jewels one by one;
Loosens her fragrant bodice, by degrees
Her rich attire creeps rustling to her knees: 230
Half-hidden, like a mermaid in seaweed,
Pensive awhile she dreams awake, and sees,
In fancy, fair St. Agnes in her bed,
But dares not look behind, or all the charm is fled.

Soon, trembling in her soft and chilly nest,   235
In sort of wakeful swoon, perplexed she lay,
Until the poppied warmth of sleep oppressed
Her soothed limbs, and soul fatigued away;
Flown, like a thought, until the morrow-day;
Blissfully havened both from joy and pain;   240
Clasped like a missal where swart Paynims pray;
Blinded alike from sunshine and from rain,
As though a rose should shut, and be a bud again.

Stolen to this paradise, and so entranced,
Porphyro gazed upon her empty dress,   245
And listened to her breathing, if it chanced
To wake into a slumberous tenderness;
Which when he heard, that minute did he bless,
And breathed himself: then from the closet crept,
Noiseless as fear in a wide wilderness,   250
And over the hushed carpet, silent, stepped
And 'tween the curtains peeped, where, lo!—how fast she slept.

Then by the bedside, where the faded moon
Made a dim, silver twilight, soft he set
A table, and, half anguished, threw thereon   255
A cloth of woven crimson, gold, and jet—
O for some drowsy Morphean amulet!

gules] heraldic red

The boisterous, midnight, festive clarion,
The kettle-drum, and far-heard clarionet,
Affray his ears, though but in dying tone: 260
The hall door shuts again, and all the noise is gone.

And still she slept an azure-lidded sleep,
In blanched linen, smooth, and lavendered,
While he from forth the closet brought a heap
Of candied apple, quince, and plum, and gourd;   265
With jellies soother than the creamy curd,
And lucent syrups, tinct with cinnamon;
Manna and dates, in argosy transferred
From Fez; and spiced dainties, every one,
From silken Samarcand to cedared Lebanon.   270

These delicates he heaped with glowing hand
On golden dishes and in baskets bright
Of wreathed silver: sumptuous they stand
In the retired quiet of the night,
Filling the chilly room with perfume light—   275
'And now, my love, my seraph fair, awake!
Thou art my heaven, and I thine eremite:
Open thine eyes, for meek St. Agnes' sake,
Or I shall drowse beside thee, so my soul doth ache.'

Thus whispering, his warm, unnerved arm   280
Sank in her pillow. Shaded was her dream
By the dusk curtains— 'twas a midnight charm
Impossible to melt as iced stream:
The lustrous salvers in the moonlight gleam;
Broad golden fringe upon the carpet lies: 285
It seemed he never, never could redeem
From such a steadfast spell his lady's eyes;
So mused awhile, entoiled in woofèd phantasies.

Awakening up, he took her hollow lute—
Tumultuous—and, in chords that tenderest be,   290
He played an ancient ditty, long since mute,
In Provence called, 'La belle dame sans mercy,'
Close to her ear touching the melody;
Wherewith disturbed, she uttered a soft moan:
He ceased—she panted quick—and suddenly   295
Her blue affrayed eyes wide open shone:
Upon his knees he sank, pale as smooth-sculptured stone.

Her eyes were open, but she still beheld,
Now wide awake, the vision of her sleep:
There was a painful change, that nigh expelled   300
The blisses of her dream so pure and deep;
At which fair Madeline began to weep,
And moan forth witless words with many a sigh;
While still her gaze on Porphyro would keep;
Who knelt, with joined hands and piteous eye,   305
Fearing to move or speak, she looked so dreamingly.

'Ah, Porphyro!' said she, 'but even now
Thy voice was at sweet tremble in mine ear,
Made tuneable with every sweetest vow;
And those sad eyes were spiritual and clear: 310
How changed thou art! how pallid, chill, and drear!
Give me that voice again, my Porphyro,
Those looks immortal, those complainings dear!
Oh leave me not in this eternal woe,
For if thou diest, my love, I know not where to go.'   315

Beyond a mortal man impassioned far
At these voluptuous accents, he arose,
Ethereal, flushed, and like a throbbing star
Seen mid the sapphire heaven's deep repose;
Into her dream he melted, as the rose   320
Blendeth its odour with the violet—
Solution sweet: meantime the frost-wind blows
Like love's alarum pattering the sharp sleet
Against the window-panes; St. Agnes' moon hath set.

'Tis dark: quick pattereth the flaw-blown sleet: 325
'This is no dream, my bride, my Madeline!'
'Tis dark: the iced gusts still rave and beat:
'No dream, alas! alas! and woe is mine!
Porphyro will leave me here to fade and pine—
Cruel! what traitor could thee hither bring?   330
I curse not, for my heart is lost in thine,
Though thou forsakest a deceived thing—
A dove forlorn and lost with sick unpruned wing.'

'My Madeline! sweet dreamer! lovely bride!
Say, may I be for aye thy vassal blest?   335
Thy beauty's shield, heart-shaped and vermeil dyed?
Ah, silver shrine, here will I take my rest
After so many hours of toil and quest,

flaw-blown] gust-blown

A famished pilgrim, saved by miracle.
Though I have found, I will not rob thy nest   340
Saving of thy sweet self; if thou think'st well
To trust, fair Madeline, to no rude infidel.

'Hark! 'tis an elfin-storm from faery land,
Of haggard seeming but a boon indeed:
Arise—arise! the morning is at hand;   345
The bloated wassaillers will never heed:
Let us away, my love, with happy speed;
There are no ears to hear, or eyes to see—
Drowned all in Rhenish and the sleepy mead:
Awake! arise! my love, and fearless be,   350
For o'er the southern moors I have a home for thee.'

She hurried at his words, beset with fears,
For there were sleeping dragons all around—
At glaring watch, perhaps, with ready spears:
Down the wide stairs a darkling way they found: 355
In all the house was heard no human sound.
A chain-drooped lamp was flickering by each door;
The arras, rich with horseman, hawk, and hound,
Fluttered in the besieging wind's uproar;
And the long carpets rose along the gusty floor.   360

They glide, like phantoms, into the wide hall;
Like phantoms, to the iron porch, they glide;
Where lay the porter, in uneasy sprawl,
With a huge empty flagon by his side:
The wakeful bloodhound rose, and shook his hide,   365
But his sagacious eyes an inmate owns:
By one, and one, the bolts full easy slide:
The chains lie silent on the footworn stones;
The key turns, and the door upon its hinges groans.

And they are gone: ay, ages long ago   370
These lovers fled away into the storm.
That night the Baron dreamt of many a woe,
And all his warrior-guests, with shade and form
Of witch, and demon, and large coffin-worm,
Were long be-nightmared. Angela the old   375
Died palsy-twitched, with meagre face deform;
The Beadsman, after thousand aves told,
For aye unsought for slept among his ashes cold.

THOMAS HOOD
1799–1845

Faithless Sally Brown

YOUNG Ben he was a nice young man,
   A carpenter by trade;
And he fell in love with Sally Brown,
   That was a lady's maid.

But as they fetched a walk one day,   5
   They met a press-gang crew;
And Sally she did faint away,
   Whilst Ben he was brought to.

The boatswain swore with wicked words,
   Enough to shock a saint,   10
That though she did seem in a fit,
   'Twas nothing but a feint.

'Come, girl,' said he, 'hold up your head,
   He'll be as good as me;
For when your swain is in our boat,   15
   A boatswain he will be.'

So when they'd made their game of her,
   And taken off her elf,
She roused, and found she only was
   A coming to herself.   20

'And is he gone, and is he gone?'
   She cried, and wept outright:
'Then I will to the water side,
   And see him out of sight.'

A waterman came up to her,   25
   'Now, young woman,' said he,
'If you weep on so, you will make
   Eye-water in the sea.'

elf] young man

188

'Alas! they've taken my beau Ben,
   To sail with old Benbow;'
And her woe began to run afresh,
   As if she'd said, Gee woe!   30

Says he, 'They've only taken him
   To the Tender-ship, you see;'
'The Tender-ship,' cried Sally Brown,   35
   'What a hard-ship that must be!

'Oh! would I were a mermaid now,
   For then I'd follow him;
But Oh!—I'm not a fish-woman,
   And so I cannot swim.   40

'Alas! I was not born beneath
   The virgin and the scales,
So I must curse my cruel stars,
   And walk about in Wales.'

Now Ben had sailed to many a place   45
   That's underneath the world;
But in two years the ship came home,
   And all her sails were furled.

But when he called on Sally Brown,
   To see how she got on,
He found she'd got another Ben,   50
   Whose Christian name was John.

'Oh, Sally Brown, oh, Sally Brown,
   How could you serve me so,
I've met with many a breeze before,   55
   But never such a blow!'

Then reading on his 'bacco box,
   He heaved a heavy sigh,
And then began to eye his pipe,
   And then to pipe his eye.   60

And then he tried to sing 'All's Well',
   But could not, though he tried;
His head was turned, and so he chewed
   His pigtail till he died.

His death, which happened in his berth,   65
  At forty-odd befell:
They went and told the sexton, and
  The sexton tolled the bell.

ALFRED, LORD TENNYSON
1809–1892

The Lady of Shalott

PART I

ON either side the river lie
Long fields of barley and of rye,
That clothe the wold and meet the sky;
And thro' the field the road runs by
        To many-towered Camelot;   5
And up and down the people go,
Gazing where the lilies blow
Round an island there below,
        The island of Shalott.

Willows whiten, aspens quiver,   10
Little breezes dusk and shiver
Thro' the wave that runs for ever
By the island in the river
        Flowing down to Camelot.
Four grey walls, and four grey towers,   15
Overlook a space of flowers,
And the silent isle embowers
        The Lady of Shalott.

By the margin, willow-veiled,
Slide the heavy barges trailed   20
By slow horses; and unhailed
The shallop flitteth silken-sailed
        Skimming down to Camelot:
But who hath seen her wave her hand?
Or at the casement seen her stand?   25
Or is she known in all the land,
        The Lady of Shalott?

Only reapers, reaping early
In among the bearded barley,
Hear a song that echoes cheerly   30
From the river winding clearly,
     Down to towered Camelot:
And by the moon the reaper weary,
Piling sheaves in uplands airy,
Listening, whispers ''Tis the fairy   35
     Lady of Shalott'.

PART II

There she weaves by night and day
A magic web with colours gay.
She has heard a whisper say,
A curse is on her if she stay   40
     To look down to Camelot.
She knows not what the curse may be,
And so she weaveth steadily,
And little other care hath she,
     The Lady of Shalott.   45

And moving thro' a mirror clear
That hangs before her all the year,
Shadows of the world appear.
There she sees the highway near
     Winding down to Camelot: 50
There the river eddy whirls,
And there the surly village churls,
And the red cloaks of market girls,
     Pass onward from Shalott.

Sometimes a troop of damsels glad,   55
An abbot on an ambling pad,
Sometimes a curly shepherd lad,
Or long-haired page in crimson clad,
     Goes by to towered Camelot;
And sometimes thro' the mirror blue   60
The knights come riding two and two:
She hath no loyal knight and true,
     The Lady of Shalott.

But in her web she still delights
To weave the mirror's magic sights,   65
For often thro' the silent nights
A funeral, with plumes and lights,
     And music, went to Camelot:

Or when the moon was overhead,
Came two young lovers lately wed; 70
'I am half sick of shadows,' said
    The Lady of Shalott.

PART III

A bow-shot from her bower-eaves,
He rode between the barley sheaves,
The sun came dazzling thro' the leaves, 75
And flamed upon the brazen greaves
    Of bold Sir Lancelot.
A red-cross knight for ever kneeled
To a lady in his shield,
That sparkled on the yellow field, 80
    Beside remote Shalott.

The gemmy bridle glittered free,
Like to some branch of stars we see
Hung in the golden Galaxy.
The bridle bells rang merrily 85
    As he rode down to Camelot:
And from his blazoned baldric slung
A mighty silver bugle hung,
And as he rode his armour rung,
    Beside remote Shalott. 90

All in the blue unclouded weather
Thick-jewelled shone the saddle-leather,
The helmet and the helmet-feather
Burned like one burning flame together,
    As he rode down to Camelot. 95
As often thro' the purple night,
Below the starry clusters bright,
Some bearded meteor, trailing light,
    Moves over still Shalott.

His broad clear brow in sunlight glowed; 100
On burnished hooves his war-horse trode;
From underneath his helmet flowed
His coal-black curls as on he rode,
    As he rode down to Camelot.
From the bank and from the river 105
He flashed into the crystal mirror,
'Tirra lirra,' by the river
    Sang Sir Lancelot.

She left the web, she left the loom,
She made three paces thro' the room, 110
She saw the water-lily bloom,
She saw the helmet and the plume,
     She looked down to Camelot.
Out flew the web and floated wide;
The mirror cracked from side to side; 115
'The curse is come upon me,' cried
     The Lady of Shalott.

PART IV

In the stormy east wind straining,
The pale yellow woods were waning,
The broad stream in his banks complaining, 120
Heavily the low sky raining
     Over towered Camelot;
Down she came and found a boat
Beneath a willow left afloat,
And round about the prow she wrote 125
     The Lady of Shalott.

And down the river's dim expanse—
Like some bold seer in a trance,
Seeing all his own mischance—
With a glassy countenance 130
     Did she look to Camelot.
And at the closing of the day
She loosed the chain, and down she lay;
The broad stream bore her far away,
     The Lady of Shalott. 135

Lying, robed in snowy white
That loosely flew to left and right—
The leaves upon her falling light—
Thro' the noises of the night
     She floated down to Camelot: 140
And as the boat-head wound along
The willowy hills and fields among,
They heard her singing her last song,
     The Lady of Shalott.

Heard a carol, mournful, holy, 145
Chanted loudly, chanted lowly,
Till her blood was frozen slowly,
And her eyes were darkened wholly,
     Turned to towered Camelot;

For ere she reached upon the tide   150
The first house by the waterside,
Singing in her song she died,
      The Lady of Shalott.

Under tower and balcony,
By garden wall and gallery,   155
A gleaming shape she floated by,
Dead-pale between the houses high,
      Silent into Camelot.
Out upon the wharfs they came,
Knight and burgher, lord and dame,   160
And round the prow they read her name,
      The Lady of Shalott.

Who is this? and what is here?
And in the lighted palace near
Died the sound of royal cheer;   165
And they crossed themselves for fear,
      All the knights at Camelot:
But Lancelot mused a little space;
He said, 'She has a lovely face;
God in his mercy lend her grace,   170
      The Lady of Shalott.'

Morte d'Arthur

So all day long the noise of battle rolled
Among the mountains by the winter sea;
Until King Arthur's table, man by man,
Had fallen in Lyonnesse about their Lord,
King Arthur: then, because his wound was deep,   5
The bold Sir Bedivere uplifted him,
Sir Bedivere, the last of all his knights,
And bore him to a chapel nigh the field,
A broken chancel with a broken cross,
That stood on a dark strait of barren land.   10
On one side lay the ocean, and on one
Lay a great water, and the moon was full.

  Then spake King Arthur to Sir Bedivere:
'The sequel of today unsolders all
The goodliest fellowship of famous knights   15

Whereof this world holds record. Such a sleep
They sleep—the men I loved. I think that we
Shall never more, at any future time,
Delight our souls with talk of knightly deeds,
Walking about the gardens and the halls   20
Of Camelot, as in the days that were.
I perish by this people which I made—
Tho' Merlin sware that I should come again
To rule once more—but let what will be, be,
I am so deeply smitten thro' the helm   25
That without help I cannot last till morn.
Thou therefore take my brand Excalibur,
Which was my pride: for thou rememberest how
In those old days, one summer noon, an arm
Rose up from out the bosom of the lake,   30
Clothed in white samite, mystic, wonderful,
Holding the sword—and how I rowed across
And took it, and have worn it, like a king:
And, wheresoever I am sung or told
In aftertime, this also shall be known: 35
But now delay not: take Excalibur,
And fling him far into the middle mere:
Watch what thou seest, and lightly bring me word.'

    To him replied the bold Sir Bedivere:
'It is not meet, Sir King, to leave thee thus,   40
Aidless, alone, and smitten thro' the helm.
A little thing may harm a wounded man.
Yet I thy hest will all perform at full,
Watch what I see, and lightly bring thee word.'

    So saying, from the ruined shrine he stept   45
And in the moon athwart the place of tombs,
Where lay the mighty bones of ancient men,
Old knights, and over them the sea-wind sang
Shrill, chill, with flakes of foam. He, stepping down
By zig-zag paths, and juts of pointed rock,   50
Came on the shining levels of the lake.

    There drew he forth the brand Excalibur,
And o'er him, drawing it, the winter moon,
Brightening the skirts of a long cloud, ran forth
And sparkled keen with frost against the hilt: 55
For all the haft twinkled with diamond sparks,
Myriads of topaz lights, and jacinth-work

Of subtlest jewellery. He gazed so long
That both his eyes were dazzled, as he stood,
This way and that dividing the swift mind,   60
In act to throw: but at the last it seemed
Better to leave Excalibur concealed
There in the many-knotted waterflags,
That whistled stiff and dry about the marge.
So strode he back slow to the wounded King.   65

    Then spake King Arthur to Sir Bedivere:
'Hast thou performed my mission which I gave?
What is it thou hast seen? or what hast heard?'

    And answer made the bold Sir Bedivere:
'I heard the ripple washing in the reeds,   70
And the wild water lapping on the crag.'

    To whom replied King Arthur, faint and pale:
'Thou hast betrayed thy nature and thy name,
Not rendering true answer, as beseemed
Thy fealty, nor like a noble knight: 75
For surer sign had followed, either hand,
Or voice, or else a motion of the mere.
This is a shameful thing for men to lie.
Yet now, I charge thee, quickly go again
As thou art lief and dear, and do the thing   80
I bad thee, watch, and lightly bring me word.'

    Then went Sir Bedivere the second time
Across the ridge, and paced beside the mere,
Counting the dewy pebbles, fixed in thought;
But when he saw the wonder of the hilt,   85
How curiously and strangely chased, he smote
His palms together, and he cried aloud,

    'And if indeed I cast the brand away,
Surely a precious thing, one worthy note,
Should thus be lost for ever from the earth,   90
Which might have pleased the eyes of many men.
What good should follow this, if this were done?
What harm, undone? deep harm to disobey,
Seeing obedience is the bond of rule.
Were it well to obey then, if a king demand   95
An act unprofitable, against himself?
The King is sick, and knows not what he does.

What record, or what relic of my lord
Should be to aftertime, but empty breath
And rumours of a doubt? But were this kept,   100
Stored in some treasure-house of mighty kings,
Some one might show it at a joust of arms,
Saying, "King Arthur's sword, Excalibur,
Wrought by the lonely maiden of the Lake.
Nine years she wrought it, sitting in the deeps   105
Upon the hidden bases of the hills."
So might some old man speak in the aftertime
To all the people, winning reverence.
But now much honour and much fame were lost.'

   So spake he, clouded with his own conceit,   110
And hid Excalibur the second time,
And so strode back slow to the wounded King.

   Then spoke King Arthur, breathing heavily:
'What is it thou hast seen? or what hast heard?'

   And answer made the bold Sir Bedivere: 115
'I heard the water lapping on the crag,
And the long ripple washing in the reeds.'

   To whom replied King Arthur, much in wrath:
'Ah, miserable and unkind, untrue,
Unknightly, traitor-hearted! Woe is me!   120
Authority forgets a dying king,
Laid widowed of the power in his eye
That bowed the will. I see thee what thou art,
For thou, the latest-left of all my knights,
In whom should meet the offices of all,   125
Thou wouldst betray me for the precious hilt;
Either from lust of gold, or like a girl
Valuing the giddy pleasure of the eyes.
Yet, for a man may fail in duty twice,
And the third time may prosper, get thee hence: 130
But, if thou spare to fling Excalibur,
I will arise and slay thee with my hands.'

   Then quickly rose Sir Bedivere, and ran,
And, leaping down the ridges lightly, plunged
Among the bulrush-beds, and clutched the sword,   135
And strongly wheeled and threw it. The great brand
Made lightnings in the splendour of the moon,

And flashing round and round, and whirled in an arch,
Shot like a streamer of the northern morn,
Seen where the moving isles of winter shock   140
By night, with noises of the northern sea.
So flashed and fell the brand Excalibur:
But ere he dipt the surface, rose an arm
Clothed in white samite, mystic, wonderful,
And caught him by the hilt, and brandished him   145
Three times, and drew him under in the mere.
And lightly went the other to the King.

   Then spoke King Arthur, drawing thicker breath:
'Now see I by thine eyes that this is done.
Speak out: what is it thou hast heard, or seen?'   150

   And answer made the bold Sir Bedivere:
'Sir King, I closed mine eyelids, lest the gems
Should blind my purpose, for I never saw,
Nor shall see, here or elsewhere, till I die,
Not tho' I live three lives of mortal men,   155
So great a miracle as yonder hilt.
Then with both hands I flung him, wheeling him;
But when I looked again, behold an arm,
Clothed in white samite, mystic, wonderful,
That caught him by the hilt, and brandished him   160
Three times, and drew him under in the mere.'

   And answer made King Arthur, breathing hard:
'My end draws nigh; 'tis time that I were gone.
Make broad thy shoulders to receive my weight,
And bear me to the margin; yet I fear   165
My wound hath taken cold, and I shall die.'

   So saying, from the pavement he half rose,
Slowly, with pain, reclining on his arm,
And looking wistfully with wide blue eyes
As in a picture. Him Sir Bedivere   170
Remorsefully regarded thro' his tears,
And would have spoken, but he found not words,
Then took with care, and kneeling on one knee,
O'er both his shoulders drew the languid hands,
And rising bore him thro' the place of tombs.   175

   But, as he walked, King Arthur panted hard,
Like one that feels a nightmare on his bed

When all the house is mute. So sighed the King,
Muttering and murmuring at his ear, 'Quick, quick!
I fear it is too late, and I shall die.'   180
But the other swiftly strode from ridge to ridge,
Clothed with his breath, and looking, as he walked,
Larger than human on the frozen hills.
He heard the deep behind him, and a cry
Before. His own thought drove him, like a goad.   185
Dry clashed his harness in the icy caves
And barren chasms, and all to left and right
The bare black cliff clanged round him, as he based
His feet on juts of slippery crag that rang
Sharp-smitten with the dint of armed heels—   190
And on a sudden, lo! the level lake,
And the long glories of the winter moon.

Then saw they how there hove a dusky barge,
Dark as a funeral scarf from stem to stern,
Beneath them; and descending they were ware   195
That all the decks were dense with stately forms
Black-stoled, black-hooded, like a dream—by these
Three Queens with crowns of gold—and from them rose
A cry that shivered to the tingling stars,
And, as it were one voice, an agony   200
Of lamentation, like a wind, that shrills
All night in a waste land, where no one comes,
Or hath come, since the making of the world.

Then murmured Arthur, 'Place me in the barge,'
And to the barge they came. There those three Queens   205
Put forth their hands, and took the King, and wept.
But she, that rose the tallest of them all
And fairest, laid his head upon her lap,
And loosed the shattered casque, and chafed his hands,
And called him by his name, complaining loud,   210
And dropping bitter tears against his brow
Striped with dark blood: for all his face was white
And colourless, and like the withered moon
Smote by the fresh beam of the springing east;
And all his greaves and cuisses dashed with drops   215
Of onset; and the light and lustrous curls—
That made his forehead like a rising sun
High from the dais-throne—were parched with dust;
Or, clotted into points and hanging loose,
Mixed with the knightly growth that fringed his lips.   220

So like a shattered column lay the King;
Not like that Arthur who, with lance in rest,
From spur to plume a star of tournament,
Shot thro' the lists at Camelot, and charged
Before the eyes of ladies and of kings.   225
  Then loudly cried the bold Sir Bedivere,
'Ah! my lord Arthur, whither shall I go?
Where shall I hide my forehead and my eyes?
For now I see the true old times are dead,
When every morning brought a noble chance,   230
And every chance brought out a noble knight.
Such times have been not since the light that led
The holy Elders with the gift of myrrh.
But now the whole Round Table is dissolved
Which was an image of the mighty world;   235
And I, the last, go forth companionless,
And the days darken round me, and the years,
Among new men, strange faces, other minds.'

  And slowly answered Arthur from the barge:
'The old order changeth, yielding place to new,   240
And God fulfils Himself in many ways,
Lest one good custom should corrupt the world.
Comfort thyself: what comfort is in me?
I have lived my life, and that which I have done
May He within Himself make pure! but thou,   245
If thou shouldst never see my face again,
Pray for my soul. More things are wrought by prayer
Than this world dreams of. Wherefore, let thy voice
Rise like a fountain for me night and day.
For what are men better than sheep or goats   250
That nourish a blind life within the brain,
If, knowing God, they lift not hands of prayer
Both for themselves and those who call them friend?
For so the whole round earth is every way
Bound by gold chains about the feet of God.   255
But now farewell. I am going a long way
With these thou seest—if indeed I go—
(For all my mind is clouded with a doubt)
To the island-valley of Avilion;
Where falls not hail, or rain, or any snow,   260
Nor ever wind blows loudly; but it lies
Deep-meadowed, happy, fair with orchard-lawns
And bowery hollows crowned with summer sea,
Where I will heal me of my grievous wound.'

So said he, and the barge with oar and sail   265
Moved from the brink, like some full-breasted swan
That, fluting a wild carol ere her death,
Ruffles her pure cold plume, and takes the flood
With swarthy webs. Long stood Sir Bedivere
Revolving many memories, till the hull   270
Looked one black dot against the verge of dawn,
And on the mere the wailing died away.

WILLIAM MAKEPEACE THACKERAY
1811–1863

From *The King of Brentford's Testament*

THE noble King of Brentford
  Was old and very sick,
He summoned his physicians
  To wait upon him quick;
They stepped into their coaches   5
  And brought their best physic.

They crammed their gracious master
  With potion and with pill;
They drenched him and they bled him:
  They could not cure his ill.   10
'Go fetch,' says he, 'my lawyer;
  I'd better make my will.'

The monarch's royal mandate
  The lawyer did obey;
The thought of six-and-eightpence   15
  Did make his heart full gay.
'What is't,' says he, 'your Majesty
  Would wish of me today?'

'The doctors have belaboured me
  With potion and with pill:
My hours of life are counted,   20
  O man of tape and quill!
Sit down and mend a pen or two;
  I want to make my will.

'O'er all the land of Brentford   25
  I'm lord, and eke of Kew:
I've three-per-cents and five-per-cents;
  My debts are but a few;
And to inherit after me
  I have but children two.   30

'Prince Thomas is my eldest son;
  A sober prince is he,
And from the day we breeched him
  Till now—he's twenty-three—
He never caused disquiet   35
  To his poor mamma or me.

'At school they never flogged him;
  At college, though not fast,
Yet his little-go and great-go
  He creditably passed,   40
And made his year's allowance
  For eighteen months to last.

'He never owed a shilling,
  Went never drunk to bed,
He has not two ideas   45
  Within his honest head—
In all respects he differs
  From my second son, Prince Ned.

'When Tom has half his income
  Laid by at the year's end,   50
Poor Ned has ne'er a stiver
  That rightly he may spend,
But sponges on a tradesman,
  Or borrows from a friend.

'While Tom his legal studies   55
  Most soberly pursues,
Poor Ned must pass his mornings
  A-dawdling with the Muse:
While Tom frequents his banker,
  Young Ned frequents the Jews.   60

'Ned drives about in buggies,
  Tom sometimes takes a 'bus;
Ah, cruel fate, why made you
  My children differ thus?
Why make of Tom a *dullard*,   65
  And Ned a *genius*?'

'You'll cut him with a shilling!'
  Exclaimed the man of wits:
'I'll leave my wealth,' said Brentford,
  'Sir Lawyer, as befits,   70
And portion both their fortunes
  Unto their several wits.'

'Your Grace knows best,' the lawyer said;
  'On your commands I wait.'
'Be silent, sir,' says Brentford,   75
  'A plague upon your prate!
Come take your pen and paper,
  And write as I dictate.'

The will as Brentford spoke it
  Was writ and signed and closed;   80
He bade the lawyer leave him,
  And turned him round and dozed;
And next week in the churchyard
  The good old King reposed.

Tom, dressed in crape and hatband,   85
  Of mourners was the chief;
In bitter self-upbraidings
  Poor Edward showed his grief:
Tom hid his fat white countenance
  In his pocket-handkerchief.   90

And when the bones of Brentford—
  That gentle King and just—
With bell and book and candle
  Were duly laid in dust,
'Now, gentlemen,' says Thomas,   95
  'Let business be discussed.

'When late our sire beloved
  Was taken deadly ill,
Sir Lawyer, you attended him
  (I mean to tax your bill);   100
And, as you signed and wrote it,
  I prithee read the will.'

The lawyer wiped his spectacles,
  And drew the parchment out;
And all the Brentford family   105
  Sat eager round about:
Poor Ned was somewhat anxious,
  But Tom had ne'er a doubt.

'My son, as I make ready
  To seek my last long home,   110
Some cares I had for Neddy,
  But none for thee, my Tom:
Sobriety and order
  You ne'er departed from.
                                                      115
'Ned hath a brilliant genius,
  And thou a plodding brain;
On thee I think with pleasure,
  On him with doubt and pain.'
('You see, good Ned,' says Thomas,
  'What he thought about us twain.')   120

'Though small was your allowance,
  You saved a little store;
And those who save a little
  Shall get a plenty more.'
As the lawyer read this compliment,   125
  Tom's eyes were running o'er.

'And though my lands are wide,
  And plenty is my gold,
Still better gifts from Nature,
  My Thomas, do you hold—   130
A brain that's thick and heavy,
  A heart that's dull and cold.'

'Too dull to feel depression,
  Too hard to heed distress,
Too cold to yield to passion   135
  Or silly tenderness.
March on—your road is open
  To wealth, Tom, and success.

'Ned sinneth in extravagance,
  And you in greedy lust.'   140
('I' faith,' says Ned, 'our father
  Is less polite than just.')
'In you, son Tom, I've confidence,
  But Ned I cannot trust.

'Wherefore my lease and copyholds,   145
  My lands and tenements,
My parks, my farms, and orchards,
  My houses and my rents,
My Dutch stock and my Spanish stock,
  My five and three per cents,   150

'I leave to you, my Thomas'—
  ('What, all?' poor Edward said.
'Well, well, I should have spent them,
  And Tom's a prudent head')—
'I leave to you, my Thomas—   155
  To you IN TRUST for Ned.'

The wrath and consternation
  What poet e'er could trace
That at this fatal passage
  Came o'er Prince Tom his face;   160
The wonder of the company,
  And honest Ned's amaze?

''Tis surely some mistake,'
  Good-naturedly cries Ned;
The lawyer answered gravely,   165
  ''Tis even as I said;
'Twas thus his gracious Majesty
  Ordained on his death-bed.

'See, here the will is witnessed.
   And here's his autograph.'   170
'In truth, our father's writing,'
   Says Edward, with a laugh;
'But thou shalt not be a loser, Tom;
   We'll share it half and half.'

'Alas! my kind young gentleman,   175
   This sharing cannot be;
'Tis written in the testament
   That Brentford spoke to me,
"I do forbid Prince Ned to give
   Prince Tom a halfpenny."   180

'He hath a store of money,
   But ne'er was known to lend it;
He never helped his brother;
   The poor he ne'er befriended;
He hath no need of property   185
   Who knows not how to spend it.

'Poor Edward knows but how to spend,
   And thrifty Tom to hoard;
Let Thomas be the steward then,
   And Edward be the lord;   190
And as the honest labourer
   Is worthy his reward,

'I pray Prince Ned, my second son,
   And my successor dear,
To pay to his intendant   195
   Five hundred pounds a year;
And to think of his old father,
   And live and make good cheer.'

Such was old Brentford's honest testament,
   He did devise his moneys for the best,   200
   And lies in Brentford church in peaceful rest.
Prince Edward lived, and money made and spent;
   But his good sire was wrong, it is confessed,
To say his son, young Thomas, never lent.
   He did. Young Thomas lent at interest,   205
And nobly took his twenty-five per cent.

Long time the famous reign of Ned endured
  O'er Chiswick, Fulham, Brentford, Putney, Kew,
But of extravagance he ne'er was cured.
  And when both died, as mortal men will do,   210
'Twas commonly reported that the steward
  Was very much the richer of the two.

RICHARD HARRIS BARHAM
1788–1845

The Jackdaw of Rheims

THE jackdaw sat on the Cardinal's chair!
Bishop, and abbot, and prior were there;
  Many a monk, and many a friar,
  Many a knight, and many a squire,
With a great many more of lesser degree—   5
In sooth a goodly company;
And they served the Lord Primate on bended knee.
  Never, I ween,
  Was a prouder seen,
Read of in books, or dreamt of in dreams,   10
Than the Cardinal Lord Archbishop of Rheims!

  In and out
  Through the motley rout,
That little jackdaw kept hopping about;
  Here and there   15
  Like a dog in a fair,
  Over comfits and cates,
  And dishes and plates,
Cowl and cope, and rochet and pall,
Mitre and crosier! he hopped upon all!   20
  With saucy air,
  He perched on the chair
Where, in state, the great Lord Cardinal sat
In the great Lord Cardinal's great red hat;
  And he peered in the face   25
  Of his Lordship's Grace,
With a satisfied look, as if he would say,
'We two are the greatest folks here today!'

And the priests with awe,
As such freaks they saw,   30
Said, 'The Devil must be in that little jackdaw!'

The feast was over, the board was cleared,
The flawns and the custards had all disappeared,
And six little singing-boys—dear little souls!
In nice clean faces, and nice white stoles,   35
   Came, in order due,
   Two by two,
Marching that grand refectory through.
A nice little boy held a golden ewer,
Embossed and filled with water, as pure   40
As any that flows between Rheims and Namur,
Which a nice little boy stood ready to catch
In a fine golden hand-basin made to match.
Two nice little boys, rather more grown,
Carried lavender water, and Eau de Cologne;   45
And a nice little boy had a nice cake of soap,
Worthy of washing the hands of the Pope.
   One little boy more
   A napkin bore,
Of the best white diaper, fringed with pink,   50
And a Cardinal's Hat marked in permanent ink.

The great Lord Cardinal turns at the sight
Of these nice little boys dressed all in white:
   From his finger he draws
   His costly turquoise;   55
And, not thinking at all about little jackdaws,
   Deposits it straight
   By the side of his plate,
While the nice little boys on his Eminence wait;
Till, when nobody's dreaming of any such thing,   60
That little jackdaw hops off with the ring!

   There's a cry and a shout,
   And a deuce of a rout,
And nobody seems to know what they're about,
But the monks have their pockets all turned inside out.   65
   The friars are kneeling,
   And hunting and feeling
The carpet, the floor, and the walls, and the ceiling.
   The Cardinal drew
   Off each plum-coloured shoe,   70
And left his red stockings exposed to the view;

208

He peeps and he feels
In the toes and the heels;
They turn up the dishes, they turn up the plates,
They take up the poker and poke out the grates,   75
   —They turn up the rugs,
   They examine the mugs:
   But, no!—no such thing—
   They can't find THE RING!
And the Abbot declared that 'when nobody twigged it,   80
Some rascal or other had popped in and prigged it'.

The Cardinal rose with a dignified look,
He called for his candle, his bell, and his book.
   In holy anger and pious grief,
   He solemnly cursed that rascally thief.   85
   He cursed him at board, he cursed him in bed;
   From the sole of his foot to the crown of his head;
   He cursed him in sleeping, that every night
   He should dream of the devil, and wake in a fright;
   He cursed him in eating, he cursed him in drinking,   90
   He cursed him in coughing, in sneezing, in winking;
   He cursed him in sitting, in standing, in lying;
   He cursed him in walking, in riding, in flying;
   He cursed him in living, he cursed him in dying.
Never was heard such a terrible curse!   95
   But what gave rise
   To no little surprise,
Nobody seemed one penny the worse!

   The day was gone,
   The night came on,   100
The monks and the friars they searched till dawn;
   When the Sacristan saw,
   On crumpled claw,
Come limping a poor little lame jackdaw!
   No longer gay,   105
   As on yesterday;
His feathers all seemed to be turned the wrong way;
His pinions drooped, he could hardly stand,
His head was as bald as the palm of your hand;
   His eye so dim,   110
   So wasted each limb,
That, heedless of grammar, they all cried, 'THAT'S HIM!—
That's the scamp that has done this scandalous thing!
That's the thief that has got my Lord Cardinal's ring!'

The poor little jackdaw,   115
When the monks he saw,
Feebly gave vent to the ghost of a caw;
And turned his bald head, as much as to say,
'Pray, be so good as to walk this way!'
    Slower and slower   120
    He limped on before,
Till they came to the back of the belfry door,
    Where the first thing they saw,
    Midst the sticks and the straw,
Was the RING in the nest of that little jackdaw!   125

Then the great Lord Cardinal called for his book,
And off that terrible curse he took;
    The mute expression
    Served in lieu of confession,
And, being thus coupled with full restitution,   130
The jackdaw got plenary absolution.
    —When those words were heard,
    That poor little bird
Was so changed in a moment, 'twas really absurd.
    He grew sleek and fat;   135
    In addition to that,
A fresh crop of feathers came thick as a mat.
    His tail waggled more
    Even than before;
But no longer it wagged with an impudent air,   140
No longer he perched on the Cardinal's chair.

    He hopped now about
    With a gait devout;
At Matins, at Vespers, he never was out;
And, so far from any more pilfering deeds,   145
He always seemed telling the Confessor's beads.
If anyone lied, or if anyone swore,
Or slumbered in prayer-time and happened to snore,
    That good jackdaw
    Would give a great 'Caw!'   150
As much as to say, 'Don't do so any more!'
While many remarked, as his manners they saw,
That they 'never had known such a pious jackdaw!'
    He long lived the pride
    Of that countryside,   155
And at last in the odour of sanctity died;

When, as words were too faint
    His merits to paint,
The Conclave determined to make him a Saint;
And on newly-made Saints and Popes, as you know,   160
It's the custom at Rome, new names to bestow,
So they canonized him by the name of Jim Crow!

HENRY WADSWORTH LONGFELLOW

1807–1882

The Wreck of the Hesperus

IT was the schooner Hesperus,
    That sailed the wintry sea;
And the skipper had taken his little daughter,
    To bear him company.

Blue were her eyes as the fairy-flax,   5
    Her cheeks like the dawn of day,
And her bosom white as the hawthorn buds
    That ope in the month of May.

The skipper he stood beside the helm,
    His pipe was in his mouth,   10
And he watched how the veering flaw did blow
    The smoke now west, now south.

Then up and spake an old sailor,
    Had sailed the Spanish Main,
'I pray thee, put into yonder port,   15
    For I fear a hurricane.

'Last night the moon had a golden ring,
    And tonight no moon we see!'
The skipper he blew a whiff from his pipe,
    And a scornful laugh laughed he.   20

Colder and louder blew the wind,
    A gale from the north-east,
The snow fell hissing in the brine,
    And the billows frothed like yeast.

211

Down came the storm, and smote amain   25
  The vessel in its strength;
She shuddered and paused, like a frighted steed,
  Then leaped her cable's length.

'Come hither! come hither! my little daughter,
  And do not tremble so;   30
For I can weather the roughest gale
  That ever wind did blow.'

He wrapped her warm in his seaman's coat
  Against the stinging blast;
He cut a rope from a broken spar,   35
  And bound her to the mast.

'O father! I hear the church bells ring,
  O say, what may it be?'
''Tis a fog-bell on a rock-bound coast!'—
  And he steered for the open sea.   40

'O father! I hear the sound of guns,
  O say, what may it be?'
'Some ship in distress, that cannot live
  In such an angry sea!'

'O father! I see a gleaming light,   45
  O say, what may it be?'
But the father answered never a word,
  A frozen corpse was he.

Lashed to the helm, all stiff and stark,
  With his face turned to the skies,   50
The lantern gleamed through the gleaming snow
  On his fixed and glassy eyes.

Then the maiden clasped her hands and prayed
  That savèd she might be;
And she thought of Christ, who stilled the wave   55
  On the Lake of Galilee.

And fast through the midnight dark and drear,
  Through the whistling sleet and snow,
Like a sheeted ghost the vessel swept
  Towards the reef of Norman's Woe.   60

And ever the fitful gusts between
  A sound came from the land;
It was the sound of the trampling surf
  On the rocks and the hard sea-sand.

The breakers were right beneath her bows,   65
  She drifted a dreary wreck,
And a whooping billow swept the crew
  Like icicles from her deck.

She struck where the white and fleecy waves
  Looked soft as carded wool,   70
But the cruel rocks they gored her side
  Like the horns of an angry bull.

Her rattling shrouds, all sheathed in ice,
  With the masts went by the board;
Like a vessel of glass she stove and sank—   75
  Ho! ho! the breakers roared!

At daybreak on the bleak sea-beach
  A fisherman stood aghast,
To see the form of a maiden fair
  Lashed close to a drifting mast.   80

The salt sea was frozen on her breast,
  The salt tears in her eyes;
And he saw her hair, like the brown sea-weed,
  On the billows fall and rise.

Such was the wreck of the Hesperus,   85
  In the midnight and the snow!
Christ save us all from a death like this,
  On the reef of Norman's Woe!

Paul Revere's Ride

LISTEN, my children, and you shall hear
Of the midnight ride of Paul Revere,
On the eighteenth of April, in Seventy-five;
Hardly a man is now alive
Who remembers that famous day and year.   5

He said to his friend, 'If the British march
By land or sea from the town tonight,
Hang a lantern aloft in the belfry arch
Of the North Church tower as a signal light—
One, if by land, and two, if by sea;   10
And I on the opposite shore will be,
Ready to ride and spread the alarm
Through every Middlesex village and farm,
For the country folk to be up and to arm.'

Then he said 'Good night!' and with muffled oar   15
Silently rowed to the Charlestown shore,
Just as the moon rose over the bay,
Where swinging wide at her moorings lay
The *Somerset*, British man-of-war;
A phantom ship, with each mast and spar   20
Across the moon like a prison bar,
And a huge black hulk, that was magnified
By its own reflection in the tide.

Meanwhile, his friend, through alley and street,
Wanders and watches with eager ears,   25
Till in the silence around him he hears
The muster of men at the barrack door,
The sound of arms, and the tramp of feet,
And the measured tread of the grenadiers
Marching down to their boats on the shore.   30

Then he climbed the tower of the Old North Church,
By the wooden stairs, with stealthy tread,
To the belfry chamber overhead,
And startled the pigeons from their perch
On the sombre rafters, that round him made   35
Masses and moving shapes of shade—
By the trembling ladder, steep and tall,
To the highest window in the wall,
Where he paused to listen and look down
A moment on the roofs of the town,   40
And the moonlight flowing over all.

Beneath, in the churchyard, lay the dead,
In their night-encampment on the hill,
Wrapped in silence so deep and still
That he could hear, like a sentinel's tread,   45

The watchful night-wind, as it went
Creeping along from tent to tent,
And seeming to whisper, 'All is well!'
A moment only he feels the spell
Of the place and the hour, and the secret dread   50
Of the lonely belfry and the dead;
For suddenly all his thoughts are bent
On a shadowy something far away,
Where the river widens to meet the bay—
A line of black that bends and floats   55
On the rising tide, like a bridge of boats.

Meanwhile, impatient to mount and ride,
Booted and spurred, with a heavy stride
On the opposite shore walked Paul Revere.
Now he patted his horse's side,   60
Now gazed at the landscape far and near,
Then, impetuous, stamped the earth,
And turned and tightened his saddle-girth;
But mostly he watched with eager search
The belfry-tower of the Old North Church,   65
As it rose above the graves on the hill,
Lonely and spectral and sombre and still.
And lo! as he looks, on the belfry's height
A glimmer, and then a gleam of light!
He springs to the saddle, the bridle he turns,   70
But lingers and gazes, till full on his sight
A second lamp in the belfry burns!

A hurry of hoofs in a village street,
A shape in the moonlight, a bulk in the dark,
And beneath, from the pebbles, in passing, a spark   75
Struck out by a steed flying fearless and fleet:
That was all! And yet, through the gloom and the light,
The fate of a nation was riding that night;
And the spark struck out by that steed, in his flight,
Kindled the land into flame with its heat.   80

He has left the village and mounted the steep,
And beneath him, tranquil and broad and deep,
Is the Mystic, meeting the ocean tides;
And under the alders, that skirt its edge,
Now soft on the sand, now loud on the ledge,   85
Is heard the tramp of his steed as he rides.

It was twelve by the village clock
When he crossed the bridge into Medford town.
He heard the crowing of the cock,
And the barking of the farmer's dog,   90
And felt the damp of the river fog,
That rises after the sun goes down.

It was one by the village clock,
When he galloped into Lexington.
He saw the gilded weathercock   95
Swim in the moonlight as he passed,
And the meeting-house windows, blank and bare,
Gaze at him with a spectral glare,
As if they already stood aghast
At the bloody work they would look upon.   100

It was two by the village clock,
When he came to the bridge in Concord town.
He heard the bleating of the flock,
And the twitter of birds among the trees,
And felt the breath of the morning breeze   105
Blowing over the meadows brown.
And one was safe and asleep in his bed
Who at the bridge would be first to fall,
Who that day would be lying dead,
Pierced by a British musket-ball.   110

You know the rest. In the books you have read,
How the British Regulars fired and fled,
How the farmers gave them ball for ball,
From behind each fence and farmyard wall;
Chasing the red-coats down the lane,   115
Then crossing the fields to emerge again
Under the trees at the turn of the road,
And only pausing to fire and load.

So through the night rode Paul Revere;
And so through the night went his cry of alarm   120
To every Middlesex village and farm—
A cry of defiance and not of fear,
A voice in the darkness, a knock at the door,
And a word that shall echo for evermore!
For, borne on a night-wind of the Past,   125
Through all our history, to the last,

216

In the hour of darkness and peril and need,
The people will waken and listen to hear
The hurrying hoof-beats of that steed,
And the midnight message of Paul Revere.   130

THOMAS BABINGTON MACAULAY,
LORD MACAULAY

1800–1859

From *Horatius*

LARS PORSENA of Clusium
   By the Nine Gods he swore
That the great house of Tarquin
   Should suffer wrong no more.
By the Nine Gods he swore it,   5
   And named a trysting day,
And bade his messengers ride forth,
East and west and south and north,
   To summon his array.

East and west and south and north   10
   The messengers ride fast,
And tower and town and cottage
   Have heard the trumpet's blast.
Shame on the false Etruscan
   Who lingers in his home,   15
When Porsena of Clusium
   Is on the march for Rome.

The horsemen and the footmen
   Are pouring in amain
From many a stately market-place;   20
   From many a fruitful plain;
From many a lonely hamlet,
   Which, hid by beech and pine,
Like an eagle's nest, hangs on the crest
   Of purple Apennine.   25

The harvests of Arretium,
  This year, old men shall reap;
This year, young boys in Umbro
  Shall plunge the struggling sheep;
And in the vats of Luna,   30
  This year, the must shall foam
Round the white feet of laughing girls
  Whose sires have marched to Rome.

And now hath every city
  Sent up her tale of men;   35
The foot are fourscore thousand,
  The horse are thousands ten.
Before the gates of Sutrium
  Is met the great array.
A proud man was Lars Porsena   40
  Upon the trysting day.

But by the yellow Tiber
  Was tumult and affright:
From all the spacious champaign
  To Rome men took their flight.   45
A mile around the city,
  The throng stopped up the ways;
A fearful sight it was to see
  Through two long nights and days.

Now, from the rock Tarpeian,   50
  Could the wan burghers spy
The line of blazing villages
  Red in the midnight sky.
The Fathers of the City,
  They sat all night and day,   55
For every hour some horseman came
  With tidings of dismay.

I wis, in all the Senate,
  There was no heart so bold,
But sore it ached, and fast it beat,   60
  When that ill news was told.
Forthwith up rose the Consul,
  Up rose the Fathers all;
In haste they girded up their gowns,
  And hied them to the wall.   65

218

They held a council standing
  Before the River Gate;
Short time was there, ye well may guess,
  For musing or debate.
Out spake the Consul roundly: 70
  'The bridge must straight go down;
For, since Janiculum is lost,
  Nought else can save the town.'

Just then a scout came flying,
  All wild with haste and fear: 75
'To arms! to arms! Sir Consul:
  Lars Porsena is here.'
On the low hills to westward
  The Consul fixed his eye,
And saw the swarthy storm of dust   80
  Rise fast along the sky.

And nearer fast and nearer
  Doth the red whirlwind come;
And louder still and still more loud,
From underneath that rolling cloud,   85
Is heard the trumpet's war-note proud,
  The trampling, and the hum.
And plainly and more plainly
  Now through the gloom appears,
Far to left and far to right,   90
In broken gleams of dark-blue light,
The long array of helmets bright,
  The long array of spears.

But the Consul's brow was sad,
  And the Consul's speech was low,   95
And darkly looked he at the wall,
  And darkly at the foe.
'Their van will be upon us
  Before the bridge goes down;
And if they once may win the bridge,   100
  What hope to save the town?'

Then out spake brave Horatius,
  The Captain of the Gate:
'To every man upon this earth
  Death cometh soon or late.   105

And how can man die better
  Than facing fearful odds,
For the ashes of his fathers,
  And the temples of his Gods?

'Hew down the bridge, Sir Consul,   110
  With all the speed ye may;
I, with two more to help me,
  Will hold the foe in play.
In yon straight path a thousand
  May well be stopped by three.   115
Now who will stand on either hand,
  And keep the bridge with me?'

Then out spake Spurius Lartius;
  A Ramnian proud was he:
'Lo, I will stand at thy right hand,   120
  And keep the bridge with thee.'
And out spake strong Herminius;
  Of Titian blood was he:
'I will abide on thy left side,
  And keep the bridge with thee.'   125

'Horatius,' quoth the Consul,
  'As thou sayest, so let it be.'
And straight against that great array
  Forth went the dauntless Three.
For Romans in Rome's quarrel   130
  Spared neither land nor gold,
Nor son nor wife, nor limb nor life,
  In the brave days of old.

Then none was for a party;
  Then all were for the state;   135
Then the great man helped the poor,
  And the poor man loved the great:
Then lands were fairly portioned;
  Then spoils were fairly sold:
The Romans were like brothers   140
  In the brave days of old.

Now while the Three were tightening
  Their harness on their backs,
The Consul was the foremost man
  To take in hand an axe: 145

And Fathers mixed with Commons
  Seized hatchet, bar, and crow,
And smote upon the planks above,
  And loosed the props below.

Meanwhile the Tuscan army,   150
  Right glorious to behold,
Came, flashing back the noonday light,
Rank behind rank, like surges bright
  Of a broad sea of gold.
Four hundred trumpets sounded   155
  A peal of warlike glee,
As that great host, with measured tread,
And spears advanced, and ensigns spread,
Rolled slowly towards the bridge's head,
  Where stood the dauntless Three.   160

The Three stood calm and silent,
  And looked upon the foes,
And a great shout of laughter
  From all the vanguard rose:
And forth three chiefs came spurring   165
  Before that deep array;
To earth they sprang, their swords they drew,
And lifted high their shields, and flew
  To win the narrow way;

Aunus from green Tifernum,   170
  Lord of the Hill of Vines;
And Seius, whose eight hundred slaves
  Sicken in Ilva's mines;
And Picus, long to Clusium
  Vassal in peace and war,   175
Who led to fight his Umbrian powers
From that grey crag where, girt with towers,
The fortress of Nequinum lowers
  O'er the pale waves of Nar.

Stout Lartius hurled down Aunus   180
  Into the stream beneath:
Herminius struck at Seius,
  And clove him to the teeth:
At Picus brave Horatius
  Darted one fiery thrust;   185
And the proud Umbrian's gilded arms
  Clashed in the bloody dust.

Then Ocnus of Falerii
  Rushed on the Roman Three;
And Lausulus of Urgo,   190
  The rover of the sea;
And Aruns of Volsinium,
  Who slew the great wild boar,
The great wild boar that had his den
Amidst the reeds of Cosa's fen,   195
And wasted fields, and slaughtered men,
  Along Albinia's shore.

Herminius smote down Aruns:
  Lartius laid Ocnus low:
Right to the heart of Lausulus   200
  Horatius sent a blow.
'Lie there,' he cried, 'fell pirate!
  No more, aghast and pale,
From Ostia's walls the crowd shall mark
The track of thy destroying bark.   205
No more Campania's hinds shall fly
To woods and caverns when they spy
  Thy thrice accursed sail.'

But now no sound of laughter
  Was heard among the foes.   210
A wild and wrathful clamour
  From all the vanguard rose.
Six spears' lengths from the entrance
  Halted that deep array,
And for a space no man came forth   215
  To win the narrow way.

But hark! the cry is Astur:
  And lo! the ranks divide;
And the great Lord of Luna
  Comes with his stately stride.   220
Upon his ample shoulders
  Clangs loud the four-fold shield,
And in his hand he shakes the brand
  Which none but he can wield.

He smiled on those bold Romans   225
  A smile serene and high;
He eyed the flinching Tuscans,
  And scorn was in his eye.

Quoth he, 'The she-wolf's litter
   Stand savagely at bay: 230
But will ye dare to follow,
   If Astur clears the way?'

Then, whirling up his broadsword
   With both hands to the height,
He rushed against Horatius,   235
   And smote with all his might.
With shield and blade Horatius
   Right deftly turned the blow.
The blow, though turned, came yet too nigh;
It missed his helm, but gashed his thigh: 240
The Tuscans raised a joyful cry
   To see the red blood flow.

He reeled, and on Herminius
   He leaned one breathing-space;
Then, like a wild cat mad with wounds,   245
   Sprang right at Astur's face.
Through teeth, and skull, and helmet
   So fierce a thrust he sped,
The good sword stood a hand-breadth out
   Behind the Tuscan's head.   250

And the great Lord of Luna
   Fell at that deadly stroke,
As falls on Mount Alvernus
   A thunder-smitten oak.
Far o'er the crashing forest   255
   The giant arms lie spread;
And the pale augurs, muttering low,
   Gaze on the blasted head.

On Astur's throat Horatius
   Right firmly pressed his heel,   260
And thrice and four times tugged amain,
   Ere he wrenched out the steel.
'And see,' he cried, 'the welcome,
   Fair guests, that waits you here!
What noble Lucumo comes next   265
   To taste our Roman cheer?'

But at his haughty challenge
  A sullen murmur ran,
Mingled of wrath, and shame, and dread,
  Along that glittering van.   270
There lacked not men of prowess,
  Nor men of lordly race;
For all Etruria's noblest
  Were round the fatal place.

But all Etruria's noblest   275
  Felt their hearts sink to see
On the earth the bloody corpses,
  In the path the dauntless Three:
And, from the ghastly entrance
  Where those bold Romans stood,   280
All shrank, like boys who unaware,
Ranging the woods to start a hare,
Come to the mouth of the dark lair
Where, growling low, a fierce old bear
  Lies amidst bones and blood.   285

Was none who would be foremost
  To lead such dire attack:
But those behind cried 'Forward!'
  And those before cried 'Back!'
And backward now and forward   290
  Wavers the deep array;
And on the tossing sea of steel,
To and fro the standards reel;
And the victorious trumpet-peal
  Dies fitfully away.   295

But meanwhile axe and lever
  Have manfully been plied;
And now the bridge hangs tottering
  Above the boiling tide.
'Come back, come back, Horatius!'   300
  Loud cried the Fathers all.
'Back, Lartius! back, Herminius!
  Back, ere the ruin fall!'

Back darted Spurius Lartius;
  Herminius darted back:
And, as they passed, beneath their feet   305
  They felt the timbers crack.

But when they turned their faces,
  And on the farther shore
Saw brave Horatius stand alone,   310
  They would have crossed once more.

But with a crash like thunder
  Fell every loosened beam,
And, like a dam, the mighty wreck
  Lay right athwart the stream: 315
And a long shout of triumph
  Rose from the walls of Rome,
As to the highest turret-tops
  Was splashed the yellow foam.

And, like a horse unbroken   320
  When first he feels the rein,
The furious river struggled hard,
  And tossed his tawny mane,
And burst the curb, and bounded,
  Rejoicing to be free,   325
And whirling down, in fierce career,
Battlement, and plank, and pier,
  Rushed headlong to the sea.

Alone stood brave Horatius,
  But constant still in mind;   330
Thrice thirty thousand foes before,
  And the broad flood behind.
'Down with him!' cried false Sextus,
  With a smile on his pale face.
'Now yield thee,' cried Lars Porsena,   335
  'Now yield thee to our grace.'

Round turned he, as not deigning
  Those craven ranks to see;
Nought spake he to Lars Porsena
  To Sextus nought spake he;   340
But he saw on Palatinus
  The white porch of his home;
And he spake to the noble river
  That rolls by the towers of Rome.

'Oh, Tiber! father Tiber!   345
  To whom the Romans pray,
A Roman's life, a Roman's arms,
  Take thou in charge this day!'

So he spake, and speaking sheathed
   The good sword by his side,   350
And with his harness on his back,
   Plunged headlong in the tide.

No sound of joy or sorrow
   Was heard from either bank;
But friends and foes in dumb surprise,   355
With parted lips and straining eyes,
   Stood gazing where he sank;
And when above the surges
   They saw his crest appear,
All Rome sent forth a rapturous cry,   360
And even the ranks of Tuscany
   Could scarce forbear to cheer.

But fiercely ran the current,
   Swollen high by months of rain:
And fast his blood was flowing;   365
   And he was sore in pain,
And heavy with his armour,
   And spent with changing blows:
And oft they thought him sinking,
   But still again he rose.   370

Never, I ween, did swimmer,
   In such an evil case,
Struggle through such a raging flood
   Safe to the landing place:
But his limbs were borne up bravely   375
   By the brave heart within,
And our good father Tiber
   Bare bravely up his chin.

And now he feels the bottom;
   Now on dry earth he stands;   380
Now round him throng the Fathers
   To press his gory hands;
And now, with shouts and clapping,
   And noise of weeping loud,
He enters through the River Gate,   385
   Borne by the joyous crowd.

They gave him of the corn-land,
  That was of public right,
As much as two strong oxen
  Could plough from morn till night;   390
And they made a molten image,
  And set it up on high,
And there it stands unto this day
  To witness if I lie.

It stands in the Comitium,   395
  Plain for all folk to see;
Horatius in his harness,
  Halting upon one knee:
And underneath is written,
  In letters all of gold,   400
How valiantly he kept the bridge
  In the brave days of old.

ROBERT BROWNING
1812–1889

The Pied Piper of Hamelin

HAMELIN TOWN's in Brunswick,
  By famous Hanover city;
The river Weser, deep and wide,
Washes its wall on the southern side;
A pleasanter spot you never spied;   5
  But, when begins my ditty,
Almost five hundred years ago,
To see the townsfolk suffer so
  From vermin, was a pity.

  Rats!   10
They fought the dogs and killed the cats,
  And bit the babies in the cradles,
And ate the cheeses out of the vats,
  And licked the soup from the cooks' own ladles,
Split open the kegs of salted sprats,   15
Made nests inside men's Sunday hats,

And even spoiled the women's chats
   By drowning their speaking
   With shrieking and squeaking
In fifty different sharps and flats.   20

At last the people in a body
   To the Town Hall came flocking:
''Tis clear,' cried they, 'our Mayor's a noddy;
   And as for our Corporation—shocking
To think we buy gowns lined with ermine   25
For dolts that can't or won't determine
What's best to rid us of our vermin!
You hope, because you're old and obese,
To find in the furry civic robe ease?
Rouse up, sirs! Give your brains a racking   30
To find the remedy we're lacking,
Or, sure as fate, we'll send you packing!'
At this the Mayor and Corporation
Quaked with a mighty consternation.

An hour they sat in council,   35
   At length the Mayor broke silence:
'For a guilder I'd my ermine gown sell,
   I wish I were a mile hence!
It's easy to bid one rack one's brain—
I'm sure my poor head aches again,   40
I've scratched it so, and all in vain.
Oh for a trap, a trap, a trap!'
Just as he said this, what should hap
At the chamber door but a gentle tap?
'Bless us,' cried the Mayor, 'what's that?'   45
(With the Corporation as he sat,
Looking little though wondrous fat;
Nor brighter was his eye, nor moister
Than a too-long-opened oyster,
Save when at noon his paunch grew mutinous   50
For a plate of turtle, green and glutinous)
'Only a scraping of shoes on the mat?
Anything like the sound of a rat
Makes my heart go pit-a-pat!'

'Come in!' the Mayor cried, looking bigger: 55
And in did come the strangest figure!
His queer long coat from heel to head
Was half of yellow and half of red,

And he himself was tall and thin,
With sharp blue eyes, each like a pin,   60
And light loose hair, yet swarthy skin,
No tuft on cheek nor beard on chin,
But lips where smiles went out and in;
There was no guessing his kith and kin:
And nobody could enough admire   65
The tall man and his quaint attire.
Quoth one: 'It's as my great-grandsire,
Starting up at the Trump of Doom's tone,
Had walked this way from his painted tombstone!'

He advanced to the council-table: 70
And, 'Please your honours,' said he, 'I'm able,
By means of a secret charm, to draw
   All creatures living beneath the sun,
   That creep or swim or fly or run,
After me so as you never saw!   75
And I chiefly use my charm
On creatures that do people harm,
The mole and toad and newt and viper;
And people call me the Pied Piper.'
(And here they noticed round his neck   80
   A scarf of red and yellow stripe,
To match with his coat of the self-same check;
   And at the scarf's end hung a pipe;
And his fingers, they noticed, were ever straying
As if impatient to be playing   85
Upon this pipe, as low it dangled
Over his vesture so old-fangled.)
'Yet,' said he, 'poor piper as I am,
In Tartary I freed the Cham,
   Last June, from his huge swarms of gnats;   90
I eased in Asia the Nizam
   Of a monstrous brood of vampire-bats:
And as for what your brain bewilders,
   If I can rid your town of rats
Will you give me a thousand guilders?'   95
'One? fifty thousand!'—was the exclamation
Of the astonished Mayor and Corporation.

Into the street the Piper stept,
   Smiling first a little smile,
As if he knew what magic slept   100
   In his quiet pipe the while;

Then, like a musical adept,
To blow the pipe his lips he wrinkled,
And green and blue his sharp eyes twinkled,
Like a candle-flame where salt is sprinkled;   105
And ere three shrill notes the pipe uttered,
You heard as if an army muttered;
And the muttering grew to a grumbling;
And the grumbling grew to a mighty rumbling;
And out of the houses the rats came tumbling.   110
Great rats, small rats, lean rats, brawny rats,
Brown rats, black rats, grey rats, tawny rats,
Grave old plodders, gay young friskers,
    Fathers, mothers, uncles, cousins,
Cocking tails and pricking whiskers,   115
    Families by tens and dozens,
Brothers, sisters, husbands, wives—
Followed the Piper for their lives.
From street to street he piped advancing,
And step for step they followed dancing,   120
Until they came to the river Weser,
    Wherein all plunged and perished!
—Save one who, stout as Julius Caesar,
Swam across and lived to carry
    (As he, the manuscript he cherished)   125
To Rat-land home his commentary:
Which was, 'At the first shrill notes of the pipe,
I heard a sound as of scraping tripe,
And putting apples, wondrous ripe,
Into a cider-press's gripe: 130
And a moving away of pickle-tub-boards,
And a leaving ajar of conserve-cupboards,
And a drawing the corks of train-oil-flasks,
And a breaking the hoops of butter-casks;
And it seemed as if a voice   135
    (Sweeter far than by harp or by psaltery
Is breathed) called out, "Oh rats, rejoice!
    The world is grown to one vast drysaltery!
So munch on, crunch on, take your nuncheon,
Breakfast, supper, dinner, luncheon!"   140
And just as a bulky sugar-puncheon,
All ready staved, like a great sun shone
Glorious scarce an inch before me,
Just as methought it said, "Come, bore me!"
—I found the Weser rolling o'er me.'   145

You should have heard the Hamelin people
Ringing the bells till they rocked the steeple.
'Go,' cried the Mayor, 'and get long poles,
Poke out the nests and block up the holes!
Consult with carpenters and builders,   150
And leave in our town not even a trace
Of the rats!'—when suddenly, up the face
Of the Piper perked in the market-place,
With a 'First, if you please, my thousand guilders!'

A thousand guilders! The Mayor looked blue;   155
So did the Corporation too.
For council dinners made rare havoc
With Claret, Moselle, Vin-de-Grave, Hock;
And half the money would replenish
Their cellar's biggest butt with Rhenish.   160
To pay this sum to a wandering fellow
With a gipsy coat of red and yellow!
'Beside,' quoth the Mayor with a knowing wink,
'Our business was done at the river's brink;
We saw with our eyes the vermin sink,   165
And what's dead can't come to life, I think.
So, friend, we're not the folks to shrink
From the duty of giving you something for drink,
And a matter of money to put in your poke;
But as for the guilders, what we spoke   170
Of them, as you very well know, was in joke.
Besides, our losses have made us thrifty.
A thousand guilders! Come, take fifty!'

The Piper's face fell, and he cried
'No trifling! I can't wait, beside!   175
I've promised to visit by dinnertime
Baghdad, and accept the prime
Of the Head-Cook's pottage, all he's rich in,
For having left, in the Caliph's kitchen,
Of a nest of scorpions no survivor: 180
With him I proved no bargain-driver,
With you, don't think I'll bate a stiver!
And folks who put me in a passion
May find me pipe after another fashion.'

'How?' cried the Mayor, 'd'ye think I brook   185
Being worse treated than a cook?

Insulted by a lazy ribald
With idle pipe and vesture piebald?
You threaten us, fellow? Do your worst,
Blow your pipe there till you burst!'   190

Once more he stepped into the street
  And to his lips again
  Laid his long pipe of smooth straight cane;
And ere he blew three notes (such sweet
Soft notes as yet musician's cunning   195
  Never gave the enraptured air)
There was a rustling that seemed like a bustling
Of merry crowds justling at pitching and hustling
Small feet were pattering, wooden shoes clattering,
Little hands clapping and little tongues chattering,   200
And, like fowls in a farmyard when barley is scattering,
Out came the children running.
All the little boys and girls,
With rosy cheeks and flaxen curls,
And sparkling eyes and teeth like pearls,   205
Tripping and skipping, ran merrily after
The wonderful music with shouting and laughter.

The Mayor was dumb, and the Council stood
As if they were changed into blocks of wood,
Unable to move a step, or cry   210
To the children merrily skipping by
—Could only follow with the eye
That joyous crowd at the Piper's back.
But how the Mayor was on the rack,
And the wretched Council's bosoms beat,   215
As the Piper turned from the High Street
To where the Weser rolled its waters
Right in the way of their sons and daughters!
However he turned from south to west,
And to Koppelberg Hill his steps addressed,   220
And after him the children pressed;
Great was the joy in every breast.
'He never can cross that mighty top!
He's forced to let the piping drop,
And we shall see our children stop!'   225
When, lo, as they reached the mountain-side,
A wondrous portal opened wide,
As if a cavern was suddenly hollowed;
And the Piper advanced and the children followed,

And when all were in to the very last,   230
The door in the mountain-side shut fast.
Did I say, all? No! One was lame,
   And could not dance the whole of the way;
And in after years, if you would blame
   His sadness, he was used to say—   235
'It's dull in our town since my playmates left!
I can't forget that I'm bereft
Of all the pleasant sights they see,
Which the Piper also promised me.
For he led us, he said, to a joyous land,   240
Joining the town and just at hand,
Where waters gushed and fruit trees grew
And flowers put forth a fairer hue,
And everything was strange and new;
The sparrows were brighter than peacocks here,   245
And their dogs outran our fallow deer,
And honey-bees had lost their stings,
And horses were born with eagles' wings:
And just as I became assured
My lame foot would be speedily cured,   250
The music stopped and I stood still,
And found myself outside the hill,
Left alone against my will,
To go now limping as before,
And never hear of that country more!'   255

Alas, alas for Hamelin!
   There came into many a burgher's pate
   A text which says that heaven's gate
   Opes to the rich at as easy rate
As the needle's eye takes a camel in!   260
The Mayor sent east, west, north, and south,
To offer the Piper, by word of mouth,
   Wherever it was men's lot to find him,
Silver and gold to his heart's content,
If he'd only return the way he went,   265
   And bring the children behind him.
But when they saw 'twas a lost endeavour,
And Piper and dancers were gone for ever,
They made a decree that lawyers never
   Should think their records dated duly   270
If, after the day of the month and year,
These words did not as well appear,

233

'And so long after what happened here
  On the Twenty-second of July,
Thirteen hundred and seventy-six':   275
And the better in memory to fix
The place of the children's last retreat,
They called it the Pied Piper's Street—
Where anyone playing on pipe or tabor
Was sure for the future to lose his labour.   280
Nor suffered they hostelry or tavern
  To shock with mirth a street so solemn;
But opposite the place of the cavern
  They wrote the story on a column;
And on the great church-window painted   285
The same, to make the world acquainted
How their children were stolen away,
And there it stands to this very day.
And I must not omit to say
That in Transylvania there's a tribe   290
Of alien people who ascribe
The outlandish ways and dress
On which their neighbours lay such stress,
To their fathers and mothers having risen
Out of some subterraneous prison   295
Into which they were trepanned
Long time ago in a mighty band
Out of Hamelin town in Brunswick land,
But how or why, they don't understand.

The Italian in England

THAT second time they hunted me
From hill to plain, from shore to sea,
And Austria, hounding far and wide
Her bloodhounds through the countryside,
Breathed hot and instant on my trace—   5
I made six days a hiding-place
Of that dry green old aqueduct
Where I and Charles, when boys, have plucked
The fireflies from the roof above,
Bright creeping through the moss they love: 10
—How long it seems since Charles was lost!
Six days the soldiers crossed and crossed

The country in my very sight;
And when that peril ceased at night,
The sky broke out in red dismay   15
With signal fires; well, there I lay
Close covered o'er in my recess,
Up to the neck in ferns and cress,
Thinking on Metternich our friend,
And Charles's miserable end,   20
And much beside, two days; the third,
Hunger o'ercame me when I heard
The peasants from the village go
To work among the maize; you know,
With us in Lombardy, they bring   25
Provisions packed on mules, a string
With little bells that cheer their task,
And casks, and boughs on every cask
To keep the sun's heat from the wine;
These I let pass in jingling line,   30
And, close on them, dear noisy crew,
The peasants from the village, too;
For at the very rear would troop
Their wives and sisters in a group
To help, I knew. When these had passed,   35
I threw my glove to strike the last,
Taking the chance: she did not start,
Much less cry out, but stooped apart,
One instant rapidly glanced round,
And saw me beckon from the ground.   40
A wild bush grows and hides my crypt;
She picked my glove up while she stripped
A branch off, then rejoined the rest
With that; my glove lay in her breast.
Then I drew breath; they disappeared: 45
It was for Italy I feared.

   An hour, and she returned alone
Exactly where my glove was thrown.
Meanwhile came many thoughts: on me
Rested the hopes of Italy.   50
I had devised a certain tale
Which, when 't was told her, could not fail
Persuade a peasant of its truth;
I meant to call a freak of youth
This hiding, and give hopes of pay,   55
And no temptation to betray.

But when I saw that woman's face,
Its calm simplicity of grace,
Our Italy's own attitude
In which she walked thus far, and stood,   60
Planting each naked foot so firm,
To crush the snake and spare the worm—
At first sight of her eyes, I said,
'I am that man upon whose head
They fix the price, because I hate   65
The Austrians over us: the State
Will give you gold—oh, gold so much!—
If you betray me to their clutch,
And be your death, for aught I know,
If once they find you saved their foe.   70
Now, you must bring me food and drink,
And also paper, pen and ink,
And carry safe what I shall write
To Padua, which you'll reach at night
Before the duomo shuts; go in,   75
And wait till Tenebræ begin;
Walk to the third confessional,
Between the pillar and the wall,
And kneeling whisper, *Whence comes peace?*
Say it a second time, then cease;   80
And if the voice inside returns,
*From Christ and Freedom; what concerns
The cause of Peace?*—for answer, slip
My letter where you placed your lip;
Then come back happy we have done   85
Our mother service—I, the son,
As you the daughter of our land!'

   Three mornings more, she took her stand
In the same place, with the same eyes:
I was no surer of sunrise   90
Than of her coming. We conferred
Of her own prospects, and I heard
She had a lover—stout and tall,
She said—then let her eyelids fall,
'He could do much'—as if some doubt   95
Entered her heart,—then, passing out,
'She could not speak for others, who
Had other thoughts; herself she knew:'
And so she brought me drink and food.
After four days, the scouts pursued   100

Another path; at last arrived
The help my Paduan friends contrived
To furnish me: she brought the news.
For the first time I could not choose
But kiss her hand, and lay my own   105
Upon her head—'This faith was shown
To Italy, our mother; she
Uses my hand and blesses thee.'
She followed down to the sea-shore;
I left and never saw her more.   110

   How very long since I have thought
Concerning—much less wished for—aught
Beside the good of Italy,
For which I live and mean to die!
I never was in love; and since   115
Charles proved false, what shall now convince
My inmost heart I have a friend?
However, if I pleased to spend
Real wishes on myself—say, three—
I know at least what one should be.   120
I would grasp Metternich until
I felt his red wet throat distil
In blood through these two hands. And next
—Nor much for that am I perplexed—
Charles, perjured traitor, for his part,   125
Should die slow of a broken heart
Under his new employers. Last
—Ah, there, what should I wish? For fast
Do I grow old and out of strength.
If I resolved to seek at length   130
My father's house again, how scared
They all would look, and unprepared!
My brothers live in Austria's pay
—Disowned me long ago, men say;
And all my early mates who used   135
To praise me so—perhaps induced
More than one early step of mine—
Are turning wise: while some opine
'Freedom grows license,' some suspect
'Haste breeds delay,' and recollect   140
They always said, such premature
Beginnings never could endure.
So, with a sullen 'All's for best,'
The land seems settling to its rest.

I think then, I should wish to stand   145
This evening in that dear, lost land,
Over the sea the thousand miles,
And know if yet that woman smiles
With the calm smile; some little farm
She lives in there, no doubt: what harm   150
If I sat on the doorside bench,
And, while her spindle made a trench
Fantastically in the dust,
Inquired of all her fortunes—just
Her children's ages and their names,   155
And what may be the husband's aims
For each of them. I'd talk this out,
And sit there, for an hour about,
Then kiss her hand once more, and lay
Mine on her head, and go my way.   160

So much for idle wishing—how
It steals the time! To business now.

'Childe Roland to the Dark Tower Came'

MY first thought was, he lied in every word,
   That hoary cripple, with malicious eye
   Askance to watch the working of his lie
On mine, and mouth scarce able to afford
Suppression of the glee, that pursed and scored   5
   Its edge, at one more victim gained thereby.

What else should he be set for, with his staff?
   What, save to waylay with his lies, ensnare
   All travellers who might find him posted there,
And ask the road? I guessed what skull-like laugh   10
Would break, what crutch 'gin write my epitaph
   For pastime in the dusty thoroughfare,

If at his counsel I should turn aside
   Into that ominous tract which, all agree,
   Hides the Dark Tower. Yet acquiescingly   15
I did turn as he pointed: neither pride
Nor hope rekindling at the end descried,
   So much as gladness that some end might be.

For, what with my whole world-wide wandering,
  What with my search drawn out through years, my hope   20
  Dwindled into a ghost not fit to cope
With that obstreperous joy success would bring—
I hardly tried now to rebuke the spring
  My heart made, finding failure in its scope.

As when a sick man very near to death   25
  Seems dead indeed, and feels begin and end
  The tears and takes the farewell of each friend,
And hears one bid the other go, draw breath
Freelier outside ('since all is o'er,' he saith,
  'And the blow fallen no grieving can amend');   30

While some discuss if near the other graves
  Be room enough for this, and when a day
  Suits best for carrying the corpse away,
With care about the banners, scarves and staves:
And still the man hears all, and only craves   35
  He may not shame such tender love and stay.

Thus, I had so long suffered in this quest,
  Heard failure prophesied so oft, been writ
  So many times among 'The Band'—to wit,
The knights who to the Dark Tower's search addressed   40
Their steps—that just to fail as they, seemed best,
  And all the doubt was now—should I be fit?

So, quiet as despair, I turned from him,
  That hateful cripple, out of his highway
  Into the path he pointed. All the day   45
Had been a dreary one at best, and dim
Was settling to its close, yet shot one grim
  Red leer to see the plain catch its estray.

For mark! no sooner was I fairly found
  Pledged to the plain, after a pace or two,   50
  Than, pausing to throw backward a last view
O'er the safe road, 'twas gone; grey plain all round:
Nothing but plain to the horizon's bound.
  I might go on; nought else remained to do.

So, on I went. I think I never saw   55
  Such starved ignoble nature; nothing throve:
  For flowers—as well expect a cedar grove!

But cockle, spurge, according to their law
Might propagate their kind, with none to awe,
   You'd think; a burr had been a treasure trove.   60

No! penury, inertness and grimace,
   In some strange sort, were the land's portion. 'See
   Or shut your eyes,' said Nature peevishly,
'It nothing skills: I cannot help my case:
   'Tis the Last Judgment's fire must cure this place,   65
   Calcine its clods and set my prisoners free.'

If there pushed any ragged thistle stalk
   Above its mates, the head was chopped; the bents
   Were jealous else. What made those holes and rents
In the dock's harsh swarth leaves, bruised as to baulk   70
All hope of greenness? 'tis a brute must walk
   Pashing their life out, with a brute's intents.

As for the grass, it grew as scant as hair
   In leprosy; thin dry blades pricked the mud
   Which underneath looked kneaded up with blood.   75
One stiff blind horse, his every bone a-stare,
Stood stupefied, however he came there:
   Thrust out past service from the devil's stud!

Alive? he might be dead for aught I know,
   With that red gaunt and colloped neck a-strain,   80
   And shut eyes underneath the rusty mane;
Seldom went such grotesqueness with such woe;
I never saw a brute I hated so;
   He must be wicked to deserve such pain.

I shut my eyes and turned them on my heart.   85
   As a man calls for wine before he fights,
   I asked one draught of earlier, happier sights,
Ere fitly I could hope to play my part.
Think first, fight afterwards—the soldier's art:
   One taste of the old time sets all to rights.   90

Not it! I fancied Cuthbert's reddening face
   Beneath its garniture of curly gold,
   Dear fellow, till I almost felt him fold
An arm in mine to fix me to the place,
That way he used. Alas, one night's disgrace!   95
   Out went my heart's new fire and left it cold.

Giles then, the soul of honour—there he stands
  Frank as ten years ago when knighted first.
  What honest men should dare (he said) he durst.
Good—but the scene shifts—faugh! what hangman-hands   100
Pin to his breast a parchment? his own bands
  Read it. Poor traitor, spit upon and curst!

Better this present than a past like that;
  Back therefore to my darkening path again!
  No sound, no sight as far as eye could strain.   105
Will the night send a howlet or a bat?
I asked: when something on the dismal flat
  Came to arrest my thoughts and change their train.

A sudden little river crossed my path
  As unexpected as a serpent comes.   110
  No sluggish tide congenial to the glooms;
This, as it frothed by, might have been a bath
For the fiend's glowing hoof—to see the wrath
  Of its black eddy bespate with flakes and spumes.

So petty yet so spiteful! All along,   115
  Low scrubby alders kneeled down over it;
  Drenched willows flung them headlong in a fit
Of mute despair, a suicidal throng:
The river which had done them all the wrong,
  Whate'er that was, rolled by, deterred no whit.   120

Which, while I forded—good saints, how I feared
  To set my foot upon a dead man's cheek,
  Each step, or feel the spear I thrust to seek
For hollows, tangled in his hair or beard!
—It may have been a water-rat I speared,   125
  But, ugh! it sounded like a baby's shriek.

Glad was I when I reached the other bank.
  Now for a better country. Vain presage!
  Who were the strugglers, what war did they wage,
Whose savage trample thus could pad the dank   130
Soil to a plash? Toads in a poisoned tank,
  Or wild cats in a red-hot iron cage—

The fight must so have seemed in that fell cirque.
  What penned them there, with all the plain to choose?
  No footprint leading to that horrid mews,   135

None out of it. Mad brewage set to work
Their brains, no doubt, like galley-slaves the Turk
   Pits for his pastime, Christians against Jews.

And more than that—a furlong on—why, there!
   What bad use was that engine for, that wheel,   140
   Or brake, not wheel—that harrow fit to reel
Men's bodies out like silk? with all the air
Of Tophet's tool, on earth left unaware,
   Or brought to sharpen its rusty teeth of steel.

Then came a bit of stubbed ground, once a wood,   145
   Next a marsh, it would seem, and now mere earth
   Desperate and done with (so a fool finds mirth,
Makes a thing and then mars it, till his mood
Changes and off he goes!) within a rood—
   Bog, clay and rubble, sand and stark black dearth.   150

Now blotches rankling, coloured gay and grim,
   Now patches where some leanness of the soil's
   Broke into moss or substances like boils;
Then came some palsied oak, a cleft in him
Like a distorted mouth that splits its rim   155
   Gaping at death, and dies while it recoils.

And just as far as ever from the end!
   Nought in the distance but the evening, nought
   To point my footstep further! At the thought,
A great black bird, Apollyon's bosom friend,   160
Sailed past, nor beat his wide wing dragon-penned
   That brushed my cap—perchance the guide I sought.

For, looking up, aware I somehow grew,
   'Spite of the dusk, the plain had given place
   All round to mountains—with such name to grace   165
Mere ugly heights and heaps now stolen in view.
How thus they had surprised me—solve it, you!
   How to get from them was no clearer case.

Yet half I seemed to recognize some trick
   Of mischief happened to me, God knows when—   170
   In a bad dream perhaps. Here ended, then,
Progress this way. When, in the very nick
Of giving up, one time more, came a click
   As when a trap shuts—you're inside the den!

Burningly it came on me all at once,   175
    This was the place! those two hills on the right,
Crouched like two bulls locked horn in horn in fight;
While to the left, a tall scalped mountain ... Dunce,
Dotard, a-dozing at the very nonce,
    After a life spent training for the sight!   180

What in the midst lay but the Tower itself?
    The round squat turret, blind as the fool's heart,
    Built of brown stone, without a counterpart
In the whole world. The tempest's mocking elf
Points to the shipman thus the unseen shelf   185
    He strikes on, only when the timbers start.

Not see? because of night perhaps?—why, day
    Came back again for that! before it left,
    The dying sunset kindled through a cleft:
The hills, like giants at a hunting, lay,   190
Chin upon hand, to see the game at bay—
    'Now stab and end the creature—to the heft!'

Not hear? when noise was everywhere! it tolled
    Increasing like a bell. Names in my ears
    Of all the lost adventurers my peers—   195
How such a one was strong, and such was bold,
And such was fortunate, yet each of old
    Lost, lost! one moment knelled the woe of years.

There they stood, ranged along the hillsides, met
    To view the last of me, a living frame   200
    For one more picture! in a sheet of flame
I saw them and I knew them all. And yet
Dauntless the slug-horn to my lips I set,
    And blew. '*Childe Roland to the Dark Tower came.*'

EDGAR ALLAN POE
1809–1849

The Raven

ONCE upon a midnight dreary, while I pondered, weak and weary,
Over many a quaint and curious volume of forgotten lore—
While I nodded, nearly napping, suddenly there came a tapping,
As of someone gently rapping, rapping at my chamber door.
''Tis some visitor,' I muttered, 'tapping at my chamber door—   5
        Only this and nothing more.'

Ah, distinctly I remember it was in the bleak December;
And each separate dying ember wrought its ghost upon the floor.
Eagerly I wished the morrow; vainly I had sought to borrow
From my books surcease of sorrow—sorrow for the lost Lenore—   10
For the rare and radiant maiden whom the angels name Lenore—
        Nameless *here* for evermore.

And the silken, sad, uncertain rustling of each purple curtain
Thrilled me— filled me with fantastic terrors never felt before;
So that now, to still the beating of my heart, I stood repeating,   15
''Tis some visitor entreating entrance at my chamber door—
Some late visitor entreating entrance at my chamber door—
        This it is and nothing more.'

Presently my soul grew stronger; hesitating then no longer,
'Sir,' said I, 'or Madam, truly your forgiveness I implore;   20
But the fact is I was napping, and so gently you came rapping,
And so faintly you came tapping, tapping at my chamber door,
That I scarce was sure I heard you'—here I opened wide the
    door—
        Darkness there and nothing more.

Deep into that darkness peering, long I stood there wondering,
    fearing,   25
Doubting, dreaming dreams no mortal ever dared to dream before;
But the silence was unbroken, and the stillness gave no token,
And the only word there spoken was the whispered word, 'Lenore?'
This I whispered, and an echo murmured back the word, 'Lenore!'
        Merely this and nothing more.   30

Back into the chamber turning, all my soul within me burning,
Soon again I heard a tapping somewhat louder than before.
'Surely,' said I, 'surely that is something at my window lattice;
Let me see, then, what thereat is, and this mystery explore—
Let my heart be still a moment and this mystery explore— 35
      'Tis the wind and nothing more!'

Open here I flung the shutter, when, with many a flirt and flutter,
In there stepped a stately Raven of the saintly days of yore;
Not the least obeisance made he; not a minute stopped or stayed he;
But, with mien of lord or lady, perched above my chamber door— 40
Perched upon a bust of Pallas just above my chamber door—
      Perched, and sat, and nothing more.

Then this ebony bird beguiling my sad fancy into smiling,
By the grave and stern decorum of the countenance it wore,
'Though thy crest be shorn and shaven, thou,' I said, 'art sure no
   craven, 45
Ghastly grim and ancient Raven wandering from the Nightly shore—
Tell me what thy lordly name is on the Night's Plutonian shore!'
      Quoth the Raven, 'Nevermore.'

Much I marvelled this ungainly fowl to hear discourse so plainly,
Though its answer little meaning—little relevancy bore; 50
For we cannot help agreeing that no living human being
Ever yet was blessed with seeing bird above his chamber door—
Bird or beast upon the sculptured bust above his chamber door,
      With such name as 'Nevermore.'

But the Raven, sitting lonely on the placid bust, spoke only 55
That one word, as if his soul in that one word he did outpour.
Nothing farther then he uttered—not a feather then he fluttered—
Till I scarcely more than muttered, 'Other friends have flown
   before—
On the morrow *he* will leave me, as my Hopes have flown before.'
      Then the bird said, 'Nevermore.' 60

Startled at the stillness broken by reply so aptly spoken,
'Doubtless,' said I, 'what it utters is its only stock and store
Caught from some unhappy master whom unmerciful Disaster
Followed fast and followed faster till his songs one burden bore—
Till the dirges of his Hope that melancholy burden bore 65
      Of "Never—nevermore." '

But the Raven still beguiling my sad fancy into smiling,
Straight I wheeled a cushioned seat in front of bird and bust and
    door;
Then, upon the velvet sinking, I betook myself to linking
Fancy unto fancy, thinking what this ominous bird of yore—   70
What this grim, ungainly, ghastly, gaunt, and ominous bird of yore
               Meant in croaking 'Nevermore.'

This I sat engaged in guessing, but no syllable expressing
To the fowl whose fiery eyes now burned into my bosom's core;
This and more I sat divining, with my head at ease reclining   75
On the cushion's velvet lining that the lamplight gloated o'er,
But whose velvet-violet lining with the lamplight gloating o'er,
               She shall press, ah, nevermore!

Then, methought, the air grew denser, perfumed from an unseen
    censer
Swung by seraphim whose footfalls tinkled on the tufted floor.   80
'Wretch,' I cried, 'thy God hath lent thee—by these angels he hath
    sent thee
Respite—respite and nepenthe from thy memories of Lenore;
Quaff, oh quaff this kind nepenthe and forget this lost Lenore!'
               Quoth the Raven, 'Nevermore.'

'Prophet!' said I, 'thing of evil!—prophet still, if bird or devil!—   85
Whether Tempter sent, or whether tempest tossed thee here ashore,
Desolate yet all undaunted, on this desert land enchanted—
On this home by Horror haunted—tell me truly, I implore—
Is there—*is* there balm in Gilead?—tell me—tell me, I implore!'
               Quoth the Raven, 'Nevermore.'   90

'Prophet!' said I, 'thing of evil!—prophet still, if bird or devil!
By that Heaven that bends above us—by that God we both adore—
Tell this soul with sorrow laden if, within the distant Aidenn,
It shall clasp a sainted maiden whom the angels name Lenore—
Clasp a rare and radiant maiden whom the angels name Lenore.'   95
               Quoth the Raven, 'Nevermore.'

'Be that word our sign of parting, bird or fiend!' I shrieked,
    upstarting—
'Get thee back into the tempest and the Night's Plutonian shore!
Leave no black plume as a token of that lie thy soul hath spoken!
Leave my loneliness unbroken!—quit the bust above my door!   100
Take thy beak from out my heart, and take thy form from off my
    door!'
               Quoth the Raven, 'Nevermore.'

And the Raven, never flitting, still is sitting, *still* is sitting
On the pallid bust of Pallas just above my chamber door;
And his eyes have all the seeming of a demon's that is dreaming,   105
And the lamplight o'er him streaming throws his shadow on the floor;
And my soul from out that shadow that lies floating on the floor
       Shall be lifted—nevermore!

MATTHEW ARNOLD
1822–1888

The Forsaken Merman

  COME, dear children, let us away;
    Down and away below!
Now my brothers call from the bay,
Now the great winds shoreward blow,
Now the salt tides seaward flow,   5
Now the wild white horses play,
Champ and chafe and toss in the spray.
  Children dear, let us away!
    This way, this way!

Call her once before you go—   10
    Call once yet.
In a voice that she will know:
  'Margaret! Margaret!'
Children's voices should be dear
(Call once more) to a mother's ear;   15
Children's voices, wild with pain—
Surely she will come again.
Call her once and come away;
    This way, this way!
'Mother dear, we cannot stay.   20
The wild white horses foam and fret.'
  Margaret! Margaret!

  Come, dear children, come away down;
    Call no more.
    One last look at the white-walled town,   25
And the little grey church on the windy shore.
    Then come down.
    She will not come though you call all day.
    Come away, come away!

Children dear, was it yesterday   30
We heard the sweet bells over the bay?
In the caverns where we lay,
Through the surf and through the swell,
The far-off sound of a silver bell?
Sand-strewn caverns, cool and deep,   35
Where the winds are all asleep;
Where the spent lights quiver and gleam,
Where the salt weed sways in the stream,
Where the sea-beasts, ranged all round,
Feed in the ooze of their pasture-ground;   40
Where the sea-snakes coil and twine,
Dry their mail and bask in the brine;
Where great whales come sailing by,
Sail and sail, with unshut eye,
Round the world for ever and aye?   45
When did music come this way?
Children dear, was it yesterday?

Children dear, was it yesterday
(Call yet once) that she went away?
Once she sate with you and me,   50
On a red gold throne in the heart of the sea,
    And the youngest sate on her knee.
She combed its bright hair, and she tended it well,
When down swung the sound of the far-off bell.
She sighed, she looked up through the clear green sea;   55
She said, 'I must go, for my kinsfolk pray
In the little grey church on the shore today.
'Twill be Easter-time in the world—ah me!
And I lose my poor soul, Merman, here with thee.'
I said, 'Go up, dear heart, through the waves.   60
Say thy prayer, and come back to the kind sea-caves.'
She smiled, she went up through the surf in the bay.
    Children dear, was it yesterday?

    Children dear, were we long alone?
'The sea grows stormy, the little ones moan.   65
Long prayers,' I said, 'in the world they say.
Come,' I said, and we rose through the surf in the bay.
We went up the beach, by the sandy down
Where the sea-stocks bloom, to the white-walled town;
Through the narrow paved streets, where all was still,   70
To the little grey church on the windy hill.

From the church came a murmur of folk at their prayers,
But we stood without in the cold blowing airs.
We climbed on the graves, on the stones worn with rains,
And we gazed up the aisle through the small leaded panes. 75
    She sate by the pillar; we saw her clear:
    'Margaret, hist! come quick, we are here.
    Dear heart,' I said, 'we are long alone.
    The sea grows stormy, the little ones moan.'
But ah! she gave me never a look, 80
For her eyes were sealed to the holy book.
Loud prays the priest; shut stands the door.
    Come away, children, call no more.
    Come away, come down, call no more.

    Down, down, down; 85
    Down to the depth of the sea.
She sits at her wheel in the humming town,
    Singing most joyfully.
Hark what she sings: 'O joy, O joy,
For the humming street, and the child with its toy. 90
For the priest, and the bell, and the holy well;
For the wheel where I spun,
And the blessed light of the sun.'
And so she sings her fill,
Singing most joyfully, 95
Till the spindle falls from her hand,
And the whizzing wheel stands still.
She steals to the window, and looks at the sand,
    And over the sand at the sea;
    And her eyes are set in a stare; 100
    And anon there breaks a sigh,
    And anon there drops a tear,
    From a sorrow-clouded eye,
    And a heart sorrow-laden,
    A long, long sigh; 105
For the cold strange eyes of a little mermaiden,
    And the gleam of her golden hair.

    Come away, away, children.
    Come children, come down!
The hoarse wind blows coldly; 110
Lights shine in the town.
She will start from her slumber
When gusts shake the door;
She will hear the winds howling,
Will hear the waves roar. 115

We shall see, while above us
The waves roar and whirl,
A ceiling of amber,
A pavement of pearl.
Singing, 'Here came a mortal,   120
But faithless was she:
And alone dwell for ever
The kings of the sea.'

But, children, at midnight,
When soft the winds blow,   125
When clear falls the moonlight,
When spring-tides are low;
When sweet airs come seaward
From heaths starred with broom;
And high rocks throw mildly   130
On the blanched sands a gloom;
Up the still, glistening beaches,
Up the creeks we will hie;
Over banks of bright seaweed
The ebb-tide leaves dry.   135
We will gaze, from the sand-hills,
At the white, sleeping town;
At the church on the hillside—
    And then come back down.
Singing, 'There dwells a loved one,   140
    But cruel is she.
She left lonely for ever
    The kings of the sea.'

Sohrab and Rustum

AND the first grey of morning filled the east,
And the fog rose out of the Oxus stream.
But all the Tartar camp along the stream
Was hushed, and still the men were plunged in sleep:
Sohrab alone, he slept not: all night long   5
He had lain wakeful, tossing on his bed;
But when the grey dawn stole into his tent,
He rose, and clad himself, and girt his sword,
And took his horseman's cloak, and left his tent,
And went abroad into the cold wet fog,   10
Through the dim camp to Peran-Wisa's tent.

Through the black Tartar tents he passed, which stood
Clustering like bee-hives on the low flat strand
Of Oxus, where the summer floods o'erflow
When the sun melts the snows in high Pamere: 15
Through the black tents he passed, o'er that low strand,
And to a hillock came, a little back
From the stream's brink, the spot where first a boat,
Crossing the stream in summer, scrapes the land.
The men of former times had crowned the top   20
With a clay fort: but that was fallen; and now
The Tartars built there Peran-Wisa's tent,
A dome of laths, and o'er it felts were spread.
And Sohrab came there, and went in, and stood
Upon the thick-piled carpets in the tent,   25
And found the old man sleeping on his bed
Of rugs and felts, and near him lay his arms.
And Peran-Wisa heard him, though the step
Was dulled; for he slept light, an old man's sleep;
And he rose quickly on one arm, and said: 30
    'Who art thou? for it is not yet clear dawn.
Speak! is there news, or any night alarm?'
    But Sohrab came to the bedside, and said:
'Thou know'st me, Peran-Wisa: it is I.
The sun is not yet risen, and the foe   35
Sleep; but I sleep not; all night long I lie
Tossing and wakeful, and I come to thee.
For so did King Afrasiab bid me seek
Thy counsel, and to heed thee as thy son,
In Samarcand, before the army marched;   40
And I will tell thee what my heart desires.
Thou know'st if, since from Ader-baijan first
I came among the Tartars, and bore arms,
I have still served Afrasiab well, and shown,
At my boy's years, the courage of a man.   45
This too thou know'st, that, while I still bear on
The conquering Tartar ensigns through the world,
And beat the Persians back on every field,
I seek one man, one man, and one alone—
Rustum, my father; who, I hoped, should greet,   50
Should one day greet, upon some well-fought field
His not unworthy, not inglorious son.
So I long hoped, but him I never find.
Come then, hear now, and grant me what I ask.
Let the two armies rest today: but I   55
Will challenge forth the bravest Persian lords

To meet me, man to man: if I prevail,
Rustum will surely hear it; if I fall—
Old man, the dead need no one, claim no kin.
Dim is the rumour of a common fight, 60
Where host meets host, and many names are sunk:
But of a single combat fame speaks clear.'
  He spoke: and Peran-Wisa took the hand
Of the young man in his, and sighed, and said:
  'O Sohrab, an unquiet heart is thine! 65
Canst thou not rest among the Tartar chiefs,
And share the battle's common chance with us
Who love thee, but must press for ever first,
In single fight incurring single risk,
To find a father thou hast never seen? 70
That were far best, my son, to stay with us
Unmurmuring; in our tents, while it is war,
And when 'tis truce, then in Afrasiab's towns.
But, if this one desire indeed rules all,
To seek out Rustum—seek him not through fight: 75
Seek him in peace, and carry to his arms,
O Sohrab, carry an unwounded son!
But far hence seek him, for he is not here.
For now it is not as when I was young,
When Rustum was in front of every fray: 80
But now he keeps apart, and sits at home,
In Seistan, with Zal, his father old.
Whether that his own mighty strength at last
Feels the abhorred approaches of old age;
Or in some quarrel with the Persian King. 85
There go!—Thou wilt not? Yet my heart forebodes
Danger or death awaits thee on this field.
Fain would I know thee safe and well, though lost
To us: fain therefore send thee hence, in peace
To seek thy father, not seek single fights 90
In vain:—but who can keep the lion's cub
From ravening? and who govern Rustum's son?
Go: I will grant thee what thy heart desires.'
  So said he, and dropped Sohrab's hand, and left
His bed, and the warm rugs whereon he lay, 95
And o'er his chilly limbs his woollen coat
He passed, and tied his sandals on his feet,
And threw a white cloak round him, and he took
In his right hand a ruler's staff, no sword;
And on his head he set his sheepskin cap, 100
Black, glossy, curled, the fleece of Kara-Kul;

And raised the curtain of his tent, and called
His herald to his side, and went abroad.
　　The sun, by this, had risen, and cleared the fog
From the broad Oxus and the glittering sands:　　　　105
And from their tents the Tartar horsemen filed
Into the open plain; so Haman bade;
Haman, who next to Peran-Wisa ruled
The host, and still was in his lusty prime.
From their black tents, long files of horse, they streamed:　110
As when, some grey November morn, the files,
In marching order spread, of long-necked cranes,
Stream over Casbin, and the southern slopes
Of Elburz, from the Aralian estuaries.
Or some frore Caspian reed-bed, southward bound　　　115
For the warm Persian sea-board: so they streamed.
The Tartars of the Oxus, the King's guard,
First, with black sheepskin caps and with long spears;
Large men, large steeds; who from Bokhara come
And Khiva, and ferment the milk of mares.　　　　　120
Next the more temperate Toorkmuns of the south,
The Tukas, and the lances of Salore,
And those from Attruck and the Caspian sands;
Light men, and on light steeds, who only drink
The acrid milk of camels, and their wells.　　　　　125
And then a swarm of wandering horse, who came
From far, and a more doubtful service owned;
The Tartars of Ferghana, from the banks
Of the Jaxartes, men with scanty beards
And close-set skull-caps; and those wilder hordes　　130
Who roam o'er Kipchak and the northern waste,
Kalmuks and unkemped Kuzzaks, tribes who stray
Nearest the Pole, and wandering Kirghizzes,
Who come on shaggy ponies from Pamere.
These all filed out from camp into the plain.　　　　135
And on the other side the Persians formed:
First a light cloud of horse, Tartars they seemed,
The Ilyats of Khorassan: and behind,
The royal troops of Persia, horse and foot,
Marshalled battalions bright in burnished steel.　　　140
But Peran-Wisa with his herald came
Threading the Tartar squadrons to the front,
And with his staff kept back the foremost ranks.
And when Ferood, who led the Persians, saw
That Peran-Wisa kept the Tartars back,　　　　　　145
He took his spear, and to the front he came,

MATTHEW ARNOLD

And checked his ranks, and fixed them where they stood.
And the old Tartar came upon the sand
Betwixt the silent hosts, and spake, and said:
   'Ferood, and ye, Persians and Tartars, hear!   150
Let there be truce between the hosts today.
But choose a champion from the Persian lords
To fight our champion Sohrab, man to man.'
   As, in the country, on a morn in June,
When the dew glistens on the pearled ears,   155
A shiver runs through the deep corn for joy—
So, when they heard what Peran-Wisa said,
A thrill through all the Tartar squadrons ran
Of pride and hope for Sohrab, whom they loved.
   But as a troop of pedlars, from Cabool,   160
Cross underneath the Indian Caucasus,
That vast sky-neighbouring mountain of milk snow;
Winding so high, that, as they mount, they pass
Long flocks of travelling birds dead on the snow,
Choked by the air, and scarce can they themselves   165
Slake their parched throats with sugared mulberries—
In single file they move, and stop their breath,
For fear they should dislodge the o'erhanging snows—
So the pale Persians held their breath with fear.
   And to Ferood his brother chiefs came up   170
To counsel: Gudurz and Zoarrah came,
And Feraburz, who ruled the Persian host
Second, and was the uncle of the King:
These came and counselled; and then Gudurz said:
   'Ferood, shame bids us take their challenge up,   175
Yet champion have we none to match this youth.
He has the wild stag's foot, the lion's heart.
But Rustum came last night; aloof he sits
And sullen, and has pitched his tents apart:
Him will I seek, and carry to his ear   180
The Tartar challenge, and this young man's name.
Haply he will forget his wrath, and fight.
Stand forth the while, and take their challenge up.'
   So spake he; and Ferood stood forth and said:
'Old man, be it agreed as thou hast said.   185
Let Sohrab arm, and we will find a man.'
   He spoke; and Peran-Wisa turned, and strode
Back through the opening squadrons to his tent.
But through the anxious Persians Gudurz ran,
And crossed the camp which lay behind, and reached,   190
Out on the sands beyond it, Rustum's tents.

Of scarlet cloth they were, and glittering gay,
Just pitched: the high pavilion in the midst
Was Rustum's, and his men lay camped around.
And Gudurz entered Rustum's tent, and found   195
Rustum: his morning meal was done, but still
The table stood before him, charged with food—
A side of roasted sheep, and cakes of bread,
And dark green melons; and there Rustum sate
Listless, and held a falcon on his wrist,   200
And played with it; but Gudurz came and stood
Before him; and he looked, and saw him stand;
And with a cry sprang up, and dropped the bird,
And greeted Gudurz with both hands, and said:

   'Welcome! these eyes could see no better sight. 205
What news? but sit down first, and eat and drink.'

   But Gudurz stood in the tent door, and said:
'Not now: a time will come to eat and drink,
But not today: today has other needs.
The armies are drawn out, and stand at gaze: 210
For from the Tartars is a challenge brought
To pick a champion from the Persian lords
To fight their champion—and thou know'st his name—
Sohrab men call him, but his birth is hid.
O Rustum, like thy might is this young man's!   215
He has the wild stag's foot, the lion's heart.
And he is young, and Iran's chiefs are old,
Or else too weak; and all eyes turn to thee.
Come down and help us, Rustum, or we lose.'

   He spoke: but Rustum answered with a smile: 220
'Go to! if Iran's chiefs are old, then I
Am older: if the young are weak, the King
Errs strangely: for the King, for Kai Khosroo,
Himself is young, and honours younger men,
And lets the aged moulder to their graves.   225
Rustum he loves no more, but loves the young—
The young may rise at Sohrab's vaunts, not I.
For what care I, though all speak Sohrab's fame?
For would that I myself had such a son,
And not that one slight helpless girl I have,   230
A son so famed, so brave, to send to war.
And I to tarry with the snow-haired Zal,
My father, whom the robber Afghans vex,
And clip his borders short, and drive his herds,
And he has none to guard his weak old age.   235
There would I go, and hang my armour up,

And with my great name fence that weak old man,
And spend the goodly treasures I have got,
And rest my age, and hear of Sohrab's fame,
And leave to death the hosts of thankless kings,   240
And with these slaughterous hands draw sword no more.'
    He spoke, and smiled; and Gudurz made reply:
'What then, O Rustum, will men say to this,
When Sohrab dares our bravest forth, and seeks
Thee most of all, and thou, whom most he seeks,   245
Hidest thy face? Take heed, lest men should say,
Like some old miser, Rustum hoards his fame,
And shuns to peril it with younger men.'
    And greatly moved, then Rustum made reply:
'O Gudurz, wherefore dost thou say such words?   250
Thou knowest better words than this to say.
What is one more, one less, obscure or famed,
Valiant or craven, young or old, to me?
Are not they mortal, am not I myself?
But who for men of naught would do great deeds?   255
Come, thou shalt see how Rustum hoards his fame.
But I will fight unknown, and in plain arms;
Let not men say of Rustum, he was matched
In single fight with any mortal man.'
    He spoke, and frowned; and Gudurz turned, and ran   260
Back quickly through the camp in fear and joy,
Fear at his wrath, but joy that Rustum came.
But Rustum strode to his tent door, and called
His followers in, and bade them bring his arms,
And clad himself in steel: the arms he chose   265
Were plain, and on his shield was no device,
Only his helm was rich, inlaid with gold,
And from the fluted spine atop a plume
Of horsehair waved, a scarlet horsehair plume.
So armed he issued forth; and Ruksh, his horse,   270
Followed him, like a faithful hound, at heel—
Ruksh, whose renown was noised through all the earth,
The horse, whom Rustum on a foray once
Did in Bokhara by the river find
A colt beneath its dam, and drove him home,   275
And reared him; a bright bay, with lofty crest;
Dight with a saddle-cloth of broidered green
Crusted with gold, and on the ground were worked
All beasts of chase, all beasts which hunters know:
So followed, Rustum left his tents, and crossed   280
The camp, and to the Persian host appeared.

And all the Persians knew him, and with shouts
Hailed; but the Tartars knew not who he was.
And dear as the wet diver to the eyes
Of his pale wife who waits and weeps on shore,   285
By sandy Bahrein, in the Persian Gulf,
Plunging all day in the blue waves, at night,
Having made up his tale of precious pearls,
Rejoins her in their hut upon the sands—
So dear to the pale Persians Rustum came.   290
   And Rustum to the Persian front advanced,
And Sohrab armed in Haman's tent, and came.
And as afield the reapers cut a swathe
Down through the middle of a rich man's corn,
And on each side are squares of standing corn,   295
And in the midst a stubble, short and bare;
So on each side were squares of men, with spears
Bristling, and in the midst, the open sand.
And Rustum came upon the sand, and cast
His eyes towards the Tartar tents, and saw   300
Sohrab come forth, and eyed him as he came.
   As some rich woman, on a winter's morn,
Eyes through her silken curtains the poor drudge
Who with numb blackened fingers makes her fire—
At cock-crow, on a starlit winter's morn,   305
When the frost flowers the whitened window panes—
And wonders how she lives, and what the thoughts
Of that poor drudge may be; so Rustum eyed
The unknown adventurous youth, who from afar
Came seeking Rustum, and defying forth   310
All the most valiant chiefs: long he perused
His spirited air, and wondered who he was.
For very young he seemed, tenderly reared;
Like some young cypress, tall, and dark, and straight,
Which in a queen's secluded garden throws   315
Its slight dark shadow on the moonlit turf,
By midnight, to a bubbling fountain's sound—
So slender Sohrab seemed, so softly reared.
And a deep pity entered Rustum's soul
As he beheld him coming; and he stood,   320
And beckoned to him with his hand, and said:
   'O thou young man, the air of Heaven is soft,
And warm, and pleasant; but the grave is cold.
Heaven's air is better than the cold dead grave.
Behold me: I am vast, and clad in iron,   325
And tried; and I have stood on many a field

257

Of blood, and I have fought with many a foe:
Never was that field lost, or that foe saved.
O Sohrab, wherefore wilt thou rush on death?
Be governed: quit the Tartar host, and come   330
To Iran, and be as my son to me,
And fight beneath my banner till I die.
There are no youths in Iran brave as thou.'
  So he spake, mildly: Sohrab heard his voice,
The mighty voice of Rustum; and he saw   335
His giant figure planted on the sand,
Sole, like some single tower, which a chief
Has builded on the waste in former years
Against the robbers; and he saw that head,
Streaked with its first grey hairs: hope filled his soul;   340
And he ran forwards and embraced his knees,
And clasped his hand within his own and said:
  'Oh, by thy father's head! by thine own soul!
Art thou not Rustum? Speak! art thou not he?'
  But Rustum eyed askance the kneeling youth,   345
And turned away, and spoke to his own soul:
  'Ah me, I muse what this young fox may mean.
False, wily, boastful, are these Tartar boys.
For if I now confess this thing he asks,
And hide it not, but say—*Rustum is here*—   350
He will not yield indeed, nor quit our foes,
But he will find some pretext not to fight,
And praise my fame, and proffer courteous gifts,
A belt or sword perhaps, and go his way.
And on a feast-tide, in Afrasiab's hall,   355
In Samarcand, he will arise and cry—
"I challenged once, when the two armies camped
Beside the Oxus, all the Persian lords
To cope with me in single fight; but they
Shrank; only Rustum dared: then he and I   360
Changed gifts, and went on equal terms away."
So will he speak, perhaps, while men applaud.
Then were the chiefs of Iran shamed through me.'
  And then he turned, and sternly spake aloud:
'Rise! wherefore dost thou vainly question thus   365
Of Rustum? I am here, whom thou hast called
By challenge forth: make good thy vaunt, or yield.
Is it with Rustum only thou wouldst fight?
Rash boy, men look on Rustum's face and flee.
For well I know, that did great Rustum stand   370

Before thy face this day, and were revealed,
There would be then no talk of fighting more.
But being what I am, I tell thee this;
Do thou record it in thine inmost soul:
Either thou shalt renounce thy vaunt, and yield;   375
Or else thy bones shall strew this sand, till winds
Bleach them, or Oxus with his summer floods,
Oxus in summer wash them all away.'
    He spoke: and Sohrab answered, on his feet:
'Art thou so fierce? Thou wilt not fright me so.   380
I am no girl, to be made pale by words.
Yet this thou hast said well, did Rustum stand
Here on this field, there were no fighting then.
But Rustum is far hence, and we stand here.
Begin: thou art more vast, more dread than I,   385
And thou art proved, I know, and I am young—
But yet success sways with the breath of Heaven.
And though thou thinkest that thou knowest sure
Thy victory, yet thou canst not surely know.
For we are all, like swimmers in the sea,   390
Poised on the top of a huge wave of fate,
Which hangs uncertain to which side to fall.
And whether it will heave us up to land,
Or whether it will roll us out to sea,
Back out to sea, to the deep waves of death,   395
We know not, and no search will make us know:
Only the event will teach us in its hour.'
    He spoke; and Rustum answered not, but hurled
His spear: down from the shoulder, down it came,
As on some partridge in the corn a hawk   400
That long has towered in the airy clouds
Drops like a plummet: Sohrab saw it come,
And sprang aside, quick as a flash: the spear
Hissed, and went quivering down into the sand,
Which it sent flying wide: then Sohrab threw   405
In turn, and full struck Rustum's shield: sharp rang,
The iron plates rang sharp, but turned the spear.
And Rustum seized his club, which none but he
Could wield: an unlopped trunk it was, and huge,
Still rough; like those which men in treeless plains   410
To build them boats fish from the flooded rivers,
Hyphasis or Hydaspes, when, high up
By their dark springs, the wind in winter time
Has made in Himalayan forests wrack,
And strewn the channels with torn boughs; so huge   415

The club which Rustum lifted now, and struck
One stroke; but again Sohrab sprang aside
Lithe as the glancing snake, and the club came
Thundering to earth, and leapt from Rustum's hand.
And Rustum followed his own blow, and fell   420
To his knees, and with his fingers clutched the sand:
And now might Sohrab have unsheathed his sword,
And pierced the mighty Rustum while he lay
Dizzy, and on his knees, and choked with sand:
But he looked on, and smiled, nor bared his sword,   425
But courteously drew back, and spoke, and said:
    'Thou strik'st too hard: that club of thine will float
Upon the summer floods, and not my bones.
But rise, and be not wroth; not wroth am I:
No, when I see thee, wrath forsakes my soul.   430
Thou say'st, thou art not Rustum: be it so.
Who art thou then, that canst so touch my soul?
Boy as I am, I have seen battles too;
Have waded foremost in their bloody waves,
And heard their hollow roar of dying men;   435
But never was my heart thus touched before.
Are they from Heaven, these softenings of the heart?
O thou old warrior, let us yield to Heaven!
Come, plant we here in earth our angry spears,
And make a truce, and sit upon this sand,   440
And pledge each other in red wine, like friends,
And thou shalt talk to me of Rustum's deeds.
There are enough foes in the Persian host
Whom I may meet, and strike, and feel no pang;
Champions enough Afrasiab has, whom thou   445
Mayst fight; fight them, when they confront thy spear.
But oh, let there be peace 'twixt thee and me!'
    He ceased: but while he spake, Rustum had risen,
And stood erect, trembling with rage: his club
He left to lie, but had regained his spear,   450
Whose fiery point now in his mailed right hand
Blazed bright and baleful, like that autumn star,
The baleful sign of fevers: dust had soiled
His stately crest, and dimmed his glittering arms.
His breast heaved; his lips foamed; and twice his voice   455
Was choked with rage: at last these words broke way:
    'Girl! nimble with thy feet, not with thy hands!
Curled minion, dancer, coiner of sweet words!
Fight; let me hear thy hateful voice no more!
Thou art not in Afrasiab's gardens now   460

With Tartar girls, with whom thou art wont to dance;
But on the Oxus sands, and in the dance
Of battle, and with me, who make no play
Of war: I fight it out, and hand to hand.
Speak not to me of truce, and pledge, and wine!   465
Remember all thy valour: try thy feints
And cunning: all the pity I had is gone:
Because thou hast shamed me before both the hosts
With thy light skipping tricks, and thy girl's wiles.'
    He spoke; and Sohrab kindled at his taunts.   470
And he too drew his sword: at once they rushed
Together, as two eagles on one prey
Come rushing down together from the clouds,
One from the east, one from the west: their shields
Dashed with a clang together, and a din   475
Rose, such as that the sinewy woodcutters
Make often in the forest's heart at morn,
Of hewing axes, crashing trees: such blows
Rustum and Sohrab on each other hailed.
And you would say that sun and stars took part   480
In that unnatural conflict; for a cloud
Grew suddenly in Heaven, and darked the sun
Over the fighters' heads; and a wind rose
Under their feet, and moaning swept the plain,
And in a sandy whirlwind wrapped the pair.   485
In gloom they twain were wrapped, and they alone;
For both the on-looking hosts on either hand
Stood in broad daylight, and the sky was pure,
And the sun sparkled on the Oxus stream.
But in the gloom they fought, with bloodshot eyes   490
And labouring breath; first Rustum struck the shield
Which Sohrab held stiff out: the steel-spiked spear
Rent the tough plates, but failed to reach the skin,
And Rustum plucked it back with angry groan.
Then Sohrab with his sword smote Rustum's helm,   495
Nor clove its steel quite through; but all the crest
He shore away, and that proud horsehair plume,
Never till now defiled, sunk to the dust;
And Rustum bowed his head; but then the gloom
Grew blacker: thunder rumbled in the air,   500
And lightnings rent the cloud; and Ruksh, the horse,
Who stood at hand, uttered a dreadful cry:
No horse's cry was that, most like the roar
Of some pained desert lion, who all day
Has trailed the hunter's javelin in his side,   505

261

And comes at night to die upon the sand:
The two hosts heard that cry, and quaked for fear,
And Oxus curdled as it crossed his stream.
But Sohrab heard, and quailed not, but rushed on,
And struck again; and again Rustum bowed   510
His head; but this time all the blade, like glass,
Sprang in a thousand shivers on the helm,
And in his hand the hilt remained alone.
Then Rustum raised his head: his dreadful eyes
Glared, and he shook on high his menacing spear,   515
And shouted, *Rustum*! Sohrab heard that shout,
And shrank amazed: back he recoiled one step,
And scanned with blinking eyes the advancing form:
And then he stood bewildered; and he dropped
His covering shield, and the spear pierced his side.   520
He reeled, and staggering back, sunk to the ground.
And then the gloom dispersed, and the wind fell,
And the bright sun broke forth, and melted all
The cloud; and the two armies saw the pair;
Saw Rustum standing, safe upon his feet,   525
And Sohrab, wounded, on the bloody sand.
    Then, with a bitter smile, Rustum began:
'Sohrab, thou thoughtest in thy mind to kill
A Persian lord this day, and strip his corpse,
And bear thy trophies to Afrasiab's tent.   530
Or else that the great Rustum would come down
Himself to fight, and that thy wiles would move
His heart to take a gift, and let thee go.
And then that all the Tartar host would praise
Thy courage or thy craft, and spread thy fame,   535
To glad thy father in his weak old age.
Fool! thou art slain, and by an unknown man!
Dearer to the red jackals shalt thou be,
Than to thy friends, and to thy father old.'
    And with a fearless mien Sohrab replied: 540
'Unknown thou art; yet thy fierce vaunt is vain.
Thou dost not slay me, proud and boastful man!
No! Rustum slays me, and this filial heart.
For were I matched with ten such men as thee,
And I were he who till today I was,   545
They should be lying here, I standing there.
But that beloved name unnerved my arm—
That name, and something, I confess, in thee,
Which troubles all my heart, and made my shield
Fall; and thy spear transfixed an unarmed foe.   550

And now thou boastest, and insult'st my fate.
But hear thou this, fierce man, tremble to hear!
The mighty Rustum shall avenge my death!
My father, whom I seek through all the world,
He shall avenge my death, and punish thee!'   555
   As when some hunter in the spring hath found
A breeding eagle sitting on her nest,
Upon the craggy isle of a hill lake,
And pierced her with an arrow as she rose,
And followed her to find out where she fell   560
Far off;—anon her mate comes winging back
From hunting, and a great way off descries
His huddling young left sole; at that, he checks
His pinion, and with short uneasy sweeps
Circles above his eyrie, with loud screams   565
Chiding his mate back to her nest; but she
Lies dying, with the arrow in her side,
In some far stony gorge out of his ken,
A heap of fluttering feathers: never more
Shall the lake glass her, flying over it;   570
Never the black and dripping precipices
Echo her stormy scream as she sails by:—
As that poor bird flies home, nor knows his loss—
So Rustum knew not his own loss, but stood
Over his dying son, and knew him not.   575
   But with a cold, incredulous voice, he said:
'What prate is this of fathers and revenge?
The mighty Rustum never had a son.'
   And, with a failing voice, Sohrab replied:
'Ah yes, he had! and that lost son am I.   580
Surely the news will one day reach his ear,
Reach Rustum, where he sits, and tarries long,
Somewhere, I know not where, but far from here;
And pierce him like a stab, and make him leap
To arms, and cry for vengeance upon thee.   585
Fierce man, bethink thee, for an only son!
What will that grief, what will that vengeance be!
Oh, could I live, till I that grief had seen!
Yet him I pity not so much, but her,
My mother, who in Ader-baijan dwells   590
With that old King, her father, who grows grey
With age, and rules over the valiant Koords.
Her most I pity, who no more will see
Sohrab returning from the Tartar camp,
With spoils and honour, when the war is done.   595

263

But a dark rumour will be bruited up,
From tribe to tribe, until it reach her ear;
And then will that defenceless woman learn
That Sohrab will rejoice her sight no more;
But that in battle with a nameless foe,   600
By the far-distant Oxus, he is slain.'
    He spoke; and as he ceased he wept aloud,
Thinking of her he left, and his own death.
He spoke; but Rustum listened, plunged in thought.
Nor did he yet believe it was his son   605
Who spoke, although he called back names he knew;
For he had had sure tidings that the babe,
Which was in Ader-baijan born to him,
Had been a puny girl, no boy at all:
So that sad mother sent him word, for fear   610
Rustum should take the boy, to train in arms;
And so he deemed that either Sohrab took,
By a false boast, the style of Rustum's son;
Or that men gave it him, to swell his fame.
So deemed he; yet he listened, plunged in thought;   615
And his soul set to grief, as the vast tide
Of the bright rocking ocean sets to shore
At the full moon: tears gathered in his eyes;
For he remembered his own early youth,
And all its bounding rapture; as, at dawn,   620
The shepherd from his mountain lodge descries
A far bright city, smitten by the sun,
Through many rolling clouds;—so Rustum saw
His youth; saw Sohrab's mother, in her bloom;
And that old King, her father, who loved well   625
His wandering guest, and gave him his fair child
With joy; and all the pleasant life they led,
They three, in that long-distant summer time—
The castle, and the dewy woods, and hunt
And hound, and morn on those delightful hills   630
In Ader-baijan. And he saw that youth,
Of age and looks to be his own dear son,
Piteous and lovely, lying on the sand,
Like some rich hyacinth, which by the scythe
Of an unskilful gardener has been cut,   635
Mowing the garden grass-plots near its bed,
And lies, a fragrant tower of purple bloom,
On the mown, dying grass;—so Sohrab lay,
Lovely in death, upon the common sand.

And Rustum gazed on him with grief, and said: 640
    'O Sohrab, thou indeed art such a son
Whom Rustum, wert thou his, might well have loved!
Yet here thou errest, Sohrab, or else men
Have told thee false;—thou art not Rustum's son.
For Rustum had no son: one child he had—   645
But one—a girl: who with her mother now
Plies some light female task, nor dreams of us—
Of us she dreams not, nor of wounds, nor war.'
    But Sohrab answered him in wrath; for now
The anguish of the deep-fixed spear grew fierce,   650
And he desired to draw forth the steel,
And let the blood flow free, and so to die;
But first he would convince his stubborn foe—
And, rising sternly on one arm, he said:
    'Man, who art thou who dost deny my words?   655
Truth sits upon the lips of dying men,
And falsehood, while I lived, was far from mine.
I tell thee, pricked upon this arm I bear
That seal which Rustum to my mother gave,
That she might prick it on the babe she bore.'   660
    He spoke; and all the blood left Rustum's cheeks,
And his knees tottered, and he smote his hand
Against his breast, his heavy mailed hand,
That the hard iron corslet clanked aloud;
And to his heart he pressed the other hand,   665
And in a hollow voice he spake, and said:
    'Sohrab, that were a proof which could not lie.
If thou shew this, then art thou Rustum's son.'
    Then, with weak hasty fingers, Sohrab loosed
His belt, and near the shoulder bared his arm,   670
And shewed a sign in faint vermilion points
Pricked; as a cunning workman, in Pekin,
Pricks with vermilion some clear porcelain vase,
An emperor's gift—at early morn he paints,
And all day long, and, when night comes, the lamp   675
Lights up his studious forehead and thin hands—
So delicately pricked the sign appeared
On Sohrab's arm, the sign of Rustum's seal.
It was that griffin, which of old reared Zal,
Rustum's great father, whom they left to die,   680
A helpless babe, among the mountain rocks.
Him that kind creature found, and reared, and loved—
Then Rustum took it for his glorious sign.

And Sohrab bared that figure on his arm,
And himself scanned it long with mournful eyes,   685
And then he touched it with his hand and said:
  'How say'st thou? Is that sign the proper sign
Of Rustum's son, or of some other man's?'
  He spoke: but Rustum gazed, and gazed, and stood
Speechless; and then he uttered one sharp cry—   690
O boy—thy father!—and his voice choked there.
And then a dark cloud passed before his eyes,
And his head swam, and he sank down to earth.
But Sohrab crawled to where he lay, and cast
His arms about his neck, and kissed his lips,   695
And with fond faltering fingers stroked his cheeks,
Trying to call him back to life: and life
Came back to Rustum, and he oped his eyes,
And they stood wide with horror; and he seized
In both his hands the dust which lay around,   700
And threw it on his head, and smirched his hair,
His hair, and face, and beard, and glittering arms:
And strong convulsive groanings shook his breast,
And his sobs choked him; and he clutched his sword,
To draw it, and for ever let life out.   705
But Sohrab saw his thought, and held his hands,
And with a soothing voice he spoke, and said:
  'Father, forbear: for I but meet today
The doom that at my birth was written down
In Heaven, and thou art Heaven's unconscious hand.   710
Surely my heart cried out that it was thou,
When first I saw thee; and thy heart spoke too,
I know it: but fate trod those promptings down
Under its iron heel; fate, fate engaged
The strife and hurled me on my father's spear.   715
But let us speak no more of this: I find
My father; let me feel that I have found.
Come, sit beside me on this sand, and take
My head betwixt thy hands, and kiss my cheeks,
And wash them with thy tears, and say, *My son!*   720
Quick! quick! for numbered are my sands of life,
And swift; for like the lightning to this field
I came, and like the wind I go away—
Sudden, and swift, and like a passing wind.
But it was writ in Heaven that this should be.'   725
  So said he: and his voice released the heart
Of Rustum, and his tears broke forth; he cast
His arms round his son's neck, and wept aloud,

And kissed him. And awe fell on both the hosts
When they saw Rustum's grief: and Ruksh, the horse,   730
With his head bowing to the ground, and mane
Sweeping the dust, came near, and in mute woe
First to the one then to the other moved
His head, as if inquiring what their grief
Might mean; and from his dark compassionate eyes   735
The big warm tears rolled down, and caked the sand.
But Rustum chid him with stern voice, and said:
    'Ruksh, now thou grievest; but, O Ruksh, thy feet
Should then have rotted on their nimble joints,
When first they bore thy master to this field.'   740
    But Sohrab looked upon the horse and said:
'Is this then Ruksh? How often, in past days,
My mother told me of thee, thou brave steed!
My terrible father's terrible horse; and said,
That I should one day find thy lord and thee.   745
Come, let me lay my hand upon thy mane.
O Ruksh, thou art more fortunate than I;
For thou hast gone where I shall never go,
And snuffed the breezes of my father's home.
And thou hast trod the sands of Seistan,   750
And seen the River of Helmund, and the Lake
Of Zirrah; and the aged Zal himself
Has often stroked thy neck, and given thee food,
Corn in a golden platter soaked with wine,
And said—*O Ruksh! bear Rustum well!*—but I   755
Have never known my grandsire's furrowed face,
Nor seen his lofty house in Seistan,
Nor slaked my thirst at the clear Helmund stream:
But lodged among my father's foes, and seen
Afrasiab's cities only, Samarcand,   760
Bokhara, and lone Khiva in the waste,
And the black Toorkmun tents; and only drunk
The desert rivers, Moorghab and Tejend,
Kohik, and where the Kalmuks feed their sheep,
The northern Sir; and this great Oxus stream—   765
The yellow Oxus, by whose brink I die.'
    And, with a heavy groan, Rustum replied:
'Oh that its waves were flowing over me!
Oh that I saw its grains of yellow silt
Roll tumbling in the current o'er my head!'   770
    And, with a grave mild voice, Sohrab replied:
'Desire not that, my father; thou must live.
For some are born to do great deeds, and live,

As some are born to be obscured, and die.
Do thou the deeds I die too young to do,   775
And reap a second glory in thine age.
Thou art my father, and thy gain is mine.
But come: thou seest this great host of men
Which follow me; I pray thee, slay not these:
Let me entreat for them: what have they done?   780
They followed me, my hope, my fame, my star.
Let them all cross the Oxus back in peace.
But me thou must bear hence, not send with them,
But carry me with thee to Seistan,
And place me on a bed, and mourn for me,   785
Thou, and the snow-haired Zal, and all thy friends.
And thou must lay me in that lovely earth,
And heap a stately mound above my bones,
And plant a far-seen pillar over all:
That so the passing horseman on the waste   790
May see my tomb a great way off, and say—
Sohrab, the mighty Rustum's son, lies there,
Whom his great father did in ignorance kill—
And I be not forgotten in my grave.'

      And, with a mournful voice, Rustum replied: 795
'Fear not; as thou hast said, Sohrab, my son,
So shall it be: for I will burn my tents,
And quit the host, and bear thee hence with me,
And carry thee away to Seistan,
And place thee on a bed, and mourn for thee,   800
With the snow-headed Zal, and all my friends.
And I will lay thee in that lovely earth,
And heap a stately mound above thy bones,
And plant a far-seen pillar over all:
And men shall not forget thee in thy grave.   805
And I will spare thy host: yea, let them go:
Let them all cross the Oxus back in peace.
What should I do with slaying any more?
For would that all whom I have ever slain
Might be once more alive; my bitterest foes,   810
And they who were called champions in their time,
And through whose death I won that fame I have;
And I were nothing but a common man,
A poor, mean soldier, and without renown,
So thou mightest live, too, my son, my son!   815
Or rather would that I, even I myself,
Might now be lying on this bloody sand,

Near death, and by an ignorant stroke of thine,
Not thou of mine; and I might die, not thou;
And I, not thou, be borne to Seistan;   820
And Zal might weep above my grave, not thine;
And say—*O son, I weep thee not too sore,*
For willingly, I know, thou met'st thine end.
But now in blood and battles was my youth,
And full of blood and battles is my age;   825
And I shall never end this life of blood.'
   Then, at the point of death, Sohrab replied:
'A life of blood indeed, thou dreadful man!
But thou shalt yet have peace; only not now;
Not yet: but thou shalt have it on that day,   830
When thou shalt sail in a high-masted ship,
Thou and the other peers of Kai Khosroo,
Returning home over the salt blue sea,
From laying thy dear master in his grave.'
   And Rustum gazed on Sohrab's face, and said: 835
'Soon be that day, my son, and deep that sea!
Till then, if fate so wills, let me endure.'
   He spoke; and Sohrab smiled on him, and took
The spear, and drew it from his side, and eased
His wound's imperious anguish: but the blood   840
Came welling from the open gash, and life
Flowed with the stream: all down his cold white side
The crimson torrent ran, dim now, and soiled,
Like the soiled tissue of white violets
Left, freshly gathered, on their native bank,   845
By romping children, whom their nurses call
From the hot fields at noon: his head drooped low,
His limbs grew slack; motionless, white, he lay—
White, with eyes closed; only when heavy gasps,
Deep, heavy gasps, quivering through all his frame,   850
Convulsed him back to life, he opened them,
And fixed them feebly on his father's face:
Till now all strength was ebbed, and from his limbs
Unwillingly the spirit fled away,
Regretting the warm mansion which it left,   855
And youth and bloom, and this delightful world.
   So, on the bloody sand, Sohrab lay dead.
And the great Rustum drew his horseman's cloak
Down o'er his face, and sat by his dead son.
As those black granite pillars, once high-reared   860
By Jemshid in Persepolis, to bear

His house, now, mid their broken flights of steps
Lie prone, enormous, down the mountain side—
So in the sand lay Rustum by his son.

    And night came down over the solemn waste,   865
And the two gazing hosts, and that sole pair,
And darkened all; and a cold fog, with night,
Crept from the Oxus. Soon a hum arose,
As of a great assembly loosed, and fires
Began to twinkle through the fog: for now   870
Both armies moved to camp, and took their meal:
The Persians took it on the open sands
Southward; the Tartars by the river marge:
And Rustum and his son were left alone.

    But the majestic river floated on,   875
Out of the mist and hum of that low land,
Into the frosty starlight, and there moved,
Rejoicing, through the hushed Chorasmian waste,
Under the solitary moon: he flowed
Right for the Polar Star, past Orgunjè,   880
Brimming, and bright, and large: then sands begin
To hem his watery march, and dam his streams,
And split his currents; that for many a league
The shorn and parcelled Oxus strains along
Through beds of sand and matted rushy isles—   885
Oxus, forgetting the bright speed he had
In his high mountain cradle in Pamere,
A foiled circuitous wanderer: till at last
The longed-for dash of waves is heard, and wide
His luminous home of waters opens, bright   890
And tranquil, from whose floor the new-bathed stars
Emerge, and shine upon the Aral Sea.

WILLIAM MORRIS
1834–1896

The Haystack in the Floods

HAD she come all the way for this,
To part at last without a kiss?
Yea, had she borne the dirt and rain
That her own eyes might see him slain
Beside the haystack in the floods?   5

Along the dripping leafless woods,
The stirrup touching either shoe,
She rode astride as troopers do;
With kirtle kilted to her knee,
To which the mud splashed wretchedly;   10
And the wet dripped from every tree
Upon her head and heavy hair,
And on her eyelids broad and fair;
The tears and rain ran down her face.
By fits and starts they rode apace,   15
And very often was his place
Far off from her; he had to ride
Ahead, to see what might betide
When the roads crossed; and sometimes, when
There rose a murmuring from his men,   20
Had to turn back with promises;
Ah me! she had but little ease;
And often for pure doubt and dread
She sobbed, made giddy in the head
By the swift riding; while, for cold   25
Her slender fingers scarce could hold
The wet reins; yea, and scarcely, too,
She felt the foot within her shoe
Against the stirrup; all for this,
To part at last without a kiss   30
Beside the haystack in the floods.

For when they neared that old soaked hay,
They saw across the only way
That Judas, Godmar, and the three
Red running lions dismally   35
Grinned from his pennon, under which,
In one straight line along the ditch,
They counted thirty heads.

So then,
While Robert turned round to his men,   40
She saw at once the wretched end,
And, stooping down, tried hard to rend
Her coif the wrong way from her head,
And hid her eyes; while Robert said:
'Nay, love, 'tis scarcely two to one,   45
At Poictiers where we made them run
So fast—why, sweet my love, good cheer.
The Gascon frontier is so near,
Nought after this.'

But, 'O,' she said,   50
'My God! my God! I have to tread
The long way back without you; then
The court at Paris; those six men;
The gratings of the Chatelet;
The swift Seine on some rainy day   55
Like this, and people standing by,
And laughing, while my weak hands try
To recollect how strong men swim.
All this, or else a life with him,
For which I should be damned at last,   60
Would God that this next hour were past!'

He answered not, but cried his cry,
'St. George for Marny!' cheerily;
And laid his hand upon her rein.
Alas! no man of all his train   65
Gave back that cheery cry again;
And, while for rage his thumb beat fast
Upon his sword-hilts, some one cast
About his neck a kerchief long,
And bound him.   70

                    Then they went along
To Godmar; who said: 'Now, Jehane,
Your lover's life is on the wane
So fast, that, if this very hour
You yield not as my paramour,   75
He will not see the rain leave off—
Nay, keep your tongue from gibe and scoff,
Sir Robert, or I slay you now.'

She laid her hand upon her brow,
Then gazed upon the palm, as though   80
She thought her forehead bled, and—'No,'
She said, and turned her head away,
As there were nothing else to say,
And everything were settled: red
Grew Godmar's face from chin to head: 85
'Jehane, on yonder hill there stands
My castle, guarding well my lands:
What hinders me from taking you,
And doing that I list to do
To your fair wilful body, while   90
Your knight lies dead?'

A wicked smile
Wrinkled her face, her lips grew thin,
A long way out she thrust her chin:
'You know that I should strangle you   95
While you were sleeping; or bite through
Your throat, by God's help—ah!' she said,
'Lord Jesus, pity your poor maid!
For in such wise they hem me in,
I cannot choose but sin and sin,   100
Whatever happens: yet I think
They could not make me eat or drink,
And so should I just reach my rest.'
'Nay, if you do not my behest,
O Jehane! though I love you well,'   105
Said Godmar, 'would I fail to tell
All that I know.' 'Foul lies,' she said.
'Eh? lies my Jehane? by God's head,
At Paris folks would deem them true!
Do you know, Jehane, they cry for you,   110
"Jehane the brown, Jehane the brown!
Give us Jehane to burn or drown!"—
Eh—gag me Robert!—sweet my friend,
This were indeed a piteous end
For those long fingers, and long feet,   115
And long neck, and smooth shoulders sweet;
An end that few men would forget
That saw it—So, an hour yet:
Consider, Jehane, which to take
Of life or death!'   120

So, scarce awake,
Dismounting, did she leave that place,
And totter some yards: with her face
Turned upward to the sky she lay,
Her head on a wet heap of hay,   125
And fell asleep: and while she slept,
And did not dream, the minutes crept
Round to the twelve again; but she,
Being waked at last, sighed quietly,
And strangely childlike came, and said: 130
'I will not.' Straightway Godmar's head,
As though it hung on strong wires, turned
Most sharply round, and his face burned.

For Robert—both his eyes were dry.
He could not weep, but gloomily   135
He seemed to watch the rain; yea, too,
His lips were firm; he tried once more
To touch her lips; she reached out, sore
And vain desire so tortured them,
The poor grey lips, and now the hem   140
Of his sleeve brushed them.

                     With a start
Up Godmar rose, thrust them apart;
From Robert's throat he loosed the bands
Of silk and mail; with empty hands
Held out, she stood and gazed, and saw,   145
The long bright blade without a flaw
Glide out from Godmar's sheath, his hand
In Robert's hair; she saw him bend
Back Robert's head; she saw him send   150
The thin steel down; the blow told well,
Right backward the knight Robert fell,
And moaned as dogs do, being half dead,
Unwitting, as I deem: so then
Godmar turned grinning to his men,   155
Who ran, some five or six, and beat
His head to pieces at their feet.
Then Godmar turned again, and said:
'So, Jehane, the first fitte is read!
Take note, my lady, that your way   160
Lies backward to the Chatelet!'
She shook her head and gazed awhile
At her cold hands with a rueful smile,
As though this thing had made her mad.

This was the parting that they had   165
Beside the haystack in the floods.

CHRISTINA ROSSETTI
1830–1894

Goblin Market

MORNING and evening
Maids heard the goblins cry:
'Come buy our orchard fruits,
Come buy, come buy:
Apples and quinces,   5
Lemons and oranges,
Plump unpecked cherries,
Melons and raspberries,
Bloom-down-cheeked peaches,
Swart-headed mulberries,   10
Wild free-born cranberries,
Crab-apples, dewberries,
Pineapples, blackberries,
Apricots, strawberries;
All ripe together   15
In summer weather—
Morns that pass by,
Fair eves that fly;
Come buy, come buy:
Our grapes fresh from the vine,   20
Pomegranates full and fine,
Dates and sharp bullaces,
Rare pears and greengages,
Damsons and bilberries,
Taste them and try: 25
Currants and gooseberries,
Bright-fire-like barberries,
Figs to fill your mouth,
Citrons from the South,
Sweet to tongue and sound to eye;   30
Come buy, come buy.'

    Evening by evening
Among the brookside rushes,
Laura bowed her head to hear,
Lizzie veiled her blushes: 35
Crouching close together
In the cooling weather,

With clasping arms and cautioning lips,
With tingling cheeks and finger tips.
'Lie close,' Laura said,   40
Pricking up her golden head:
'We must not look at goblin men,
We must not buy their fruits:
Who knows upon what soil they fed
Their hungry thirsty roots?'   45
'Come buy,' call the goblins
Hobbling down the glen.
'Oh,' cried Lizzie, 'Laura, Laura,
You should not peep at goblin men.'
Lizzie covered up her eyes,   50
Covered close lest they should look;
Laura reared her glossy head,
And whispered like the restless brook:
'Look, Lizzie, look, Lizzie,
Down the glen tramp little men.   55
One hauls a basket,
One bears a plate,
One lugs a golden dish
Of many pounds weight.
How fair the vine must grow   60
Whose grapes are so luscious;
How warm the wind must blow
Through those fruit bushes.'
'No,' said Lizzie: 'No, no, no;
Their offers should not charm us,   65
Their evil gifts would harm us.'
She thrust a dimpled finger
In each ear, shut eyes and ran:
Curious Laura chose to linger
Wondering at each merchant man.   70
One had a cat's face,
One whisked a tail,
One tramped at a rat's pace,
One crawled like a snail,
One like a wombat prowled obtuse and furry,   75
One like a ratel tumbled hurry skurry.
She heard a voice like voice of doves
Cooing all together:
They sounded kind and full of loves
In the pleasant weather.   80

Laura stretched her gleaming neck
Like a rush-imbedded swan,
Like a lily from the beck,
Like a moonlit poplar branch,
Like a vessel at the launch   85
When its last restraint is gone.

Backwards up the mossy glen
Turned and trooped the goblin men,
With their shrill repeated cry,
'Come buy, come buy.'   90
When they reached where Laura was
They stood stock still upon the moss,
Leering at each other,
Brother with queer brother;
Signalling each other,   95
Brother with sly brother.
One set his basket down,
One reared his plate;
One began to weave a crown
Of tendrils, leaves and rough nuts brown   100
(Men sell not such in any town);
One heaved the golden weight
Of dish and fruit to offer her:
'Come buy, come buy,' was still their cry.
Laura stared but did not stir,   105
Longed but had no money:
The whisk-tailed merchant bade her taste
In tones as smooth as honey,
The cat-faced purred,
The rat-paced spoke a word   110
Of welcome, and the snail-paced even was heard;
One parrot-voiced and jolly
Cried 'Pretty Goblin' still for 'Pretty Polly;'
One whistled like a bird.

But sweet-tooth Laura spoke in haste: 115
'Good folk, I have no coin;
To take were to purloin:
I have no copper in my purse,
I have no silver either,
And all my gold is on the furze   120
That shakes in windy weather
Above the rusty heather.'

'You have much gold upon your head,'
They answered all together:
'Buy from us with a golden curl.'   125
She clipped a precious golden lock,
She dropped a tear more rare than pearl,
Then sucked their fruit globes fair or red:
Sweeter than honey from the rock,
Stronger than man-rejoicing wine,   130
Clearer than water flowed that juice;
She never tasted such before,
How should it cloy with length of use?
She sucked and sucked and sucked the more
Fruits which that unknown orchard bore;   135
She sucked until her lips were sore;
Then flung the emptied rinds away
But gathered up one kernel-stone,
And knew not was it night or day
As she turned home alone.   140

    Lizzie met her at the gate
Full of wise upbraidings:
'Dear, you should not stay so late,
Twilight is not good for maidens;
Should not loiter in the glen   145
In the haunts of goblin men.
Do you not remember Jeanie,
How she met them in the moonlight,
Took their gifts both choice and many,
Ate their fruits and wore their flowers   150
Plucked from bowers
Where summer ripens at all hours?
But ever in the noonlight
She pined and pined away;
Sought them by night and day,   155
Found them no more, but dwindled and grew grey;
Then fell with the first snow,
While to this day no grass will grow
Where she lies low:
I planted daisies there a year ago   160
That never blow.
You should not loiter so.'
'Nay, hush,' said Laura:
'Nay, hush, my sister:
I ate and ate my fill,   165
Yet my mouth waters still;

Tomorrow night I will
Buy more;' and kissed her:
'Have done with sorrow;
I'll bring you plums tomorrow   170
Fresh on their mother twigs,
Cherries worth getting;
You cannot think what figs
My teeth have met in,
What melons icy-cold   175
Piled on a dish of gold
Too huge for me to hold,
What peaches with a velvet nap,
Pellucid grapes without one seed:
Odorous indeed must be the mead   180
Whereon they grow, and pure the wave they drink
With lilies at the brink,
And sugar-sweet their sap.'

   Golden head by golden head,
Like two pigeons in one nest   185
Folded in each other's wings,
They lay down in their curtained bed:
Like two blossoms on one stem,
Like two flakes of new-fall'n snow,
Like two wands of ivory   190
Tipped with gold for awful kings.
Moon and stars gazed in at them,
Wind sang to them lullaby,
Lumbering owls forbore to fly,
Not a bat flapped to and fro   195
Round their rest:
Cheek to cheek and breast to breast
Locked together in one nest.

   Early in the morning
When the first cock crowed his warning,   200
Neat like bees, as sweet and busy,
Laura rose with Lizzie:
Fetched in honey, milked the cows,
Aired and set to rights the house,
Kneaded cakes of whitest wheat,   205
Cakes for dainty mouths to eat,
Next churned butter, whipped up cream,
Fed their poultry, sat and sewed;
Talked as modest maidens should:

Lizzie with an open heart,   210
Laura in an absent dream,
One content, one sick in part;
One warbling for the mere bright day's delight,
One longing for the night.

  At length slow evening came: 215
They went with pitchers to the reedy brook;
Lizzie most placid in her look,
Laura most like a leaping flame.
They drew the gurgling water from its deep;
Lizzie plucked purple and rich golden flags,   220
Then turning homewards said: 'The sunset flushes
Those furthest loftiest crags;
Come, Laura, not another maiden lags,
No wilful squirrel wags,
The beasts and birds are fast asleep.'   225
But Laura loitered still among the rushes
And said the bank was steep.

  And said the hour was early still,
The dew not fall'n, the wind not chill;
Listening ever, but not catching   230
The customary cry,
'Come buy, come buy,'
With its iterated jingle
Of sugar-baited words:
Not for all her watching   235
Once discerning even one goblin
Racing, whisking, tumbling, hobbling;
Let alone the herds
That used to tramp along the glen,
In groups or single,   240
Of brisk fruit-merchant men.

  Till Lizzie urged, 'O Laura, come;
I hear the fruit-call but I dare not look:
You should not loiter longer at this brook:
Come with me home.   245
The stars rise, the moon bends her arc,
Each glowworm winks her spark,
Let us get home before the night grows dark:
For clouds may gather
Though this is summer weather,   250
Put out the lights and drench us through;
Then if we lost our way what should we do?'

Laura turned cold as stone
To find her sister heard that cry alone,
That goblin cry,   255
'Come buy our fruits, come buy.'
Must she then buy no more such dainty fruit?
Must she no more such succous pasture find,
Gone deaf and blind?
Her tree of life drooped from the root: 260
She said not one word in her heart's sore ache;
But peering thro' the dimness, nought discerning,
Trudged home, her pitcher dripping all the way;
So crept to bed, and lay
Silent till Lizzie slept;   265
Then sat up in a passionate yearning,
And gnashed her teeth for baulked desire, and wept
As if her heart would break.

Day after day, night after night,
Laura kept watch in vain   270
In sullen silence of exceeding pain.
She never caught again the goblin cry:
'Come buy, come buy;'—
She never spied the goblin men
Hawking their fruits along the glen: 275
But when the noon waxed bright
Her hair grew thin and grey;
She dwindled, as the fair full moon doth turn
To swift decay and burn
Her fire away.   280

One day remembering her kernel-stone
She set it by a wall that faced the south;
Dewed it with tears, hoped for a root,
Watched for a waxing shoot,
But there came none;   285
It never saw the sun,
It never felt the trickling moisture run:
While with sunk eyes and faded mouth
She dreamed of melons, as a traveller sees
False waves in desert drouth   290
With shade of leaf-crowned trees,
And burns the thirstier in the sandful breeze.

She no more swept the house,
Tended the fowls or cows,

Fetched honey, kneaded cakes of wheat,   295
Brought water from the brook:
But sat down listless in the chimney-nook
And would not eat.

   Tender Lizzie could not bear
To watch her sister's cankerous care   300
Yet not to share.
She night and morning
Caught the goblins' cry:
'Come buy our orchard fruits,
Come buy, come buy:'—   305
Beside the brook, along the glen,
She heard the tramp of goblin men,
The voice and stir
Poor Laura could not hear;
Longed to buy fruit to comfort her,   310
But feared to pay too dear.
She thought of Jeanie in her grave,
Who should have been a bride;
But who for joys brides hope to have
Fell sick and died   315
In her gay prime,
In earliest winter time,
With the first glazing rime,
With the first snowfall of crisp winter time.

   Till Laura dwindling   320
Seemed knocking at death's door:
Then Lizzie weighed no more
Better and worse;
But put a silver penny in her purse,
Kissed Laura, crossed the heath with clumps of furze   325
At twilight, halted by the brook:
And for the first time in her life
Began to listen and look.

   Laughed every goblin
When they spied her peeping: 330
Came towards her hobbling,
Flying, running, leaping,
Puffing and blowing,
Chuckling, clapping, crowing,
Clucking and gobbling,   335
Mopping and mowing,

Full of airs and graces,
Pulling wry faces,
Demure grimaces,
Cat-like and rat-like,   340
Ratel- and wombat-like,
Snail-paced in a hurry,
Parrot-voiced and whistler,
Helter skelter, hurry skurry,
Chattering like magpies,   345
Fluttering like pigeons,
Gliding like fishes—
Hugged her and kissed her,
Squeezed and caressed her:
Stretched up their dishes,   350
Panniers, and plates:
'Look at our apples
Russet and dun,
Bob at our cherries,
Bite at our peaches,   355
Citrons and dates,
Grapes for the asking,
Pears red with basking
Out in the sun,
Plums on their twigs;   360
Pluck them and suck them,
Pomegranates, figs.'

 'Good folk,' said Lizzie,
Mindful of Jeanie:
'Give me much and many'—   365
Held out her apron,
Tossed them her penny.
'Nay, take a seat with us,
Honour and eat with us,'
They answered grinning: 370
'Our feast is but beginning.
Night yet is early,
Warm and dew-pearly,
Wakeful and starry:
Such fruits as these   375
No man can carry;
Half their bloom would fly,
Half their dew would dry,
Half their flavour would pass by.

Sit down and feast with us,   380
Be welcome guest with us,
Cheer you and rest with us.'
'Thank you,' said Lizzie: 'But one waits
At home alone for me:
So without further parleying,   385
If you will not sell me any
Of your fruits though much and many,
Give me back my silver penny
I tossed you for a fee.'
They began to scratch their pates,   390
No longer wagging, purring,
But visibly demurring,
Grunting and snarling.
One called her proud,
Cross-grained, uncivil;   395
Their tones waxed loud,
Their looks were evil.
Lashing their tails
They trod and hustled her,
Elbowed and jostled her,   400
Clawed with their nails,
Barking, mewing, hissing, mocking,
Tore her gown and soiled her stocking,
Twitched her hair out by the roots,
Stamped upon her tender feet,   405
Held her hands and squeezed their fruits
Against her mouth to make her eat.

  White and golden Lizzie stood,
Like a lily in a flood—
Like a rock of blue-veined stone   410
Lashed by tides obstreperously—
Like a beacon left alone
In a hoary roaring sea,
Sending up a golden fire—
Like a fruit-crowned orange tree   415
White with blossoms honey-sweet
Sore beset by wasp and bee—
Like a royal virgin town
Topped with gilded dome and spire
Close beleaguered by a fleet   420
Mad to tug her standard down.

One may lead a horse to water,
Twenty cannot make him drink.
Though the goblins cuffed and caught her,
Coaxed and fought her, 425
Bullied and besought her,
Scratched her, pinched her black as ink,
Kicked and knocked her,
Mauled and mocked her,
Lizzie uttered not a word; 430
Would not open lip from lip
Lest they should cram a mouthful in:
But laughed in heart to feel the drip
Of juice that syrupped all her face,
And lodged in dimples of her chin, 435
And streaked her neck which quaked like curd.
At last the evil people
Worn out by her resistance
Flung back her penny, kicked their fruit
Along whichever road they took, 440
Not leaving root or stone or shoot;
Some writhed into the ground,
Some dived into the brook
With ring and ripple,
Some scudded on the gale without a sound, 445
Some vanished in the distance.

In a smart, ache, tingle,
Lizzie went her way;
Knew not was it night or day;
Sprang up the bank, tore through the furze, 450
Threaded copse and dingle,
And heard her penny jingle
Bouncing in her purse—
Its bounce was music to her ear.
She ran and ran 455
As if she feared some goblin man
Dogged her with gibe or curse
Or something worse:
But not one goblin skurried after,
Nor was she pricked by fear; 460
The kind heart made her windy-paced
That urged her home quite out of breath with haste
And inward laughter.

She cried 'Laura,' up the garden,
'Did you miss me?   465
Come and kiss me.
Never mind my bruises,
Hug me, kiss me, suck my juices
Squeezed from goblin fruits for you,
Goblin pulp and goblin dew.   470
Eat me, drink me, love me;
Laura, make much of me;
For your sake I have braved the glen
And had to do with goblin merchant men.'

Laura started from her chair,   475
Flung her arms up in the air,
Clutched her hair:
'Lizzie, Lizzie, have you tasted
For my sake the fruit forbidden?
Must your light like mine be hidden,   480
Your young life like mine be wasted,
Undone in mine undoing
And ruined in my ruin,
Thirsty, cankered, goblin-ridden?'
She clung about her sister,   485
Kissed and kissed and kissed her:
Tears once again
Refreshed her shrunken eyes,
Dropping like rain
After long sultry drouth;   490
Shaking with aguish fear, and pain,
She kissed and kissed her with a hungry mouth.

Her lips began to scorch,
That juice was wormwood to her tongue,
She loathed the feast: 495
Writhing as one possessed she leaped and sung,
Rent all her robe, and wrung
Her hands in lamentable haste,
And beat her breast.
Her locks streamed like the torch   500
Borne by a racer at full speed,
Or like the mane of horses in their flight,
Or like an eagle when she stems the light
Straight toward the sun,
Or like a caged thing freed,   505
Or like a flying flag when armies run.

Swift fire spread through her veins, knocked at her heart,
Met the fire smouldering there
And overbore its lesser flame;
She gorged on bitterness without a name: 510
Ah! fool, to choose such part
Of soul-consuming care!
Sense failed in the mortal strife:
Like the watch-tower of a town
Which an earthquake shatters down, 515
Like a lightning-stricken mast,
Like a wind-uprooted tree
Spun about,
Like a foam-topped waterspout
Cast down headlong in the sea, 520
She fell at last;
Pleasure past and anguish past,
Is it death or is it life?

   Life out of death.
That night long Lizzie watched by her, 525
Counted her pulse's flagging stir,
Felt for her breath,
Held water to her lips, and cooled her face
With tears and fanning leaves:
But when the first birds chirped about their eaves, 530
And early reapers plodded to the place
Of golden sheaves,
And dew-wet grass
Bowed in the morning winds so brisk to pass,
And new buds with new day 535
Opened of cup-like lilies on the stream,
Laura awoke as from a dream,
Laughed in the innocent old way,
Hugged Lizzie but not twice or thrice;
Her gleaming locks showed not one thread of grey, 540
Her breath was sweet as May
And light danced in her eyes.

   Days, weeks, months, years
Afterwards, when both were wives
With children of their own; 545
Their mother-hearts beset with fears,
Their lives bound up in tender lives;
Laura would call the little ones
And tell them of her early prime,

Those pleasant days long gone 550
Of not-returning time:
Would talk about the haunted glen,
The wicked, quaint fruit-merchant men,
Their fruits like honey to the throat
But poison in the blood 555
(Men sell not such in any town);
Would tell them how her sister stood
In deadly peril to do her good,
And win the fiery antidote:
Then joining hands to little hands 560
Would bid them cling together,
'For there is no friend like a sister
In calm or stormy weather;
To cheer one on the tedious way,
To fetch one if one goes astray, 565
To lift one if one totters down,
To strengthen whilst one stands.'

BRET HARTE
1836–1902

The Tale of a Pony

NAME of my heroine, simply 'Rose;'
Surname, tolerable only in prose;
Habitat, Paris,—that is where
She resided for change of air;
Ætat. twenty; complexion fair, 5
Rich, good-looking, and *débonnaire*,
Smarter than Jersey-lightning—There!
That's her photograph, done with care.

In Paris, whatever they do besides,
EVERY LADY IN FULL DRESS RIDES! 10
Moiré antique you never meet
Sweeping the filth of a dirty street;
But every woman's claim to *ton*
   Depends upon
The team she drives, whether phaeton, 15

Landau, or britzka. Hence it's plain
That Rose, who was of her toilet vain,
Should have a team that ought to be
Equal to any in all *Paris!*

'Bring forth the horse!' The *commissaire*   20
Bowed, and brought Miss Rose a pair
Leading an equipage rich and rare.
Why doth that lovely lady stare?
Why? The tail of the off grey mare
Is bobbed, by all that's good and fair!   25
Like the shaving-brushes that soldiers wear,
Scarcely showing as much back-hair
As Tam o'Shanter's 'Meg'—and there,
Lord knows, she'd little enough to spare.

That stare and frown the Frenchman knew,   30
But did as well-bred Frenchmen do:
Raised his shoulders above his crown,
Joined his thumbs with the fingers down,
And said, 'Ah Heaven!'—then, 'Mademoiselle
Delay one minute, and all is well!'   35
He went—returned; by what good chance
These things are managed so well in France
I cannot say, but he made the sale,
And the bob-tailed mare had a flowing tail.

All that is false in this world below   40
Betrays itself in a love of show;
Indignant Nature hides her lash
In the purple-black of a dyed moustache;
The shallowest fop will trip in French,
The would-be critic will misquote Trench;   45
In short, you're always sure to detect
A sham in the things folks most affect;
Bean-pods are noisiest when dry,
And you always wink with your weakest eye:
And that's the reason the old grey mare   50
Forever had her tail in the air,
With flourishes beyond compare,
    Though every whisk
    Incurred the risk
Of leaving that sensitive region bare: 55
She did some things that you couldn't but feel
She wouldn't have done had her tail been real.

Champs-Élysées: time, past five;
There go the carriages—look alive!
Everything that man can drive,   60
Or his inventive skill contrive—
Yankee buggy or English 'chay,'
Dog-cart, droschky, and smart coupé,
A *désobligeante* quite bulky
(French idea of a Yankee *sulky*);   65
Band in the distance playing a march,
Footmen standing stiff as starch;
Savans, lorettes, deputies, Arch-
Bishops, and there together range
Sous-lieutenants and *cent*-gardes (strange   70
Way these soldier-chaps make change),
Mixed with black-eyed Polish dames,
With unpronounceable awful names;
Laces tremble and ribbons flout,
Coachmen wrangle and gendarmes shout—   75
Bless us! what is the row about?
Ah! here comes Rosy's new turn-out!
Smart! You bet your life 'twas that!
Nifty! (short for *magnificat*).
Mulberry panels, heraldic spread,   80
Ebony wheels picked out with red,
And two grey mares that were thorough-bred;
No wonder that every dandy's head
Was turned by the turn-out; and 'twas said
That Caskowhisky (friend of the Czar),   85
A very good *whip* (as Russians are),
Was tied to Rosy's triumphal car,
Entranced, the reader will understand,
By 'ribbons' that graced her head and hand.

Alas! the hour you think would crown   90
Your highest wishes should let you down!
Or Fate should turn, by your own mischance,
Your victor's car to an ambulance;
From cloudless heavens her lightnings glance
(And these things happen, even in France).   95
And so Miss Rose, as she trotted by,
The cynosure of every eye,
Saw to her horror the off mare shy—
Flourish her tail so exceedingly high
That, disregarding the closest tie,   100
And without giving a reason why,

She flung that tail so free and frisky
Off in the face of Caskowhisky.

Excuses, blushes, smiles: in fine,
End of the pony's tail, and mine!   105

LEWIS CARROLL
(CHARLES LUTWIDGE DODGSON)

1832–1898

The Hunting of the Snark

FIT THE FIRST

THE LANDING

'JUST the place for a Snark!' the Bellman cried,
    As he landed his crew with care;
Supporting each man on the top of the tide
    By a finger entwined in his hair.

'Just the place for a Snark! I have said it twice: 5
    That alone should encourage the crew.
Just the place for a Snark! I have said it thrice:
    What I tell you three times is true.'

The crew was complete: it included a Boots—
    A maker of Bonnets and Hoods—   10
A Barrister, brought to arrange their disputes—
    And a Broker, to value their goods.

A Billiard-marker, whose skill was immense,
    Might perhaps have won more than his share—
But a Banker, engaged at enormous expense,   15
    Had the whole of their cash in his care.

There was also a Beaver, that paced on the deck,
    Or would sit making lace in the bow:
And had often (the Bellman said) saved them from wreck,
    Though none of the sailors knew how.   20

There was one who was famed for the number of things
    He forgot when he entered the ship:
His umbrella, his watch, all his jewels and rings,
    And the clothes he had bought for the trip.

He had forty-two boxes, all carefully packed,   25
    With his name painted clearly on each:
But, since he omitted to mention the fact,
    They were all left behind on the beach.

The loss of his clothes hardly mattered, because
    He had seven coats on when he came,   30
With three pair of boots—but the worst of it was,
    He had wholly forgotten his name.

He would answer to 'Hi!' or to any loud cry,
    Such as 'Fry me!' or 'Fritter my wig!'
To 'What-you-may-call-um!' or 'What-was-his-name!'   35
    But especially 'Thing-um-a-jig!'

While, for those who preferred a more forcible word,
    He had different names from these:
His intimate friends called him 'Candle-ends',
    And his enemies 'Toasted-cheese'.   40

'His form is ungainly—his intellect small—'
    (So the Bellman would often remark)
'But his courage is perfect! And that, after all,
    Is the thing that one needs with a Snark.'

He would joke with hyænas, returning their stare   45
    With an impudent wag of the head:
And he once went a walk, paw-in-paw, with a bear,
    'Just to keep up its spirits,' he said.

He came as a Baker: but owned, when too late—
    And it drove the poor Bellman half-mad—   50
He could only bake Bridecake—for which, I may state,
    No materials were to be had.

The last of the crew needs especial remark,
    Though he looked an incredible dunce:
He had just one idea—but, that one being 'Snark',   55
    The good Bellman engaged him at once.

He came as a Butcher: but gravely declared,
  When the ship had been sailing a week,
He could only kill Beavers. The Bellman looked scared,
  And was almost too frightened to speak: 60

But at length he explained, in a tremulous tone,
  There was only one Beaver on board;
And that was a tame one he had of his own,
  Whose death would be deeply deplored.

The Beaver, who happened to hear the remark,   65
  Protested, with tears in its eyes,
That not even the rapture of hunting the Snark
  Could atone for that dismal surprise!

It strongly advised that the Butcher should be
  Conveyed in a separate ship: 70
But the Bellman declared that would never agree
  With the plans he had made for the trip;

Navigation was always a difficult art,
  Though with only one ship and one bell:
And he feared he must really decline, for his part,   75
  Undertaking another as well.

The Beaver's best course was, no doubt, to procure
  A second-hand dagger-proof coat—
So the Baker advised it—and next, to insure
  Its life in some Office of note: 80

This the Banker suggested, and offered for hire
  (On moderate terms), or for sale,
Two excellent Policies, one Against Fire,
  And one Against Damage From Hail.

Yet still, ever after that sorrowful day,   85
  Whenever the Butcher was by,
The Beaver kept looking the opposite way,
  And appeared unaccountably shy.

FIT THE SECOND

THE BELLMAN'S SPEECH

The Bellman himself they all praised to the skies—
  Such a carriage, such ease and such grace!   90
Such solemnity, too! One could see he was wise,
  The moment one looked in his face!

He had bought a large map representing the sea,
    Without the least vestige of land:
And the crew were much pleased when they found it to be   95
    A map they could all understand.

'What's the good of Mercator's North Poles and Equators,
    Tropics, Zones, and Meridian Lines?'
So the Bellman would cry: and the crew would reply
    'They are merely conventional signs!   100

'Other maps are such shapes, with their islands and capes!
    But we've got our brave Captain to thank'
(So the crew would protest) 'that he's bought us the best—
    A perfect and absolute blank!'

This was charming, no doubt: but they shortly found out   105
    That the Captain they trusted so well
Had only one notion for crossing the ocean,
    And that was to tingle his bell.

He was thoughtful and grave—but the orders he gave
    Were enough to bewilder a crew.   110
When he cried 'Steer to starboard, but keep her head larboard!'
    What on earth was the helmsman to do?

Then the bowsprit got mixed with the rudder sometimes:
    A thing, as the Bellman remarked,
That frequently happens in tropical climes,   115
    When a vessel is, so to speak, 'snarked'.

But the principal failing occurred in the sailing,
    And the Bellman, perplexed and distressed,
Said he *had* hoped, at least, when the wind blew due East
    That the ship would *not* travel due West!   120

But the danger was past—they had landed at last,
    With their boxes, portmanteaus, and bags:
Yet at first sight the crew were not pleased with the view,
    Which consisted of chasms and crags.

The Bellman perceived that their spirits were low,   125
    And repeated in musical tone
Some jokes he had kept for a season of woe—
    But the crew would do nothing but groan.

He served out some grog with a liberal hand,
   And bade them sit down on the beach: 130
And they could not but own that their Captain looked grand,
   As he stood and delivered his speech.

'Friends, Romans, and countrymen, lend me your ears!'
   (They were all of them fond of quotations:
So they drank to his health, and they gave him three cheers,   135
   While he served out additional rations).

'We have sailed many months, we have sailed many weeks
   (Four weeks to the month you may mark),
But never as yet ('tis your Captain who speaks)
   Have we caught the least glimpse of a Snark!   140

'We have sailed many weeks, we have sailed many days
   (Seven days to the week I allow),
But a Snark, on the which we might lovingly gaze,
   We have never beheld till now!

'Come, listen, my men, while I tell you again   145
   The five unmistakable marks
By which you may know, wheresoever you go,
   The warranted genuine Snarks.

'Let us take them in order. The first is the taste,
   Which is meagre and hollow, but crisp: 150
Like a coat that is rather too tight in the waist,
   With a flavour of Will-o'-the-wisp.

'Its habit of getting up late you'll agree
   That it carries too far, when I say
That it frequently breakfasts at five-o'clock tea,   155
   And dines on the following day.

'The third is its slowness in taking a jest,
   Should you happen to venture on one,
It will sigh like a thing that is deeply distressed:
   And it always looks grave at a pun.   160

'The fourth is its fondness for bathing-machines,
   Which it constantly carries about,
And believes that they add to the beauty of scenes—
   A sentiment open to doubt.

'The fifth is ambition. It next will be right 165
  To describe each particular batch:
Distinguishing those that have feathers, and bite,
  From those that have whiskers, and scratch.

'For, although common Snarks do no manner of harm,
  Yet, I feel it my duty to say,
Some are Boojums—' The Bellman broke off in alarm, 170
  For the Baker had fainted away.

Fit the Third

the baker's tale

They roused him with muffins—they roused him with ice—
  They roused him with mustard and cress—
They roused him with jam and judicious advice— 175
  They set him conundrums to guess.

When at length he sat up and was able to speak,
  His sad story he offered to tell;
And the Bellman cried 'Silence! not even a shriek!'
  And excitedly tingled his bell. 180

There was silence supreme! Not a shriek, not a scream,
  Scarcely even a howl or a groan,
As the man they called 'Ho!' told his story of woe
  In an antediluvian tone.

'My father and mother were honest, though poor—' 185
  'Skip all that!' cried the Bellman in haste.
'If it once becomes dark, there's no chance of a Snark—
  We have hardly a minute to waste!'

'I skip forty years,' said the Baker, in tears,
  'And proceed without further remark 190
To the day when you took me aboard of your ship
  To help you in hunting the Snark.

'A dear uncle of mine (after whom I was named)
  Remarked, when I bade him farewell—'
'Oh, skip your dear uncle!' the Bellman exclaimed, 195
  As he angrily tingled his bell.

'He remarked to me then,' said that mildest of men,
  ' "If your Snark be a Snark, that is right:
Fetch it home by all means—you may serve it with greens,
  And it's handy for striking a light. 200

THE HUNTING OF THE SNARK

' "You may seek it with thimbles—and seek it with care;
   You may hunt it with forks and hope;
You may threaten its life with a railway-share;
   You may charm it with smiles and soap—" '

('That's exactly the method,' the Bellman bold   205
   In a hasty parenthesis cried,
'That's exactly the way I have always been told
   That the capture of Snarks should be tried!')

' "But oh, beamish nephew, beware of the day,
   If your Snark be a Boojum! For then   210
You will softly and suddenly vanish away,
   And never be met with again!"

'It is this, it is this that oppresses my soul,
   When I think of my uncle's last words:
And my heart is like nothing so much as a bowl   215
   Brimming over with quivering curds!

'It is this, it is this—' 'We have had that before!'
   The Bellman indignantly said.
And the Baker replied 'Let me say it once more.
   It is this, it is this that I dread!   220

'I engage with the Snark—every night after dark—
   In a dreamy delirious fight:
I serve it with greens in those shadowy scenes,
   And I use it for striking a light;

'But if ever I meet with a Boojum, that day,   225
   In a moment (of this I am sure),
I shall softly and suddenly vanish away—
   And the notion I cannot endure!'

Fit the Fourth

THE HUNTING

The Bellman looked uffish, and wrinkled his brow.
   'If only you'd spoken before!   230
It's excessively awkward to mention it now,
   With the Snark, so to speak, at the door!

'We should all of us grieve, as you well may believe,
   If you never were met with again—
But surely, my man, when the voyage began,   235
   You might have suggested it then?

297

'It's excessively awkward to mention it now—
   As I think I've already remarked.'
And the man they called 'Hi!' replied, with a sigh,
   'I informed you the day we embarked.   240

'You may charge me with murder—or want of sense—
   (We are all of us weak at times):
But the slightest approach to a false pretence
   Was never among my crimes!

'I said it in Hebrew—I said it in Dutch—   245
   I said it in German and Greek;
But I wholly forgot (and it vexes me much)
   That English is what you speak!'

''Tis a pitiful tale,' said the Bellman, whose face
   Had grown longer at every word;   250
'But, now that you've stated the whole of your case,
   More debate would be simply absurd.

'The rest of my speech' (he explained to his men)
   'You shall hear when I've leisure to speak it.
But the Snark is at hand, let me tell you again!   255
   'Tis your glorious duty to seek it!

'To seek it with thimbles, to seek it with care;
   To pursue it with forks and hope;
To threaten its life with a railway-share;
   To charm it with smiles and soap!   260

'For the Snark's a peculiar creature, that won't
   Be caught in a commonplace way.
Do all that you know, and try all that you don't:
   Not a chance must be wasted today!

'For England expects—I forbear to proceed: 265
   'Tis a maxim tremendous, but trite:
And you'd best be unpacking the things that you need
   To rig yourselves out for the fight.'

Then the Banker endorsed a blank cheque (which he crossed),
   And changed his loose silver for notes.   270
The Baker with care combed his whiskers and hair,
   And shook the dust out of his coats.

The Boots and the Broker were sharpening a spade—
    Each working the grindstone in turn;
But the Beaver went on making lace, and displayed   275
    No interest in the concern:

Though the Barrister tried to appeal to its pride,
    And vainly proceeded to cite
A number of cases, in which making laces
    Had been proved an infringement of right.   280

The maker of Bonnets ferociously planned
    A novel arrangement of bows:
While the Billiard-marker with quivering hand
    Was chalking the tip of his nose.

But the Butcher turned nervous, and dressed himself fine,   285
    With yellow kid gloves and a ruff—
Said he felt it exactly like going to dine,
    Which the Bellman declared was all 'stuff'.

'Introduce me, now there's a good fellow,' he said,
    'If we happen to meet it together!'   290
And the Bellman, sagaciously nodding his head,
    Said 'That must depend on the weather'.

The Beaver went simply galumphing about,
    At seeing the Butcher so shy:
And even the Baker, though stupid and stout,   295
    Made an effort to wink with one eye.

'Be a man!' said the Bellman in wrath, as he heard
    The Butcher beginning to sob.
'Should we meet with a Jubjub, that desperate bird,
    We shall need all our strength for the job!'   300

FIT THE FIFTH

THE BEAVER'S LESSON

They sought it with thimbles, they sought it with care;
    They pursued it with forks and hope;
They threatened its life with a railway-share;
    They charmed it with smiles and soap.

Then the Butcher contrived an ingenious plan   305
    For making a separate sally;
And had fixed on a spot unfrequented by man,
    A dismal and desolate valley.

But the very same plan to the Beaver occurred:
  It had chosen the very same place;   310
Yet neither betrayed, by a sign or a word,
  The disgust that appeared in his face.

Each thought he was thinking of nothing but 'Snark'
  And the glorious work of the day;
And each tried to pretend that he did not remark   315
  That the other was going that way.

But the valley grew narrow and narrower still,
  And the evening got darker and colder,
Till (merely from nervousness, not from goodwill)
  They marched along shoulder to shoulder.   320

Then a scream, shrill and high, rent the shuddering sky,
  And they knew that some danger was near:
The Beaver turned pale to the tip of its tail,
  And even the Butcher felt queer.

He thought of his childhood, left far far behind—   325
  That blissful and innocent state—
The sound so exactly recalled to his mind
  A pencil that squeaks on a slate!

''Tis the voice of the Jubjub!' he suddenly cried.
  (This man, that they used to call 'Dunce'.)   330
'As the Bellman would tell you,' he added with pride,
  'I have uttered that sentiment once.

''Tis the note of the Jubjub! Keep count, I entreat;
  You will find I have told it you twice.
'Tis the song of the Jubjub! The proof is complete,   335
  If only I've stated it thrice.'

The Beaver had counted with scrupulous care,
  Attending to every word:
But it fairly lost heart, and outgrabe in despair,
  When the third repetition occurred.   340

It felt that, in spite of all possible pains,
  It had somehow contrived to lose count,
And the only thing now was to rack its poor brains
  By reckoning up the amount.

'Two added to one—if that could but be done,'   345
   It said, 'with one's fingers and thumbs!'
Recollecting with tears how, in earlier years,
   It had taken no pains with its sums.

'The thing can be done,' said the Butcher, 'I think.
   The thing must be done, I am sure.   350
The thing shall be done! Bring me paper and ink,
   The best there is time to procure.'

The Beaver brought paper, portfolio, pens,
   And ink in unfailing supplies:
While strange creepy creatures came out of their dens,   355
   And watched them with wondering eyes.

So engrossed was the Butcher, he heeded them not,
   As he wrote with a pen in each hand,
And explained all the while in a popular style
   Which the Beaver could well understand.   360

'Taking Three as the subject to reason about—
   A convenient number to state—
We add Seven, and Ten, and then multiply out
   By One Thousand diminished by Eight.

'The result we proceed to divide, as you see,   365
   By Nine Hundred and Ninety and Two:
Then subtract Seventeen, and the answer must be
   Exactly and perfectly true.

'The method employed I would gladly explain,
   While I have it so clear in my head,   370
If I had but the time and you had but the brain—
   But much yet remains to be said.

'In one moment I've seen what has hitherto been
   Enveloped in absolute mystery,
And without extra charge I will give you at large   375
   A Lesson in Natural History.'

In his genial way he proceeded to say
   (Forgetting all laws of propriety,
And that giving instruction, without introduction,
   Would have caused quite a thrill in Society),   380

'As to temper the Jubjub's a desperate bird,
  Since it lives in perpetual passion:
Its taste in costume is entirely absurd—
  It is ages ahead of the fashion:

'But it knows any friend it has met once before: 385
  It never will look at a bribe:
And in charity meetings it stands at the door,
  And collects—though it does not subscribe.

'Its flavour when cooked is more exquisite far
  Than mutton, or oysters, or eggs: 390
(Some think it keeps best in an ivory jar,
  And some, in mahogany kegs:)

'You boil it in sawdust: you salt it in glue:
  You condense it with locusts and tape:
Still keeping one principal object in view—   395
  To preserve its symmetrical shape.'

The Butcher would gladly have talked till next day,
  But he felt that the Lesson must end,
And he wept with delight in attempting to say
  He considered the Beaver his friend.   400

While the Beaver confessed, with affectionate looks
  More eloquent even than tears,
It had learnt in ten minutes far more than all books
  Would have taught it in seventy years.

They returned hand-in-hand, and the Bellman, unmanned 405
  (For a moment) with noble emotion,
Said 'This amply repays all the wearisome days
  We have spent on the billowy ocean!'

Such friends, as the Beaver and Butcher became,
  Have seldom if ever been known;   410
In winter or summer, 'twas always the same—
  You could never meet either alone.

And when quarrels arose—as one frequently finds
  Quarrels will, spite of every endeavour—
The song of the Jubjub recurred to their minds,   415
  And cemented their friendship for ever!

Fit the Sixth

the barrister's dream

They sought it with thimbles, they sought it with care;
    They pursued it with forks and hope;
They threatened its life with a railway-share;
    They charmed it with smiles and soap.   420

But the Barrister, weary of proving in vain
    That the Beaver's lace-making was wrong,
Fell asleep, and in dreams saw the creature quite plain
    That his fancy had dwelt on so long.

He dreamed that he stood in a shadowy Court,   425
    Where the Snark, with a glass in its eye,
Dressed in gown, bands, and wig, was defending a pig
    On the charge of deserting its sty.

The Witnesses proved, without error or flaw,
    That the sty was deserted when found: 430
And the judge kept explaining the state of the law
    In a soft under-current of sound.

The indictment had never been clearly expressed,
    And it seemed that the Snark had begun,
And had spoken three hours, before any one guessed   435
    What the pig was supposed to have done.

The Jury had each formed a different view
    (Long before the indictment was read),
And they all spoke at once, so that none of them knew
    One word that the others had said.   440

'You must know—' said the Judge: but the Snark exclaimed
      'Fudge!
    That statute is obsolete quite!
Let me tell you, my friends, the whole question depends
    On an ancient manorial right.

'In the matter of Treason the pig would appear   445
    To have aided, but scarcely abetted:
While the charge of Insolvency fails, it is clear,
    If you grant the plea "never indebted".

'The fact of Desertion I will not dispute:
  But its guilt, as I trust, is removed
(So far as relates to the costs of this suit)
  By the Alibi which has been proved.

'My poor client's fate now depends on your votes.'
  Here the speaker sat down in his place,
And directed the Judge to refer to his notes
  And briefly to sum up the case.

But the Judge said he never had summed up before;
  So the Snark undertook it instead,
And summed it so well that it came to far more
  Than the Witnesses ever had said!

When the verdict was called for, the Jury declined,
  As the word was so puzzling to spell;
But they ventured to hope that the Snark wouldn't mind
  Undertaking that duty as well.

So the Snark found the verdict, although as it owned,
  It was spent with the toils of the day:
When it said the word 'GUILTY!' the Jury all groaned,
  And some of them fainted away.

Then the Snark pronounced sentence, the Judge being quite
  Too nervous to utter a word:
When it rose to its feet, there was silence like night,
  And the fall of a pin might be heard.

'Transportation for life' was the sentence it gave,
  'And *then* to be fined forty pound.'
The Jury all cheered, though the Judge said he feared
  That the phrase was not legally sound.

But their wild exultation was suddenly checked
  When the jailer informed them, with tears,
Such a sentence would have not the slightest effect,
  As the pig had been dead for some years.

The Judge left the Court, looking deeply disgusted:
  But the Snark, though a little aghast,
As the lawyer to whom the defence was intrusted,
  Went bellowing on to the last.

450

455

460

465

470

475

480

Thus the Barrister dreamed, while the bellowing seemed   485
    To grow every moment more clear:
Till he woke to the knell of a furious bell,
    Which the Bellman rang close at his ear.

FIT THE SEVENTH

THE BANKER'S FATE

They sought it with thimbles, they sought it with care;
    They pursued it with forks and hope;   490
They threatened its life with a railway-share;
    They charmed it with smiles and soap.

And the Banker, inspired with a courage so new
    It was matter for general remark,
Rushed madly ahead and was lost to their view   495
    In his zeal to discover the Snark.

But while he was seeking with thimbles and care,
    A Bandersnatch swiftly drew nigh
And grabbed at the Banker, who shrieked in despair,
    For he knew it was useless to fly.   500

He offered large discount—he offered a cheque
    (Drawn 'to bearer') for seven-pounds-ten:
But the Bandersnatch merely extended its neck
    And grabbed at the Banker again.

Without rest or pause—while those frumious jaws   505
    Went savagely snapping around—
He skipped and he hopped, and he floundered and flopped,
    Till fainting he fell to the ground.

The Bandersnatch fled as the others appeared:
    Led on by that fear-stricken yell: 510
And the Bellman remarked 'It is just as I feared!'
    And solemnly tolled on his bell.

He was black in the face, and they scarcely could trace
    The least likeness to what he had been:
While so great was his fright that his waistcoat turned white—   515
    A wonderful thing to be seen!

To the horror of all who were present that day,
    He uprose in full evening dress,
And with senseless grimaces endeavoured to say
    What his tongue could no longer express.   520

Down he sank in a chair—ran his hands through his hair—
  And chanted in mimsiest tones
Words whose utter inanity proved his insanity,
  While he rattled a couple of bones.

'Leave him here to his fate—it is getting so late!'   525
  The Bellman exclaimed in a fright.
'We have lost half the day. Any further delay,
  And we shan't catch a Snark before night!'

FIT THE EIGHTH

THE VANISHING

They sought it with thimbles, they sought it with care;
  They pursued it with forks and hope;   530
They threatened its life with a railway-share;
  They charmed it with smiles and soap.

They shuddered to think that the chase might fail,
  And the Beaver, excited at last,
Went bounding along on the tip of its tail,   535
  For the daylight was nearly past.

'There is Thingumbob shouting!' the Bellman said.
  'He is shouting like mad, only hark!
He is waving his hands, he is wagging his head,
  He has certainly found a Snark!'   540

They gazed in delight, while the Butcher exclaimed
  'He was always a desperate wag!'
They beheld him—their Baker—their hero unnamed—
  On the top of a neighbouring crag,

Erect and sublime, for one moment of time.   545
  In the next, that wild figure they saw
(As if stung by a spasm) plunge into a chasm,
  While they waited and listened in awe.

'It's a Snark!' was the sound that first came to their ears,
  And seemed almost too good to be true.   550
Then followed a torrent of laughter and cheers:
  Then the ominous words 'It's a Boo—'

Then, silence. Some fancied they heard in the air
  A weary and wandering sigh
That sounded like '—jum!' but the others declare   555
  It was only a breeze that went by.

306

They hunted till darkness came on, but they found
  Not a button, or feather, or mark,
By which they could tell that they stood on the ground
  Where the Baker had met with the Snark. 560

In the midst of the word he was trying to say
  In the midst of his laughter and glee,
He had softly and suddenly vanished away—
  For the Snark *was* a Boojum, you see.

DANTE GABRIEL ROSSETTI
1828–1882

The White Ship

By none but me can the tale be told,
The butcher of Rouen, poor Berold.
  (*Lands are swayed by a King on a throne.*)
'Twas a royal train put forth to sea,
Yet the tale can be told by none but me. 5
  (*The sea hath no King but God alone.*)

King Henry held it as life's whole gain
That after his death his son should reign.

'Twas so in my youth I heard men say,
And my old age calls it back today. 10

King Henry of England's realm was he,
And Henry Duke of Normandy.

The times had changed when on either coast
'Clerkly Harry' was all his boast.

Of ruthless strokes full many an one 15
He had struck to crown himself and his son;
And his elder brother's eyes were gone.

And when to the chase his court would crowd,
The poor flung ploughshares on his road,
And shrieked: 'Our cry is from King to God!' 20

But all the chiefs of the English land
Had knelt and kissed the Prince's hand.

And next with his son he sailed to France
To claim the Norman allegiance:

And every baron in Normandy   25
Had taken the oath of fealty.

'Twas sworn and sealed, and the day had come
When the King and the Prince might journey home:

For Christmas cheer is to home hearts dear,
And Christmas now was drawing near.   30

Stout Fitz-Stephen came to the King—
A pilot famous in seafaring;

And he held to the King, in all men's sight,
A mark of gold for his tribute's right.

'Liege Lord! my father guided the ship   35
From whose boat your father's foot did slip
When he caught the English soil in his grip,

'And cried: "By this clasp I claim command
O'er every rood of English land!"

'He was borne to the realm you rule o'er now   40
In that ship with the archer carved at her prow:

'And thither I'll bear, an it be my due,
Your father's son and his grandson too.

'The famed White Ship is mine in the bay;
From Harfleur's harbour she sails today,   45

'With masts fair-pennoned as Norman spears
And with fifty well-tried mariners.'

Quoth the King: 'My ships are chosen each one,
But I'll not say nay to Stephen's son.

'My son and daughter and fellowship   50
Shall cross the water in the White Ship.'

The King set sail with eve's south wind,
And soon he left that coast behind.

The Prince and all his, a princely show,
Remained in the good White Ship to go.   55

With noble knights and with ladies fair,
With courtiers and sailors gathered there,
Three hundred living souls we were:

And I Berold was the meanest hind
In all that train to the Prince assigned.   60

The Prince was a lawless shameless youth;
From his father's loins he sprang without ruth:

Eighteen years till then he had seen,
And the devil's dues in him were eighteen.

And now he cried: 'Bring wine from below;   65
Let the sailors revel ere yet they row:

'Our speed shall o'ertake my father's flight
Though we sail from the harbour at midnight.'

The rowers made good cheer without check:
The lords and ladies obeyed his beck;
The night was light, and they danced on the deck.   70

But at midnight's stroke they cleared the bay,
And the White Ship furrowed the water-way.

The sails were set, and the oars kept tune
To the double flight of the ship and the moon: 75

Swifter and swifter the White Ship sped
Till she flew as the spirit flies from the dead:

As white as a lily glimmered she
Like a ship's fair ghost upon the sea.

And the Prince cried, 'Friends, 'tis the hour to sing!   80
Is a songbird's course so swift on the wing?'

And under the winter stars' still throng,
From brown throats, white throats, merry and strong,
The knights and the ladies raised a song.

A song—nay, a shriek that rent the sky,　　　　　　85
That leaped o'er the deep!—the grievous cry
Of three hundred living that now must die.

An instant shriek that sprang to the shock
As the ship's keel felt the sunken rock.

'Tis said that afar—a shrill strange sigh—　　　　　90
The King's ships heard it and knew not why.

Pale Fitz-Stephen stood by the helm
'Mid all those folks that the wave must whelm.

A great King's heir for the waves to whelm,
And the helpless pilot pale at the helm!　　　　　　95

The ship was eager and sucked athirst,
By the stealthy stab of the sharp reef pierced:

And like the moil round a sinking cup
The waters against her crowded up.

A moment the pilot's senses spin—　　　　　　100
The next he snatched the Prince 'mid the din,
Cut the boat loose, and the youth leaped in.

A few friends leaped with him, standing near.
'Row! the sea's smooth and the night is clear!'

'What! none to be saved but these and I?'　　　　　　105
'Row, row as you'd live! All here must die!'

Out of the churn of the choking ship,
Which the gulf grapples and the waves strip,
They struck with the strained oars' flash and dip.

'Twas then o'er the splitting bulwarks' brim　　　　　　110
The Prince's sister screamed to him.

He gazed aloft, still rowing apace,
And through the whirled surf he knew her face.

To the toppling decks clave one and all
As a fly cleaves to a chamber-wall.   115

I Berold was clinging anear;
I prayed for myself and quaked with fear,
But I saw his eyes as he looked at her.

He knew her face and he heard her cry,
And he said, 'Put back! she must not die!'   120

And back with the current's force they reel
Like a leaf that's drawn to a water-wheel.

'Neath the ship's travail they scarce might float,
But he rose and stood in the rocking boat.

Low the poor ship leaned on the tide: 125
O'er the naked keel as she best might slide,
The sister toiled to the brother's side.

He reached an oar to her from below,
And stiffened his arms to clutch her so.

But now from the ship some spied the boat,   130
And 'Saved!' was the cry from many a throat.

And down to the boat they leaped and fell:
It turned as a bucket turns in a well,
And nothing was there but the surge and swell.

The Prince that was and the King to come,   135
There in an instant gone to his doom,

Despite of all England's bended knee
And maugre the Norman fealty!

He was a Prince of lust and pride;
He showed no grace till the hour he died.   140

When he should be King, he oft would vow,
He'd yoke the peasant to his own plough.
O'er him the ships score their furrows now.

God only knows where his soul did wake,
But I saw him die for his sister's sake.   145

By none but me can the tale by told,
The butcher of Rouen, poor Berold.
   (*Lands are swayed by a King on a throne.*)
'Twas a royal train put forth to sea,
Yet the tale can be told by none but me.   150
   (*The sea hath no King but God alone.*)

And now the end came o'er the waters' womb
Like the last great Day that's yet to come.

With prayers in vain and curses in vain,
The White Ship sundered on the mid-main: 155

And what were men and what was a ship
Were toys and splinters in the sea's grip.

I Berold was down in the sea;
And passing strange though the thing may be,
Of dreams then known I remember me.   160

Blithe is the shout on Harfleur's strand
When morning lights the sails to land:

And blithe is Honfleur's echoing gloam
When mothers call the children home:

And high do the bells of Rouen beat   165
When the Body of Christ goes down the street.

These things and the like were heard and shown
In a moment's trance 'neath the sea alone;

And when I rose, 'twas the sea did seem,
And not these things, to be all a dream.   170

The ship was gone and the crowd was gone,
And the deep shuddered and the moon shone:

And in a strait grasp my arms did span
The mainyard rent from the mast where it ran;
And on it with me was another man.   175

Where lands were none 'neath the dim sea-sky,
We told our names, that man and I.

'O I am Godefroy de l'Aigle hight,
And son I am to a belted knight.'

'And I am Berold the butcher's son   180
Who slays the beasts in Rouen town.'

Then cried we upon God's name, as we
Did drift on the bitter winter sea.

But lo! a third man rose o'er the wave,
And we said, 'Thank God! us three may He save!'   185

He clutched to the yard with panting stare,
And we looked and knew Fitz-Stephen there.

He clung, and 'What of the Prince?' quoth he.
'Lost, lost!' we cried. He cried, 'Woe on me!'
And loosed his hold and sank through the sea.   190

And soul with soul again in that space
We two were together face to face:

And each knew each, as the moments sped,
Less for one living than for one dead:

And every still star overhead   195
Seemed an eye that knew we were but dead.

And the hours passed; till the noble's son
Sighed, 'God be thy help! my strength's fordone!

'O farewell, friend, for I can no more!'
'Christ take thee!' I moaned; and his life was o'er.   200

Three hundred souls were all lost but one,
And I drifted over the sea alone.

At last the morning rose on the sea
Like an angel's wing that beat tow'rds me.

Sore numbed I was in my sheepskin coat;   205
Half dead I hung, and might nothing note,
Till I woke sun-warmed in a fisher-boat.

The sun was high o'er the eastern brim
As I praised God and gave thanks to Him.

That day I told my tale to a priest, 210
Who charged me, till the shrift were released,
That I should keep it in mine own breast.

And with the priest I thence did fare
To King Henry's court at Winchester.

We spoke with the King's high chamberlain, 215
And he wept and mourned again and again,
As if his own son had been slain:

And round us ever there crowded fast
Great men with faces all aghast:

And who so bold that might tell the thing 220
Which now they knew to their lord the King?
Much woe I learnt in their communing.

The King had watched with a heart sore stirred
For two whole days, and this was the third:

And still to all his court would he say, 225
'What keeps my son so long away?'

And they said: 'The ports lie far and wide
That skirt the swell of the English tide;

'And England's cliffs are not more white
Than her women are, and scarce so light 230
Her skies as their eyes are blue and bright;

'And in some port that he reached from France
The Prince has lingered for his pleasaùnce.'

But once the King asked: 'What distant cry
Was that we heard 'twixt the sea and sky?' 235

And one said: 'With suchlike shouts, pardie!
Do the fishers fling their nets at sea.'

And one: 'Who knows not the shrieking quest
When the sea-mew misses its young from the nest?'

'Twas thus till now they had soothed his dread,   240
Albeit they knew not what they said:

But who should speak today of the thing
That all knew there except the King?

Then pondering much they found a way,
And met round the King's high seat that day: 245

And the King sat with a heart sore stirred,
And seldom he spoke and seldom heard.

'Twas then through the hall the King was 'ware
Of a little boy with golden hair,

As bright as the golden poppy is   250
That the beach breeds for the surf to kiss:

Yet pale his cheek as the thorn in spring,
And his garb black like the raven's wing.

Nothing heard but his foot through the hall,
For now the lords were silent all.   255

And the King wondered, and said, 'Alack!
Who sends me a fair boy dressed in black?

'Why, sweet heart, do you pace through the hall
As though my court were a funeral?'

Then lowly knelt the child at the dais,   260
And looked up weeping in the King's face.

'O wherefore black, O King, ye may say,
For white is the hue of death today.

'Your son and all his fellowship
Lie low in the sea with the White Ship.'   265

King Henry fell as a man struck dead;
And speechless still he stared from his bed
When to him next day my rede I read.

There's many an hour must needs beguile
A King's high heart that he should smile—   270

Full many a lordly hour, full fain
Of his realm's rule and pride of his reign—

But this King never smiled again.

By none but me can the tale be told,
The butcher of Rouen, poor Berold.   275
    (Lands are swayed by a King on a throne.)
'Twas a royal train put forth to sea,
Yet the tale can be told by none but me.
    (The sea hath no King but God alone.)

ROBERT LOUIS STEVENSON

1850–1894

Ticonderoga: a Legend of the West Highlands

THIS is the tale of the man
    Who heard a word in the night
In the land of the heathery hills,
    In the days of the feud and the fight.
By the sides of the rainy sea,   5
    Where never a stranger came,
On the awful lips of the dead,
    He heard the outlandish name.
It sang in his sleeping ears,
    It hummed in his waking head: 10
The name—Ticonderoga,
    The utterance of the dead.

THE SAYING OF THE NAME

On the loch-sides of Appin,
    When the mist blew from the sea,
A Stewart stood with a Cameron: 15
    An angry man was he.
The blood beat in his ears,
    The blood ran hot to his head,
The mist blew from the sea,
    And there was the Cameron dead.   20

O, what have I done to my friend,
    O, what have I done to mysel',
That he should be cold and dead,
    And I in the danger of all?

'Nothing but danger about me,   25
    Danger behind and before,
Death at wait in the heather
    In Appin and Mamore,
Hate at all of the ferries
    And death at each of the fords,   30
Camerons priming gunlocks
    And Camerons sharpening swords.'

But this was a man of counsel,
    This was a man of a score,
There dwelt no pawkier Stewart   35
    In Appin or Mamore.
He looked on the blowing mist,
    He looked on the awful dead,
And there came a smile on his face
    And there slipped a thought in his head.   40

Out over cairn and moss,
    Out over scrog and scaur,
He ran as runs the clansman
    That bears the cross of war.
His heart beat in his body,   45
    His hair clove to his face,
When he came at last in the gloaming
    To the dead man's brother's place.
The east was white with the moon,
    The west with the sun was red,   50
And there, in the house-doorway,
    Stood the brother of the dead.

'I have slain a man to my danger,
    I have slain a man to my death,
I put my soul in your hands,'   55
    The panting Stewart saith.
'I lay it bare in your hands,
    For I know your hands are leal;
And be you my targe and bulwark
    From the bullet and the steel.'   60

Then up and spoke the Cameron,
  And gave him his hand again:
'There shall never a man in Scotland
  Set faith in me in vain;
And whatever man you have slaughtered, 65
  Of whatever name or line,
By my sword and yonder mountain,
  I make your quarrel mine.
I bid you in to my fireside,
  I share with you house and hall; 70
It stands upon my honour
  To see you safe from all.'

It fell in the time of midnight,
  When the fox barked in the den,
And the plaids were over the faces 75
  In all the houses of men,
That as the living Cameron
  Lay sleepless on his bed,
Out of the night and the other world
  Came in to him the dead. 80

'My blood is on the heather,
  My bones are on the hill;
There is joy in the home of ravens
  That the young shall eat their fill.
My blood is poured in the dust, 85
  My soul is spilled in the air;
And the man that has undone me
  Sleeps in my brother's care.'

'I'm wae for your death, my brother,
  But if all of my house were dead, 90
I couldnae withdraw the plighted hand
  Nor break the word once said.'

'O, what shall I say to our father,
  In the place to which I fare?
O, what shall I say to our mother, 95
  Who greets to see me there?
And to all the kindly Camerons
  That have lived and died long-syne—
Is this the word you send them,
  Fause-hearted brother mine?' 100

'It's neither fear nor duty,
  It's neither quick nor dead
Shall gar me withdraw the plighted hand,
  Or break the word once said.'

Thrice in the time of midnight,   105
  When the fox barked in the den,
And the plaids were over the faces
  In all the houses of men,
Thrice as the living Cameron
  Lay sleepless on his bed,   110
Out of the night and the other world
  Came in to him the dead,
And cried to him for vengeance
  On the man that laid him low;
And thrice the living Cameron   115
  Told the dead Cameron, no.

'Thrice have you seen me, brother,
  But now shall see me no more,
Till you meet your angry fathers
  Upon the farther shore.   120
Thrice have I spoken, and now,
  Before the cock be heard,
I take my leave for ever
  With the naming of a word.
It shall sing in your sleeping ears,   125
  It shall hum in your waking head,
The name—Ticonderoga,
  And the warning of the dead.'

Now when the night was over
  And the time of people's fears,   130
The Cameron walked abroad,
  And the word was in his ears.
'Many a name I know,
  But never a name like this;
O, where shall I find a skilly man   135
  Shall tell me what it is?'
With many a man he counselled
  Of high and low degree,
With the herdsmen on the mountains
  And the fishers of the sea.   140
And he came and went unweary,
  And read the books of yore,

And the runes that were written of old
  On stones upon the moor.
And many a name he was told,   145
  But never the name of his fears—
Never, in east or west,
  The name that rang in his ears:
Names of men and of clans;
  Names for the grass and the tree,   150
For the smallest tarn in the mountains,
  The smallest reef in the sea:
Names for the high and low
  The names of the craig and the flat;
But in all the land of Scotland,   155
  Never a name like that.

THE SEEKING OF THE NAME

And now there was speech in the south,
    And a man of the south that was wise,
A periwigged lord of London,*
  Called on the clans to rise.   160
And the riders rode, and the summons
  Came to the western shore,
To the land of the sea and the heather,
  To Appin and Mamore.
It called on all to gather   165
  From every scrog and scaur,
That loved their father's tartan
  And the ancient game of war.
And down the watery valley
  And up the windy hill,   170
Once more, as in the olden,
  The pipes were sounding shrill.
Again in highland sunshine
  The naked steel was bright;
And the lads, once more in tartan,   175
  Went forth again to fight.

'O, why should I dwell here
  With a weird upon my life,
When the clansmen shout for battle
  And the war-swords clash in strife?   180
I cannae joy at feast,
  I cannae sleep in bed,

*A periwigged lord of London] The first Pitt [R.L.S.]   weird] doom

For the wonder of the word
  And the warning of the dead.
It sings in my sleeping ears,   185
  It hums in my waking head,
The name—Ticonderoga,
  The utterance of the dead.
Then up, and with the fighting men
  To march away from here,   190
Till the cry of the great war-pipe
  Shall drown it in my ear!'

Where flew King George's ensign
  The plaided soldiers went:
They drew the sword in Germany,   195
  In Flanders pitched the tent.
The bells of foreign cities
  Rang far across the plain:
They passed the happy Rhine,
  They drank the rapid Main.   200
Through Asiatic jungles
  The Tartans filed their way,
And the neighing of the war-pipes
  Struck terror in Cathay.

'Many a name have I heard,' he thought,   205
  'In all the tongues of men,
Full many a name both here and there,
  Full many both now and then.
When I was at home in my father's house
  In the land of the naked knee,   210
Between the eagles that fly in the lift
  And the herrings that swim in the sea,
And now that I am a captain-man
  With a braw cockade in my hat—
Many a name have I heard,' he thought,   215
  'But never a name like that.'

THE PLACE OF THE NAME

There fell a war in a woody place,
  Lay far across the sea,
A war of the march in the mirk midnight
  And the shot from behind the tree,   220
The shaven head and the painted face,
  The silent foot in the wood,
In a land of a strange, outlandish tongue
  That was hard to be understood.

It fell about the gloaming,   225
  The general stood with his staff,
He stood and he looked east and west
  With little mind to laugh.
'Far have I been and much have I seen,
  And kent both gain and loss,   230
But here we have woods on every hand
  And a kittle water to cross.
Far have I been and much have I seen,
  But never the beat of this;
And there's one must go down to that waterside   235
  To see how deep it is.'

It fell in the dusk of the night
  When unco things betide,
The skilly captain, the Cameron,
  Went down to that waterside.   240
Canny and soft the captain went;
  And a man of the woody land,
With the shaven head and the painted face,
  Went down at his right hand.
It fell in the quiet night,   245
  There was never a sound to ken;
But all the woods to the right and the left
  Lay filled with the painted men.

'Far have I been and much have I seen,
  Both as a man and boy,   250
But never have I set forth a foot
  On so perilous an employ.'
It fell in the dusk of the night
  When unco things betide,
That he was aware of a captain-man   255
  Drew near to the waterside.
He was aware of his coming
  Down in the gloaming alone;
And he looked in the face of the man,
  And lo! the face was his own.   260
'This is my weird,' he said,
  'And now I ken the worst;
For many shall fall with the morn,
  But I shall fall with the first.
O, you of the outland tongue,   265
  You of the painted face,
This is the place of my death;
  Can you tell me the name of the place?'

'Since the Frenchmen have been here
  They have called it Sault-Marie;   270
But that is a name for priests,
  And not for you and me.
It went by another word,'
  Quoth he of the shaven head:
'It was called Ticonderoga   275
  In the days of the great dead.'

And it fell on the morrow's morning,
  In the fiercest of the fight,
That the Cameron bit the dust
  As he foretold at night;   280
And far from the hills of heather
  Far from the isles of the sea,
He sleeps in the place of the name
  As it was doomed to be.

RUDYARD KIPLING

1865–1936

The Ballad of East and West

Oh, East is East, and West is West, and never the twain shall meet,
Till Earth and Sky stand presently at God's great Judgment Seat;
But there is neither East nor West, Border nor Breed, nor Birth,
When two strong men stand face to face, though they come from the ends of
*   the earth!*

Kamal is out with twenty men to raise the Border-side,   5
And he has lifted the Colonel's mare that is the Colonel's pride.
He has lifted her out of the stable-door between the dawn and the
    day,
And turned the calkins upon her feet, and ridden her far away.
Then up and spoke the Colonel's son that led a troop of the Guides:
'Is there never a man of all my men can say where Kamal hides?' 10
Then up and spoke Mohammed Khan, the son of the Ressaldar:
'If ye know the track of the morning mist, ye know where his pickets
    are.

calkins] turned-down ends of a horseshoe

At dusk he harries the Abazai—at dawn he is into Bonair,
But he must go by Fort Bukloh to his own place to fare.
So if ye gallop to Fort Bukloh as fast as a bird can fly,   15
By the favour of God ye may cut him off ere he win to the Tongue
    of Jagai.
But if he be past the Tongue of Jagai, right swiftly turn ye then,
For the length and the breadth of that grisly plain is sown with
    Kamal's men.
There is rock to the left, and rock to the right, and low lean thorn
    between,
And ye may hear a breech-bolt snick where never a man is seen.'   20
The Colonel's son has taken horse, and a raw rough dun was he,
With the mouth of a bell and the heart of Hell and the head of a
    gallows-tree.
The Colonel's son to the Fort has won, they bid him stay to eat—
Who rides at the tail of a Border thief, he sits not long at his meat.
He's up and away from Fort Bukloh as fast as he can fly,   25
Till he was aware of his father's mare in the gut of the Tongue of
    Jagai,
Till he was aware of his father's mare with Kamal upon her back,
And when he could spy the white of her eye, he made the pistol crack.
He has fired once, he has fired twice, but the whistling ball went
    wide.   30
'Ye shoot like a soldier,' Kamal said. 'Show now if ye can ride!'
It's up and over the Tongue of Jagai, as blown dust-devils go,
The dun he fled like a stag of ten, but the mare like a barren doe.
The dun he leaned against the bit and slugged his head above,
But the red mare played with the snaffle-bars, as a maiden plays with
    a glove.
There was rock to the left and rock to the right, and low lean thorn
    between,   35
And thrice he heard a breech-bolt snick tho' never a man was seen.
They have ridden the low moon out of the sky, their hoofs drum up
    the dawn,
The dun he went like a wounded bull, but the mare like a new-roused
    fawn.
The dun he fell at a water-course—in a woeful heap fell he,
And Kamal has turned the red mare back, and pulled the rider free. 40
He has knocked the pistol out of his hand—small room was there to
    strive,
''Twas only by favour of mine,' quoth he, 'ye rode so long alive:
There was not a rock for twenty mile, there was not a clump of tree,
But covered a man of my own men with his rifle cocked on his knee.
If I had raised my bridle-hand, as I have held it low,   45
The little jackals that flee so fast were feasting all in a row.

If I had bowed my head on my breast, as I have held it high,
The kite that whistles above us now were gorged till she could not fly.'
Lightly answered the Colonel's son: 'Do good to bird and beast,
But count who come for the broken meats before thou makest a feast.
If there should follow a thousand swords to carry my bones away, 51
Belike the price of a jackal's meal were more than a thief could pay.
They will feed their horse on the standing crop, their men on the
garnered grain.
The thatch of the byres will serve their fires when all the cattle are
slain.
But if thou thinkest the price be fair—thy brethren wait to sup, 55
The hound is kin to the jackal-spawn—howl, dog, and call them up!
And if thou thinkest the price be high, in steer and gear and stack,
Give me my father's mare again, and I'll fight my own way back!'
Kamal has gripped him by the hand and set him upon his feet.
'No talk shall be of dogs,' said he, 'when wolf and grey wolf meet. 60
May I eat dirt if thou hast hurt of me in deed or breath;
What dam of lances brought thee forth to jest at the dawn with
Death?'
Lightly answered the Colonel's son: 'I hold by the blood of my clan:
Take up the mare for my father's gift—by God, she has carried a
man!'
The red mare ran to the Colonel's son, and nuzzled against his
breast; 65
'We be two strong men,' said Kamal then, 'but she loveth the younger
best.
So she shall go with a lifter's dower, my turquoise-studded rein,
My 'broidered saddle and saddle-cloth, and silver stirrups twain.'
The Colonel's son a pistol drew, and held it muzzle-end,
'Ye have taken the one from a foe,' said he. 'Will ye take the mate
from a friend?' 70
'A gift for a gift,' said Kamal straight; 'a limb for the risk of a limb.
Thy father has sent his son to me, I'll send my son to him!'
With that he whistled his only son, that dropped from a
mountain-crest—
He trod the ling like a buck in spring, and he looked like a lance in
rest.
'Now here is thy master,' Kamal said, 'who leads a troop of the
Guides,
And thou must ride at his left side as shield on shoulder rides. 75
Till Death or I cut loose the tie, at camp and board and bed,
Thy life is his—thy fate it is to guard him with thy head.
So, thou must eat the White Queen's meat, and all her foes are thine,
And thou must harry thy father's hold for the peace of the
Border-line. 80

And thou must make a trooper tough and hack thy way to power—
Belike they will raise thee to Ressaldar when I am hanged in
    Peshawur!'

They have looked each other between the eyes, and there they found
    no fault.
They have taken the Oath of the Brother-in-Blood on leavened bread
    and salt:
They have taken the Oath of the Brother-in-Blood on fire and
    fresh-cut sod,   85
On the hilt and the haft of the Khyber knife, and the Wondrous
    Names of God.
The Colonel's son he rides the mare and Kamal's boy the dun,
And two have come back to Fort Bukloh where there went forth but
    one.
And when they drew to the Quarter-Guard, full twenty swords flew
    clear—
There was not a man but carried his feud with the blood of the
    mountaineer.   90
'Ha' done! ha' done!' said the Colonel's son. 'Put up the steel at your
    sides!
Last night ye had struck at a Border thief—tonight 'tis a man of the
    Guides!'

Oh, East is East, and West is West, and never the twain shall meet,
Till Earth and Sky stand presently at God's great Judgment Seat;
But there is neither East nor West, Border, nor Breed, nor Birth,   95
When two strong men stand face to face, though they come from the ends of
    the earth!

OSCAR WILDE
1856–1900

The Ballad of Reading Gaol

I

HE did not wear his scarlet coat,
    For blood and wine are red,
And blood and wine were on his hands
    When they found him with the dead,
The poor dear woman whom he loved,   5
    And murdered in her bed.

He walked amongst the Trial Men
  In a suit of shabby grey;
A cricket cap was on his head,
  And his step seemed light and gay;   10
But I never saw a man who looked
  So wistfully at the day.

I never saw a man who looked
  With such a wistful eye
Upon that little tent of blue   15
  Which prisoners call the sky,
And at every drifting cloud that went
  With sails of silver by.

I walked, with other souls in pain,
  Within another ring,   20
And was wondering if the man had done
  A great or little thing,
When a voice behind me whispered low,
  'That fellow's got to swing.'

Dear Christ! the very prison walls   25
  Suddenly seemed to reel,
And the sky above my head became
  Like a casque of scorching steel;
And, though I was a soul in pain,
  My pain I could not feel.   30

I only knew what hunted thought
  Quickened his step, and why
He looked upon the garish day
  With such a wistful eye;
The man had killed the thing he loved,   35
  And so he had to die.

Yet each man kills the thing he loves,
  By each let this be heard,
Some do it with a bitter look,
  Some with a flattering word,   40
The coward does it with a kiss,
  The brave man with a sword!

Some kill their love when they are young,
   And some when they are old;
Some strangle with the hands of Lust,   45
   Some with the hands of Gold:
The kindest use a knife, because
   The dead so soon grow cold.

Some love too little, some too long,
   Some sell, and others buy;
Some do the deed with many tears,   50
   And some without a sigh:
For each man kills the thing he loves,
   Yet each man does not die.

He does not die a death of shame   55
   On a day of dark disgrace,
Nor have a noose about his neck,
   Nor a cloth upon his face,
Nor drop feet-foremost through the floor
   Into an empty space.   60

He does not sit with silent men
   Who watch him night and day;
Who watch him when he tries to weep,
   And when he tries to pray;
Who watch him lest himself should rob   65
   The prison of its prey.

He does not wake at dawn to see
   Dread figures throng his room,
The shivering Chaplain robed in white,
   The Sheriff stern with gloom,   70
And the Governor all in shiny black,
   With the yellow face of Doom.

He does not rise in piteous haste
   To put on convict-clothes,
While some coarse-mouthed Doctor gloats, and notes   75
   Each new and nerve-twitched pose,
Fingering a watch whose little ticks
   Are like horrible hammer-blows.

He does not know that sickening thirst
   That sands one's throat, before   80
The hangman with his gardener's gloves
   Comes through the padded door,
And binds one with three leathern thongs,
   That the throat may thirst no more.

He does not bend his head to hear   85
   The Burial Office read,
Now, while the anguish of his soul
   Tells him he is not dead,
Cross his own coffin, as he moves
   Into the hideous shed.   90

He does not stare upon the air
   Through a little roof of glass:
He does not pray with lips of clay
   For his agony to pass;
Nor feel upon his shuddering cheek   95
   The kiss of Caiaphas.

II

Six weeks our guardsman walked the yard
   In the suit of shabby grey:
His cricket cap was on his head,
   And his step seemed light and gay,   100
But I never saw a man who looked
   So wistfully at the day.

I never saw a man who looked
   With such a wistful eye
Upon that little tent of blue   105
   Which prisoners call the sky,
And at every wandering cloud that trailed
   Its ravelled fleeces by.

He did not wring his hands, as do
   Those witless men who dare   110
To try to rear the changeling Hope
   In the cave of black Despair:
He only looked upon the sun,
   And drank the morning air.

He did not wring his hands nor weep, 115
  Nor did he peek or pine,
But he drank the air as though it held
  Some healthful anodyne;
With open mouth he drank the sun
  As though it had been wine! 120

And I and all the souls in pain,
  Who tramped the other ring,
Forgot if we ourselves had done
  A great or little thing,
And watched with gaze of dull amaze 125
  The man who had to swing.

For strange it was to see him pass
  With a step so light and gay,
And strange it was to see him look
  So wistfully at the day, 130
And strange it was to think that he
  Had such a debt to pay.

For oak and elm have pleasant leaves
  That in the springtime shoot:
But grim to see is the gallows-tree, 135
  With its adder-bitten root,
And, green or dry, a man must die
  Before it bears its fruit.

The loftiest place is that seat of grace
  For which all worldlings try: 140
But who would stand in hempen band
  Upon a scaffold high,
And through a murderer's collar take
  His last look at the sky?

It is sweet to dance to violins 145
  When Love and Life are fair:
To dance to flutes, to dance to lutes,
  Is delicate and rare:
But it is not sweet with nimble feet
  To dance upon the air! 150

So with curious eyes and sick surmise
  We watched him day by day,
And wondered if each one of us
  Would end the selfsame way,
For none can tell to what red Hell   155
  His sightless soul may stray.

At last the dead man walked no more
  Amongst the Trial Men,
And I knew that he was standing up
  In the black dock's dreadful pen,   160
And that never would I see his face
  In God's sweet world again.

Like two doomed ships that pass in storm
  We had crossed each other's way:
But we made no sign, we said no word,   165
  We had no word to say;
For we did not meet in the holy night,
  But in the shameful day.

A prison wall was round us both,
  Two outcast men we were: 170
The world had thrust us from its heart,
  And God from out His care:
And the iron gin that waits for Sin
  Had caught us in its snare.

III

In Debtors' Yard the stones are hard,   175
  And the dripping wall is high,
So it was there he took the air
  Beneath the leaden sky,
And by each side a warder walked,
  For fear the man might die.   180

Or else he sat with those who watched
  His anguish night and day;
Who watched him when he rose to weep,
  And when he crouched to pray;
Who watched him lest himself should rob   185
  Their scaffold of its prey.

The Governor was strong upon
   The Regulations Act:
The Doctor said that Death was but
   A scientific fact: 190
And twice a day the Chaplain called,
   And left a little tract.

And twice a day he smoked his pipe,
   And drank his quart of beer:
His soul was resolute, and held   195
   No hiding-place for fear;
He often said that he was glad
   The hangman's day was near.

But why he said so strange a thing
   No warder dared to ask: 200
For he to whom a watcher's doom
   Is given as his task,
Must set a lock upon his lips
   And make his face a mask.

Or else he might be moved, and try   205
   To comfort or console:
And what should Human Pity do
   Pent up in Murderer's Hole?
What word of grace in such a place
   Could help a brother's soul?   210

With slouch and swing around the ring
   We trod the Fools' Parade!
We did not care: we knew we were
   The Devil's Own Brigade:
And shaven head and feet of lead   215
   Make a merry masquerade.

We tore the tarry rope to shreds
   With blunt and bleeding nails;
We rubbed the doors, and scrubbed the floors,
   And cleaned the shining rails: 220
And, rank by rank, we soaped the plank,
   And clattered with the pails.

We sewed the sacks, we broke the stones,
  We turned the dusty drill:
We banged the tins, and bawled the hymns,   225
  And sweated on the mill:
But in the heart of every man
  Terror was lying still.

So still it lay that every day
  Crawled like a weed-clogged wave: 230
And we forgot the bitter lot
  That waits for fool and knave,
Till once, as we tramped in from work,
  We passed an open grave.

With yawning mouth the yellow hole   235
  Gaped for a living thing;
The very mud cried out for blood
  To the thirsty asphalt ring;
And we knew that ere one dawn grew fair
  Some prisoner had to swing.   240

Right in we went, with soul intent
  On Death and Dread and Doom:
The hangman, with his little bag,
  Went shuffling through the gloom:
And I trembled as I groped my way   245
  Into my numbered tomb.

That night the empty corridors
  Were full of forms of Fear,
And up and down the iron town
  Stole feet we could not hear,
And through the bars that hide the stars   250
  White faces seemed to peer.

He lay as one who lies and dreams
  In a pleasant meadow-land,
The watchers watched him as he slept,   255
  And could not understand
How one could sleep so sweet a sleep
  With a hangman close at hand.

But there is no sleep when men must weep
  Who never yet have wept: 260
So we—the fool, the fraud, the knave—
  That endless vigil kept,
And through each brain on hands of pain
  Another's terror crept.

Alas! it is a fearful thing 265
  To feel another's guilt!
For, right within, the Sword of Sin
  Pierced to its poisoned hilt,
And as molten lead were the tears we shed
  For the blood we had not spilt. 270

The warders with their shoes of felt
  Crept by each padlocked door,
And peeped and saw, with eyes of awe,
  Grey figures on the floor,
And wondered why men knelt to pray 275
  Who never prayed before.

All through the night we knelt and prayed,
  Mad mourners of a corse!
The troubled plumes of midnight shook
  Like the plumes upon a hearse: 280
The bitter wine upon a sponge
  Was the savour of Remorse.

The grey cock crew, the red cock crew,
  But never came the day:
And crooked shapes of Terror crouched, 285
  In the corners where we lay:
And each evil sprite that walks by night
  Before us seemed to play.

They glided past, they glided fast,
  Like travellers through a mist: 290
They mocked the moon in a rigadoon
  Of delicate turn and twist,
And with formal pace and loathsome grace
  The phantoms kept their tryst.

With mop and mow, we saw them go,   295
    Slim shadows hand in hand:
About, about, in ghostly rout
    They trod a saraband:
And the damned grotesques made arabesques,
    Like the wind upon the sand!   300

With the pirouettes of marionettes,
    They tripped on pointed tread:
But with flutes of Fear they filled the ear,
    As their grisly masque they led,
And loud they sang, and long they sang,   305
    For they sang to wake the dead.

'Oho!' they cried, 'The world is wide,
    But fettered limbs go lame!
And once, or twice, to throw the dice
    Is a gentlemanly game,   310
But he does not win who plays with Sin
    In the secret House of Shame.'

No things of air these antics were,
    That frolicked with such glee:
To men whose lives were held in gyves,   315
    And whose feet might not go free,
Ah, wounds of Christ! they were living things,
    Most terrible to see.

Around, around, they waltzed and wound;
    Some wheeled in smirking pairs;   320
With the mincing step of a demirep
    Some sidled up the stairs;
And with subtle sneer, and fawning leer,
    Each helped us at our prayers.

The morning wind began to moan,   325
    But still the night went on:
Through its giant loom the web of gloom
    Crept till each thread was spun:
And, as we prayed, we grew afraid
    Of the Justice of the Sun.   330

335

The moaning wind went wandering round
   The weeping prison-wall:
Till like a wheel of turning steel
   We felt the minutes crawl:
O moaning wind! what had we done   335
   To have such a seneschal?

At last I saw the shadowed bars,
   Like a lattice wrought in lead,
Move right across the whitewashed wall
   That faced my three-plank bed,   340
And I knew that somewhere in the world
   God's dreadful dawn was red.

At six o'clock we cleaned our cells,
   At seven all was still,
But the sough and swing of a mighty wing   345
   The prison seemed to fill,
But the Lord of Death with icy breath
   Had entered in to kill.

He did not pass in purple pomp,
   Nor ride a moon-white steed.   350
Three yards of cord and a sliding board
   Are all the gallows' need:
So with rope of shame the Herald came
   To do the secret deed.

We were as men who through a fen   355
   Of filthy darkness grope:
We did not dare to breathe a prayer,
   Or to give our anguish scope:
Something was dead in each of us,
   And what was dead was Hope.   360

For Man's grim Justice goes its way,
   And will not swerve aside:
It slays the weak, it slays the strong,
   It has a deadly stride:
With iron heel it slays the strong,   365
   The monstrous parricide!

We waited for the stroke of eight:
　Each tongue was thick with thirst:
For the stroke of eight is the stroke of Fate
　That makes a man accursed,　　　　　　　　370
And Fate will use a running noose
　For the best man and the worst.

We had no other thing to do,
　Save to wait for the sign to come:
So, like things of stone in a valley lone,　　375
　Quiet we sat and dumb:
But each man's heart beat thick and quick,
　Like a madman on a drum!

With sudden shock the prison-clock
　Smote on the shivering air,　　　　　　　　380
And from all the gaol rose up a wail
　Of impotent despair,
Like the sound that frightened marshes hear
　From some leper in his lair.

And as one sees most fearful things
　In the crystal of a dream,　　　　　　　　385
We saw the greasy hempen rope
　Hooked to the blackened beam,
And heard the prayer the hangman's snare
　Strangled into a scream.　　　　　　　　390

And all the woe that moved him so
　That he gave that bitter cry,
And the wild regrets, and the bloody sweats,
　None knew so well as I:
For he who lives more lives than one　　　395
　More deaths than one must die.

IV

There is no chapel on the day
　On which they hang a man:
The Chaplain's heart is far too sick,
　Or his face is far too wan,　　　　　　　　400
Or there is that written in his eyes
　Which none should look upon.

So they kept us close till nigh on noon,
  And then they rang the bell,
And the warders with their jingling keys   405
  Opened each listening cell,
And down the iron stair we tramped,
  Each from his separate Hell.

Out into God's sweet air we went,
  But not in wonted way,   410
For this man's face was white with fear,
  And that man's face was grey,
And I never saw sad men who looked
  So wistfully at the day.

I never saw sad men who looked   415
  With such a wistful eye
Upon that little tent of blue
  We prisoners called the sky,
And at every happy cloud that passed
  In happy freedom by.   420

But there were those amongst us all
  Who walked with downcast head,
And knew that, had each got his due,
  They should have died instead:
He had but killed a thing that lived,   425
  Whilst they had killed the dead.

For he who sins a second time
  Wakes a dead soul to pain,
And draws it from its spotted shroud,
  And makes it bleed again,   430
And makes it bleed great gouts of blood,
  And makes it bleed in vain.

Like ape or clown, in monstrous garb
  With crooked arrows starred,
Silently we went round and round   435
  The slippery asphalt yard;
Silently we went round and round,
  And no man spoke a word.

Silently we went round and round,
   And through each hollow mind
The Memory of dreadful things
   Rushed like a dreadful wind,
And Horror stalked before each man,
   And Terror crept behind.

440

The warders strutted up and down,
   And watched their herd of brutes,
Their uniforms were spick and span,
   And they wore their Sunday suits,
But we knew the work they had been at
   By the quicklime on their boots.

445

450

For where a grave had opened wide,
   There was no grave at all:
Only a stretch of mud and sand
   By the hideous prison-wall,
And a little heap of burning lime,
   That the man should have his pall.

455

For he has a pall, this wretched man,
   Such as few men can claim:
Deep down below a prison-yard,
   Naked for greater shame,
He lies, with fetters on each foot,
   Wrapt in a sheet of flame!

460

And all the while the burning lime
   Eats flesh and bone away,
It eats the brittle bone by night,
   And the soft flesh by day,
It eats the flesh and bone by turns,
   But it eats the heart alway.

465

For three long years they will not sow
   Or root or seedling there:
For three long years the unblessed spot
   Will sterile be and bare,
And look upon the wondering sky
   With unreproachful stare.

470

They think a murderer's heart would taint 475
   Each simple seed they sow.
It is not true! God's kindly earth
   Is kindlier than men know,
And the red rose would but blow more red,
   The white rose whiter blow. 480

Out of his mouth a red, red rose!
   Out of his heart a white!
For who can say by what strange way,
   Christ brings His will to light, 485
Since the barren staff the pilgrim bore
   Bloomed in the great Pope's sight?

But neither milk-white rose nor red
   May bloom in prison air;
The shard, the pebble, and the flint, 490
   Are what they give us there:
For flowers have been known to heal
   A common man's despair.

So never will wine-red rose or white,
   Petal by petal, fall 495
On that stretch of mud and sand that lies
   By the hideous prison-wall,
To tell the men who tramp the yard
   That God's Son died for all.

Yet though the hideous prison-wall 500
   Still hems him round and round,
And a spirit may not walk by night
   That is with fetters bound,
And a spirit may but weep that lies
   In such unholy ground,

He is at peace—this wretched man— 505
   At peace, or will be soon:
There is no thing to make him mad,
   Nor does Terror walk at noon,
For the lampless Earth in which he lies
   Has neither Sun nor Moon. 510

They hanged him as a beast is hanged:
  They did not even toll
A requiem that might have brought
  Rest to his startled soul,
They stripped him of his canvas clothes,
  And hid him in a hole.

The warders stripped him of his clothes,
  And gave him to the flies:
They mocked the swollen purple throat,
  And the stark and staring eyes:
And with laughter loud they heaped the shroud
  In which their convict lies.

The Chaplain would not kneel to pray
  By his dishonoured grave:
Nor mark it with that blessed Cross
  That Christ for sinners gave,
Because the man was one of those
  Whom Christ came down to save.

Yet all is well; he has but passed
  To Life's appointed bourne:
And alien tears will fill for him
  Pity's long-broken urn,
For his mourners will be outcast men,
  And outcasts always mourn.

ALFRED NOYES
1880–1958

The Highwayman

I

THE wind was a torrent of darkness among the gusty trees.
The moon was a ghostly galleon tossed upon cloudy seas.
The road was a ribbon of moonlight over the purple moor,
And the highwayman came riding—
    Riding—riding—
The highwayman came riding, up to the old inn-door.

He'd a French cocked-hat on his forehead, a bunch of lace at his
    chin,
A coat of the claret velvet, and breeches of brown doe-skin;
They fitted with never a wrinkle: his boots were up to the thigh.
And he rode with a jewelled twinkle,   10
    His pistol butts a-twinkle,
His rapier hilt a-twinkle, under the jewelled sky.

Over the cobbles he clattered and clashed in the dark inn-yard.
He tapped with his whip on the shutters, but all was locked and
    barred.
He whistled a tune to the window, and who should be waiting there   15
But the landlord's black-eyed daughter,
    Bess, the landlord's daughter,
Plaiting a dark red love-knot into her long black hair.

And dark in the dark old inn-yard a stable-wicket creaked
Where Tim the ostler listened; his face was white and peaked;   20
His eyes were hollows of madness, his hair like mouldy hay,
But he loved the landlord's daughter,
    The landlord's red-lipped daughter.
Dumb as a dog he listened, and he heard the robber say—

'One kiss, my bonny sweetheart, I'm after a prize tonight,   25
But I shall be back with the yellow gold before the morning light;
Yet, if they press me sharply, and harry me through the day,
Then look for me by moonlight,
    Watch for me by moonlight,
I'll come to thee by moonlight, though hell should bar the way.'   30

He rose upright in the stirrups. He scarce could reach her hand,
But she loosened her hair in the casement. His face burnt like a brand
As the black cascade of perfume came tumbling over his breast;
And he kissed its waves in the moonlight,
    (O, sweet black waves in the moonlight!)   35
Then he tugged at his rein in the moonlight, and galloped away to the
    west.

II

He did not come in the dawning. He did not come at noon;
And out of the tawny sunset, before the rise of the moon,
When the road was a gypsy's ribbon, looping the purple moor,
A red-coat troop came marching—   40
    Marching—marching—
King George's men came marching, up to the old inn-door.

They said no word to the landlord. They drank his ale instead.
But they gagged his daughter, and bound her, to the foot of her
    narrow bed.
Two of them knelt at her casement, with muskets at their side.   45
There was death at every window;
    And hell at one dark window;
For Bess could see, through her casement, the road that *he* would
    ride.

They had tied her up to attention, with many a sniggering jest.
They had bound a musket beside her, with the muzzle beneath her
    breast.   50
'Now, keep good watch!' and they kissed her. She heard the doomed
    man say—
Look for me by moonlight;
    Watch for me by moonlight;
I'll come to thee by moonlight, though hell should bar the way!

She twisted her hands behind her; but all the knots held good.   55
She writhed her hands till her fingers were wet with sweat or blood.
They stretched and strained in the darkness, and the hours crawled by
    like years,
Till, now, on the stroke of midnight,
    Cold, on the stroke of midnight,
The tip of one finger touched it! The trigger at least was hers!   60

The tip of one finger touched it. She strove no more for the rest.
Up, she stood up to attention, with the muzzle beneath her breast.
She would not risk their hearing; she would not strive again;
For the road lay bare in the moonlight;
    Blank and bare in the moonlight;   65
And the blood of her veins, in the moonlight, throbbed to her love's
    refrain.

Tlot-tlot;tlot-tlot! Had they heard it? The horsehoofs ringing clear;
Tlot-tlot, tlot-tlot, in the distance? Were they deaf that they did not
    hear?
Down the ribbon of moonlight, over the brow of the hill,
The highwayman came riding—   70
    Riding—riding—
The red-coats looked to their priming! She stood up, straight and
    still.

Tlot-tlot, in the frosty silence! *Tlot-tlot,* in the echoing night!
Nearer he came and nearer. Her face was like a light.

Her eyes grew wide for a moment; she drew one last deep breath,   75
Then her finger moved in the moonlight,
  Her musket shattered the moonlight,
Shattered her breast in the moonlight and warned him—with her
  death.

He turned. He spurred to the west; he did not know who stood
Bowed, with her head o'er the musket, drenched with her own
  blood.   80
Not till the dawn he heard it, and his face grew grey to hear
How Bess, the landlord's daughter,
  The landlord's black-eyed daughter,
Had watched for her love in the moonlight, and died in the darkness
  there.

Back, he spurred like a madman, shouting a curse to the sky,   85
With the white road smoking behind him and his rapier brandished
  high.
Blood-red were his spurs in the golden noon; wine-red was his velvet
  coat;
When they shot him down on the highway,
  Down like a dog on the highway,
And he lay in his blood on the highway, with a bunch of lace at his
  throat.   90

  . . . .

And still of a winter's night, they say, when the wind is in the trees,
When the moon is a ghostly galleon tossed upon cloudy seas,
When the road is a ribbon of moonlight over the purple moor,
A highwayman comes riding—
  Riding—riding—   95
A highwayman comes riding, up to the old inn-door.

Over the cobbles he clatters and clangs in the dark inn-yard.
He taps with his whip on the shutters, but all is locked and barred.
He whistles a tune to the window, and who should be waiting there
But the landlord's black-eyed daughter,   100
  Bess, the landlord's daughter,
Plaiting a dark red love-knot into her long black hair.

344

ROBERT W. SERVICE
1874–1958

The Cremation of Sam McGee

There are strange things done in the midnight sun
 By the men who moil for gold;
The Arctic trails have their secret tales
 That would make your blood run cold;
The Northern Lights have seen queer sights,   5
 But the queerest they ever did see
Was that night on the marge of Lake Lebarge
 I cremated Sam McGee.

Now Sam McGee was from Tennessee, where the cotton blooms and
 blows.
Why he left his home in the South to roam 'round the Pole, God only
 knows.   10
He was always cold, but the land of gold seemed to hold him like a
 spell;
Though he'd often say in his homely way that 'he'd sooner live in
 hell'.

On a Christmas Day we were mushing our way over the Dawson trail.
Talk of your cold! through the parka's fold it stabbed like a driven
 nail.
If our eyes we'd close, then the lashes froze till sometimes we couldn't
 see;   15
It wasn't much fun, but the only one to whimper was Sam McGee.

And that very night, as we lay packed tight in our robes beneath the
 snow,
And the dogs were fed, and the stars o'erhead were dancing heel and
 toe,
He turned to me, and 'Cap,' says he, 'I'll cash in this trip, I guess;
And if I do, I'm asking that you won't refuse my last request.'   20

Well, he seemed so low that I couldn't say no; then he says with a sort
 of moan:
'It's the cursèd cold, and it's got right hold till I'm chilled clean
 through to the bone.
Yet 'tain't being dead—it's my awful dread of the icy grave that pains;
So I want you to swear that, foul or fair, you'll cremate my last
 remains.'

A pal's last need is a thing to heed, so I swore I would not fail;   25
And we started on at the streak of dawn; but God! he looked ghastly
    pale.
He crouched on the sleigh, and he raved all day of his home in
    Tennessee;
And before nightfall a corpse was all that was left of Sam McGee.

There wasn't a breath in that land of death, and I hurried,
    horror-driven,
With a corpse half hid that I couldn't get rid, because of a promise
    given;   30
It was lashed to the sleigh, and it seemed to say: 'You may tax your
    brawn and brains,
But you promised true, and it's up to you to cremate those last
    remains.'

Now a promise made is a debt unpaid, and the trail has its own stern
    code.
In the days to come, though my lips were dumb, in my heart how I
    cursed that load.
In the long, long night, by the lone firelight, while the huskies, round
    in a ring,   35
Howled out their woes to the homeless snows—O God! how I
    loathed the thing.

And every day that quiet clay seemed to heavy and heavier grow;
And on I went, though the dogs were spent and the grub was
    getting low;
The trail was bad, and I felt half mad, but I swore I would not give
    in;
And I'd often sing to the hateful thing, and it hearkened with a
    grin.   40

Till I came to the marge of Lake Lebarge, and a derelict there lay;
It was jammed in the ice, but I saw in a trice it was called the
    'Alice May'.
And I looked at it, and I thought a bit, and I looked at my frozen
    chum;
Then 'Here,' said I, with a sudden cry, 'is my cre-ma-tor-eum.'

Some planks I tore from the cabin floor, and I lit the boiler fire;   45
Some coal I found that was lying around, and I heaped the fuel
    higher;

THE CREMATION OF SAM McGEE

The flames just soared, and the furnace roared—such a blaze you
    seldom see;
And I burrowed a hole in the glowing coal, and I stuffed in Sam
    McGee.

Then I made a hike, for I didn't like to hear him sizzle so;
And the heavens scowled, and the huskies howled, and the wind
    began to blow.   50
It was icy cold, but the hot sweat rolled down my cheeks, and I
    don't know why;
And the greasy smoke in an inky cloak went streaking down the
    sky.

I do not know how long in the snow I wrestled with grisly fear;
But the stars came out and they danced about ere again I ventured
    near;
I was sick with dread, but I bravely said: 'I'll just take a peep
    inside.
I guess he's cooked, and it's time I looked'—then the door I   55
    opened wide.

And there sat Sam, looking cool and calm, in the heart of the
    furnace roar;
And he wore a smile you could see a mile, and he said: 'Please
    close that door.
It's fine in here, but I greatly fear you'll let in the cold and storm—
Since I left Plumtree, down in Tennessee, it's the first time I've
    been warm.'   60

> *There are strange things done in the midnight sun*
>   *By the men who moil for gold;*
> *The Arctic trails have their secret tales*
>   *That would make your blood run cold;*
> *The Northern Lights have seen queer sights,*   65
>   *But the queerest they ever did see*
> *Was the night on the marge of Lake Lebarge*
>   *I cremated Sam McGee.*

THOMAS HARDY
1840–1928

A Trampwoman's Tragedy

FROM Wynyard's Gap the livelong day,
  The livelong day,
We beat afoot the northward way
  We had travelled times before.
The sun-blaze burning on our backs,   5
Our shoulders sticking to our packs,
By fosseway, fields, and turnpike tracks
  We skirted sad Sedge-Moor.

Full twenty miles we jaunted on,
  We jaunted on—   10
My fancy-man, and jeering John,
  And Mother Lee, and I.
And, as the sun drew down to west,
We climbed the toilsome Poldon crest,
And saw, of landskip sights the best,   15
  The inn that beamed thereby.

For months we had padded side by side,
  Ay, side by side
Through the Great Forest, Blackmoor wide,
  And where the Parret ran.   20
We'd faced the gusts on Mendip ridge,
Had crossed the Yeo unhelped by bridge,
Been stung by every Marshwood midge,
  I and my fancy-man.

Lone inns we loved, my man and I,   25
  My man and I;
'King's Stag', 'Windwhistle' high and dry,
  'The Horse' on Hintock Green,
The cosy house at Wynyard's Gap,
'The Hut' renowned on Bredy Knap,   30
And many another wayside tap
  Where folk might sit unseen.

Now as we trudged—O deadly day,
    O deadly day!—
I teased my fancy-man in play   35
    And wanton idleness.
I walked alongside jeering John,
I laid his hand my waist upon;
I would not bend my glances on
    My lover's dark distress.   40

Thus Poldon top at last we won,
    At last we won,
And gained the inn at sink of sun
    Far-famed as 'Marshal's Elm'.
Beneath us figured tor and lea,   45
From Mendip to the western sea—
I doubt if finer sight there be
    Within this royal realm.

Inside the settle all a-row—
    All four a-row   50
We sat, I next to John, to show
    That he had wooed and won.
And then he took me on his knee,
And swore it was his turn to be
My favoured mate, and Mother Lee   55
    Passed to my former one.

Then in a voice I had never heard,
    I had never heard,
My only Love to me: 'One word,
    My lady, if you please!   60
Whose is the child you are like to bear?—
His? After all my months o' care?'
God knows 'twas not! But, O despair!
    I nodded—still to tease.

Then up he sprung, and with his knife—   65
    And with his knife
He let out jeering Johnny's life,
    Yes; there, at set of sun.
The slant ray through the window nigh
Gilded John's blood and glazing eye,   70
Ere scarcely Mother Lee and I
    Knew that the deed was done.

The taverns tell the gloomy tale,
    The gloomy tale,
How that at Ivel-chester jail   75
    My Love, my sweetheart swung;
Though stained till now by no misdeed
Save one horse ta'en in time o' need;
(Blue Jimmy stole right many a steed
    Ere his last fling he flung.)   80

Thereaft I walked the world alone,
    Alone, alone!
On his death-day I gave my groan
    And dropt his dead-born child.
'Twas nigh the jail, beneath a tree,   85
None tending me; for Mother Lee
Had died at Glaston, leaving me
    Unfriended on the wild.

And in the night as I lay weak,
    As I lay weak,   90
The leaves a-falling on my cheek,
    The red moon low declined—
The ghost of him I'd die to kiss
Rose up and said: 'Ah, tell me this!
Was the child mine, or was it his?   95
    Speak, that I rest may find!'

O doubt not but I told him then,
    I told him then,
That I had kept me from all men
    Since we joined lips and swore.   100
Whereat he smiled, and thinned away
As the wind stirred to call up day . . .
—'Tis past! And here alone I stray
    Haunting the Western Moor.

G. K. CHESTERTON
1874–1936

Lepanto

WHITE founts falling in the courts of the sun,
And the Soldan of Byzantium is smiling as they run;
There is laughter like the fountains in that face of all men feared,
It stirs the forest darkness, the darkness of his beard,
It curls the blood-red crescent, the crescent of his lips,   5
For the inmost sea of all the earth is shaken with his ships.
They have dared the white republics up the capes of Italy,
They have dashed the Adriatic round the Lion of the Sea,
And the Pope has cast his arms abroad for agony and loss,
And called the kings of Christendom for swords about the Cross.   10
The cold queen of England is looking in the glass,
The shadow of the Valois is yawning at the Mass;
From evening isles fantastical rings faint the Spanish gun,
And the Lord upon the Golden Horn is laughing in the sun.

Dim drums throbbing, in the hills half heard,   15
Where only on a nameless throne a crownless prince has stirred,
Where, risen from a doubtful seat and half attainted stall,
The last knight of Europe takes weapons from the wall,
The last and lingering troubadour to whom the bird has sung,
That once went singing southward when all the world was young.   20
In that enormous silence, tiny and unafraid,
Comes up along a winding road the noise of the Crusade.
Strong gongs groaning as the guns boom far,
Don John of Austria is going to the war,
Stiff flags straining in the night-blasts cold   25
In the gloom black-purple, in the glint old-gold,
Torchlight crimson on the copper kettle-drums,
Then the tuckets, then the trumpets, then the cannon, and he comes.
Don John laughing in the brave beard curled,
Spurning of his stirrups like the thrones of all the world,   30
Holding his head up for a flag of all the free.
Love-light of Spain—hurrah!
Deathlight of Africa!
Don John of Austria
Is riding to the sea.   35

Mahound is in his paradise above the evening star,
(*Don John of Austria is going to the war.*)
He moves a mighty turban on the timeless houri's knees,
His turban that is woven of the sunsets and the seas.
He shakes the peacock gardens as he rises from his ease, 40
And he strides among the tree-tops and is taller than the trees,
And his voice through all the garden is a thunder sent to bring
Black Azrael and Ariel and Ammon on the wing.
Giants and the Genii,
Multiplex of wing and eye, 45
Whose strong obedience broke the sky
When Solomon was king.

They rush in red and purple from the red clouds of the morn,
From temples where the yellow gods shut up their eyes in scorn;
They rise in green robes roaring from the green hells of the sea 50
Where fallen skies and evil hues and eyeless creatures be;
On them the sea-valves cluster and the grey sea-forests curl,
Splashed with a splendid sickness, the sickness of the pearl;
They swell in sapphire smoke out of the blue cracks of the ground—
They gather and they wonder and give worship to Mahound. 55
And he saith, 'Break up the mountains where the hermit-folk can
    hide,
And sift the red and silver sands lest bone of saint abide,
And chase the Giaours flying night and day, not giving rest,
For that which was our trouble comes again out of the west.
We have set the seal of Solomon on all things under sun, 60
Of knowledge and of sorrow and endurance of things done;
But a noise is in the mountains, in the mountains, and I know
The voice that shook our palaces—four hundred years ago:
It is he that saith not 'Kismet'; it is he that knows not Fate;
It is Richard, it is Raymond, it is Godfrey in the gate! 65
It is he whose loss is laughter when he counts the wager worth:
Put down your feet upon him, that our peace be on the earth.'
For he heard drums groaning and he heard guns jar,
(*Don John of Austria is going to the war.*)
Sudden and still—hurrah! 70
Bolt from Iberia!
Don John of Austria
Is gone by Alcalar.

St. Michael's on his Mountain in the sea-roads of the north,
(*Don John of Austria is girt and going forth.*) 75
Where the grey seas glitter and the sharp tides shift
And the sea-folk labour and the red sails lift.

He shakes his lance of iron and he claps his wings of stone;
The noise is gone through Normandy; the noise is gone alone;
The North is full of tangled things and texts and aching eyes,   80
And dead is all the innocence of anger and surprise,
And Christian killeth Christian in a narrow dusty room,
And Christian dreadeth Christ that hath a newer face of doom,
And Christian hateth Mary that God kissed in Galilee,
But Don John of Austria is riding to the sea.   85
Don John calling through the blast and the eclipse,
Crying with the trumpet, with the trumpet of his lips,
Trumpet that sayeth ha!
Domino gloria!
Don John of Austria   90
Is shouting to the ships.

King Philip's in his closet with the Fleece about his neck,
(*Don John of Austria is armed upon the deck.*)
The walls are hung with velvet that is black and soft as sin,
And little dwarfs creep out of it and little dwarfs creep in.   95
He holds a crystal phial that has colours like the moon,
He touches, and it tingles, and he trembles very soon,
And his face is as a fungus of a leprous white and grey,
Like plants in the high houses that are shuttered from the day,
And death is the phial and the end of noble work,   100
But Don John of Austria has fired upon the Turk.
Don John's hunting, and his hounds have bayed—
Booms away past Italy the rumour of his raid.
Gun upon gun, ha! ha!
Gun upon gun, hurrah!   105
Don John of Austria
Has loosed the cannonade.

The Pope was in his chapel before day or battle broke,
(*Don John of Austria is hidden in the smoke.*)
The hidden room in man's house where God sits all the year.   110
The secret window whence the world looks small and very dear.
He sees as in a mirror on the monstrous twilight sea
The crescent of his cruel ships whose name is mystery;
They fling great shadows foe-wards, making Cross and Castle dark;
They veil the plumèd lions on the galleys of St. Mark;   115
And above the ships are palaces of brown, black-bearded chiefs,
And below the ships are prisons, where with multitudinous griefs,
Christian captives sick and sunless, all a labouring race repines
Like a race in sunken cities, like a nation in the mines.

They are lost like slaves that swat, and in the skies of morning hung 120
The stairways of the tallest gods when tyranny was young.
They are countless, voiceless, hopeless as those fallen or fleeing on
Before the high Kings' horses in the granite of Babylon.
And many a one grows witless in his quiet room in hell,
Where a yellow face looks inward through the lattice of his cell, 125
And he finds his God forgotten, and he seeks no more a sign—
(*But Don John of Austria has burst the battle line!*)
Don John pounding from the slaughter-painted poop,
Purpling all the ocean like a bloody pirate's sloop,
Scarlet running over on the silvers and the golds, 130
Breaking of the hatches up and bursting of the holds,
Thronging of the thousands up that labour under sea,
White for bliss and blind for sun and stunned for liberty.
Vivat Hispania!
Domino gloria! 135
Don John of Austria
Has set his people free!

Cervantes on his galley sets the sword back in the sheath
(*Don John of Austria rides homeward with a wreath.*)
And he sees across a weary land a straggling road in Spain, 140
Up which a lean and foolish knight forever rides in vain,
And he smiles, but not as Sultans smile, and settles back the blade—
(*But Don John of Austria rides home from the Crusade.*)

ROBERT FROST
1874–1963

The Code

THERE were three in the meadow by the brook
Gathering up windrows, piling cocks of hay,
With an eye always lifted toward the west
Where an irregular sun-bordered cloud
Darkly advanced with a perpetual dagger 5
Flickering across its bosom. Suddenly
One helper, thrusting pitchfork in the ground,
Marched himself off the field and home. One stayed.
The town-bred farmer failed to understand.

'What is there wrong?' 10

THE CODE

'Something you just now said.'

'What did I say?'

'About our taking pains.'

'To cock the hay?—because it's going to shower?
I said that more than half an hour ago.   15
I said it to myself as much as you.'

'You didn't know. But James is one big fool.
He thought you meant to find fault with his work.
That's what the average farmer would have meant.
James would take time, of course, to chew it over   20
Before he acted: he's just got round to act.'

'He is a fool if that's the way he takes me.'

'Don't let it bother you. You've found out something.
The hand that knows his business won't be told
To do work better or faster—those two things.   25
I'm as particular as anyone:
Most likely I'd have served you just the same.
But I know you don't understand our ways.
You were just talking what was in your mind,
What was in all our minds, and you weren't hinting.   30
Tell you a story of what happened once:
I was up here in Salem at a man's
Named Sanders with a gang of four or five
Doing the haying. No one liked the boss.
He was one of the kind sports call a spider,   35
All wiry arms and legs that spread out wavy
From a humped body nigh as big's a biscuit.
But work! that man could work, especially
If by so doing he could get more work
Out of his hired help. I'm not denying   40
He was hard on himself. I couldn't find
That he kept any hours—not for himself.
Daylight and lantern-light were one to him:
I've heard him pounding in the barn all night.
But what he liked was someone to encourage.   45
Them that he couldn't lead he'd get behind
And drive, the way you can, you know, in mowing—
Keep at their heels and threaten to mow their legs off.
I'd seen about enough of his bulling tricks
(We call that bulling). I'd been watching him.   50

355

So when he paired off with me in the hayfield
To load the load, thinks I, Look out for trouble.
I built the load and topped it off; old Sanders
Combed it down with a rake and says, "O.K."
Everything went well till we reached the barn   55
With a big jag to empty in a bay.
You understand that meant the easy job
For the man up on top of throwing *down*
The hay and rolling it off wholesale,
Where on a mow it would have been slow lifting.   60
You wouldn't think a fellow'd need much urging
Under those circumstances, would you now?
But the old fool seizes his fork in both hands,
And looking up bewhiskered out of the pit,
Shouts like an army captain, "Let her come!"   65
Thinks I, D'ye mean it? "What was that you said?"
I asked out loud, so's there'd be no mistake,
"Did you say, Let her come?" "Yes, let her come."
He said it over, but he said it softer.
Never you say a thing like that to a man,   70
Not if he values what he is. God, I'd as soon
Murdered him as left out his middle name.
I'd built the load and knew right where to find it.
Two or three forkfuls I picked lightly round for
Like meditating, and then I just dug in   75
And dumped the rackful on him in ten lots.
I looked over the side once in the dust
And caught sight of him treading-water-like,
Keeping his head above. "Damn ye," I says,
"That gets ye!" He squeaked like a squeezed rat.   80
That was the last I saw or heard of him.
I cleaned the rack and drove out to cool off.
As I sat mopping hayseed from my neck,
And sort of waiting to be asked about it,
One of the boys sings out, "Where's the old man?"   85
"I left him in the barn under the hay.
If ye want him, ye can go and dig him out."
They realized from the way I swabbed my neck
More than was needed something must be up.
They headed for the barn; I stayed where I was.   90
They told me afterward. First they forked hay,
A lot of it, out into the barn floor.
Nothing! They listened for him. Not a rustle.
I guess they thought I'd spiked him in the temple
Before I buried him, or I couldn't have managed.   95

They excavated more. "Go keep his wife
Out of the barn." Someone looked in a window,
And curse me if he wasn't in the kitchen
Slumped way down in a chair, with both his feet
Against the stove, the hottest day that summer.   100
He looked so clean disgusted from behind
There was no one that dared to stir him up,
Or let him know that he was being looked at.
Apparently I hadn't buried him
(I may have knocked him down); but my just trying   105
To bury him had hurt his dignity.
He had gone to the house so's not to meet me.
He kept away from us all afternoon.
We tended to his hay. We saw him out
After a while picking peas in his garden: 110
He couldn't keep away from doing something.'

'Weren't you relieved to find he wasn't dead?'

'No! and yet I don't know—it's hard to say.
I went about to kill him fair enough.'

'You took an awkward way. Did he discharge you?'   115

'Discharge me? No! He knew I did just right.'

JOHN MASEFIELD

1878–1967

From *Reynard the Fox*

THE fox knew well, that before they tore him,
They should try their speed on the downs before him,
There were three more miles to the Wan Dyke Hill,
But his heart was high, that he beat them still.
The wind of the downland charmed his bones   5
So off he went for the Sarsen Stones.

The moan of the three great firs in the wind,
And the Ai of the foxhounds died behind,
Wind-dapples followed the hill-wind's breath
On the Kill Down gorge where the Danes found death;   10

357

Larks scattered up; the peewits feeding
Rose in a flock from the Kill Down Steeding.
The hare leaped up from her form and swerved
Swift left for the Starveall, harebell-turved.
On the wind-bare thorn some longtails prinking   15
Cried sweet, as though wind-blown glass were chinking.
Behind came thudding and loud halloo,
Or a cry from hounds as they came to view.

The pure clean air came sweet to his lungs,
Till he thought foul scorn of those crying tongues.   20
In a three mile more he would reach the haven
In the Wan Dyke croaked on by the raven.
In a three mile more he would make his berth
On the hard cool floor of a Wan Dyke earth,
Too deep for spade, too curved for terrier,   25
With the pride of the race to make rest the merrier.
In a three mile more he would reach his dream,
So his game heart gulped and he put on steam.

Like a rocket shot to a ship ashore
The lean red bolt of his body tore,   30
Like a ripple of wind running swift on grass,
Like a shadow on wheat when a cloud blows past,
Like a turn at the buoy in a cutter sailing
When the bright green gleam lips white at the railing,
Like the April snake whipping back to sheath,   35
Like the gannet's hurtle on fish beneath,
Like a kestrel chasing, like a sickle reaping,
Like all things swooping, like all things sweeping,
Like a hound for stay, like a stag for swift,
With his shadow beside like spinning drift.   40

Past the gibbet-stock all stuck with nails,
Where they hanged in chains what had hung at jails,
Past Ashmundshowe where Ashmund sleeps,
And none but the tumbling peewit weeps,
Past Curlew Calling, the gaunt grey corner   45
Where the curlew comes as a summer mourner,
Past Blowbury Beacon shaking his fleece,
Where all winds hurry and none brings peace;
Then down, on the mile-long green decline
Where the turf's like spring and the air's like wine,   50
Where the sweeping spurs of the downland spill
Into Wan Brook Valley and Wan Dyke Hill.

On he went with a galloping rally
Past Maesbury Clump for Wan Brook Valley.
The blood in his veins went romping high,   55
'Get on, on, on to the earth or die.'
The air of the downs went purely past
Till he felt the glory of going fast,
Till the terror of death, though there indeed,
Was lulled for a while by his pride of speed;   60
He was romping away from hounds and hunt,
He had Wan Dyke Hill and his earth in front,
In a one mile more when his point was made,
He would rest in safety from dog or spade;
Nose between paws he would hear the shout   65
Of the 'gone to earth' to the hounds without,
The whine of the hounds, and their cat feet gadding,
Scratching the earth, and their breath pad-padding;
He would hear the horn call hounds away,
And rest in peace till another day.   70
In one mile more he would lie at rest
So for one mile more he would go his best.
He reached the dip at the long droop's end
And he took what speed he had still to spend.

So down past Maesbury beech clump grey,   75
That would not be green till the end of May,
Past Arthur's Table, the white chalk boulder,
Where pasque flowers purple the down's grey shoulder,
Past Quichelm's Keeping, past Harry's Thorn,
To Thirty Acre all thin with corn.   80
As he raced the corn towards Wan Dyke Brook,
The pack had view of the way he took,
Robin hallooed from the downland's crest,
He capped them on till they did their best.
The quarter mile to the Wan Brook's brink   85
Was raced as quick as a man can think.
And here, as he ran to the huntsman's yelling,
The fox first felt that the pace was telling;
His body and lungs seemed all grown old,
His legs less certain, his heart less bold,   90
The hound-noise nearer, the hill slope steeper,
The thud in the blood of his body deeper,
His pride in his speed, his joy in the race,
Were withered away, for what use was pace?
He had run his best, and the hounds ran better.   95
Then the going worsened, the earth was wetter.

359

Then his brush drooped down till it sometimes dragged,
And his fur felt sick and his chest was tagged
With taggles of mud, and his pads seemed lead,
It was well for him he'd an earth ahead.   100
Down he went to the brook and over,
Out of the corn and into the clover,
Over the slope that the Wan Brook drains,
Past Battle Tump where they earthed the Danes,
Then up the hill that the Wan Dyke rings   105
Where the Sarsen Stones stand grand like kings.

Seven Sarsens of granite grim,
As he ran them by they looked at him;
As he leaped the lip of their earthen paling
The hounds were gaining and he was failing.   110

He passed the Sarsens, he left the spur,
He pressed up hill to the blasted fir,
He slipped as he leaped the hedge; he slithered;
'He's mine,' thought Robin. 'He's done; he's dithered.'
At the second attempt he cleared the fence,   115
He turned half right where the gorse was dense,
He was leading hounds by a furlong clear.
He was past his best, but his earth was near.
He ran up gorse to the spring of the ramp,
The steep green wall of the dead men's camp,   120
He sidled up it and scampered down
To the deep green ditch of the dead men's town.

Within, as he reached that soft green turf,
The wind, blowing lonely, moaned like surf,
Desolate ramparts rose up steep,   125
On either side, for the ghosts to keep.
He raced the trench, past the rabbit warren,
Close-grown with moss which the wind made barren,
He passed the spring where the rushes spread,
And there in the stones was his earth ahead.   130
One last short burst upon failing feet—
There life lay waiting, so sweet, so sweet,
Rest in a darkness, balm for aches.

The earth was stopped. It was barred with stakes.

With the hounds at head so close behind   135
He had to run as he changed his mind.

This earth, as he saw, was stopped, but still
There was one earth more on the Wan Dyke Hill
A rabbit burrow a furlong on,
He could kennel there till the hounds were gone.   140
Though his death seemed near he did not blench,
He upped his brush and ran the trench.

He ran the trench while the wind moaned treble,
Earth trickled down, there were falls of pebble.
Down in the valley of that dark gash   145
The wind-withered grasses looked like ash.
Trickles of stones and earth fell down
In that dark valley of dead men's town.
A hawk arose from a fluff of feathers,
From a distant fold came a bleat of wethers.   150
He heard no noise from the hounds behind
But the hill-wind moaning like something blind.

He turned the bend in the hill and there
Was his rabbit-hole with its mouth worn bare;
But there with a gun tucked under his arm   155
Was young Sid Kissop of Purlpits Farm,
With a white hob ferret to drive the rabbit
Into a net which was set to nab it.
And young Jack Cole peered over the wall,
And loosed a pup with a 'Z'bite en, Saul!'   160
The terrier pup attacked with a will,
So the fox swerved right and away down hill.

Down from the ramp of the Dyke he ran
To the brackeny patch where the gorse began,
Into the gorse, where the hill's heave hid   165
The line he took from the eyes of Sid;
He swerved downwind and ran like a hare
For the wind-blown spinney below him there.

He slipped from the gorse to the spinney dark
(There were curled grey growths on the oak tree bark);   170
He saw no more of the terrier pup,
But he heard men speak and the hounds come up.

He crossed the spinney with ears intent
For the cry of hounds on the way he went;
His heart was thumping, the hounds were near now,   175
He could make no sprint at a cry and cheer now,

He was past his perfect, his strength was failing,
His brush sag-sagged and his legs were ailing.
He felt as he skirted Dead Men's Town,
That in one mile more they would have him down.   180
Through the withered oak's wind-crouching tops
He saw men's scarlet above the copse,
He heard men's oaths, yet he felt hounds slacken
In the frondless stalks of the brittle bracken.
He felt that the unseen link which bound   185
His spine to the nose of the leading hound
Was snapped, that the hounds no longer knew
Which way to follow nor what to do;
That the threat of the hounds' teeth left his neck,
They had ceased to run, they had come to check,   190
They were quartering wide on the Wan Hill's bent.

The terrier's chase had killed his scent.

He heard bits chink as the horses shifted,
He heard hounds cast, then he heard hounds lifted,
But there came no cry from a new attack;   195
His heart grew steady, his breath came back.

He left the spinney and ran its edge
By the deep dry ditch of the blackthorn hedge;
Then out of the ditch and down the meadow,
Trotting at ease in the blackthorn shadow   200
Over the track called Godsdown Road,
To the great grass heave of the gods' abode.
He was moving now upon land he knew:
Up Clench Royal and Morton Tew,
The Pol Brook, Cheddesdon and East Stoke Church,   205
High Clench St. Lawrence and Tinker's Birch,
Land he had roved on night by night,
For hot blood-suckage or furry bite,
The threat of the hounds behind was gone;
He breathed deep pleasure and trotted on.   210

MARRIOTT EDGAR
1880–1951

The Lion and Albert

THERE'S a famous seaside place called Blackpool,
 That's noted for fresh air and fun,
And Mr and Mrs Ramsbottom
 Went there with young Albert, their son.

A grand little lad was young Albert, 5
 All dressed in his best; quite a swell
With a stick with an 'orse's 'ead 'andle,
 The finest that Woolworth's could sell.

They didn't think much to the Ocean:
 The waves, they was fiddlin' and small, 10
There was no wrecks and nobody drownded,
 Fact, nothing to laugh at at all.

So, seeking for further amusement,
 They paid and went into the Zoo,
Where they'd Lions and Tigers and Camels, 15
 And old ale and sandwiches too.

There was one great big Lion called Wallace;
 His nose were all covered with scars—
He lay in a somnolent posture
 With the side of his face on the bars. 20

Now Albert had heard about Lions,
 How they was ferocious and wild—
To see Wallace lying so peaceful,
 Well, it didn't seem right to the child.

So straightway the brave little feller, 25
 Not showing a morsel of fear,
Took his stick with its 'orse's 'ead 'andle
 And pushed it in Wallace's ear.

You could see that the Lion didn't like it,
 For giving a kind of a roll, 30
He pulled Albert inside the cage with 'im,
 And swallowed the little lad 'ole.

Then Pa, who had seen the occurrence,
    And didn't know what to do next,
Said 'Mother! Yon Lion's 'et Albert,'   35
    And Mother said 'Well, I am vexed!'

Then Mr and Mrs Ramsbottom—
    Quite rightly, when all's said and done—
Complained to the Animal Keeper
    That the Lion had eaten their son.   40

The keeper was quite nice about it;
    He said 'What a nasty mishap.
Are you sure that it's *your* boy he's eaten?'
    Pa said 'Am I sure? There's his cap!'

The manager had to be sent for.   45
    He came and he said 'What's to do?'
Pa said 'Yon Lion's 'et Albert,
    And 'im in his Sunday clothes, too.'

Then Mother said, 'Right's right, young feller;
    I think it's a shame and a sin   50
For a lion to go and eat Albert,
    And after we've paid to come in.'

The manager wanted no trouble,
    He took out his purse right away,
Saying 'How much to settle the matter?'   55
    And Pa said 'What do you usually pay?'

But Mother had turned a bit awkward
    When she thought where her Albert had gone.
She said 'No! someone's got to be summonsed'—
    So that was decided upon.   60

Then off they went to the P'lice Station,
    In front of the Magistrate chap;
They told 'im what happened to Albert,
    And proved it by showing his cap.

The Magistrate gave his opinion   65
    That no one was really to blame
And he said that he hoped the Ramsbottoms
    Would have further sons to their name.

At that Mother got proper blazing,
 'And thank you, sir, kindly,' said she.   70
'What, waste all our lives raising children
 To feed ruddy Lions? Not me!'

C. DAY-LEWIS
1904–1972

The Nabara

*'They preferred, because of the rudeness of their heart, to die
rather than to surrender.'*

PHASE ONE

Freedom is more than a word, more than the base coinage
Of statesmen, the tyrant's dishonoured cheque, or the dreamer's mad
Inflated currency. She is mortal, we know, and made
In the image of simple men who have no taste for carnage
But sooner kill and are killed than see that image betrayed. 5
Mortal she is, yet rising always refreshed from her ashes:
She is bound to earth, yet she flies as high as a passage bird
To home wherever man's heart with seasonal warmth is stirred:
Innocent is her touch as the dawn's, but still it unleashes
The ravisher shades of envy. Freedom is more than a word. 10

I see man's heart two-edged, keen both for death and creation.
As a sculptor rejoices, stabbing and mutilating the stone
Into a shapelier life, and the two joys make one—
So man is wrought in his hour of agony and elation
To efface the flesh to reveal the crying need of his bone. 15
Burning the issue was beyond their mild forecasting
For those I tell of—men used to the tolerable joy and hurt
Of simple lives: they coveted never an epic part;
But history's hand was upon them and hewed an everlasting
Image of freedom out of their rude and stubborn heart. 20

The year, Nineteen-thirty-seven: month, March: the men,
  descendants
Of those Iberian fathers, the inquiring ones who would go
Wherever the sea-ways led: a pacific people, slow
To feel ambition, loving their laws and their independence—
Men of the Basque country, the Mar Cantabrico. 25

365

Fishermen, with no guile outside their craft, they had weathered
Often the sierra-ranked Biscayan surges, the wet
Fog of the Newfoundland Banks: they were fond of *pelota*: they met
No game beyond their skill as they swept the sea together,
Until the morning they found the leviathan in their net.   30

Government trawlers *Nabara, Guipuzkoa, Bizkaya,*
Donostia, escorting across blockaded seas
Galdames with her cargo of nickel and refugees
From Bayonne to Bilbao, while the crest of war curled higher
Inland over the glacial valleys, the ancient ease.   35
On the morning of March the fifth, a chill North-Wester fanned them,
Fogging the glassy waves: what uncharted doom lay low
There in the fog athwart their course, they could not know:
Stout were the armed trawlers, redoubtable those who manned
        them—   40
Men of the Basque country, the Mar Cantabrico.

Slowly they nosed ahead, while under the chill North-Wester
Nervous the sea crawled and twitched like the skin of a beast
That dreams of the chase, the kill, the blood-beslavered feast:
They too, the light-hearted sailors, dreamed of a fine fiesta,
Flags and their children waving, when they won home from the east.   45
Vague as images seen in a misted glass or the vision
Of crystal-gazer, the ships huddled, receded, neared,
Threading the weird fog-maze that coiled their funnels and bleared
Day's eye. They were glad of the fog till *Galdames* lost position
—Their convoy, precious in life and metal—and disappeared.   50

But still they held their course, the confident ear-ringed captains,
Unerring towards the landfall, nor guessed how the land lay,
How the guardian fog was a guide to lead them all astray.
For now, at a wink, the mist rolled up like the film that curtains
A saurian's eye; and into the glare of an evil day   55
Bizkaya, Guipuzkoa, Nabara, and the little
Donostia stepped at intervals; and sighted, alas,
Blocking the sea and sky a mountain they might not pass,
An isle thrown up volcanic and smoking, a giant in metal
Astride their path—the rebel cruiser, *Canarias.*   60

A ship of ten thousand tons she was, a heavyweight fighter
To the cocky bantam trawlers: and under her armament
Of eight- and four-inch guns there followed obedient
Towards Pasajes a prize just seized, an Estonian freighter
Laden with arms the exporters of death to Spain had sent.   65

THE NABARA

A hush, the first qualm of conflict, falls on the cruiser's burnished
Turrets, the trawlers' grimy decks: fiercer the lime-
Light falls, and out of the solemn ring the late mists climb,
And ship to ship the antagonists gaze at each other astonished
Across the quaking gulf of the sea for a moment's time.   70

The trawlers' men had no chance or wish to elude the fated
Encounter. Freedom to these was natural pride that runs
Hot as the blood, their climate and heritage, dearer than sons.
Bizkaya, Guipuzkoa, knowing themselves outweighted,
Drew closer to draw first blood with their pairs of four-inch guns.   75
Aboard *Canarias* the German gun-layers stationed
Brisk at their intricate batteries—guns and men both trained
To a hair in accuracy, aimed at a pitiless end—
Fired, and the smoke rolled forth over the unimpassioned
Face of a day where nothing certain but death remained.   80

PHASE TWO

The sound of the first salvo skimmed the ocean and thumped
Cape Machichaco's granite ribs: it rebounded where
The salt-sprayed trees grow tough from wrestling the wind: it
     jumped
From isle to rocky isle: it was heard by women while
They walked to shrine or market, a warning they must fear.   85
But, beyond their alarm, as
Though that sound were also a signal for fate to strip
Luck's last green shoot from the falling stock of the Basques,
     Guldames
Emerged out of the mist that lingered to the west
Under the reeking muzzles of the rebel battleship: 90

Which instantly threw five shells over her funnel, and threw
Her hundred women and children into a slaughter-yard panic
On the deck they imagined smoking with worse than the foggy dew,
So that *Galdames* rolled as they slipped, clawed, trampled, reeled
Away from the gape of the cruiser's guns. A spasm galvanic,   95
Fear's chemistry, shocked the women's bodies, a moment before
Huddled like sheep in a mist, inert as bales of rag,
A mere deck-cargo; but more
Than furies now, for they stormed *Galdames'* bridge and swarmed
Over her captain and forced him to run up the white flag.   100

Signalling the Estonian, 'Heave-to', *Canarias* steamed
Leisurely over to make sure of this other prize:
Over-leisurely was her reckoning—she never dreamed

The Estonian in that pause could be snatched from her shark-shape
    jaws
By ships of minnow size.   105
Meanwhile *Nabara* and *Guipuzkoa*, not reluctant
For closer grips while their guns and crews were still entire,
Thrust forward: twice *Guipuzkoa* with a deadly jolt was rocked, and
The sea spat up in geysers of boiling foam, as the cruiser's
Heavier guns boxed them in a torrid zone of fire.   110

And now the little *Donostia* who lay with her 75's
Dumb in the offing—her weapons against that leviathan
Impotent as pen-knives—
Witnessed a bold manoeuvre, a move of genius, never
In naval history told. She saw *Bizkaya* run   115
Ahead of her consorts, a berserk atom of steel, audacious,
Her signal-flags soon to flutter like banderillas, straight
Towards the Estonian speeding, a young bull over the spacious
And foam-distraught arena, till the sides of the freight-ship screen
    her
From *Canarias* that will see the point of her charge too late.   120

'Who are you and where are you going?' the flags of *Bizkaya*
    questioned.
'Carrying arms and forced to go to Pasajes' replied
The Estonian. 'Follow me to harbour.' 'Cannot, am threatened.'
Bizkaya's last word—'Turn at once!'—and she points her peremptory
    guns
Against the freighter's mountainous flanks that blankly hide   125
This fluttering language and flaunt of signal insolence
From the eyes of *Canarias*. At last the rebels can see
That the two ships' talk meant a practical joke at their expense:
They see the Estonian veering away, to Bermeo steering,
Bizkaya under her lee.   130

(To the Basques that ship was a tonic, for she carried some million
    rounds
Of ammunition: to hearts grown sick with hope deferred
And the drain of their country's wounds
She brought what most they needed in face of the aid evaded
And the cold delay of those to whom freedom was only a word.)   135
Owlish upon the water sat the *Canarias*
Mobbed by those darting trawlers, and her signals blinked in vain
After the freighter, that still she believed too large to pass
Into Bermeo's port—a prize she fondly thought,
When she'd blown the trawlers out of the water, she'd take again.   140

THE NABARA

Brisk at their intricate batteries the German gun-layers go
About death's business, knowing their longer reach must foil
The impetus, break the heart of the government ships: each blow
Deliberately they aim, and tiger-striped with flame
Is the jungle mirk of the smoke as their guns leap and recoil.   145
The Newfoundland trawlers feel
A hail and hurricane the like they have never known
In all their deep-sea life: they wince at the squalls of steel
That burst on their open decks, rake them and leave them wrecks,
But still they fight on long into the sunless afternoon.   150

—Fought on, four guns against the best of the rebel navy,
Until *Guipuzkoa*'s crew could stanch the fires no more
That gushed from her gashes and seeped nearer the magazine. Heavy
At heart they turned away for the Nervion that day:
Their ship, *Guipuzkoa*, wore   155
Flame's rose on her heart like a decoration of highest honour
As listing she reeled into Las Arenas; and in a row
On her deck there lay, smoke-palled, that oriflamme's crackling banner
Above them, her dead—a quarter of the fishermen who had fought
  her—
Men of the Basque country, the Mar Cantabrico.   160

PHASE THREE

And now the gallant *Nabara* was left in the ring alone,
The sky hollow around her, the fawning sea at her side:
But the ear-ringed crew in their berets stood to the guns, and cried
A fresh defiance down
The ebb of the afternoon, the battle's darkening tide.   165
Honour was satisfied long since; they had held and harried
A ship ten times their size; they well could have called it a day.
But they hoped, if a little longer they kept the cruiser in play,
Galdames with the wealth of life and metal she carried
Might make her getaway.   170

Canarias, though easily she outpaced and out-gunned her,
Finding this midge could sting
Edged off, and beneath a wedge of smoke steamed in a ring
On the rim of the trawler's range, a circular storm of thunder.
But always *Nabara* turned her broadside, manoeuvring   175
To keep both guns on the target, scorning safety devices.
Slower now battle's tempo, irregular the beat
Of gunfire in the heart
Of the afternoon, the distempered sky sank to the crisis,
Shell-shocked the sea tossed and hissed in delirious heat.   180

369

The battle's tempo slowed, for the cruiser could take her time,
And the guns of *Nabara* grew
Red-hot, and of fifty-two Basque seamen had been her crew
Many were dead already, the rest filthy with grime
And their comrades' blood, weary with wounds all but a few.   185
Between two fires they fought, for the sparks that flashing spoke
From the cruiser's thunder-bulk were answered on their own craft
By traitor flames that crawled out of every cranny and rift
Blinding them all with smoke.
At half-past four *Nabara* was burning fore and aft.   190

What buoyancy of will
Was theirs to keep her afloat, no vessel now but a sieve—
So jarred and scarred, the rivets starting, no inch of her safe
From the guns of the foe that wrapped her in a cyclone of shrieking
     steel!
Southward the sheltering havens showed clear, the cliffs and the
     surf   195
Familiar to them from childhood, the shapes of a life still dear:
But dearer still to see
Those shores insured for life from the shadow of tyranny.
Freedom was not on their lips; it was what made them endure,
A steel spring in the yielding flesh, a thirst to be free.   200

And now from the little *Donostia* that lay with her 75's
Dumb in the offing, they saw *Nabara* painfully lower
A boat, which crawled like a shattered crab slower and slower
Towards them. They cheered the survivors, thankful to save these
     lives
At least. They saw each rower,   205
As the boat dragged alongside, was wounded—the oars they held
Dripping with blood, a bloody skein reeled out in their wake:
And they swarmed down the rope-ladders to rescue these men so
     weak
From wounds they must be hauled
Aboard like babies. And then they saw they had made a mistake.   210

For, standing up in the boat,
A man of that grimy boat's-crew hailed them: 'Our officer asks
You give us your bandages and all your water-casks,
Then run for Bermeo. We're going to finish this game of *pelota*.'
Donostia's captain begged them with tears to escape: but the Basques
Would play their game to the end.   216
They took the bandages, and cursing at his delay
They took the casks that might keep the fires on their ship at bay;

And they rowed back to *Nabara*, trailing their blood behind
Over the water, the sunset and crimson ebb of their day.   220

For two hours more they fought, while *Nabara* beneath their feet
Was turned to a heap of smouldering scrap-iron. Once again
The flames they had checked a while broke out. When the forward
    gun
Was hit, they turned about
Bringing the after gun to bear. They fought in pain   225
And the instant knowledge of death: but the waters filling their riven
Ship could not quench the love that fired them. As each man fell
To the deck, his body took fire as if death made visible
That burning spirit. For two more hours they fought, and at seven
They fired their last shell.   230

Of her officers all but one were dead. Of her engineers
All but one were dead. Of the fifty-two that had sailed
In her, all were dead but fourteen—and each of these half killed
With wounds. And the night-dew fell in a hush of ashen tears,
And *Nabara*'s tongue was stilled.   235
Southward the sheltering havens grew dark, the cliffs and the green
Shallows they knew; where their friends had watched them as evening
    wore
To a glowing end, who swore
Nabara must show a white flag now, but saw instead the fourteen
Climb into their matchwood boat and fainting pull for the shore.   240

Canarias lowered a launch that swept in a greyhound's curve
Pitiless to pursue
And cut them off. But that bloodless and all-but-phantom crew
Still gave no soft concessions to fate: they strung their nerve
For one last fling of defiance, they shipped their oars and threw   245
Hand-grenades at the launch as it circled about to board them.
But the strength of the hands that had carved them a hold on history
Failed them at last: the grenades fell short of the enemy,
Who grappled and overpowered them,
While *Nabara* sank by the stern in the hushed Cantabrian sea.   250

     *   *   *   *   *

They bore not a charmed life. They went into battle foreseeing
Probable loss, and they lost. The tides of Biscay flow
Over the obstinate bones of many, the winds are sighing
Round prison walls where the rest are doomed like their ship to
    rust—
Men of the Basque country, the Mar Cantabrico.   255

Simple men who asked of their life no mythical splendour,
They loved its familiar ways so well that they preferred
In the rudeness of their heart to die rather than to surrender . . .
Mortal these words and the deed they remember, but cast a seed
Shall flower for an age when freedom is man's creative word.   260

Freedom was more than a word, more than the base coinage
Of politicians who hiding behind the skirts of peace
They had defiled, gave up that country to rack and carnage:
For whom, indelibly stamped with history's contempt,   265
Remains but to haunt the blackened shell of their policies.
For these I have told of, freedom was flesh and blood—a mortal
Body, the gun-breech hot to its touch: yet the battle's height
Raised it to love's meridian and held it awhile immortal;
And its light through time still flashes like a star's that has turned to
     ashes,
Long after *Nabara*'s passion was quenched in the sea's heart.   270

CHARLES CAUSLEY
1917–

The Song of Samuel Sweet

As I leaned at my window
All in the white of noon,
The sun his silken volleys
Firing at the moon,
Over the dying valley   5
Slain by the sword of heat,
I heard a horseman riding
And the sound of running feet.

I live in the grassy meadow
     Where the little houses lie,   10
Hoisting their naked chimneys
     Like sails upon the sky.
I live where the honey-heather
     In a tide comes down the street,
Down to the hurling river,   15
     And my name is Samuel Sweet.

When the cock with crow of silver
  Splits as a stone the night,
And over the snoring water
  There comes the morning light,   20
I rise from my strawy pallet
  To the leaping light's alarm
And go about my business
  Upon my father's farm.

Down in the silent stackyard   25
  I met the maiden, day,
Her skin as soft as summer
  Her fears all cast away.
And she and I together
  Under the sky did sing,   30
Till I met by the barnyard
  The soldiers of the King.

From the flowery field of battle
  That blooms all red and white
They had ridden for the rebels   35
  Through all the steely night.
Far from the field of battle
  That blossoms white and red
There rode three tossing troopers,
  A captain at their head.   40

'O halt not by my barnyard!
  Ride to the west, away!
No rebel here is hiding
  Among the friendly hay!
Only the wealthy spider   45
  Building his diamond house,
The bat on the beam, the beetle,
  And the secret harvest-mouse.'

The captain reined and answered
  Beneath the hawthorn tree,   50
'If a rebel thou art hiding
  We'll hang both him and thee.
By the tongues of my three troopers
  And the springing hawthorn spray
We'll hang you, boy, as surely   55
  As night relieves the day.

'If a rebel you are hoarding
  Among the golden hay
We'll hang you high as moonlight
  When we ride back this way.   60
Lighter than any angel,
  Whiter than any dove,
We'll knit a knot of innocence
  With a string as strong as love.'

'Farewell, my bonny captain!   65
  Farewell, you troopers three!
Seize your sailing standards,
  Never seize you me!
Keep your courage handy,
  Keep your justice dry,   70
You will never like a banner
  Hang me from the sky!'

I watched them as they galloped
  Down the leaf-hung lane,
The hooves beating a warning   75
  Over the wheeling plain.
I climbed the leaning ladder
  And in the brittle hay,
His face as pale as morning,
  A wounded soldier lay.   80

He wore no scarlet jacket
  Nor shirt of linen fine,
He wore no silver buckles
  Nor campaign medals nine.
He wore no lace at his pocket   85
  Nor of diamond spurs the best,
Only the badge of battle
  Pinned to his bleeding breast.

I watched his slow surrender
  To the daggers of the hay,   90
The blood that from his body
  Poured like wine away.
I saw death smile and enter
  Trailing his coat so smart,
On sentry-go to plunder   95
  The jewel of the heart.

'Goodbye, goodbye, dear father
  Whom I did never meet,
And goodbye now to mother
  Who lives on easy street.   100
I was not meant for a soldier,
  I do not want to die,
But I must take a journey
  Across the silver sky.

'Part my hair in the middle,   105
  Put a clean shirt on my back!
Hark, I hear the bugle
  And the mourning muskets' crack!
Cover me with a banner,
  Ring the funeral bell!   110
But first, O comrade, fetch me
  Some water from the well.'

I could not give a pillow
  Nor comb his hair so fine,
I had no shirt of linen,   115
  Nor cruse of oil and wine.
But as I fetched the water
  From the dazzling spring
I saw within the barnyard
  The soldiers of the King.   120

'O captain, but I knew not
  Dying among the hay
When you rode by at sunrise
  A rebel soldier lay.
Speak, and he will answer!   125
  Stand in your stirrup, call!
Ere death shall freeze his fingers
  And silent spread its shawl.'

The mirror of the morning,
  Broken by troopers three,
Flashed its brilliant warning—   130
  But never a word spoke he.
Never a word he answered
  From his yellow bed,
Lying asleep for ever   135
  In the bivouac of the dead.

'Rig the gallows, troopers!
　Make the ship shine!
Here's a likely cabin-boy
　For the death or glory line!　　　　　　140
Give him a hempen collar
　As he heavenward steers,
The clouds about his ankles,
　The stars about his ears.'

'O captain, do not hang me　　　　　　145
　From the mast so high,
Nor stand me like a trooper
　In the barrack of the sky.
Hang me not for a rebel,
　Nor fire the fatal gun,　　　　　　　150
I was not made for a hero,
　I was made to run.

'Faster than the storm-bird
　Beating up the west,
Swifter than the serpent　　　　　　　155
　In the sea's breast,
Lighter than the lariat
　Falling from the sun,
Faster than fear,
　My captain, I run!'　　　　　　　　160

'Cut him down, troopers,
　From the forest skies,
Break away the bandage
　That binds his clear eyes.
Let him go a-coursing　　　　　　　　165
　My charger and me!
If he be the victor
　He shall go free!

'If he flies faster
　Than the sea-foam,　　　　　　　　170
Faster than my war-horse,
　He shall fly home.
As I ride over
　The valley's open knife,
If the boy pass me:　　　　　　　　　175
　He shall have his life!'

'Where the glass river
  Runs his sword through
The green breast of the valley,
  I am running too!   180
Lend me your wings, eagle!
  Strong winds, your breath!
That I may race the rider
  And his drummer, death.'

'As the happy hunter   185
  Aims the accurate gun,
As the raving rifleman
  Knows the battle's won,
Come away, charger,
  With your hooves fleet!   190
If we win or if we lose
  The prize is Samuel Sweet!'

'O captain, I am waiting
  By the empty tree
As your horse of fire   195
  Comes blazing on the lea.
See, my feet are bloody,
  With salt my eyes are blind
For captain, I have left you
  Far, far behind.   200

'Why do you frown, captain,
  As I bend the knee,
Nor tell your tossing troopers
  That I may go free?
Why do you tie my collar   205
  With a shining strand,
Nor send me home to mother,
  A ring-dove in my hand?'

'Launch the gallows, hangman,
  On the bay of heaven.   210
Take aboard a passenger
  And his sins all seven.
Pull him up the rigging
  As high as he will fly,
A captain's request-man   215
  In the sessions of the sky.'

'Lord, the drunken gibbet
  Steering in the clouds
With his wooden fingers
  Wraps me in his shrouds.   220
Murdered by my captain,
  Murdered by my King,
Murdered by the water
  From the weeping spring.

'Murdered by the rebel   225
  In the reeking hay,
Murdered by the bragging night
  Who has ransomed day.
When the shepherd, morning,
  Shoots his golden sling,   230
Listen to the warning
  And the song I sing:

'When the gangs of battle
  Press all through the day,
The innocent and guilty   235
  Are stolen all away.
Fire the starting pistol,
  Fire a parting prayer,
For I run for ever
  In the alleys of the air.'   240

As I leaned at my window
  All in the white of noon,
The sun his silken volleys
  Firing at the moon,
Over the dying valley   245
  Slain by the sword of heat,
I heard a horseman riding
  And the sound of running feet.

WILLIAM PLOMER

1903–1973

Atheling Grange: or, The Apotheosis of
Lotte Nussbaum

I

A HEAVY mist. A muffled sea.
A cloth of cobwebs veils the grass.
Upstairs alone the refugee
  Sees autumn in her glass:

A touch of autumn in the air,   5
The knife of autumn in the heart
Of one too constantly aware
  Of living half apart.

Is comfort peace? Can it restore
The severed root within the mind?   10
Domestic service evermore
  Is not what hope designed:

Kindly and rich and not a fool
The widow whom she housekeeps for,
But unadventurous, so cool,   15
  So English, such a bore.

Today the harmless Mrs Clunch
Went up to London on her own,
And Lotte, dreamy after lunch,
  Feels even more alone: 20

She has no one to whom to turn
And reminisce of those lost lives
The autumn smell of leaf and fern
  So poignantly revives;

It quickens an old appetite,   25
This dank and thrilling smell;
She feels a craving now to bite
  Mushroom or Chanterelle;

Off with a basket she will go
To find if, where the fields begin,   30
Some palatable fungi grow,
   And if so, bring them in;

She knows the very ones to look for—
Fresh, firm, not too mature—
There'll only be herself to cook for,   35
   A secret epicure!

2

Lotte acquired upon her native hills
   The caution of a fungivore,
Knew how to look a *Giftpilz* in the gills
And where for *Steinpilz* one had best explore,   40
So now with confidence she reconnoitres,
Steps forward, backward, stoops, intently loiters.

Though no mycophagist could be more eager,
   She finds she isn't doing well,
After an hour her harvesting is meagre—   45
Two Puffballs, and a not too fresh Morel;
But strolling on beyond her usual range
She comes to the deserted Atheling Grange.

3

Where formerly curlews were calling
And orchises fell with the hay   50
The last of the meadows are falling
To bungalows gnawing their way;

The seaboard is doubly eroded—
To seaward by gale-driven water,
And inland, where fields are outmoded   55
By inroads of bricks and of mortar;

But still, though its owners have died out,
An island of ilex encloses
A nineteenth-century hide-out
Once lovely with lawns and with roses;   60

The owls, who succeeded its owners,
Would quit it with screeches tonight
If they knew that the place is now known as
A 'ripe-for-development' site.

The state of the place is appalling—   65
What is wrongly described as a shambles;
Everywhere ivy is crawling
And striving to strangle the brambles;

Everywhere brambles are clinging
And creepers are climbing and creeping,   70
The nettles are ready for stinging,
The willows have reason for weeping;

The woods were cut down in the 'twenties,
The farm was sold off at a loss,
The lodge is kept only by woodlice,   75
The gateposts are padded with moss;

Bindweed has smothered the greenhouse,
The summer-house under the yew
Is now just a cannot-be-seen house
That commands an invisible view.   80

O house once delightfully lived in,
O Atheling Grange, did they build you
For dry rot and wet rot to feed on,
A medium for mould and for mildew?

Why ask such an imbecile question?   85
That rhetorical style has gone by,
And nothing would be more surprising
Than to hear the old ruin reply.

With bunches of bats on the ceilings
And droppings of rats in the hall,   90
The decline of the Grange is complete and
At any time now it may fall.

4

Though Lotte is aware how torn her coat is,
    Full steam ahead she ploughs and pushes
Tank-like through snags and tangled thorny bushes,   95
Quite undeterred by wire or warning notice,
Convinced this *Hintergarten* she has found
Will prove to be her happy hunting-ground.

How right she is—but God knows how she knew it!
   She's in a mycophil's Utopia   100
Where autumn, from a golden cornucopia,
Has tipped out every sort of Cèpe and Blewit.
She fills her basket quickly. New to her
Truffles one doesn't have to disinter;

Not new to her, but never yet so keen,   105
   So *appetitlich* and so rich
That mushroom smell; nor has she ever seen
The Beefsteak Fungus growing in a ditch;
Here on a stump some tender Buff Caps quiver,
There Pluteus swells, like Strasburg goose's liver;   110

And peering downward through a rusty grating
   Into what used to be the cellars
She sees there, prettily proliferating,
A multitude of little beige umbrellas,
Throngs of a choice and edible Boletus   115
That seem to say 'Come down, my dear, and eat us!'

'*Embarras de richesse!*' she might exclaim,
   If she could coin so French a phrase—
So many kinds she doesn't know by name,
All ready to be cooked in different ways: 120
But who to feed? She yearns to summon up
Her long-lost kin to sit with her and sup.

'*Himmel!*' she sighs . . . And at that very word
   Celestial choirs inflate the breeze,
Die ganze Vogelschar gets busy in the trees,   125
And then a band—a German band—is heard
Playing a waltz by Waldteufel or Strauss,
And all the lights light up inside the house.

'*Himmel!*' she cries. And so it is—she's right!
   Across the new-mown lawn advance   130
Her long-lost family, arrayed in white,
Her parents leading in a lively dance
Her brothers, sisters, nieces, uncles, aunts,
With crowns and harps—a most unearthly sight!

Oh, what a welcome for Miss Nussbaum! See,   135
   All's *himmelhoch* and *himmelblau*!
Heaven is hers, and she is Heaven's now!
She's disembodied, disencumbered, free!
Lotte is free! . . . Tomorrow Mrs Clunch
Will have no drudge to cook her blasted lunch.   140

W. H. AUDEN
1907–1973

The Ballad of Barnaby

LISTEN, good people, and you shall hear
A story of old that will gladden your ear,
The Tale of Barnaby, who was, they say,
The finest tumbler of his day.

In every town great crowds he drew,   5
And all men marvelled to see him do
The French Vault, the Vault of Champagne,
The Vault of Metz, and the Vault of Lorraine.

His eyes were blue, his figure was trim,
He liked the girls and the girls liked him;   10
For years he lived a life of vice,
Drinking in taverns and throwing the dice.

It happened one day he was riding along
Between two cities, whistling a song,
When he saw what then was quite common to see,   15
Two ravens perched on a gallows-tree.

'Barnaby,' the first raven began,
'Will one day be as this hanging man':
'Yes,' said the other, 'and we know well
That when that day comes he will go to Hell.'   20

Then Barnaby's conscience smote him sore;
He repented of all he had done heretofore:
'Woe is me! I will forsake
This wicked world and penance make.'

The evening air was grave and still 25
When he came to a monastery built on a hill:
As its bells the Angelus did begin,
He knocked at the door and they let him in.

The monks in that place were men of parts,
Learned in the sciences and the arts: 30
The Abbot could logically define
The place of all creatures in the Scheme Divine.

Brother Maurice then wrote down all that he said
In a flowing script that it might be read,
And Brother Alexander adorned the book 35
With pictures that gave it a beautiful look.

There were brothers there who could compose
Latin Sequences in verse and prose,
And a brother from Picardy, too, who sung
The praise of Our Lady in the vulgar tongue. 40

Now Barnaby had never learned to read,
Nor *Paternoster* knew nor *Creed*;
Watching them all at work and prayer,
Barnaby's heart began to despair.

Down to the crypt at massing-time 45
He crept like a man intent on crime:
In a niche there above the altar stood
A statue of Our Lady carved in wood.

'Blessed Virgin,' he cried, 'enthroned on high,
Ignorant as a beast am I: 50
Tumbling is all I have learnt to do;
Mother-of-God, let me tumble for You.'

Straightway he stripped off his jerkin,
And his tumbling acts he did begin:
So eager was he to do Her honour 55
That he vaulted higher than ever before.

The French Vault, the Vault of Champagne,
The Vault of Metz and the Vault of Lorraine,
He did them all till he sank to the ground,
His body asweat and his head in a swound. 60

Unmarked by him, Our Lady now
Steps down from her niche and wipes his brow.
'Thank you, Barnaby,' She said and smiled;
'Well have you tumbled for me, my child.'

From then on at the Office-Hours   65
Barnaby went to pay Her his devoirs.
One brother thought to himself: 'Now where
Does Barnaby go at our times of prayer?'

And so next day when Barnaby slipped
Away he followed him down to the crypt.   70
When he saw how he honoured the Mother-of-God,
This brother thought: 'This is very odd.

'It may be well: I believe it is,
But the Abbot, surely, should know of this.'
To the Abbot he went with reverent mien   75
And told him exactly what he had seen.

The Abbot said to him: 'Say no word
To the others of what you have seen and heard.
I will come tomorrow and watch with you
Before I decide what I ought to do.'   80

Next day behind a pillar they hid,
And the Abbot marked all that Barnaby did.
Watching him leap and vault and tumble,
He thought, 'This man is holy and humble.'

'Lady,' cried Barnaby, 'I beg of Thee   85
To intercede with Thy Son for me!',
Gave one more leap, then down he dropped,
And lay dead still, for his heart had stopped.

Then grinning demons, black as coal,
Swarmed out of Hell to seize his soul: 90
'In vain shall be his pious fuss,
For every tumbler belongs to us.'

But Our Lady and Her angels held them at bay,
With shining swords they drove them away,
And Barnaby's soul they bore aloft,   95
Singing with voices sweet and soft.

NOTES

The Cock and the Hen is the Nun's Priest's tale in *The Canterbury Tales*. The story of a cock being carried off by a fox, and obtaining his release by inducing the fox to open his mouth to taunt his pursuers, may have been known in medieval times as a fable. But Chaucer must also have been familiar with—or, more likely, have heard a retelling of—one of the verse tales in *Le Roman de Renart* (composed between *c.*1175 and *c.*1205), in which a cock, 'Mesire Chantecler', having been seized by a fox, not only effects his escape by the same stratagem, but first dreams he has been attacked by something wearing a red fur coat, unfolds his dream to the hen Pinte, and, in this case, refuses to believe her when she warns that a fox has already been seen in the yard. In Chaucer's retelling of the tale, supposedly in the words of a priest, the question of whether warnings in dreams should be heeded is both taken seriously and yet mocked by the scholarly outpourings of the anti-hero cock, and by the homely attitude of the uneducated hen, with her suggestion that the dreams can be dispelled by a laxative; for the principal study in this entertainment is the popular sermon of the day with its admired citation of fable and *exemplum*.

The text is an adaptation of Skeat's in the Oxford Standard Authors, with aid from F. N. Robinson's edition.

Death and the Three Revellers, the tale the Pardoner tells his fellow pilgrims on the way to Canterbury, has been described as one of the best short stories in existence: it is a realistic tale, yet one that embodies an ever-mysterious symbolic or supernatural figure; it is an adventure tale with an admirable moral, exposing the deadly sin of avarice; and, ironically, or perhaps characteristically, it is a tale told by a man—the seller of indulgences—who is, by his own admission, an avaricious fraud. The basic story, which has the essential quality of a traditional tale, in that once heard it is not likely to be forgotten, was undoubtedly old even in Chaucer's day, and one which the poet could have heard told at any time during his travels. Numerous analogues have been recorded. For instance, in an Italian manuscript collection of the early sixteenth century (Codex Panciatichiano-Palatino 138), a hermit, who finds gold in a cave, immediately flees, telling three robbers he meets he is being chased by Death, though they can see no one, and think him a fool when he directs them to the gold. They meet their deaths precisely as do Chaucer's revellers. An extra traditional element in Chaucer's tale is the ill-luck that follows disrespectful speech on meeting an old person. Compare, in *The Classic Fairy Tales* (OUP, 1974), the fate of the elder sister in 'Diamonds and Toads' and of the stepdaughter in 'The Three Heads in the Well'.

Robin Hood and the Monk is not only the earliest surviving tale of Robin Hood, it is the longest and most lively. The only source is Cambridge University Library manuscript Ff.5.48, which dates from the second half of the fifteenth century, and is a vade-mecum containing, in 135 pages, everything a minstrel might need for the solace and entertainment of a household; such as prayers, a dance-song, weather prophecies, and a variety of tales in verse. Our text is modernized from the reading of the ballad given by Dobson and Taylor in *Rymes of Robyn Hood*, 1976, who point out that this 'talkying of the munke and Robyn Hode' was more likely to have been

recited than sung. We have omitted the damaged stanza 30, where a further part of
the ballad is also clearly missing; and we have omitted stanzas 37–9, where the story
seemed to flag. We have also gratefully adopted Sir Arthur Quiller-Couch's
suggested readings for a few lines illegible in the MS.

Tam Lin is a fairy story, and has the familiar ingredients of fairy stories known to the
present day: the rose that must not be plucked; the handsome youth taken by the
Queen of the Fairies to live with her in her green hill; the tithe that must be paid to
Hell; the rescue during the fairy ride. The central theme of the story, and the most
dramatic, is the shape-shifting which Tam Lin must endure before he is free. It has
been resorted to by spirits since classical times, when they have found themselves in
the grip of a mortal. In Ovid's *Metamorphoses*, for instance, Thetis changes herself
into fire, water, wind, a tree, a bird, a tiger, a lion, and a serpent, before surrendering
in the shape of a cuttlefish. In the last stanza the Queen may simply have wished she
had taken the practical precaution of taking out Tam Lin's eyes so that he would no
longer be able to see fairies. Text of the ballad from *Johnson's Musical Museum*, vol. V,
1797, communicated by Burns.

The Tale of the Upland Mouse and the Burgess Mouse is a tale which Henryson, at one
time head-teacher in the grammar school at Dunfermline, wrote in the 1480s or
1490s in 'ornate Scottis meter'. The fable itself was already current in the time of
Christ. Horace gives a pleasant version in his *Satires* (II. 6), in which the town feast is
disturbed by the terrible noise of opening doors and the barking of mastiffs. Text
based on *The Morall Fabillis of Esope*, 1570, edited by G. Gregory Smith, *The Poems of
Robert Henryson*, II, 1906; and a 1571 printing edited by H. Harvey Wood, *The Poems
and Fables of Robert Henryson*, 1958. Stanzas 1–5, 7–10, 12–14, 16, 19–21, 23–6, 28–9.

The Babes in the Wood, the best known of all broadside ballads, was licensed to be
printed 15 October 1595 under the title 'The Norfolk gent his will and Testament
and howe he Commytted the keeping of his Children to his owne brother whoe
delte most wickedly with them and howe God plagued him for it' When Bishop
Percy published in 1765 the standard text, partly basing it on a black-letter printing
that Pepys had collected, he knew no English legend that could account for the story.
Since then, inevitably, a number of legends have gained currency, the most persistent
centring on Griston Old Hall, near Watton in Norfolk, the home in Elizabethan
times of the de Grey family, and, in particular, on the young orphan Thomas de Grey
who died in 1566, reputedly murdered by his uncle in nearby Wayland or Wailing
Wood. Percy's theory, that the ballad was derived from a stage tragedy 'of a young
childe murthered in a Wood by two Ruffians, with the consent of his Unckle', was
long discounted since the play was not published until 1601, six years after the
licensing of the ballad. It now appears, however, that Robert Yarington, to whom the
play is ascribed on the title-page, was probably only the scribe, that the play was first
performed some years earlier, and that the likely date of its composition was 1594. In
the play the scene of the murder is Padua; but no significance need be given to this
location. At the time, Italian settings for the drama were the height of fashion.

The Cave of Despair is one of the adventures in the first half of *The Faerie Queene* (Book
I, canto ix), which Spenser sent to the printer in 1589. St. George, the Red Cross
Knight, appointed protector of Una (the true religion), has been trapped by Duessa
(falsehood), and has had to be rescued by Prince Arthur; but, having languished in a

dungeon, remains weak. Una and he are now confronted by the knight Trevisan who, with a rope round his neck, is fleeing Despair, his friend having already killed himself. They ride back to the Cave of Depair; and to such effect does Despair argue life's hopelessness that the Red Cross Knight accepts a dagger, and is about to kill himself when Una snatches it from his hand.

The Ballad of Agincourt first appeared in *Poemes Lyrick and pastorall*, 1606, where it was headed 'To my frinds the Camber-britans and theyr harp' (two Welsh friends were later named in *Poly-Olbion*). Drayton was emotionally attracted by 'Th' old British Bards' whose harps stirred youth 'to Warlike Rage, Or their wyld Furie to asswage'; and he styled his poem a ballad, 'for that I labour to meet truely therein with the ould English garb'. There had been many popular ballads about Agincourt, the most celebrated English victory until supplanted by Blenheim. One, 'Agencourt, Agencourt', closely resembles Drayton's in metre. Our text follows that of *Poems*, 1619.

Sin and Death is from Book II of *Paradise Lost*, lines 629–889, and has been modernized from the second edition, 1674. The extract was chosen by Professor J. C. Smith for *A Book of Narrative Verse* (OUP, 1930). Milton considered various themes from the early history of Britain for his epic, including the story of King Arthur, but rejected them on the ground that they were partly myth. He decided that only a true story would be worthy of his grand scheme, and wrote 'Adam Unparadized'.

Cymon and Iphigenia was published in 1700, the year of the poet's death, in his *Fables Ancient and Modern*. Dryden obtained the story from the *Decameron*, the collection of a hundred tales, mostly of popular origin, written in Italy by Giovanni Boccaccio between 1348 and 1353. The story of Cymon and Iphigenia is there the first tale of the fifth day; and Dryden's rendering follows the original tale closely.

The Rape of the Lock was written to mollify an offended maiden. Young Lord Petre had stolen a lock of hair from the head of his kinswoman, Miss Arabella Fermor, and the two families were not on speaking terms. John Caryll (the 'Muse' of the poem), who was Petre's guardian, asked Pope to 'write a poem, and laugh them together again'. When the poem was published, in 1712, it only aggravated the squabble; though by the time the extended version of five cantos was published in 1714, Arabella had become proud of her fame. Partridge, who views Belinda's lock through a telescope at the end of the poem, was, Pope said, 'a ridiculous Star-gazer, who in his Almanacks every year, never fail'd to predict the downfall of the Pope, and the King of France, then at war with the English'. The text is modernized from the 1751 edition.

Elegy on the Death of a Mad Dog, which Goldsmith wrote as a kind of antidote to the sonorous elegies that had become fashionable following the publication of Gray's *Elegy written in a Country Church Yard*, first appeared in *The Vicar of Wakefield* (1766), sung by Dr Primrose's youngest son. Goldsmith probably had the idea from Voltaire's epigram on his critic Fréron:

> L'autre jour, au fond d'un vallon,
> Un serpent mordit Jean Fréron.
> Devinez ce qu'il arriva?
> Ce fut le serpent qui creva.

But the idea was not new. More than five hundred years BC, Demodocus had joked in similar vein about the despised Cappadocians of Asia Minor:

> A viper bit a Cappadocian's hide,
> And poisoned by his blood that instant died.

And such an occurrence is not, it seems, beyond the realms of possibility. According to *The Sunday Times*, 23 August 1981, a drug addict of Faizabad was bitten by a poisonous snake, and recovered. The snake it was that died.

The Double Transformation first appeared in *Essays by Mr Goldsmith*, 1765, the text given here being as revised in 1766. The statement that the lady wore 'five greasy nightcaps' means she wore them on top of each other, to keep warm, as we do today when we put on two pairs of socks.

King Estmere may have been one of the tales the shepherds told in *The Complaint of Scotland*, 1549: 'How the King of Estmure land married the King's daughter of Westmure land.' However, there is no source for this magnificent ballad other than Percy's *Reliques of Ancient English Poetry*, 1765: our text is modernized from the fourth edition, 1794. Also see Preface, p. vii.

The Diverting History of John Gilpin was written by William Cowper at Olney in October 1782. It was based on a tale his friend Lady Austen remembered from childhood, which may thus be presumed to date from the first half of the eighteenth century. Cowper wrote the verses with little thought of publication, since they had not the weight ordinarily expected of him; and when he allowed them to be printed a few weeks later in the *Public Advertiser*, 14 November, he insisted they appear anonymously. Their success was phenomenal. They were printed on broadsheets, featured in recitations, and made the subject of engravings. Whether or not the story, as retold by Cowper, is accurate, it has the trappings of truth. There was, and still is, a Bell Inn at Edmonton; and the village was, in the middle of the eighteenth century, a favourite place with small tradesmen for a family outing. The identity of John Gilpin has long been the subject of pleasant speculation. John Beyer, an eminent and 'superlatively polite' linen-draper of number 3 Cheapside, who died 11 May 1791 aged 98, is perhaps the front runner. His friends, anyway, seem to have been convinced he was the man. Cowper did not acknowledge his authorship until 1785, when he included it, after some hesitation, in the second volume of his *Poems*.

Tam o' Shanter was written by Burns in 1790, following his meeting with the antiquary Francis Grose, who was in Dumfriesshire gathering material for *The Antiquities of Scotland*. Burns was keen that Grose, an accomplished artist, should include a drawing of Alloway Kirk, where his father was buried; and Grose agreed, provided Burns could give him a good local legend for the letterpress. Burns wrote down three 'witch' stories, the most amusing of which concerned a farmer from Carrick, who, having stayed injudiciously long at Ayr market, was returning home late at night. Passing Alloway he was startled to see a light in the kirk, and without getting from his horse peered through a window, and found himself spectator to a dance of witches 'merrily footing it round their old sooty blackguard master, who was keeping them all alive with the power of his bagpipe'. The old women, a number of whom the farmer recognized as neighbours, were dressed only in their smocks; and one of them, he noticed, was in a smock considerably too short for its purpose. The farmer was so amused by this he burst out with a laugh: 'Weel luppen, Maggy wi' the short sark!' Then, quickly recollecting himself, he spurred his horse to the old bridge nearby which crossed the Doon, knowing that if he could get half over he would be safe, since no diabolic power can pursue across running water. The farmer, Burns said, just managed to escape; but as he was crossing the bridge one of the hags caught hold of his horse's tail, which immediately gave way as if blasted by a stroke of lightning. 'The unsightly, tailless condition of the vigorous steed,' he commented, 'was to the last hours of the noble creature's life, an awful warning to the Carrick farmers, not to stay too late in Ayr markets.' Having sent Grose this tale Burns evidently felt that if he gave it poetic form, and Grose printed it in his *Antiquities*—as he did, vol. ii, April 1791—an accompanying plate depicting Alloway Kirk would be essential.

The Rime of the Ancient Mariner was Coleridge's major contribution to *Lyrical Ballads*, 1798. It appeared under his own name for the first time in *Sibylline Leaves*, 1817. In old age Wordsworth recalled the genesis of the poem: 'In the autumn of 1797, he [Coleridge], my sister, and myself, started from Alfoxden pretty late in the afternoon, with a view to visit Linton, and the Valley of Stones near to it; and as our united funds were very small, we agreed to defray the expense of the tour by writing a poem. . . Accordingly we set off, and proceeded, along the Quantock Hills, towards Watchet; and in the course of this walk was planned the poem of the "Ancient Mariner," founded on a dream, as Mr Coleridge said, of his friend Mr Cruikshank [Lord Egremont's agent at Stowey]. Much the greatest part of the story was Mr Coleridge's invention; but certain parts I suggested; for example, some crime was to be committed which should bring upon the Old Navigator, as Coleridge afterwards delighted to call him, the spectral persecution, as a consequence of that crime and his own wanderings. I had been reading in Shelvocke's Voyages, a day or two before, that, while doubling Cape Horn, they frequently saw albatrosses in that latitude, the largest sort of sea-fowl, some extending their wings twelve or thirteen feet. "Suppose," said I, "you represent him as having killed one of these birds on entering the South Sea, and that the tutelary spirits of these regions take upon them to avenge the crime." . . . I also suggested the navigation of the ship by the dead men. . .' We have used the revised text, 1834, and only regret that Coleridge lost his nerve and substituted 'It ate the food it ne'er had eat' (line 67) for 'The Mariners gave it biscuit-worms', especially as it was later found that the albatross in Shelvocke was the sooty albatross, a smaller bird who might appreciate biscuit-worms.

The Idiot Boy first appeared in *Lyrical Ballads*, 1798. Wordsworth told the devoted Isabella Fenwick: 'The last stanza—"The Cocks did crow to-whoo, to-whoo, And the sun did shine so cold"—was the foundation of the whole. The words were reported to me by my dear friend, Thomas Poole; but I have since heard the same repeated of other Idiots. Let me add that this long poem was composed in the groves of Alfoxden, almost extempore; not a word, I believe, being corrected, though one stanza was omitted. I mention this in gratitude to those happy moments, for, in truth, I never wrote anything with so much glee.' The subject matter could not of course escape criticism, and in June 1802 Wordsworth defended it in a letter to John Wilson: 'I can only say that the loathing and disgust which many people have at the sight of an idiot . . . is owing in a great measure to a false delicacy, and, if I may say it without rudeness, a certain want of comprehensiveness of thinking and feeling . . . If an idiot is born in a poor man's house, it must be taken care of, and cannot be boarded out, as it would be by gentlefolks . . . I have, indeed, often looked upon the conduct of fathers and mothers of the lower classes of society towards idiots as the great triumph of the human heart'.

Alice Fell was written at the request of a friend, Mr Graham of Glasgow. Dorothy Wordsworth wrote in her journal, 16 February 1802, 'Mr Graham said he wished Wm. had been with him the other day—he was riding in a post-chaise and he heard a strange cry that he could not understand, the sound continued, and he called to the chaise driver to stop. It was a little girl that was crying as if her heart would burst. She had got up behind the chaise, and her cloak had been caught by the wheel, and was jammed in, and it hung there. She was crying after it. Poor thing. Mr Graham took her into the chaise, and the cloak was released from the wheel, but the child's misery did not cease, for her cloak was torn to rags; it had been a miserable cloak before, but she had no other, and it was the greatest sorrow that could befal her. Her name was Alice Fell. She had no parents, and belonged to the next Town. At the next Town, Mr G. left money with some respectable people in the town, to buy her a new cloak.' Later in life Wordsworth said 'The humbleness, meanness if you like, of the subject, together with the homely mode of treating it, brought upon me a world of ridicule by the small critics, so that in policy I excluded it from many editions of my Poems.' It had first been published in *Poems in Two Volumes*, 1807.

Bishop Hatto, under the title 'God's Judgement on a Wicked Bishop', appeared in the *Morning Post*, 27 November 1799; and was collected with other of the poet's work in *Metrical Tales*, 1805. Southey had taken this legend of the tenth-century Bishop of Mainz from the writings of the early English traveller Thomas Coryat, who in 1611 sought to confirm the story by saying that on a little island in the middle of the Rhine, near Bingen, a tower named 'Mowse-turn' (*Mäusethurm*) was still shown to visitors. Subsequent research has shown, however, that the legend is international. It has been told of other persons and places; and was possibly in existence even before the tenth century. The real Bishop Hatto seems to have been a man of exemplary character.

The Inchcape Rock, which was published in the *Morning Post*, 19 October 1803, was based on a legend that had been set down in the 1612 edition of John Monipennie's *True Description of the Whole Realme of Scotland*, and recently reprinted: 'By East the Ile of May twelve miles from all land in the German seas, lies a great hidden rocke called Inchcape, very dangerous for Navigators, because it is overflowed everie tide. It is reported in old times upon the said rocke, there was a Bell fixed upon a tree or timber, which rang continually, being moved by the Sea, giving notice to the Saylers of the danger. This Bell or Clocke was put there, and maintained by the Abbot of Aber-brothok, and being taken downe by a Sea Pirote, who a yeare thereafter perished upon the same rocke with ship and goods, in the righteous judgement of God'. Inchcape or Bell Rock is a reef off the east coast of Scotland, twelve miles south-east of Arbroath (Aber-brothok). Less than four years after the publication of the poem Robert Stevenson began building a lighthouse on the Rock.

Beth Gêlert; or, The Grave of the Greyhound appeared on a broadsheet printed in North Wales in 1800, and quickly became popular since it was believed to be a translation of one of the country's ancient ballads. When Spencer, a well-known London socialite and wit, included the tale in his *Poems*, 1811, he added a note: 'The story of this ballad is traditionary in a village at the foot of Snowdon, where Llewelyn the great had a house. The Greyhound, named Gêlert, was given him by his father-in-law, King John, in the year 1205, and the place to this day, is called Beth-Gêlert, or the grave of Gêlert.' Almost certainly this information emanated not from oral tradition but from Edward Jones's recently published *Musical Relicks of the Welsh Bards*. In the second edition of that work, 1794, Jones localized a story that had hitherto been general in Wales, and conveniently connected it with Llewelyn. In fact Beddgelert, four miles from Snowdon, has no ancient association with the tale, the place-name more likely commemorates a saint than a hound's burial-place (the cairn was erected to satisfy tourists), and the story is, of course, too good to be confined to any one country. Versions of this apologue against impetuosity were known in Eastern literature long before Llewelyn's day.

Young Lochinvar was based on a traditional ballad which Scott had included in his *Minstrelsy of the Scottish Border*, 1802, under the title 'The Laird of Laminton' and subsequently, when he had collected further versions, had altered and titled 'Katharine Janfarie'. In 'Katharine Janfarie' Lord Lochinvar loses the bride. But when Scott needed a ballad for Lady Heron to sing at Holyrood, the night before the Scottish army marched into England (*Marmion; A Tale of Flodden Field*, 1808, canto v), he naturally wanted the hero to carry off his treasure from the south. The Lochinvars lived in Kenmure Castle in Kirkcudbrightshire, and Netherby Hall is in Cumberland, on the south side of the Esk.

Peter Grimes is Letter xxii in Crabbe's *The Borough*, 1810, and, as might be expected, is founded on fact. Crabbe's son and namesake George Crabbe added a note in the 1834 edition: 'The original of Peter Grimes was an old fisherman of Aldborough, while Mr Crabbe was practising there as a surgeon. He had a succession of apprentices from London, and a certain sum with each. As the boys all disappeared under circumstances of strong suspicion, the man was warned by some of the principal inhabitants, that if another followed in like manner, he should certainly be charged with murder.' Benjamin Britten followed Crabbe's story fairly closely in his opera *Peter Grimes*, 1945, though of necessity he had to introduce two female characters, the soprano being, somewhat improbably, a lady Grimes wishes to marry.

Beppo: A Venetian Story was written when Byron was living at La Mira, a few miles from Venice. He heard the tale at a dinner party on 29 August 1817, told in sophisticated circumstances as if it was a recent happening; and realized that with it he could emulate John Hookham Frere whose facetious 'Whistlecraft' verses had newly arrived. Within a few weeks he was telling his publisher to expect a humorous poem of eighty-nine stanzas. Later he extended the poem to ninety-five stanzas; and—after its publication in 1818—to ninety-nine stanzas. The experiment is made here of giving only the narrative verses. Stanzas 1–3, 6, 10–13, 21–2, 24–30, 34, 53–4, 58–9, 65, 69–70, 81–2, 85–95, 97–9.

The Eve of St. Agnes was first published in *Lamia, Isabella, The Eve of St. Agnes, and other poems*, 1820. The theme had been suggested to Keats by his friend Isabella Jones in January 1819. She reminded him that the 20th was St. Agnes' Eve, when maidens were supposed to dream of their future husbands; and Keats, who was already in a romantic medieval mood, took up the idea. But although the inspiration was Isabella's, the physical background for the poem and the fact that the lover was no vision but a flesh-and-blood young man came (as Robert Gittings points out) from a book Keats had recently been reading, the ninth volume of the *Bibliothèque Universelle des Dames*, and especially the third of the three stories, 'Pierre de Provence et La Belle Maguelone'.

Faithless Sally Brown first appeared unobtrusively in the *London Magazine*, March 1822, in a section dealing with readers' letters, where it was described as 'An Old Ballad'. It soon obtained an extraordinary circulation. Hood had good reason for saying he had 'never been vainer of any verses'. They were sung at Covent Garden, were a favourite with the Thames watermen, and became part of the stock-in-trade of the ballad-mongers in the streets. Whether anyone not a cockney, appreciated the full number of the puns in the tale is another matter. 'Eye-water' should perhaps have an apostrophe, 'Wales' would have been pronounced by Sally *Veils*, and 'berth', in the last verse, not even Hood's printer could manage, spelling it 'birth'. The ballad was first collected in Hood's *Whims and Oddities*, 1826.

The Lady of Shalott, published in 1832, was the first of Tennyson's excursions into the realm of King Arthur, although he admitted he had the story from an Italian novella, *Donna di Scalotta*. 'Shalott and Astolat are the same words. The Lady of Shalott is evidently the Elaine of the Morte d'Arthur, but I do not think that I had ever heard of the latter when I wrote the former. Shalott was a softer sound than "Scalott". Stalott would have been nearer Astolat.' It is to be noted that in this Italian story Camelot is by the sea. Tennyson, who was only twenty-three when 'The Lady of Shalott' was published, returned to the theme in 'Lancelot and Elaine' (*Idylls of the King*, 1859).

Morte d'Arthur, written in 1835 and published in 1842, was subsequently incorporated by Tennyson in 'The Passing of Arthur', one of the *Idylls of the King*, 1859. King Arthur, who had been in Brittany, was faced on his return by an uprising led by his nephew, Sir Modred, whom Arthur had appointed Regent in his absence. Arthur was reluctant to fight, this battle being different from any he had fought before

> The king who fights his people fights himself.
> And they my knights, who loved me once, the stroke
> That strikes them dead is as my death to me.

Arthur chased the rebel army to Lyonnesse, the legendary country between Cornwall and the Scilly Islands, where Modred could retreat no more, having reached the sea. The battle was fought in a cold white mist, the combatants being unable to see whether they slew friend or foe. Eventually Arthur met Modred and killed him with his sword Excalibur; but not before he himself had been mortally wounded. Tennyson's story here closely follows, occasionally even in phraseology, Malory's *Morte d'Arthur* printed by Caxton in 1485.

The King of Brentford's Testament, which first appeared in *Fraser's Magazine*, May 1834, and thereafter in *The Paris Sketch Book* 'By Mr Titmarsh', was an imitation by Thackeray of one of the *chansons* of Pierre-Jean de Béranger, at that time the most popular verse-writer in France. 'Le Roi d'Yvetot', which Béranger had written about 1813, told of an easy-going monarch in a diminutive realm, and had immediately appealed to many Frenchmen who were wearying of their Emperor's unrelenting ambition. Stanzas 1–15, 17–22, 29–44.

The Jackdaw of Rheims, the best known of *The Ingoldsby Legends* 'by Thomas Ingoldsby Esquire', was written by Barham for the May number of *Bentley's Monthly Miscellany*, 1837. Although Barham was making fun in these tales both of antiquarianism and of priestly marvels, the majority of the tales were in fact based on old material, and Barham was himself a minor canon of St. Paul's. The story of the Jackdaw of Rheims had appeared long before in, for instance, the *Lectionum Memorabilium* of Joannes Wolfius, 1600. The name given to the canonized jackdaw, however, was certainly new. 'Jim Crow' was the speciality song of the American black-faced comedian Thomas D. Rice, who had taken London by storm only the previous year.

The Wreck of the Hesperus was written soon after a terrible storm had wrecked the schooner *Hesperus* on the reef known as Norman's Woe, off the Massachusetts coast, near Gloucester, in December 1839. The next morning a body had been found still lashed to a piece of the wreckage. Longfellow wrote the poem as a deliberate attempt to create an old-style ballad, something unfashionable in New England at that time. It was published in *The New World*, 14 January 1840, and collected in *Ballads and Other Poems*, 1841.

Paul Revere's Ride was written by Longfellow in April 1860 after a visit to Boston, and, in particular, after an ascent of the old North Church tower from which, he was told, the lanterns had been hung to signal that the British troops had left Boston for Concord. Curiously, Longfellow seems to have been content with a popular account of the ride rather than a historical one, as if afraid the exploit would turn out to be a legend, and the commencement of the American War of Independence on the following day, 19 April 1775, be found to be without heroics. Revere's ride from Charlestown to Lexington (he did not reach Concord) was in fact considerably more of an adventure than Longfellow makes appear. Revere was not far out of Charlestown when he was waylaid by British officers on the lookout for an 'express' rider such as himself; and he managed to give them the slip only because one of the officers got stuck in a clay pond. Further, in the early hours of the morning, having successfully delivered the warning to Hancock and Adams, he was riding on from Lexington to Concord when he was captured by the British; although, in the typically civilized manner in which both sides, at the outset, showed their reluctance for the conflict, he was released later in the day. 'Paul Revere's Ride' was published in the *Atlantic Monthly*, January 1861, and collected in *Tales of a Wayside Inn*, 1863.

Horatius was one of Macaulay's reconstructions of the kind of ballad he felt the early Romans would have been handing down until, under Greek influence, their popular literature was lost. It is supposed to be in the voice of a minstrel living about 120 years after the event it celebrates, when Horatius Cocles and two companions defended the wooden bridge across the Tiber long enough for it to be cut down, and so prevent the Etruscans entering Rome. Macaulay himself warned that the tale was not to be treated as history, pointing out that the Latin chronicles were filled with 'battles that were never fought, and Consuls that were never inaugurated'. Nevertheless when the *Lays of Ancient Rome* were published in 1842, they became immensely popular, the heroism of Horatius being justly considered an exemplar of the conduct to be expected in defence of a free state. Stanzas 1–3, 8, 11, 13, 16, 18–21, 26–7, 29–32, 34–50, 53–62, 64–6.

The Pied Piper of Hamelin was included in *Dramatic Lyrics*, 1842, as a makeweight, and is far from being consonant with the other pieces in the collection. Browning had written the poem for Willy Macready, son of the great actor, who was confined to his room with a cough and wanted a story to illustrate. The poem originally ended:

> So, Willy, let you and me be wipers
> Of scores out with all men—especially pipers!
> And, whether they pipe us free from rats or from mice,
> If we've promised them aught, let us keep our promise!

Browning had known the tale from childhood, when he was an omnivorous reader of Nathaniel Wanley's *Wonders of the Little World*, 1678. Details not in Wanley may have come to him from his father, for the Pied Piper was a family enthusiasm, and Robert Browning senior was also writing a versification of the story in 1842.

The Italian in England first appeared in *Dramatic Romances*, 1845. The poem had probably been conceived during Browning's visit to Italy in the autumn of 1844. He was an ardent supporter of the cause of Italian freedom (indeed, his Italian master in England was an Italian refugee). By 15 November 1845 Elizabeth Barrett was saying how much she liked the poems he had sent her: 'the noble, serene "Italy in England," which grows on you the more you know of it'; and it is known that she suggested changing the lines

> 'I would grasp Metternich until
> I felt his throat and had my will,'
> to
> '. . . I felt his red wet throat distil
> In blood through these two hands.'

'*Childe Roland to the Dark Tower Came*' was first published in *Men and Women*, 1855. In later years Browning told an enquirer that he had been conscious of no allegorical intention in writing it. ''Twas like this: one year in Florence, I had been very lazy; I resolved I would write something every day . . . Childe Roland came upon me as a kind of dream. I had to write it then and there, and I finished it the same day, I believe. . . I did not know then what I meant beyond that, and I'm sure I don't know now. But I'm very fond of it.' Browning always denied that the idea sprung from anything other than the phrase 'Childe Rowland to the dark tower came' from Edgar's song in *King Lear*, with which he titled his poem.

The Raven was published in the New York *Evening Mirror*, 29 January 1845, under Poe's pen-name 'Quarles', and soon afterwards in numerous other papers and journals. Later the same year it appeared in book form, in *The Raven and Other Poems*. The poem was a resounding success, and Poe was fêted in the literary salons of New York. The bird of doom was originally to have been an owl, but Poe chose instead to borrow Dickens's raven from *Barnaby Rudge*, which he had recently reviewed. Some of the scenery of the poem, such as the bust of Pallas Athene over the door, was in the rented room where 'The Raven' reached its final shape, a room previously occupied by an exiled Napoleonic officer, in a farmhouse near New York where Poe was living with his young wife and her mother. Otherwise the whole inexorable tale was the product of Poe's high-Gothic, laudanum-laden, tragedy-filled imagination. Text from 1845 edition.

The Forsaken Merman appeared in Arnold's first collection of poems, *The Strayed Reveller and other Poems*, 1849. The story is that of the Danish ballad 'Agnes and the Merman', but it is difficult to identify his exact source. Arnold could well have read it in Hans Andersen's *True Story of my Life*, translated by Mary Howitt in 1847, though surely he would have used the dramatic incident of the images in the church turning to the wall as Agnete enters. He might have seen George Borrow's review of Thiele's *Danske Folksagn* (*Universal Review*, II, 1825) in which the story of the ballad is retold, though in this version the merman buys Grete's love with gold and silver, and the parting injunction is 'let the merman himself take care of his ugly little children'. The most probable source is George Borrow's 'Deceived Merman' in *Romantic Ballads*, 1826, translated from the *Kaempe Viser* of 1695. Here the sentiments are right, though no popular ballad could equal the heart-rending pathos of Arnold's poem.

Sohrab and Rustum first appeared in *Poems, a new edition*, 1853. It recounts an incident from Firdusi's great Persian epic, the *Shah-nameh*, written in the tenth century. Arnold did not know the epic at first hand. He had read a review of Mme Mohl's French translation, 1836, and used an extract from Sir John Malcolm's *History of Persia*, 1815, as the note to his poem; showing, incidentally, how close he kept to the story as it was told there. The 'far-distant Oxus' must have seemed very far-distant in Arnold's day. That majestic river (now called the Amu-Darya) rises in the mountains of Afghanistan and after more than a thousand miles loses itself in the inland Sea of Aral. Very little was known about the region until the Russo-Afghan boundary was fixed along the line of the river in 1885. Text from 1885 edition.

The Haystack in the Floods first appeared in *The Defence of Guenevere*, 1858, a volume of poems by no means all Arthurian. Morris, like the other Pre-Raphaelites, was enthralled by the Middle Ages, and the imagined journey through French territory by the English knight and his French sweetheart took place not long after Poictiers in 1356. Andrew Lang said that he and his fellow students 'knew *The Defence of Guenevere* almost by heart... We found Froissart's people alive again in Mr Morris's poems, and we knew better what thoughts and emotions lay in the secret of their hearts, than we could learn from the bright superficial pages of Froissart'.

Goblin Market was written by Christina Rossetti in the spring of 1859 for her elder sister, Maria Francesca, then aged thirty-two. The peril of dealing with the fairies, the irreparable damage to health from partaking of fairy food, and the supreme devotion required to win a person back from the drug-pedlars of the other world, has long been part of the literature of the supernatural. When Burd Ellen's brother set out to rescue his sister, who had been carried off by the King of Elfland, in the Scottish ballad of Child Rowland, he was advised on no account to eat or drink in fairyland, 'for if he tasted or touched in Elfland, he must remain in the power of the elves, and never see middle-eard again'. When, in the old Danish story, King Gormo was passing through the domain of the giant Guthmund, and the giant pressed him to enjoy the delicacies of his garden, he knew from Thorkill that if he did, all memory of his past life would be lost to him. He would have become such a one as would Odysseus, had he accepted the honey-fruit on that island where 'the languid air did swoon, breathing like one that hath a weary dream'. Christina Rossetti would have been familiar with both Homer and Tennyson, as also with the story of Persephone and how she was unable to return permanently to her mother once she had swallowed a pomegranate seed in the underworld, but had to go back for a third of each year and let earth cope with winter. Christina Rossetti's strange goblins, however, of eccentric appearance and diversity of movement, appear to have been creatures of her imagination, though they perhaps owe something to Anna Eliza Bray's *A Peep at the Pixies; or, Legends of the West*, 1854. (Mrs Bray was a cousin.) The poem was published in *Goblin Market and Other Poems*, 1862.

The Tale of a Pony, described as 'a true story', was originally printed, 3 June 1865, in *The Californian*, a magazine which Bret Harte and a friend had launched the year before. Bret Harte was twenty-eight when he wrote the tale, had made his own living since he was a boy, and had never been abroad. Probably he picked up his European terms from his extensive reading, for instance the English 'chay' (for chaise) from *Sketches by Boz*. The tale subsequently had a place in his first book, *The Lost Galleon and other Tales*, which was published in San Francisco in 1867.

The Hunting of the Snark was written over a period of eighteen months, starting on 18 July 1874, when a solitary line came into Dodgson's mind—'For the Snark *was* a Boojum, you see'—which, although he did not realize it at the time, was to become the last line of the last of 141 stanzas. The work was published on or about April Fool's Day, 1876, and described as 'an Agony in Eight Fits'. (A fit is an old term for a division of a long poem.) Thereafter he included it in *Rhyme? and Reason?*, 1883. Hunters of allegorical significance in the poem seem to have been unaware that their exertions make an esoteric meaning unnecessary. Dodgson himself said he thought the story was nonsense; yet he added, very shrewdly, that 'words mean more than we mean to express when we use them; so a whole book ought to mean a great deal more than the writer means'.

The White Ship, which Rossetti finished writing in the spring of 1880, was included in *Ballads and Sonnets*, 1881, his last book before his death. 'Every incident in the ballad,' he told his mother, 'including that of the boy at the end, is given in one or other account of the event.' The *White Ship* set sail from Barfleur (not Harfleur) on 25 November 1120 with Henry I's son and heir Prince William on board, together with his half-brother Richard, his half-sister the Countess of Perche, and many young lords and ladies. The ship foundered, and the whole company was drowned except for a butcher from Rouen. The boy who knelt before the king and told him of his loss is recorded as having been the young son of Count Theobald.

Ticonderoga was written in May 1887 during Stevenson's last days in Edinburgh, when his father had just died, and he knew he himself was incurably ill. He had been told the legend by his friend Alfred Nutt (the publisher who was to start Robert Frost on his career); but when the ballad was published that Christmas in *Scribner's Magazine*, it brought forth immediate protests, although Stevenson seems to have been unperturbed by them. 'Two clans, the Camerons and the Campbells, lay claim to this bracing story,' he explained in his collected *Ballads*, three years later; 'and they do well: the man who preferred his plighted troth to the commands and menaces of the dead is an ancestor worth disputing'. The Campbells, he said, must rest content with their broad lands and their broad history. 'This appanage must be denied them; for between the name of "Cameron" and that of "Campbell", the muse will never hesitate.' Stevenson appears, nevertheless, to have done the Campbells an injustice. Ticonderoga, in New York State on the outlet of Lake George, was a place of strategic importance in the Seven Years War. The French built a fort there; and on 8 July 1758 a large British force under Abercrombie mounted an ineffective attack, with the loss of 1,944 officers and men. One of them was the major of the 'Forty-second' or 'Highland Regiment', Duncan Campbell of Inverawe, aged fifty-five, who was carried off the field by his clansmen, and died of his wounds nine days later. According to family tradition, current in the 1870s, Duncan Campbell had been at Inverawe House in Argyllshire when a stranger, besmeared with blood, begged asylum from the avengers of the man he had killed. Campbell swore on his dirk he would be sheltered. He then learned that the man who had been killed was his own cousin; and on three successive nights the figure of the murdered man appeared before him, warning 'Inverawe! Inverawe! blood has been shed! Shield not the murderer!' On the third night the ghost was specifically ominous: 'Farewell, Inverawe! Farewell till we meet at Ticonderoga!' Campbell never forgot this strange name; and when, years later, fighting the French and the Indians in North America, his regiment was ordered to Ticonderoga, he knew he would die. His brother officers tried to disarm his fears, saying the place they were at was Fort George not Ticonderoga. But the night before the battle the ghost came to his tent and the real name of the place was confirmed.

The Ballad of East and West was one of Kipling's earliest contributions to the English press after his arrival in London as a young man. It was published in the December number of *Macmillan's Magazine*, 1889, and afterwards in *Barrack-Room Ballads*, 1892. Soon, the saying 'East is East, and West is West' was on everyone's lips, usually being given the opposite sense to that Kipling intended. Lahore, Kipling's home for the previous seven years, was the capital of the Punjab, which at that time stretched to the North-West Frontier. The ballad is a romanticized version of an actual encounter between Colonel Lumsden of the 'Guides' and Dilawur Khan that occurred on the frontier in 1848.

The Ballad of Reading Gaol was dedicated to the memory of 'C.T.W. Sometime Trooper of the Royal Horse Guards. Obiit H.M. Prison, Reading, Berkshire, 7 July 1896.' C.T.W. was Charles Thomas Wooldridge, a thirty-year-old Berkshire man who had been in the Guards for ten years. While stationed in London he received a letter from his young wife, to whom he was devoted, making clear she was now interested in another man, and requiring him to sign a statement that he would henceforth keep away from her. His response was to arm himself with a razor, and take a train to Windsor where they lived. He cut her throat when he found her in the street; not in bed as Wilde seems to have thought. Everyone who met Wooldridge after the tragedy seems to have found him likeable, religious, and resigned. He was also, incidentally, capable of composing a better letter than his solicitor. At the time of the trial and execution Wilde was a fellow prisoner at Reading, and he wrote the ballad a year later, following his own release. It was published as a book in February 1898. As originally published the ballad had a further twenty stanzas included, said Wilde, 'to make propaganda'; and he agreed the poem would be better without them. Now that the propaganda is no longer necessary, they have been omitted. The text of the first edition has sometimes been preferred to that of the second.

The Highwayman, which is wholly imaginary, was written on the edge of the desolate stretch of land in West Surrey known as Bagshot Heath, where Noyes, then aged twenty-four, had taken rooms in a cottage. ' "The Highwayman" suggested itself to me one blustery night when the sound of the wind in the pines gave me the first line.' The poem was published in *Blackwood's Magazine*, August 1906, and soon found a place in anthologies and reciters, both in England and America, possibly due to its reputation as 'the best narrative poem in existence for oral delivery'. Noyes included 'The Highwayman' in his *Forty Singing Seamen, and Other Poems*, 1907.

The Cremation of Sam McGee was, Robert Service said, 'the keystone of my success'. When he was a bank clerk in the Yukon he used to take part in amateur entertainments, especially as a reciter of verse, and occasionally wrote verse which was published in the local paper. One day the editor suggested he should write 'something about our own bit of earth' for recitation at the next church concert, and the result was 'The Shooting of Dan McGrew'. Soon afterwards he was at a party when a big mining man, 'portly and important', suddenly said ' "I'll tell you a story Jack London never got". Then he spun a yarn of a man who cremated his pal. It had a surprise climax which occasioned much laughter. I did not join, for I had a feeling that here was a decisive moment of destiny. . . I took the woodland trail, my mind seething with excitement and a strange ecstasy. . . For six hours I tramped those silver glades, and when I rolled happily into bed, my ballad was cinched. Next day, with scarcely any effort of memory I put it on paper.' The ballad was published, with others which had come to him just as easily, in *Songs of a Sourdough*, 1907.

A Trampwoman's Tragedy, which Hardy considered possibly his most successful poem, was written in April 1902, after a bicycle excursion across the Polden hills in Somerset. The locality brought to mind an actual trampwoman of the 1820s, Mary Ann Taylor, whose desperate story he had learnt, very likely, half a century before from his mother. 'Blue Jimmy' (stanza 10) was another character from those days, a rogue who had appropriated more than a hundred horses before he was caught, and, like Mary Ann's lover, he was hanged at Ilchester (or Ivelchester). The inns the trampwoman visited were some that Hardy also knew; although he remarked that the Marshal's Elm, so picturesquely situated, was by 1902 no longer an inn. The poem was included in *Time's Laughingstocks*, 1909.

Lepanto was Chesterton's tribute to high endeavour and concerted action. The Battle of Lepanto was one of the decisive battles of history. The Turks had been proving invincible, their ships swept the Mediterranean, Cyprus had already been lost, and Christendom was threatened. Through the determination of Pope Pius V a fleet of 300 ships was assembled, and Don John of Austria, aged twenty-four, made supreme commander. He came up with the Turkish fleet, which was of a size with his own, in the Gulf of Patras; and on 7 October 1571 a murderous battle took place, in which the greater part of the Turkish fleet was destroyed. One who was in the battle, and lost his left arm, was Cervantes, author of *Don Quixote*. 'Lepanto' appeared in *The Eye-Witness*, 12 October 1911, and was collected in *Poems*, 1915.

The Code is evidence of Frost's experience as a farmer. For nine years when he was a young man—before he came to England and found literary recognition—he had his own small farm in Derry, New Hampshire, and wrote when he could poems such as this one. 'The Code' was published in England in *Poetry*, February 1914, and collected in *North of Boston*, 1914.

Reynard the Fox was written when Masefield was living on Boars Hill, outside Oxford. He was not himself a hunting man, but could hark back to his country childhood in Herefordshire; and while writing 'Reynard' he several times went by bicycle to Berkshire meets. 'I am not and never have been a fox-hunter,' he wrote, 'but it is *the* passion of English country people, and into it they put the beauty and the fervour which the English put into all things when deeply roused.' *Reynard the Fox* was published in 1919. The excerpt given here covers the whole of the fox's run to the Wan Dyke Hill. He eventually reaches safety in Mourne End Wood.

The Lion and Albert was written by Marriott Edgar (a half-brother of Edgar Wallace) as a monologue for the entertainer Stanley Holloway, who was looking for material for his part in the forthcoming *Savoy Follies*, 1932. Edgar, who was himself a variety artist, had the idea for the monologue from a press report of a boy being mauled by a lion at the London Zoo; but he changed the venue to Blackpool so that the tale could be recited in the north-country accent of a visitor to the Lancashire resort. Holloway was doubtful whether the theme would be found acceptable, and tried the monologue at the Northern Rugby League Annual Dinner and Dance at the Grand Hotel, Newcastle. Its success was immediate, and has never failed. It was published in *Albert, 'Arold and Others*, 1937.

The Nabara is a celebration of the most valiant sea-battle of the Spanish Civil War. The poem follows the events described in chapter xi of G. L. Steer's *The Tree of Gernika*, 1938, a first-hand study of the war by a *Times* correspondent. In the conflict, which had broken out in July 1936, the fortunes of the opposing sides were felt to depend largely on the arms and currency that could be obtained from outside, hence the encounter which took place off Cape Machichaco, on the north coast of Spain, could be crucial. The fourteen survivors of the *Nabara* never surrendered, and would have been put to death had not the captain of the *Canarias* made a plea for mercy, saying they were heroes and deserved to live. Day-Lewis's preface to the poem, 'They preferred, because of the rudeness of their heart, to die rather than to surrender,' were Walsingham's words after the sea-battle between English and Basques in 1350. It first appeared in *Overtures to Death*, 1938.

The Song of Samuel Sweet was, Charles Causley said, 'written with the conscious hope and intention that it might be spoken aloud as well as received through the "inner" ear from the printed page'. It was broadcast as a narrative for four voices, Poet, Samuel Sweet, Captain, and Dying Soldier, on the BBC West of England Home Service on 21 October 1952, and subsequently appeared in *Survivor's Leave*, 1953. The version printed here is the shortened, revised version, from *Collected Poems*, 1975. The story came to the poet as casually as such stories seem to do: it happened to be in a book, Berta Lawrence's *Somerset Journal*, which was about to be published by Causley's publisher, who gave him a copy. The bitter story of the boy who kept pace with a galloping horse yet could not win his own life illustrated a theme Causley was much concerned with at that time, just after the war: 'that once the shooting starts the innocent as well as the guilty are hopelessly caught up and, to various degrees, destroyed'. And he already knew and was haunted by the desolate country which was the scene of the Monmouth Rebellion.

Atheling Grange: or, The Apotheosis of Lotte Nussbaum was first printed in *Encounter*, May 1954, and in book form in *A Shot in the Park*, 1955. William Plomer gave as his

source for the story this item 'From a Sussex newspaper, October, 1953: "HOUSE-
KEEPER MISSING—Miss Lotte Nussbaum (48), who came to this country as
a refugee from Nazi Germany before the war, is reported missing from Spindrift,
Hydrangea-avenue, Atheling-on-Sea, where she has for some years resided as
housekeeper to Mrs Elvaston-Clunch. As Miss Nussbaum's shopping-basket is also
missing, it is thought that she may have gone out to gather blackberries or
mushrooms, and may be suffering from loss of memory. Search parties have failed to
find any trace of the missing woman." '

The Ballad of Barnaby, which is based on the medieval French legend 'Le Jongleur de
Notre Dame', was written as the libretto for a musical performance to be given by the
girls of Wykeham Rise School in Washington, Connecticut. The girls themselves
composed the music, and the work was performed at Wykeham Rise in May 1969.
Subsequently the ballad was published in the *New York Review of Books*, 18 December
1969, with decorations by Edward Gorey; and when Auden died, and a memorial
service was held at the Cathedral Church of St. John the Divine in New York
(3 October 1973), each member of the congregation was given a copy of the ballad.

ACKNOWLEDGEMENTS

We would like to thank a number of people who have been part of the story of the making of this book: Hugo Brunner, who suggested it; Jill Day-Lewis, who, from her poetry-filled home in Edward Thomas's village, befriended it; and Wendy Rix, who furthered it with enthusiasm and a British Library ticket. Without John Whitehead's detailed knowledge of modern poetry several of the notes would not have been as informative as they are; and without Professor George Thomas's patience under questioning we would not have understood what was probably in Edward Thomas's original 'scheme'. Finally, as always, we are grateful to Miss F. Doreen Gullen, who, being a realist herself, made sure that the book became a reality.

In addition we would like to thank the following for permission to reproduce copyright material:

W. H. Auden: 'The Ballad of Barnaby', copyright © 1969 by W. H. Auden; from *W. H. Auden: Collected Poems*, edited by Edward Mendelson. Reprinted by permission of Faber & Faber Ltd., and Random House, Inc.

Charles Causley: 'The Song of Samuel Sweet' from *Collected Poems* (Macmillan, 1975). Reprinted by permission of David Higham Associates Ltd.

G. K. Chesterton: 'Lepanto' from *The Collected Poems of G. K. Chesterton*, copyright 1932 by Dodd, Mead and Company, Inc., copyright renewed 1959 by Oliver Chesterton. Reprinted by permission of Dodd, Mead & Co., Inc.

C. Day-Lewis: 'The Nabara'. Published in the United States in *Selected Poems*, copyright 1938 by C. Day-Lewis. Published in the UK in *Collected Poems*, 1954. Reprinted by permission of the Executors of the Estate of C. Day-Lewis, Jonathan Cape Ltd., and Harper & Row, Publishers, Inc.

Marriott Edgar: 'The Lion and Albert'. © 1933 Francis Day & Hunter Ltd., London WC2H 0LD. Reproduced by permission of EMI Music Publishing Ltd. and International Music Publications, and of J. Albert & Son Pty., GPO Box 4899, Sydney, Australia.

Robert Frost: 'The Code' from *The Poetry of Robert Frost*, edited by Edward Connery Lathem, copyright 1930, 1939, by Holt, Rinehart and Winston Inc., and renewed 1958 by Robert Frost. Reprinted by permission of Jonathan Cape Ltd., the Estate of Robert Frost, and Henry Holt & Co., Inc.

Rudyard Kipling: 'The Ballad of East and West'. Reprinted by permission of A. P. Watt Ltd., on behalf of The National Trust and Eyre Methuen Ltd.

ACKNOWLEDGEMENTS

John Masefield: extract from 'Reynard the Fox', copyright 1919, and renewed 1947 by John Masefield, from *Poems*. Reprinted by permission of The Society of Authors as the literary representative of the Estate of John Masefield, and Macmillan Publishing Co., Inc.

Alfred Noyes: 'The Highwayman' from *Collected Poems*. Reprinted by permission of John Murray (Publishers) Ltd.

William Plomer: 'Atheling Grange: or, The Apotheosis of Lotte Nussbaum' from *Collected Poems*. Reprinted by permission of the Estate of William Plomer and Jonathan Cape Ltd.

Robert Service: 'The Cremation of Sam McGee' from *Songs of a Sourdough*. Used by permission, estate of Robert Service.

While every effort has been made to secure permission, we may have failed in a few cases to trace the copyright holder. We apologize for any apparent negligence.

INDEX OF FIRST LINES

INDEX OF AUTHORS

OXFORD

MORE OXFORD PAPERBACKS

Details of a selection of other Oxford Paperbacks follow. A complete list of Oxford Paperbacks, including The World's Classics, Twentieth-Century Classics, OPUS, Past Masters, Oxford Authors, Oxford Shakespeare, and Oxford Paperback Reference, is available in the UK from the General Publicity Department, Oxford University Press (RS), Walton Street, Oxford, OX2 6DP.

In the USA, complete lists are available from the Paperbacks Marketing Manager, Oxford University Press, 200 Madison Avenue, New York, NY 10016.

Oxford Paperbacks are available from all good bookshops. In case of difficulty, customers in the UK can order direct from Oxford University Press Bookshop, 116 High Street, Oxford, Freepost, OX1 4BR, enclosing full payment. Please add 10 per cent of the published price for postage and packing.

OXFORD BOOKS

Beginning in 1900 with the famous *Oxford Book of English Verse*, the Oxford Books series now boasts over 60 superb anthologies of poetry, prose, and songs.

'These anthologies—along with digests and reference books—are exactly what the general reader needs.' Auberon Waugh, *Independent*

THE NEW OXFORD BOOK OF IRISH VERSE

Edited, with Translations, by Thomas Kinsella

Verse in Irish, especially from the early and medieval periods, has long been felt to be the preserve of linguists and specialists, while Anglo-Irish poetry is usually seen as an adjunct to the English tradition. This original anthology approaches the Irish poetic tradition as a unity and presents a relationship between two major bodies of poetry that reflects a shared and painful history.

'the first coherent attempt to present the entire range of Irish poetry in both languages to an English-speaking readership' *Irish Times*

'a very satisfying and moving introduction to Irish poetry' *Listener*

Also in Oxford Paperbacks:

The Oxford Book of Travel Verse
edited by Kevin Crossley-Holland
The Oxford Book of Contemporary Verse
edited by D. J. Enright
The Oxford Book of Late Medieval Verse and Prose
edited by Douglas Gray

POETRY FROM OXFORD PAPERBACKS

Oxford's outstanding range of English poetry offers, in a single volume of convenient size, the complete poetical works of some of the most important figures in English Literature.

WORDSWORTH
Poetical Works

This edition of Wordsworth's poetry contains every piece of verse known to have been published by the poet himself, or of which he authorized the posthumous publication. The text, which Thomas Hutchinson based largely upon the 1849–50 standard edition, the last issued during the poet's lifetime, was revised for the Oxford Standard Authors series by Ernest de Selincourt.

The volume preserves the poet's famous subjective arrangement of the Minor Poems under such headings as 'Poems Referring to the Period of Childhood', 'Poems Dedicated to National Independence and Liberty', and 'Sonnets Upon the Punishment of Death'. *The Prelude* is given in the text of 1850, published shortly after Wordsworth's death, and *The Excursion* as it appears in the 1849–50 edition. Two poems of 1793 are included, 'An Evening Walk' and 'Descriptive Sketches', and a group of other pieces not appearing in the standard edition. The text reproduces Wordsworth's characteristic use of capital letters and in most cases his punctuation, though spelling has been regularized. The poet's own Notes to the 1849–50 edition, as well as to some earlier editions, are reprinted, along with his Prefaces.

The edition also contains a chronological table of Wordsworth's life, explanatory notes on the text, and chronological data for the individual poems.

Also in Oxford Paperbacks:

The Prelude   William Wordsworth
Poetical Works   John Keats
The Golden Treasury   Francis Turner Palgrave

OXFORD POETS

Oxford Paperbacks has one of the finest lists of contemporary poetry. It includes well-established and highly regarded names, as well as exciting newcomers from Britain, America, Europe, and the Commonwealth.

Winner of the 1989 Whitbread Prize for Poetry

SHIBBOLETH

Michael Donaghy

This is Michael Donaghy's first full-length collection His work has a wit and grace reminiscent of the metaphysical poets, and his subjects range widely, responding in unexpected ways to his curiosity and inventiveness. Among the varied pieces collected here are a number of love poems remarkable for their blend of tenderness and irony; a terse 'news item'; playful 'translations' of a mythical Welsh poet; and an 'interview' with Marcel Duchamp.

As the American critic Alfred Corn says:
'Michael Donaghy's poems have the fine-tuned precision of a ten-speed bike, the wit of a streetwise don, a polyphonic inventiveness . . . Poems so original, wry, and philosophical as these are hard to come by. Don't think of passing them up.'

Also in Oxford Poets:

Blood and Family   Thomas Kinsella
Selected Poems   Fleur Adcock
On Ballycastle Beach   Medbh McGuckian
Adventures with My Horse   Penelope Shuttle

OXFORD POETS

Oxford Paperbacks' well-established and highly regarded series of contemporary poetry includes the work of some of the world's most important poets, amongst them Fleur Adcock, Joseph Brodsky, D. J. Enright, Roy Fisher, Thomas Kinsella, Peter Porter, and Craig Raine.

A PORTER SELECTED

Peter Porter

This selection of about one hundred of Porter's best poems is chosen from all his works to date, including his latest book, *Possible Worlds*, and *The Automatic Oracle*, which won the 1988 Whitbread Prize for Poetry.

What the critics have said about Peter Porter:

'I can't think of any contemporary poet who is so consistently entertaining over such a variety of material.' John Lucas, *New Statesman*

'an immensely fertile, lively, informed, honest and penetrating mind.' Stephen Spender, *Observer*

'He writes vigorously, with savage erudition and wonderful expansiveness . . . No one now writing matches Porter's profoundly moral and cultured overview.' Douglas Dunn, *Punch*

Also in Oxford Poets:

Possible Worlds Peter Porter
Shibboleth Michael Donaghy
Orient Express Grete Tartler
Selected Poems 1990 D. J. Enright

CLASSIC ENGLISH SHORT STORIES

The four volumes of *Classic English Short Stories* have been compiled to reflect the excellence and variety of short fiction written in English during the twentieth century. Each volume covers a different period and represents the most distinguished writers of their day.

THE DRAGON'S HEAD

This collection contains stories written in the years between the turn of the century and the outbreak of the Second World War—'a restless and impatient age'. The authors include John Galsworthy, 'Saki', Naomi Mitchison, H. G. Wells, Dorothy L. Sayers, and Somerset Maugham.

THE KILLING BOTTLE

This collection brings together 12 very different authors whose short stories, written in the 1940s and 1950s, helped establish or extend their reputations as writers of stories, novels, or poetry. The 12 include Evelyn Waugh, Elizabeth Bowen, Graham Greene, V. S. Pritchett, Dylan Thomas, and Frank O'Connor.

CHARMED LIVES

This collection contains stories written in the 1950s and 1960s, many of which demonstrate the impressive and accomplished skills of Commonwealth writers who began to achieve world-wide reputations during that period, including Ruth Prawer Jhabvala, Nadine Gordimer, H. E. Bates, Bill Naughton, L. P. Hartley, and Peter Ustinov.

THE GREEN MAN REVISITED

This collection includes works written in the 1960s and 1970s by authors living all around the world, including Chinua Achebe, Kingsley Amis, Susan Hill, Olivia Manning, V. S. Naipaul, William Trevor, John Updike, and Patrick White.

LITERARY BIOGRAPHY AND
CRITICISM IN OXFORD PAPERBACKS

Oxford Paperbacks's impressive list of literary biography and criticism includes works ranging from specialist studies of the prominent figures of the world literature to D. J. Enright on television soap opera.

BRITISH WRITERS OF THE THIRTIES
Valentine Cunningham

'He has steeped himself in the period . . . *British Writers of the Thirties* is by far the best history of its kind published in recent years . . . and it will become required reading for those who wish to look back at a society and a culture in which writers, for all their faults, were taken seriously.' Peter Ackroyd, *The Times*

'a serious and often brilliant book, provoking one to argument, forcing one back to known texts and forward to unread ones . . . it is simply so packed with information that it will speak as much to readers with an interest in social history as to the students of literature for whom it was first intended.' Claire Tomalin, *Independent*

'this should henceforth be the standard treatment . . . a minor classic of literary history' Frank Kermode, *Guardian*

'brilliant survey and analysis . . . Mr Cunningham's narrative is cleverly constructed, wonderfully detailed, and he deploys his findings to great effect.' Charles Causley, *Times Educational Supplement*

Also in Oxford Paperbacks:

Fields of Vision   D. J. Enright
Modern English Literature   W. W. Robson
The Oxford Illustrated History of English Literature edited by Pat Rogers
The Pursuit of Happiness   Peter Quennell

THE OXFORD AUTHORS

General Editor: Frank Kermode

The Oxford Authors is a series of authoritative editions of the major English writers for the student and the general reader. Drawing on the best texts available, each volume contains a generous selection from the writings— poetry and prose, including letters—to give the essence of a writer's work and thinking. Where appropriate, texts have been tactfully modernized and all are complemented by essential Notes, an Introduction, Chronology, and suggestions for Further Reading.

'The Oxford Authors series can always be relied upon to be splendid—with good plain texts and helpful notes.' Robert Nye, *Scotsman*

OSCAR WILDE

Edited by Isobel Murray

The drama of Oscar Wilde's life has for years overshadowed his achievement in literature. This is the first large-scale edition of his work to provide unobtrusive guidance to the wealth of knowledge and allusion upon which his writing stands.

Wilde had studied Greek and Latin and was familiar with American literature, while he was as well read in French as he was in English, following Gautier and Flaubert as well as Pater and Ruskin. Through her Notes Isobel Murray enables the modern reader for the first time to read Wilde as such admiring contemporaries as Pater, Yeats, and Symons read him, in a rich, shared culture of literary and visual arts.

This edition underlines the range of his achievement in many genres, including *The Picture of Dorian Gray, Salome, The Importance of Being Earnest, The Decay of Lying,* and *The Ballad of Reading Gaol.* The text is that of the last printed edition overseen by Wilde.

Also in the Oxford Authors:

Sir Philip Sidney
Ben Jonson
Byron
Thomas Hardy

A SPLENDID QUARTET OF SHORT STORIES

CLASSIC IRISH SHORT STORIES
Selected and Introduced by Frank O'Connor

The Irish short story, Frank O'Connor believes, is 'a distinct art form' and the stories he has chosen for this collection show how the form has remained peculiarly itself while being developed in various ways in response to changing social and political conditions. Authors include James Joyce, Liam O'Flaherty, Seàn O'Faolàin, George Moore, and Elizabeth Bowen.

CLASSIC ENGLISH SHORT STORIES
Selected and Introduced by Derek Hudson

The years 1930 to 1955 marked a high point in the fortunes of the English short story. Inevitably the Second World War left its mark on many of the tales Derek Hudson has collected here, but, he argues, the dominating impression is that very English characteristic, humour. The authors include Somerset Maugham, Virginia Woolf, Evelyn Waugh, Graham Greene, H. E. Bates, and Rosamond Lehmann.

CLASSIC SCOTTISH SHORT STORIES
Selected and Introduced by J. M. Reid

CLASSIC AMERICAN SHORT STORIES
Selected and Introduced by Douglas Grant

Also in Oxford Paperbacks:

CLASSIC ENGLISH SHORT STORIES

The Dragon's Head
The Killing Bottle
Charmed Lives
The Green Man Revisited

MUSIC IN OXFORD PAPERBACKS

Whether your taste is classical or jazz, the Oxford Paperbacks range of music books is in tune with the interests of all music lovers.

ESSAYS ON MUSICAL ANALYSIS
Donald Tovey

Tovey's *Essays* are the most famous works of musical criticism in the English language. For acuteness, common sense, clarity, and wit they are probably unequalled, and they make ideal reading for anyone interested in the classical music repertory.

CHAMBER MUSIC

Chamber Music contains some of Tovey's most important essays, including those on Bach's 'Goldberg' Variations and *Art of Fugue*, and on key works by Haydn, Mozart, Beethoven, Schumann, Chopin, and Brahms.

CONCERTOS AND CHORAL WORKS

Concertos and Choral Works contains nearly all the concertos in the standard repertory, from Bach's for two violins to Walton's for viola—fifty concertos in all. The choral works include long essays on Bach's B minor Mass and Beethoven's Mass in D, amongst other famous works.

SYMPHONIES AND OTHER
ORCHESTRAL WORKS

Symphonies and Other Orchestral Works contains 115 essays: on Beethoven's overtures and symphonies (including Tovey's famous study of the Ninth Symphony), all Brahms's overtures and symphonies, and many other works by composers from Bach to Vaughan Williams.

Also in Oxford Paperbacks:

Singers and the Song   Gene Lees
The Concise Oxford Dictionary of Music 3/e
Michael Kennedy
Opera Anecdotes   Ethan Mordden